SOCIAL ISSUES IN SPORT COMMUNICATION

Combining theory with practical application, this collection of real-life, provocative case studies on social issues in sports provides students with the opportunity to make the call on ethical and professional dilemmas faced by a variety of sport and communication professionals.

The case studies examine the successes and failures of communication in the corporate culture of sport intersecting with social issues including race, gender, religion, social media, mass media, public health, and LGBTQ+ issues. Topics include the COVID-19 pandemic, the Black Lives Matter movement, sexual abuse scandals, domestic violence, cultural appropriation, and mental health. Each chapter contextualizes a specific issue, presents relevant theory and practical communication principles, and leads into discussion questions to prompt critical reflection. The book encourages students to view the evidence themselves, consider competing ethical and professional claims, and formulate practical responses.

This collection serves as a scholarly text for courses in sport communication, business, intercultural communication, public relations, journalism, media studies, and sport management.

Terry L. Rentner is Professor in the School of Media and Communication at Bowling Green State University (BGSU) in Ohio, USA.

David P. Burns is Professor in the Department of Communication at Salisbury University in Maryland, USA.

SOCIAL ISSUES IN SPORT COMMUNICATION

You Make the Call

Edited by Terry L. Rentner and David P. Burns

Routledge
Taylor & Francis Group

NEW YORK AND LONDON

Designed cover image: PeopleImages/Getty Images

First published 2023
by Routledge
605 Third Avenue, New York, NY 10158

and by Routledge
4 Park Square, Milton Park, Abingdon, Oxon, OX14 4RN

Routledge is an imprint of the Taylor & Francis Group, an informa business

Library of Congress Cataloging-in-Publication Data
Names: Rentner, Terry L., editor. | Burns, David P., editor.
Title: Social issues in sport communication : you make the call / edited by Terry L. Rentner, David P. Burns.
Description: New York, N.Y. : Routledge, 2023. | Includes bibliographical references and index.
Identifiers: LCCN 2022042236 (print) | LCCN 2022042237 (ebook) | ISBN 9781032327976 (hardback) | ISBN 9781032288963 (paperback) | ISBN 9781003316763 (ebook)
Subjects: LCSH: Communication in sports—Case studies. | Sports—Public relations—Case studies. | Sports—Social aspects—Case studies. | Racism in sports—Case studies. | Sex discrimination in sports—Case studies. | Nationalism and sports—Case studies. | Homophobia and sports—Case studies.
Classification: LCC GV567.5 .S64 2023 (print) | LCC GV567.5 (ebook) | DDC 306.4/83—dc23/eng/20221013
LC record available at https://lccn.loc.gov/2022042236
LC ebook record available at https://lccn.loc.gov/2022042237

ISBN: 978-1-032-32797-6 (hbk)
ISBN: 978-1-032-28896-3 (pbk)
ISBN: 978-1-003-31676-3 (ebk)

DOI: 10.4324/9781003316763

Typeset in Bembo
by Apex CoVantage, LLC

To family, friends, and colleagues we love but lost to pandemic, war, and time while we created this book.
To our students who fuel our passion for teaching.
Terry dedicates this book to her dad, Clarence "Kirk" Kirkpatrick, who passed away during the production stage of this book. Simply put, he was the wind beneath my wings. I also dedicate this book to my first grandchildren, Kinsley Rose and Lucas Matthew, in hopes they will grow up in a world that celebrates diversity, inclusion, and equity.
David dedicates the book to his wife, Debra, his North Star, and his daughter, Adrienne, the ultimate optimist and tireless activist.
Hope springs eternal.

CONTENTS

About the Editors   *xi*
List of Contributors   *xiv*
Preface   *xxii*
Acknowledgments   *xxiv*

PART I
Introduction to Sport and Social Issues   **1**

1 Sport and Social Issues: The Touchdowns and Strikeouts   3
   Terry L. Rentner

PART II
Diversity, Equity, and Inclusion   **15**

2 "The Rooney Ruse": Systemic Racism and Hiring NFL
   Head Coaches   17
   David P. Burns and Chris B. Geyerman

3 When Fandom Stains Your Team: Evaluating the
   Effectiveness of the Utah Jazz's Organizational Responses
   to Racist Incidents   29
   Nicola A. Corbin and Anne Bialowas

4 Concussion Settlement and Racial Norming: The NFL
   Fumbles into a Crisis   40
   Cory Young, Terry L. Rentner and Annemarie Farrell

5 Major League Soccer's Navigation of the 2019 Iron Front Crisis   53
   Caleb Bills

6 Protecting the Brees Brand: How Drew Brees Said
   "Sorry" for His National Anthem Protest Comments   64
   Steph Doehler

7 "Kicking Hate Out of Our Game": San Diego Loyal
   Soccer Club's Stand against Racism and Homophobia   75
   Jeffrey W. Kassing, Isaiah D. Utley and Steffanie M. Kiourkas

8 Issues and Crisis Management in Athlete Activism: Colin
   Kaepernick and the Take a Knee Movement   86
   Lillian Feder

9 Reputation Management Strategies at ESPN   97
   Kevin Hull and Denetra Walker

10 From *Les Esquimaux* to the Elks: Addressing Social
   Responsibility in the Canadian Football League   108
   David J. Jackson and Lori Liggett

11 In the Space of Indecision: Social and Cultural
   Challenges Facing Major League Soccer NEXT Academies   120
   Saleema Mustafa Campbell and Erin E. Gilles

12 #WeAreAllMonkeys: Eating Bananas as the Intersection
   of Hashtag Activism and Anti-Racist Solidarity   132
   Pratik Nyaupane

13 The Milwaukee Bucks: Professional Athletic Labor's
   Position in Racist Late-Stage Capitalism   141
   Kevin G. Thompson

PART III
Gender Equity, Identity, and Sexual Misconduct   **153**

14 Conquering a Boy's Club Using an Issues Management
Approach: How Women's Soccer May Pioneer a Path
to Pay Equity   155
Terry L. Rentner and David P. Burns

15 Communicating in Crisis without the Power to Act   168
Bradley J. Baker

16 Strategic Resistance through Communication Capital:
Rapinoe's Reframing of Women-Identified Athletes
through Mind–Body Performance for Social Change   178
Elesha L. Ruminski and Dorene Ciletti

17 Alysia, Allyson, and Nike's "Band of Brothers": Exposing
the Hypocrisy between Corporate Marketing and
Internal Practices   191
Amy Aldridge Sanford, Nikola Grafnetterova and RJ Loa

18 Let Them Wear Shorts! Analyzing the Norwegian
Women's Beach Handball Team's Uniform
Code Protest   202
Megan R. Hill, Karen T. Erlandson and Katey A. Price

19 Sports News Media, Major Leagues, and Intimate
Partner Violence   212
Steve Ingham, Jade Metzger-Riftkin and Tara McManus

20 "Play Like the Lady You Are": Marketing Women's
Gaelic Football   227
Niamh Kitching

21 Trans Inclusion in Sports: Assumed Advantages, (Un)
Fairness, and Athlete Well-Being   238
Aaron W. Gurlly

PART IV
Mental Health and COVID-19 Pandemic   **249**

22 Athlete Influence in Regard to Mask Wearing: An
    Application of Social Cognitive Theory   251
    Lindsey J. DiTirro and Jennifer R. Allen Catellier

23 Controlling the Narrative: NBC, USA Gymnastics,
    and Simone Biles at the 2020 Summer Olympic Games   264
    Aaron W. Gurlly

24 "We Hope to See You Soon": The Green Bay Packers'
    Crisis Management through a Letter to the Fans during
    COVID-19 Mega-Crisis   275
    Julia C. Richmond

25 Blaming Biles: Intersectionality and Organizational
    Obligations to Mental Health   287
    Jeff Nagel and Scott J. Varda

26 How Can Organizations Better Support Athletes? A Case
    Study of the Impact of COVID-19 on Minoritized
    Communities in Intercollegiate Sport   300
    Yannick Kluch, Shaun M. Anderson, and Tomika L. Ferguson

Appendix A Drew Brees' Written Apology   *312*
Appendix B Transcript from Drew Brees' Video Apology *314*
Appendix C Green Bay Packers' Letter to the Fans   *315*
Index   *316*

ABOUT THE EDITORS

Terry L. Rentner (Ph.D.), Professor, is a faculty member in the School of Media and Communication at Bowling Green State University (BGSU), Ohio. She teaches Public Relations, Sports, and Crisis Communication courses at the undergraduate level and Advertising, Public Relations, Crisis, and Health Communication at the graduate level. She was named the BGSU Master Teacher in 2019 and served for 20 years as Advisor to the Public Relations Student Society of America. She co-founded the Richard Maxwell project, which fosters student participation in sport media and communication activities and events. She was instrumental in launching the NFL Sport Media Boot Camp in 2013, a 3-day workshop for current and former NFL players. From 2018 to 2020, she taught workshops in the NFL Broadcast Boot Camp, the premier player engagement program, hosted by BGSU during that period.

Dr. Rentner is an international Health Communication and Sports Scholar. Her work as a principal or co-investigator in college student health led to over 20 state and federal grants totaling approximately $1.5 million. She received state and national awards for her health communication campaigns, including one from the U.S. Department of Education that named the university's peer-focused alcohol-reduction program as being one of eight top programs in the country. More recently, her scholarship explored international health issues, COVID-19 on college campuses, and social issues in sport, such as women's pay inequity, concussions in the NFL, equity, diversity, and inclusion.

She has presented over 50 conference papers and nine book chapters, and her refereed journal articles over the last 5 years have appeared in *Sport Management*

Education Journal, Journal of American College Health, Journal of Health Management, Atlantic Journal of Communication, Journal of Public Health Research, Journal of Media and Communication Studies, Journal of International Crisis and Risk Communication Research, and *International Journal of Communication and Health.* She is proudest of her 2019 co-edited book with Dr. David P. Burns titled *Case Studies in Sport Communication: You Make the Call.*

Dr. Rentner is former Chair of the Department of Journalism and Public Relations and Director of the School of Media and Communication at BGSU. She is a recipient of the BGSU Chairs and Directors Leadership Award and received the BGSU Lifetime Achievement Award.

She is Member of the Public Relations Society of America and the Association for Education in Journalism and Mass Communication.

David P. Burns (Ph.D.), Professor, teaches Sport Communication, Mass Media Law, International Communication, and Advanced Multimedia Journalism courses in Salisbury University's Communication Department. He is the co-editor, with Dr. Terry L. Rentner, of *Case Studies in Sport Communication: You Make the Call* (Routledge).

Dr. Burns' sport communication research focuses on women's pay inequity, controversial team names, and hiring disparities in the NFL. Besides sport communication, his research interests focus on the media–politics linkages that impact journalism and the communication industry. He is Senior Research Fellow for the University of Oregon-UNESCO Crossings Institute for Conflict-Sensitive Reporting and Intercultural Dialogue and is part of the *Central European Journal of Communication's* scientific network of scholars.

In 2018, Dr. Burns was one of six educators in the nation to receive the Scripps Howard Foundation Visiting Professor of Social Media grant. He is a two-time recipient of the Fulton School of Liberal Arts' Outstanding Academic Advisor award and has received two outstanding teaching awards at different institutions. From 2010 to 2012, he was a member of a six-person UNESCO consulting team that helped Iraqi and Kurdish educators reform and implement a National Journalism Curriculum for every higher education institution in Iraq and Kurdistan.

Dr. Burns has penned a half-dozen book chapters on topics covering sports, media, religion, and politics and has an entry on Arab nations' press systems in *The Encyclopedia of Journalism.* His refereed works are featured in *Journalism and Mass Communication Educator, Electronic News, Journal of Middle East Media,* and the *Global Media Journal.* He has numerous conference presentations and over 20 articles and columns in the popular and trade presses including *Quill,* the Society of Professional Journalists' publication, and the *American Journalism Review.*

Dr. Burns serves on the Board of Directors of the Maryland-DC Scholastic Press Association as its Treasurer and is past President of the Society of Professional Journalists Maryland Professional Chapter. He served two terms on the Board of Governors for the National Association of Television Arts and Sciences' National Capital/Chesapeake Bay Chapter, where he is still a member. He is also a member of the Association for Education in Journalism and Mass Communication, the Society of Professional Journalists, and the Broadcast Education Association.

Dr. Burns has worked for American television networks and reported for an international wire service and a Polish business newspaper. He has led and taught media and journalism workshops in the United States, Poland, Russia, Jordan, India, the United Arab Emirates, Qatar, and Afghanistan. He holds degrees from Ithaca College (B.A.), the University of Georgia (M.A.), and the University of Maryland (Ph.D.).

CONTRIBUTORS

Shaun M. Anderson, Ph.D., is an associate professor of organizational communication and faculty advisor for the Institute for Business Ethics and Sustainability at Loyola Marymount University. His research areas are at the intersection of sport, corporate social responsibility, and social justice. He has published in several peer-reviewed journals including the *International Journal of Sports Communication*, *Communication and Sport*, and *Psychology of Popular Media*. He is the author of the forthcoming book, *The Black Athlete Revolt: The Sport Justice Movement in the Age of #BlackLives-Matter*. For more information, please visit www.shaunmarqanderson.com.

Bradley J. Baker, Ph.D., is an assistant professor in the Department of Sport and Recreation Management at Temple University, Philadelphia, Pennsylvania. His research interests include consumer behavior and digital sport management, primarily brand building and identity formation in mediated spaces including social media, esports, and other contexts at the intersection of technology and sport. He has a second research area focusing on quantitative research methods and meta-science. In the classroom, he teaches sports analytics at the undergraduate and graduate levels. He has published articles in the *Journal of Sport Management*, *Sport Management Review*, *Journal of Business Research*, and *Psychological Bulletin*, among other outlets.

Anne Bialowas, Ph.D., is a professor in the Department of Communication at Weber State University, Utah. She teaches undergraduate courses in communication theory, media studies, and gender in addition to graduate courses in advanced presentations, team-building, and facilitation. Her research interests encompass sport communication, rhetoric, and gender studies. She currently is serving as the department chair.

Caleb Bills, is a Ph.D. candidate at Bowling Green State University, Ohio. He has taught courses at the undergraduate levels in public speaking and small group communication. He has also volunteered as a public speaking mentor with the Bowling Green State University College of Business yearly competition known as The Hatch. His research interests are sport communication, social movements, and social change.

Saleema Mustafa Campbell, Ph.D., is the current director of the Adolescent Literacy Project at Kentucky State University and an adjunct professor. She earned her doctorate in Pan-African studies and postcolonial literature from the University of Louisville in 2020 after teaching in both secondary and post-secondary institutions for more than a decade. She has also worked in educational training and diversity recruitment for the local state government.

Jennifer R. Allen Catellier, Ph.D., is an associate professor at Gannon University in Erie, Pennsylvania. She teaches undergraduate and graduate courses in research methods, media ethics, and communication campaigns. Her research interests are in health and risk communication. She has published her research in outlets including *Journal of American College Health*, *Journal of Communication in Healthcare*, and *Cyberpsychology, Social Networking, and Behavior*. She is currently the director for the Master of Arts in Strategic Communication program at Gannon University.

Dorene Ciletti, MBA, Ph.D., is an associate professor and director of the marketing and sales program and co-founder of the Michael P. Pitterich Sales & Innovation Center for the Rowland School of Business at Point Park University, Pittsburgh, Pennsylvania. She serves as H.J. Heinz Endowed Chair and co-director of Women in Industry, facilitating holistic resilience and intentional inclusion programs. She has authored a variety of journal articles and chapters; authored *Marketing Yourself*, a unique textbook combining marketing theory and market knowledge with career development; and co-edited *Sports Entrepreneurship: Theory and Practice*. She is active with local organizations focused on inclusion and community development.

Nicola A. Corbin, Ph.D., is an associate professor of communication at Weber State University, Utah, who teaches public relations and mass media courses and directs the university's Teaching and Learning Forum. Corbin was bestowed Weber State University's Crystal Crest Master Teacher Award in 2019 and named the 2018 Educator of the Year by the Omega Psi Phi Fraternity. Her research interests encompass exploring the impact of race-gendered representations in mass media and popular culture and critical approaches to public relations pedagogy.

Lindsey J. DiTirro, Ph.D., is an assistant professor at Gannon University. She teaches public speaking courses at the undergraduate level. At the graduate level, she teaches classes in public relations, crisis communication, and social media. Her research interests include public relations, crisis and disaster communication, and sport communication.

Steph Doehler is a sport sociologist within the School of Education, Childhood, Youth & Sport at the Open University, UK. Her research interests include media framing, sports communication, and athlete activism. She has presented at several international conferences, including the European Communication Research and Education Association and the Center for Sociocultural Sport and Olympic Research. She is a reviewer for peer-reviewed publications such as *International Journal of Sport Communication* and *Sport in Society*.

Karen T. Erlandson, Ph.D., is a professor at Albion College, a small, private liberal arts college in Michigan. She teaches a variety of undergraduate courses including persuasion, gender communication, and communication in interpersonal contexts. Her research interests include the use of gendered images in advertising and marketing, as well as interpersonal and intercultural dynamics among college roommates.

Annemarie Farrell, Ph.D., is an associate professor at Ithaca College, New York. She teaches courses in sport management, specializing in sport consumer behavior, spectator and fan motives, women's sport culture, and sports brands in crisis, among other areas. She received an MA and Ph.D. in Sport and Exercise Management from the Ohio State University.

Lillian Feder, M.S., is a doctoral student at Purdue University. She teaches courses at the undergraduate level in presentational speaking and critical writing and studies public relations and organizational behavior in sport. Her research interests include athlete activism, crisis, and social media. In addition to studying sport communication, Lillian is a former collegiate athlete and has spent a collective 5 years working as an athletic administrator at the collegiate and professional levels. In 2019, she was recognized with the Earl R. Harlan Award for Excellence in Teaching by a Master's Student.

Tomika L. Ferguson, Ph.D., is the assistant dean for student affairs and inclusive excellence and an assistant professor in the Department of Educational Leadership in the School of Education at Virginia Commonwealth University, Richmond, Virginia. Her scholarship centers on the intersection of race, gender, sport, and equity in K-20 education spaces, sport, and leadership positions. She is the founder of the Black Athlete Sister Circle, and her work has been featured in *Diverse Issues in Higher Education, Journal of College Student Development, College Student Affairs Journal,* and the *Journal of Research on Leadership Education*.

Chris B. Geyerman, Ph.D., is an associate professor at Georgia Southern University. He teaches courses in media criticism, rhetorical criticism, rhetoric of social movements, rhetoric of international relations, philosophy of communication, general semantics, and communication and conflict. Research interests include rhetorical and media criticism, cultural studies, the rhetoric of sports, and the rhetoric of social problems. He has been recognized as a University System of Georgia Governor's Teaching Fellow by the Institute for Higher Education at the University of Georgia and has received the Georgia Southern University Award for Excellence in Contributions to Service.

Erin E. Gilles, Ph.D., is an associate professor of public relations and advertising at the University of Southern Indiana, where she also directs the Master of Communication graduate program. She is the current editor of the *Kentucky Journal of Communication*. She teaches undergraduate and graduate courses in advertising, health communication, qualitative research methods, social media, and design. Dr. Gilles' research interests include social justice, health communication, and popular culture. She has been published in *Women's Reproductive Health*, *Affilia*, *the Journal of Human Services*, and the *International Journal of E-Health and Medical Communications*, among other outlets.

Nikola Grafnetterova, Ed.D., is the athletic academic coordinator for women's basketball and track and field/cross country at Texas A&M University-Corpus Christi. She also teaches the university's first-year seminar course. Her primary research interests include experiences of Latinx college athletes, leadership and administration within college athletics, and athletic academic services. Her most recent publications include peer-reviewed articles in the *Journal of Issues in Intercollegiate Athletics*, *Innovative Higher Education*, and *Journal of Latinos and Education*. Nikola is an avid runner who has completed many road and trail races, including Leadville Trail 100 and Pikes Peak Marathon.

Aaron W. Gurlly, Ph.D., is an associate professor of media production in the Communication Arts Department at Salisbury University, Salisbury, Maryland. His academic interest in communication and in media production focuses in part on the mediating functions of the camera on the visual representation of raced and gendered bodies.

Megan R. Hill, Ph.D., is an associate professor at Albion College, a small, private liberal arts college in Michigan. She teaches a wide-range of courses at the undergraduate level including sport communication, sports marketing, and public relations. Research interests include the intersections of sport and mass communication, with a particular focus on the political and health-related implications of player and coach behaviors in the public sphere.

Kevin Hull, Ph.D. from the University of Florida, is an associate professor and the sports media lead at the University of South Carolina's School of Journalism and Mass Communications. His research primarily focuses on local sports broadcasters and sports media education. A former television sports broadcaster, Dr. Hull's textbook *Sports Broadcasting* was published in 2022.

Steve Ingham is a visiting assistant professor at St. Lawrence University in the Department of Performance and Communication Arts, Canton, New York. His research as a generalist spans areas such as comedy, mental health, sports, intimate partner violence, popular culture, pornography, masculinity, and media.

David J. Jackson is a professor of political science at Bowling Green State University. His major research interest is the interactive relationship between politics and culture. He is the author of *Entertainment and Politics: The Influence of Pop Culture on Young Adult Political Socialization, 2nd Revised Edition* (2009), as well as scholarly articles in such journals as *Political Research Quarterly, Polish American Studies, International Journal of Press/Politics*, and *Journal of Political Marketing*. In 2007–2008, he was a Fulbright Fellow at the University of Łódź. His book *Classrooms and Barrooms: An American in Poland* was published in 2009.

Jeffrey W. Kassing, Ph.D., is a professor of communication studies in the School of Social and Behavioral Sciences at Arizona State University, Tempe, Arizona. His research interests include sport and identity, sports media, and soccer. He is the co-author of *The Art of Tifo: Identity, Representation, and Performing Fandom in Football/Soccer* (2022) and the co-editor of *Perspectives on the U.S.-Mexico Soccer Rivalry: Passion and Politics in Red, White, Blue, and Green* (2017). He is the co-director of the Sport, Media, and Culture Research Group at Arizona State University.

Steffanie M. Kiourkas is an MA student in the Communication Studies program at Arizona State University. Her research interests include minority representation in media and policy, identity, and women and gender studies. She is currently working on a master's thesis examining LGBTQ+ representation in sitcom televisions shows. She plans to pursue a Ph.D. in communication studies to further her research and academic goals.

Niamh Kitching, Ph.D., is a lecturer in physical education at Mary Immaculate College, University of Limerick, Ireland. She teaches at both undergraduate and postgraduate levels in physical education and wellbeing education. Her research interests include the sociology of sport and PE, sports pedagogy and coaching, and sports media. Her published research focuses on gender equality and sport, with a particular emphasis on the experiences of professional women athletes, coaches, and fans and their presence, participation, and presentation in sport and sports media. She has published in a number of sociology of sport journals and edited collections.

Yannick Kluch, Ph.D., serves as an assistant professor and director of inclusive excellence in the Center for Sport Leadership at Virginia Commonwealth University. His research areas include athlete activism, sport policy, and equity, diversity, and inclusion in sport. His research has been published in *Sport in Society, Journal of Sport Management, European Journal for Sport and Society*, and *Communication & Sport*. In 2020, he was one of only four thought leaders appointed to the inaugural Team USA Council on Racial & Social Justice by the United States Olympic and Paralympic Committee (USOPC). For more information, visit his website at www.yannickkluch.com.

Lori Liggett, Ph.D., is a teaching professor in the School of Media and Communication at Bowling Green State University, Ohio. Her teaching and research interests are critical and cultural media studies. She teaches a variety of courses including American Broadcast History; Sport Documentary; TV and Film Criticism; Principles of Sport Broadcasting; Major Events in Sport Media; and Gender, Media and Culture. Liggett was a faculty participant in the NFL Broadcast and Media Workshop held at BGSU for several years. She has served on the Faculty Senate Intercollegiate Athletics Advisory committee and the President's Advisory Committee on Intercollegiate Athletics at BGSU.

RJ Loa is a coordinator for enrollment management and a 2021 graduate of Texas A&M University-Corpus Christi, where he received a bachelor's degree in communication studies with a minor in public relations. His research focuses on interpersonal communication, family communication, mentorship, and underrepresented populations within higher education. RJ has consulted with several organizations regarding their crisis response plans. His dedication to campus groups and committees made him a sought-out panelist and speaker at university and community events in South Texas. He is an active member of the National Communication Association.

Tara McManus is a master's student in the Department of Communication at Wayne State University, Detroit, Michigan. Her research interests include news media coverage of labor issues, unions, intimate partner violence, and gender issues, particularly within professional sports.

Jade Metzger-Riftkin is a Ph.D. candidate in the Department of Communication at Wayne State University. She specializes in issues pertaining to privacy, surveillance, and information sharing practices of women and sexual minorities in online spaces. Her work can be found in *Journalism Practice, New Media and Society*, and *Medien & Kommunikationswissenschaft*.

Jeff Nagel, Ph.D., is an assistant professor at Baylor University, Texas. He teaches courses at the undergraduate and graduate levels in rhetorical theory, criticism, and argumentation. His research interests include sport, public memory, and identity, all from a rhetorical perspective. His work has appeared in several academic journals, including *Rhetoric Society Quarterly*, *Women's Studies in Communication*, and *QED: A Journal of GLBTQ Worldmaking*.

Pratik Nyaupane is a doctoral student at the Annenberg School for Communication and Journalism at the University of Southern California. He completed his undergraduate studies at Arizona State University in informatics, where he worked on his thesis, "Exploitation of Labor in Qatar: How Nepali Laborers are Victimized in Preparation for the 2022 FIFA Men's World Cup." As an interdisciplinary researcher, his scholarship focuses on looking at issues of technology, media, and politics in sports stadia and fan and athlete behaviors.

Katey A. Price, Ph.D., is an assistant professor at Albion College, a small, private liberal arts college in Michigan. She teaches a variety of courses including research methods, health communication, health disparities, and sport communication. Her research interests focus on health and aging issues in the contexts of interpersonal and family communication as well as in public domains and media.

Julia C. Richmond, Ph.D., is an assistant professor in the Department of Public Relations and Advertising at Rowan University in Glassboro, New Jersey. She teaches undergraduate public relations courses in the program of Sports Communication and Media through the Ric Edelman College of Communication and Creative Arts. She is affiliated with the Center for Sports Communication and Social Impact. Her research focuses on the intersection of crisis communication, media studies, and sport. Her work has been published in *Communication Theory* and *Public Relations Review*.

Elesha L. Ruminski, Ph.D., is a professor of communication studies and coordinator of leadership studies at Frostburg State University (FSU), Frostburg, Maryland. She researches, teaches, and facilitates communication strategies within organizations and communities. She has authored several chapters and co-edited *Communicative Understandings of Women's Leadership Development: From Ceilings of Glass to Labyrinth Paths* (2012). A past Kettering Foundation research exchange participant and chair of the National Communication Association's Public Dialogue and Deliberation Division, she has led grant-funded projects through FSU's Communication Leadership Lab. She is active with the Choose Civility: Allegany County chapter and other partners to support regional collaborations.

Amy Aldridge Sanford, Ph.D., is a communication professor and vice provost for academic programs at Middle Tennessee State University. Her research focuses on activism, social justice, allyship, not-for-profit organizations, and leadership. She is the author of the book *From Thought to Action: Developing a Social Justice Orientation*. A TEDx speaker and curator, Amy is a frequent presenter at conferences, universities, and community groups. She is past president of Central States Communication Association, a lifetime member of American Association of University Women, and the current vice chair for the Activism and Social Justice Division of the National Communication Association.

Kevin G. Thompson, M.A., is a doctoral student and instructor at The University of Alabama's College of Communication and Information Sciences. He teaches courses at the undergraduate level in public speaking, argumentation and debate, rhetoric, and sport communication. Research interests include studying the intersections of public memory, sport, and critical rhetoric. Prior to starting his doctorate, he has served as a lecturer and course coordinator at the Department of Communication, University of Texas Permian Basin.

Isaiah D. Utley, M.A., is a graduate in communication studies from the School of Social and Behavioral Sciences at Arizona State University. His research interests include sport, sports media, fandom, and social media. His favorite sports to watch and research include basketball and American football. He intends to pursue a career that blends his love for sport and communication.

Scott J. Varda, Ph.D., is an associate professor at Baylor University, Texas. He teaches graduate and undergraduate courses in argumentation, debate, rhetorical theory, and public address. His research interests include the intersections of sport and identity under modernity. His work has appeared in *Critical Studies in Media Communication*, *Communication and Critical/Cultural Studies*, and *Women's Studies in Communication*.

Denetra Walker, Ph.D. from the University of South Carolina, is an assistant professor of journalism at Grady College of Journalism and Mass Communication, University of Georgia, Athens, Georgia. Her research focuses on the experiences of journalists of color, newsroom diversity, and controversial topics including media coverage of police shootings. Prior to entering academia, she worked in management positions at several local television stations throughout the United States.

Cory Young, Ph.D., is an associate professor at Ithaca College, New York. She teaches corporate and organizational communication, specializing in crisis communication and social media. She published in communication journals, books, and trade publications and presented research at regional, national, and international conferences. She holds a Master of Social Science in Culture Studies from the University of Birmingham, England.

PREFACE

Today, societies around the world are challenging convention, rethinking cultural priorities, and shifting traditional perspectives. The voice of the voiceless is louder, the call for inclusiveness more insistent and even expectant. Just as unrelenting is the effort to rebuff change in favor of the status quo. Since sport, in its purest form, is open to any gender or ethnicity, sport often takes center stage in this push and pull as societies reconstitute norms. Today, there remain unanswered questions about who has access to the playing field, who gets to speak their mind, who gets paid an equitable wage, who gets access to vaccines and critical healthcare, and who gets to own and lead organizations worth billions of dollars. These unresolved issues do not go back 50 years, or 500 years, but rather a millennium. This textbook examines the social challenges facing sport today.

There are four parts to the book. The first introduces you to what a social issue is and ways to investigate these topics. Part II focuses on issues of diversity, equity, and race. Part III delves into issues of gender equity, identity, and cases of sexual misconduct. Part IV concentrates on mental health issues and COVID-19 pandemic challenges in sport and life. In all, each case study in the book frames a current issue in sport that transcends sport and informs social change.

The media is ubiquitous in global societies and plays a critical role in these case studies. Social media platforms allow the masses to bypass traditional "legacy" media like newspapers, television, and radio. The grassroots nature of social media provides both the catalyst and a proving ground for nascent social movements. As with every form of mass media, social media are at once empowering and imperiling. As societies resist change, they often vilify the innovators. Sport has its own social pioneers. Tennis icon and social activist Billie Jean King (2000) reminds us that "It's everyone's responsibility to lead, to honor, and to fight for everyone's basic rights for equality, regardless of our gender, our age, our race, our religion, our appearance, sexual orientation, or our ability" (12:49–13:17). You will read about pioneers like King and others in the following pages. However, it is important to keep in mind that even present-day icons like King were not always hailed as heroes within their own societies.

The Italian philosopher and historian Niccolò Machiavelli originally wrote in 1513 in *The Prince*, "There is nothing more difficult to take in hand, more perilous to conduct, or more uncertain in its success than to take the lead in the introduction of a new order of things" (Machiavelli, 2010, p. 21). In speaking out and acting out, innovators get pushback by those in power and those who benefit from the old system. Paradoxically, they may only receive wary, tepid support from others who may benefit, until those pioneering actions become more socially accepted and, therefore, palatable.

Soccer star and activist Megan Rapinoe (2020), in a recorded commencement address due to the pandemic, reminded seniors that they, too, can pioneer movements telling them,

> I know first-hand the power of a movement led by and for the next generation. You are that next generation. Take the torch and leave your mark. Put your stake in the ground and build the future that you want and you believe in and fight like hell to do it.
>
> *(Adams, 2020, para. 26)*

Social change is the measure of the task at hand. It is happening today, but it is not the work of a day.

In this book, theory and research are applied to contemporary social issues and inform each of the book's case studies. The aim of the book is to show that social issues can be empirically investigated and then scientifically and historically contextualized. After each chapter, the reader reviews the evidence of the various sport communication cases and determines whether the major players involved made the proper decision. Then, it is the reader's turn to *make the call*.

The authors of this book hope that this book demonstrates progress, promise, and providence. Change may be inevitable and ever-present, but it is not bleak and desperate. A Chinese curse goes, "May you live in interesting times." We are certainly living in interesting times, but we are not living in impossible times.

David P. Burns

References

Adams, S. (2020, May 16). Wise words to the class of COVID-19 from Oprah Winfrey, Bill Gates, Malala Yousafzai, Barack Obama, Dr. Anthony Fauci, Megan Rapinoe, Tim Cook, LeBron James and more. *Forbes*. www.forbes.com/sites/susanadams/2020/05/16/the-best-commencement-speeches-of-2020/?sh=4beaa75173f0

King, B.J. (2000, May 21). Stand for others [Video]. *C-SPAN*. www.c-span.org/video/?157273-1/university-massachusetts-commencement

Machiavelli, N. (2010). *The prince*. FastPencil, Inc. https://books.google.com/books?id=3cZ1pm8XS-gC&printsec=frontcover&source=gbs_ge_summary_r&cad=0#v=onepage&q&f=false

ACKNOWLEDGMENTS

While creating this book, a global pandemic, natural disasters, and man-made wars took too many lives and uprooted many more. Yet, during this same time period, humanity explored the heavens, discovered lifesaving vaccines, held despots to account, and persevered. The intrepid and innovative human spirit endures.

This book reflects the academic intellect and ingenuity of dozens of scholars. Each page represents hours of thought, distillation, explanation, and application, all for the benefit of the reader. As book editors, the words "thank you" do not properly capture the appreciation and admiration we have for the book's authors.

We thank our institutions – Salisbury University and Bowling Green State University – and the leaders who enabled us to write and edit this book. Salisbury University dedicated resources and funding to move this book from proposal to print. Bowling Green State University supported a Faculty Improvement Leave (FIL).

At Salisbury University, we thank Dr. Jim Burton and Dean Maarten Pereboom for their stewardship and Dr. Andrew Sharma for his sage advice and consultation. At Bowling Green State University, we thank Julie Hagenbuch for taking over advising and additional service commitments during Terry's FIL.

Our love and admiration go to our family and friends; and their patience as we "put the finishing touches on" or "just took one more look" at chapters on weekends, in the wee hours and during holidays, is appreciated beyond words. Thank you for being sounding boards for our ideas, cheerleaders for our progress, and kind critics of our work. David thanks Debra Burns and Adrienne Burns. Terry thanks the St. Louis Cardinals for instilling the love of sports at the tender age of 4; family members Jim, Jason, Kelsey, Jessie, Ryan, and Monica; her close-knit group of friends (especially Becky, Diane, and Sue); and her parents – her mom, who set the gold standard for working women, and especially her dad, who is and always will be the wind beneath her wings.

Last, we thank our students. Your resilience, patience, intelligence, and versatility during these very challenging times inspire our teaching and inform our scholarship.

PART I

Introduction to Sport and Social Issues

1

SPORT AND SOCIAL ISSUES

The Touchdowns and Strikeouts

Terry L. Rentner

Introduction

This scholarly book begins with an admission. There is no universally accepted definition of a social issue. Sociologists and other scholars have been defining and refining what constitutes a social issue, or social problem, since 1959 when Raab and Selznick said:

> A social problem exists when organized society's ability to order relationships among people seem to be failing; when its institutions are faltering, its laws are being flouted, the transmission of its values from one generation to the next is breaking down, the framework of social expectations is being shaken.
>
> *(1959, p. 6)*

A more modern definition posits that social problems are conditions or behaviors that have negative consequences for large numbers of people, which need to be addressed (University of Minnesota, 2015, 2016). This definition has both objective and subjective components. The objective component means the condition or behavior must have a serious negative impact on a large group of people while the subjective component, a perception that the condition or behavior must be addressed, recognizes the problem as being socially constructed (Rubington & Weinberg, 2010).

Non-scholars may prefer a simpler definition of social problems: "I know it when I see it. Or, I know it when I experience it."

So why is this book titled *Social **Issues** in Sport Communication* and not *Social **Problems** in Sport Communication*? A problem is defined as "a matter or situation

DOI: 10.4324/9781003316763-2

regarded as unwelcome or harmful and needed to be dealt with and overcome," while an issue is defined as "an important topic or problem for debate or discussion" (The Oxford American Dictionary and Language Guide, 1999). Therefore, *issue* better fits what we are trying to accomplish in this book – topics or matters in sport to be discussed or debated. Put simply, it is because social issues and sport intersect in our world.

Athletes as Activists

While athletes have always been vocal on social issues, Platt (2018), a writer for Global Sports Matters, argues that "since at least 2012, it's become hard to pick up a sports page and not read about an athlete taking action or weighing in on life beyond his or her field of play" (para. 8).

One of the earliest intersections of sport and social issues occurred in 1883 when the Toledo Blue Stockings baseball team started its innings with Moses Fleetwood Walker, an African American player. He was not originally scheduled to start, but when he did the other team refused to play. This was an early example of blatant racism in sport, but one that ultimately led to athletes like Jackie Robinson, who reluctantly broke sports' color barrier in professional baseball in the late 1940s, and to the National Football League's (NFL) Colin Kaepernick, who took a knee against racial injustice during the United States national anthem in 2016 (Wick, 2020).

There are numerous others who came between and after these pioneers. As examples, Irish long-jumper Peter O'Connor, an activist for Ireland's independence waving the Irish flag while the British national anthem played during an Olympic Games' medal ceremony in 1906, to track stars Tommie Smith and John Carlos, who raised their fists on a podium in 1968 to raise awareness of how Black Americans were being treated, and fighter Mohammed Ali, who refused to serve in the Vietnam War and was found guilty of draft evasion (the Supreme Court overturned his conviction in 1971), are there.

Tennis greats Althea Gibson, Arthur Ashe, Martina Navratilova, Billie Jean King, and Naomi Osaka have been advocates for multiple social issues platforms. Gibson became the first Black athlete to compete in the U.S. Open (then the U.S. Championships) in 1950 and win the Grand Slam title in 1956. She also became the first Black athlete to compete on the Women's Professional Golf Tour. Ashe exposed social injustices in South Africa and became an educator on HIV and AIDS, after contracting HIV in 1983. Navratilova has been a proponent for gay rights, the LGBTQ+ community, and animal rights. King became an advocate for gender equality during and after her career and is credited for women receiving the same prize money as men in tennis. Osaka's activism includes giving support for the Black Lives Matter movement, denouncing anti-Asian hate crimes, and most recently being a spokesperson for mental health.

After winning the gold medal in the 2012 Summer Olympics, the "Fab Five" team of Gabby Douglas, McKayla Maroney, Aly Raisman, Kyla Ross, and Jordyn Wieber was renamed the "Fierce Five" when they, along with Simone Biles and more than 350 other women, filed sexual assault claims against Michigan State University and USA Gymnastics team doctor Larry Nassar, who was convicted in 2018 and will spend his life in prison. The victims were awarded $380 million.

One of the most recent intersections of social issues and sport is in the area of mental health. As of 2021, at least 12 athletes have publicly spoken about their mental health issues. Since announcing her retirement from gymnastics in 2020, Raisman regularly talks about her anxiety issues since the Nassar trial and is an advocate of healing from past traumas. Others include Michael Phelps, the most decorated Olympian in history, who has talked about struggles with mental health, substance abuse, and depression following his guilty plea to a second Driving Under the Influence (DUI) charge in 2014 and his admission to a rehabilitation center for treatment, including suicidal thoughts. Similarly, professional wrestler Ronda Rousey, who also contemplated suicide following her UFC fight loss to Holly Holm in 2015, champions destigmatizing mental health, as do National Basketball Association (NBA) players Kevin Love and DeMar DeRozan, who tweeted about their struggles with depression.

Tennis star Serena Williams brought postpartum depression to the forefront, and Olympic swimmer Amanda Beard chronicled her issues with self-harm and poor body image. National Soccer Hall of Famer and two-time Olympic gold medalist Abby Wambach wrote about her issues with addiction and alcohol abuse following her 2016 DUI charge, and Olympic swimmer and medalist Allison Schmitt credits Phelps for her speaking out on depression. And, as aforementioned mentioned, Osaka recently became a mental health advocate after withdrawing from the 2021 French Open and being fined $15,000 for failing to attend a post-match press conference.

Arguably, the most impactful example of the intersection of athletes and social issues is the story of Pat Tillman, the NFL Arizona Cardinal safety, who turned down a 3-year, $3.6 million contract to join the Army in May 2002, presumably prompted by the devastation from the September 11, 2001 terrorists attacks in the United States Tillman was killed in 2004 by a friendly fire, but his legacy endures as the man who was more committed to fighting for his country than playing on the football field.

Athletes as Targets

Athletes have not only spoken out on social issues but also have become targets themselves. First are issues surrounding systemic racism. Such is the case of basketball superstar LeBron James being told by a Fox News Pundit in 2018 to "shut up and dribble" when James spoke out during an ESPN interview about racism, politics, and the difficulties of being a Black public figure. Former NFL quarterback Colin Kaepernick's decision to kneel rather than stand sparked a national political debate, the NFL scrambling to implement policies during the playing of the national anthem, and (some would argue) the shunning of Kaepernick by NFL teams. The backlash was so severe that one study found that nearly one-third of survey respondents said they were less likely to watch an NFL game because of player protests during the national anthem (Platt, 2018). NBA players Craig Hodges and Mahmoud Abdul-Rauf said that their protest over the national anthem presaged Kaepernick's and ended their careers (Platt, 2018). Olympians Tommie Smith and John Carlos, who, as mentioned earlier, raised their fists during their medal ceremony at the 1968 Olympics, were vilified afterward especially by sports broadcaster Brent Musburger who referred to them as "black-skinned storm troopers" (Platt, 2018 para. 11). Fast forward to June 2020, when NASCAR driver Bubba Wallace found a noose hanging in his garage (Wick, 2020).

Next are mental health issues that also have placed some athletes unwillingly in the spotlight. In baseball, it is known as the "Yips." In gymnastics, it is called the "twisties." Both are terms used when a sudden loss of motor skills prevents an athlete from performing basic skills. St. Louis Cardinals Pitcher Rick Ankiel suddenly found himself unable to pitch during a playoff game in 2000. Simone Biles, the most decorated gymnast, found herself under the microscope during the 2021 Olympics when a case of the twisties led to her withdrawing from competition. Both stepped away from their respective sports to focus on their health, sparking both support and heavy criticism. While Ankiel was spared the wrath of social media trolls, since his actions pre-dated its ubiquity, Biles was called "weak" and "a shame to our country" online with a Texas attorney general calling her "selfish, childish, and a national embarrassment" (Edwards, 2021).

Athletes also become political pawns as in the case of Women's National Basketball Association (WNBA) star Brittney Griner, detained at Moscow's Sheremetyevo Airport on February 17, 2022, for carrying hashish oil in vape cartridges. In July, Griner pleaded guilty as part of a strategy to help facilitate a prisoner swap and in recognition that she was not going to be acquitted (Quinn, 2022). A more perplexing political issue to emerge recently involves Chinese tennis star Peng Shuai, whose whereabouts became unknown after she accused a high-ranking Chinese Communist Party official of sexual assault. The social media post of the allegations was deleted, and despite purported messages from the athlete released by state-run media saying she was fine, the Women's Tennis Association voiced its concerns and suspended all events in China indefinitely, raising international attention on Shuai's safety. Shuai later denied she was sexually assaulted, but questions still remain whether she was forced to recant her allegations.

Transgender athletes also found themselves in the media spotlight. In June 2022, the International Swimming Federation (FINA) voted to restrict transgender athletes in elite women's swimming competitions. The policy is the "strictest from any Olympic sports body and effectively bans any transgender women who have gone through male puberty from competing in women's events" (CNN, 2022, para. 2). This means Lia Thomas, the first transgender National Collegiate Athletic Association (NCAA) champion in Division I history, will not be able to compete in the world championships or the Olympics. How this decision will impact transgender athletes in other sports remains to be seen.

Unwilling Participants

The COVID-19 pandemic thrust several athletes into the spotlight, but not in a positive way. NBA's Kyrie Irving was not permitted to play because he did not meet the New York City COVID-19 requirements. The NFL suspended Antonio Brown, Mike Edwards, and John Franklin for three games without pay for lying about their vaccine status.

Others have played it more coyly. NFL Green Bay Packer quarterback Aaron Rodgers misled the public about his vaccination status, saying he had been "immunized" but did not explicitly state he had received the COVID-19 vaccine (he had not). Rodgers has since taken responsibility for his obfuscation on his vaccination status, but asserted, "I'm an athlete I'm not an activist, so I'm going to get back to doing what I do best and that's playing ball" (NFL.com, 2021, para. 17). Novak Djokovic, the world's top male tennis player, was not allowed to compete in the Australian Open after admitting he made false statements on his vaccination status in his travel declaration, but blamed it on human error. Djokovic also disclosed he did not immediately isolate after testing positive for COVID-19 in December 2021, but denied knowing he had the virus during the time frame when social media posts showed him attending public events (Yeung, 2022). Australia deported Djokovic for his transgression, and he later said he preferred to miss out on future tennis trophies than be forced to get the COVID-19 vaccine (Rajan, 2022).

Athletes are not the only ones in the sports world finding themselves unwillingly involved in social issues. In October 2021, Las Vegas Raider Head Coach Jon Gruden resigned after his emails containing racist, misogynistic, and homophobic language came to light. The emails were part of the NFL's investigation into a toxic workplace culture within the Washington Commanders football team. The Commanders had earlier been the center of controversy over their former name, the Washington Redskins. Another head coach, Urban Meyer, also had been marred by controversy for a number of issues – inappropriately touching a woman in a Columbus, Ohio restaurant; using COVID-19 vaccination status to make roster cuts and to hire personal friend Tim Tebow; hiring a coach who had been fired at the University of Iowa for accusations of using racist language; calling his assistant coaches liars; violating league rules on contact during off-season practices; and kicking a player who was stretching before practice. All of these happened during Meyer's short tenure with the NFL's Jacksonville Jaguars, where he was fired after 13 games. Prior to that, as head coach at The Ohio State University, Meyer was suspended for three games after his knowledge of domestic abuse allegations against one of his assistant coaches surfaced in 2015.

Because They Can

Questions as to whether sport and social issues should intersect can either make good dinner conversation or ruin it. Song writers and singers have always addressed social issues in their works. Actors have proclaimed stances on social issues in their acceptance speeches. So, are athletes afforded the same permission to speak out on social issues? And what happens when they do?

Diversity, equity, and inclusion (DEI) are among the most talked about social issues in sport. When Jackie Robinson broke the color barrier by joining Major League Baseball (MLB), more people were inspired to challenge the social norms of segregation in 1947 (Wick, 2020) and more Black players inspired to join MLB. Kaepernick's kneeling during the national anthem not only sparked controversy, but it also sparked a national conversation on police brutality. Soccer players in the English Premier League wore "Black Lives Matter" arm patches in 2020. And the noose found in Wallace's garage prompted every driver in the next race to physically push their car around the race track in solidarity.

Equity issues affecting women sport figures parallel those of all women, particularly the topics of equal pay and motherhood. Tennis great King, as discussed earlier, was at the forefront for the fight for equal pay, and when she threatened to boycott the U.S. Open in 1973, women players were awarded equal prize money. More than 30 years later, Venus Williams successfully won the fight for equal prize money at Wimbledon, while her sister, Serena, advocated closing the gender pay gap for Black women through a 2017 *Fortune* magazine op-ed in support of Black Women's Equal Pay Day. The U.S. Women's Hockey Team's successful boycott threat of the 2017 World Championships started by "asking for a living wage and for USA Hockey to fully support its programs for women and girls and stop treating us like an afterthought," according to Captain Meghan Duggan (Lakritz, 2021, para. 8). The U.S. Women's National Soccer Team recently won its long battle for equal pay with a $24 million agreement that includes back pay and inked an historic collective bargaining agreement that guarantees equal pay and benefits as their male counterparts for present and future players. These milestone equal pay actions resulted from persistent advocacy by soccer players like Megan Rapinoe and Margaret Purce.

Also joining the conversation on gender pay equity is Women's National Basketball Association Players Association (WNBAPA) president and Los Angeles Sparks superstar Nneka Ogwumike. The WNBAPA is fighting for better sports sponsorship deals where currently "for every dollar a company invests in endorsement deals for men's sports, less than half a penny goes to the women's game" (Lakritz, 2021, para. 29). This is a battle not only for female athletes, but also according to Ogwumike, "Pay equity has always been a point of emphasis for us when we're advocating, not just for ourselves, but for women in the workplace," and "talking about supporting women is easy, but doing it takes another level of perspective and awareness to really step into that" (Lakritz, 2021, para. 31).

As a result, nearly half of the WNBA players opt to play overseas during the off-season to supplement their salaries (Amos, 2022). In the case of Brittney Griner, by doing so, she became a political pawn and, as of this writing, sits in a Russian prison.

Track and field competitors Allyson Felix and Alysia Montaño, along with long-distance runner Kara Goucher, have shed light on pregnancy and motherhood issues, speaking out against Nike for being unsupportive of pregnant women and new mothers. Montaño and Goucher were told by Nike that their contracts would be paused and they would not be paid while they were pregnant. Nike offered Felix a 70% pay cut during negotiations of her new contract, which took place while she was pregnant. The backlash did force Nike to change its policies, setting the stage for other companies to reevaluate contract guidelines and pay for pregnant women and new mothers.

Sport organizations and sponsorships have also joined the conversation on various social issues. For example, the 2021 MLB All-Star Game was moved from Atlanta in protest of restrictive voting laws recently passed in Georgia. The MLB announcement created a 626% surge in engagement levels and social reactions for both the terms "MLB" and "All-Star Game" (Nielson.com, 2021). The same Nielson Fan Insights study mentioned before found that "66% of MLB fans are passionate about combating racism and 63% are passionate about increasing inclusion and diversity – 5% and 9% more than overall sports fans, respectively" (Nielson, 2021, para. 7).

The Coca-Cola Company and Delta Air Lines, both heavy sports advertisers with headquarters in Atlanta, also opposed Georgia's new restrictive voting legislation. Sport sponsors were aware of their clout as the same Nielson study found that sports fans "are 13% more interested in brands that help fight racial inequality compared to the general population and 11% more likely to support brands that engage the local community to fight racial inequality" (Neilson.com, 2021, para. 6). This also appeared to be the case with Nike after announcing Kaepernick as its spokesperson following his "Take a Knee" controversy. First came the backlash – including calls on social media to burn Nike products – then came a reported 3% fall in stocks on Sept. 4, 2018, one day after the release of the "Dream Crazy" campaign (Handley, 2018). But, subsequently, Nike sales actually grew by 31% (Martinez, 2018), and the ad won the outstanding commercial award at the Creative Arts Emmy Awards. This supports what a sports historian and lecturer at Arizona State University said of the Kaepernick/Nike partnership – "Social justice isn't just part of the contract. It's the whole point of it" (Jackson, 2018, para. 2).

Without a doubt, athletes, sport organizations, governing boards, and sponsors can reinforce or change attitudes and behaviors, based on their stance on social issues. Athletes are often seen as heroes or role models, especially among youth, and as such can be highly influential. For example, while 74% of *Forbes'* highest-paid athletes said they were vaccinated against COVID-19 in 2021, only 13 of the 50 athletes would reveal their vaccination status, Tiger Woods being among them (Saul, 2021). Some have been misleading about their vaccination status, such as Djokovic and Rodgers, discussed earlier, while others, including Fighter Conor McGregor, *Forbes'* highest-paid athlete, has been downright defiant. Although McGregor has not publicly commented on his own vaccination status, he has proclaimed that "Forced vaccination is a war crime," and "the vaccines have not worked" in since-deleted tweets (Saul, 2021, para. 4).

While sports figures are not obligated to disclose their vaccination status, they are influencers. Sharing that they have been vaccinated could change the public conversation, allowing others to see the safety and efficacy of the shot, plus encouraging those who see them as role models to follow suit. Players such as Alvin Davis, MLB's former Mariners first baseman, are seen in a video promoting vaccinations in urban and minority communities. Similarly, NBA Hall of Famer Kareem Abdul-Jabbar expressed his support of teams and players using their public platforms to encourage vaccinations. The NBA has since launched public service announcements with high-profile former players encouraging mass vaccination. According to Harvey Fienberg, a former dean of Harvard's School of Public Health, "I can see celebrity sports figures playing a very constructive role [combating] vaccine hesitancy" and said he could envision more campaigns that enlist sports figures (Simkins, 2021, para. 27).

Sport organizations have joined in marketing campaign efforts to address vaccination hesitancy, as seen by the partnership of the Chicago Department of Public Health with their hometown teams of the Bears, White Sox, Blackhawks, Bulls, Cubs, Fire, Red Stars, and Sky. Even stadiums have gotten onboard with the vaccination effort, creating vaccination hubs in places like Phoenix's State Farm Stadium, Fenway Park in Boston, and Yankee stadium in New York City.

A columnist for *The Washington Post* called today an "unprecedented era of athlete activism" (Svrluga, 2020, para. 24), pointing to creative ways to merge sport and activism, such as players laying a Black Lives Matter T-shirt over home plate during a New York Mets/Miami Marlins baseball game and then walking off the field. This new era also includes sports figures and organizations using social media platforms as a way to connect, educate, and influence societal changes. For example, LeBron James has about 20 million followers on Instagram, where he has been quite vocal on racial issues. After he and other NBA players wore "I can't breathe" shirts during a pre-game warmup to raise awareness of police brutality, both traditional and social media erupted with fans and media discussing and debating the issue.

Sport organizations' community relations departments are ramping up efforts to address social issues. In Detroit, Michigan, for example, Red Wings' "Hockey Town Cares" partners with fans, key stakeholders, and colleagues to provide support for community investment and youth, serving the needs of those in underprivileged communities. The Detroit Tigers Foundation attends to issues related to health and wellness, military members, along with youth, education, and recreation.

Just Because They Can, Should They?

Athletes' actions matter and can inspire dialogue, leading to changing attitudes and behaviors. But, just because athletes, sport organizations, and others involved in the sports world can speak on social issues, should they? While such issues can positively impact fandom, brand reputation, and revenue, these could also be polarizing topics. As the relocation of the 2021 MLB All-Star Game demonstrated, fans and sponsors did engage in a national dialogue on voting rights that limited minority participation. Not all talk, however, supported MLB's decision to move the game, including Republican leaders who spoke out about the move and introduced punitive new antitrust legislation targeted at MLB (Nielson.com, 2021).

An ESPN survey of sports fans following protests against police shootings in 2020 found that 71% of fans supported athletes speaking against racial inequality, with 44% strongly supporting it (ESPN, 2020). When asked about NASCAR's ban of displaying the Confederate flag during races, 64% said they supported the issue. An Axios/Ipsos poll (2021), however, found that views are split on whether athletes should use their platforms to speak out on social issues, with 50% of Americans who said athletes should take a public stand on social issue, while 48% said they should not. The poll also found that the majority of White Americans and Republicans do not think that athletes should engage in activism, while most Black, Hispanic, Asian Americans, and Democrats support such engagement (Ipsos, 2021). In other findings, the majority do not want to ban sports teams from using Native American-themed mascots and think the name changes have gone too far (Ipsos, 2021). While most Americans think Native American words, symbols, and pictures/depictions are acceptable, the majority, 87%, say that using a racial slur as a sports team name is not acceptable (Ipsos, 2021). There is consensus among poll participants for protecting an athlete's ability to speak out and that speaking out against racial injustice is a form of free expression that should be protected (Ipsos, 2021).

Social media has been a game changer for weaving together sports and social issues. According to a professor of sociology at the State University of New York at New Paltz, "There is and has always been a societal backlash against athletes, particularly Black athletes, who speak out against injustice" (Platt, 2018, para. 16). Case in point – while LeBron James has gained support for his stance on systemic racism, he has also received backlash including the famous "shut up and dribble" comment from a conservative pundit.

Sport and Social Issues Agenda: What's on Deck?

It is clear that sports and social issues will continue to intersect, as a look at up-and-coming professional athletes demonstrates. A study of college athletes and staff members on activism found that 84% of athletes expressed a willingness to pursue activism, 78% felt obligated to increase awareness about justice issues, and 67% of staff members supported athlete efforts to increase awareness (RISE, 2022).

The Centre for Sport and Human Rights (2022) published its annual report identifying its top five sport and humans rights issues for 2022. These are:

1. Climate action in sport: Connect climate and human rights agendas
2. Cementing human rights in sports governance and culture: Call for leaders to fully integrate human rights in sport governance and culture, such as discrimination and sexual abuse
3. Gender fairness and inclusion: Focus includes transgender athletes with variations in sex characteristics
4. Overcoming institutional exclusion: Address institutional racism and social injustice
5. Mental health and health inequality: Address COVID-19, mental health, and global health inequalities

The goal of this chapter was to provide an overview of the discussions and debates surrounding the intersection of sport and social issues. Within these pages, together we will continue the conversation, and, then, you make the call.

References

Amos, J. (2022, May 23). The reason WNBA starts like Brittney Griner play basketball overseas? Money. *Fan Buzz*. https://fanbuzz.com/nba/wnba-stars-get-better-pay-overseas/

Centre for Sport and Human Rights (2022, February, 2). 5 sport and human rights issues to look out for in 2022. *Centre for Sport and Human Rights*. www.sporthumanrights.org/library/5-sport-and-human-rights-issues-to-look-out-for-in-2022/

CNN. (2022, June 20). Will swimming's transgender ruling lead to wider change in sports? *CNN*. www.cnn.com/2022/06/20/sport/swimming-transgender-ruling-explainer-spt-intl/index.html

Edwards, J. (2021, July 29). A Texas attorney general called Simone Biles a 'national embarrassment.' His boss publicly disagreed. *The Washington Post*. www.washingtonpost.com/nation/2021/07/29/texas-deputy-attorney-general-simone-biles/

ESPN. (2020, August, 13). Survey: Sports fans support social justice stance by athletes, teams. www.espn.com/espn/story/_/id/29654147/survey-sports-fans-support-social-justice-stance-athletes-teams

Handley, L. (2018, September 27). Nike nearly dropped Colin Kaepernick before putting him in its anniversary ads. www.cnbc.com/2018/09/27/nike-nearly-dropped-colin-kaepernick-before-putting-him-in-its-advert.html

Ipsos. (2021, March 20). Views split on whether athletes should take a stand on political, social issues. www.ipsos.com/en-us/news-polls/axios-hard-truth-sports-poll-2021

Jackson V. (2018, September 6). Colin Kaepernick's Nike sponsorship shows that athletes have more power than they realize. *The Washington Post*. www.washingtonpost.com/outlook/2018/09/06/colin-kaepernicks-nike-sponsorship-shows-that-athletes-have-more-power-than-they-realize/

Lakritz, T. (2021, August 21). 13 athletes who have fought for equal pay. *Insider*. www.insider.com/athletes-olympians-equal-pay-womens-sports

Martinez, G. (2018, September 10). Despite outrage, Nike sales increased after Kaepernick ad. *Time*. https://time.com/5390884/nike-sales-go-up-kaepernick-ad/

NFL.com (2021, November 9). Aaron Rodgers takes 'full responsibility' for comments about COVID 19 vaccination status. *NFL.com*. www.nfl.com/news/aaron-rodgers-full- responsibility-misleading-comments-covid-19-vaccine

Nielson.com (2021, April 16). Brands aren't sitting on the sidelines: The social solidarity of sports sponsorships. *Nielson.com*. www.nielsen.com/us/en/insights/article/ 2021/brands-arent-sitting-on-the-sidelines-the-social-solidarity-of-sports-sponsorships/

Platt, L. (2018, April 16), Athlete activism is on the rise, but so is the backlash. *Global Sport Matters*. https://globalsportmatters.com/culture/2018/04/16/athlete-activism-is-on-the-rise-but-so-is-the-backlash/

Quinn, T.J. (2022, July 7). Detained WNBA star Brittney Griner pleads guilty to drug charge in Russia. *ESPN*. www.espn.com/wnba/story/_/id/34205952/detained-wnba-star-brittney-griner-pleads-guilty-drug-charges-russia

Raab, E., & Selznick. (1959). *Major social problems*. Evanston, IL: Row, Peterson.

Rajan, A. (2022, February 15). Novak Djokovic willing to miss tournaments over vaccine. *BBC News*. www.bbc.com/news/world-60354068

RISE. (2022). RISE college athletics survey on racism & athlete activism. https://rise-towin.org/college-survey/index.html

Rubington, E., & Weinberg, M.S. (2010). *The study of social problems: Seven perspectives* (7th ed.). New York, NY: Oxford University Press.

Saul, D. (2021, December 31). 13 of the 50 highest-paid athletes wouldn't say if they were vaccinated in 2021. *Forbes*. www.forbes.com/sites/dereksaul/2021/ 12/31/13-of-the-50-highest-paid-athletes-wouldnt-say-if-they-were-vaccinated-in-2021/?sh=b70f6ce28161

Simkins, C. (2021, April 3). US professional sports teams promote COVID-19 vaccinations. *VOA*. www.voanews.com/a/usa_us-professional-sports-teams-promote-covid-19-vaccinations/6204094.html

Svrluga, B. (2020, September 25). Why does it matter when athletes speak out? Just ask the kids. *The Washington Post*. www.washingtonpost.com/sports/ 2020/09/25/athlete-activism-children/

The Oxford American Dictionary and Language Guide. (1999). *The Oxford American dictionary and language guide*. Oxford: Oxford University Press.

University of Minnesota. Libraries. Publishing, Ohio Library and Information Network, & Open Textbook Library. (2015/2016). *Social problems: Continuity and change*. Minneapolis, MN: University of Minnesota Libraries Publishing.

Wick, N. (2020, July 20). Athletes should continue to advocate for social issues in America *Silver Chips Online*. https://silverchips.mbhs.edu/content/athletes-should-continue-to-advocate-for-social-issues-in-america-32899/

Yeung, J. (2022, January 12). Djokovic admits he didn't immediately isolate after positive Covid test, as Australia probes possible discrepancies in tests. *CNN.com*. www.cnn.com/2022/01/11/tennis/novak-djokovic-covid-statement-intl-hnk/index.html

PART II
Diversity, Equity, and Inclusion

2

"THE ROONEY RUSE"

Systemic Racism and Hiring NFL Head Coaches

David P. Burns and Chris B. Geyerman

Introduction

It seems paradoxical that a well-intentioned organization could create policies ostensibly designed to racially diversify its management structure that when practiced perpetuates a White front office. However, this appears to be the case with the National Football League (NFL) and its so-called "Rooney Rule" especially when a Black coach, Brian Flores, presumably interviewing the next day for an NFL head coaching job with the New England Patriots, receives a misdirected text intended for a White coach congratulating the White man for getting the head coaching position, thus exposing the Rooney Rule as a mere diversity check-box step toward hiring White coaches. To understand how this occurred, and why the NFL recently revamped its Rooney Rule yet again, one must understand that U.S. organizations both reflect and constitute American customs and values. And, since America's customs and values have racist roots, it follows that many (if not most) U.S. organizations are racialized (Ray, 2019, p. 30), and the NFL is no exception.

In 2003, there were three head coaches of color in the NFL. This lack of diversity at the highest level of the coaching ranks was a cause for alarm for Dan Rooney, the one-time owner of the Pittsburgh Steelers and, at the time, head of the NFL's Diversity Committee. The result was the adoption by NFL owners of what became known as "The Rooney Rule," an NFL policy requiring every team with a head coach vacancy to interview one or more people of color for the position. In 2009, the rule was expanded to include front office personnel, like general managers, and again in 2018 to increase the accountability at the decision-making level (Blunt, 2018). However, after an initial uptick in the hiring of diverse coaches after the Rooney Rule's adoption, the numbers fell and

DOI: 10.4324/9781003316763-4

then stagnated. Now, at the time of this writing, nearly 20 years after enacting the Rooney Rule, of the 32 head coaching positions in the NFL, the number of active minority head coaches is 5 (and Black coaches is 3), and the Rooney Rule is once again being amended (Seifert, 2022).

To the extent that the goal of the Rooney Rule is to increase the number of minority head coaches, it has been an abysmal failure and the subject of scholarly attention. For example, the Rooney Rule has been studied in relation to college coaching and the possibility of Title VII litigation (Nichols, 2008). Further, it has been studied for its effect on implicit bias in the long term (Celis et al., 2020), its possible adoption to mitigate race discrimination in English professional soccer (Corapi, 2012), its relationship with the Fritz Pollard Alliance (Duru, 2008), as a case in the impact of "soft" affirmative action policies on minority hiring into executive leadership positions (DuBois, 2015), the extent to which race factors into head coach hiring decisions (Solow et al., 2011), and its relative effectiveness at addressing archaic unconscious biases regarding race and intellectual acuity (Collins, 2007).

This chapter explains how systemic racism within an organization plays a role in the perpetuation of situations like the one described earlier. The chapter describes how racialized norms are created and how even the adoption of diversity initiatives like the Rooney Rule is often ineffectual in a system that favors one group over another and that a decrease in the number of diversity hires can result without a philosophical change at the organizational level. To explain, the authors utilize racialized organizations theory (ROT).

Using ROT, the chapter explores how the NFL, as a racialized organization, created a racially biased head coaching hiring system by (1) degrading Black coaching candidates through practices like race-norming, (2) creating a hierarchical system that rewarded White players and coaches in certain positions over their Black counterparts, and (3) legitimizing the hiring of White former head coaches with inferior winning percentages over their minority counterparts with superior winning percentages, as examples.

Background

Racialized Organizations Theory (ROT)

Recently, the role that organizations play in the social construction of race and the perpetuation of systemic racism has been the subject of theorizing and analysis (Ray, 2019; Tiako et al., 2021; Enriquez et al., 2019; Bazner, 2021; Lerma et al., 2020). These organizations include medical schools, driver's license offices, and school administrations, to name a few. As an organization populated mostly by people of color at the labor level (i.e., players) by White people at the level of "management" (i.e., coaches, general managers, owners, and other administrative personnel) and which, according to the *Chicago Tribune*, generates an annual revenue of 15 billion dollars (Dixon, 2020, para 9), the NFL's implementation and administration of its Rooney Rule, understood in the context of racialized organizations theory, provide a relevant case study.

We use Ray's ROT to frame the case of the NFL's Rooney Rule. Ray defines racialized organizations as "meso-level social structures that limit the personal agency and collective efficacy of subordinate racial groups while magnifying the agency of the dominant racial group" (2019, p. 36). Whereas macro level analysis is concerned with social structures like institutional racism (cultural), and micro level analysis is concerned with social structures like prejudice or implicit bias (individual), meso level analysis is concerned with social structures that fall between the two, at the organizational level – for example, churches, schools, and, in this case, the NFL (Ray, 2019, p. 28).

The theory of racialized organizations rests on four interrelated tenets we employ in this case study (Ray, 2019, pp. 36–43). The first tenet of ROT is that racialized organizations enhance or diminish the agency of racial groups. For example, when an organizational hierarchy is practically segregated with predominantly one group (typically Whites) at the top and other groups (often people of color) farther down, this is likely to influence the resulting choices for interacting outside the formal organization.

The second tenet is that racialized organizations legitimate the unequal distribution of resources. This unequal distribution of resources is based on racial segregation, a "defining foundational characteristic of most organizations" (p. 38), and is found not only in organizational hierarchies, but in organizational practices as well. For example, "Blacks regularly shop at White-owned" businesses, "but segregation ensures Whites rarely shop at Black-owned businesses" (p. 39).

The third tenet is that Whiteness is a credential. In spite of laws against overt discrimination in terms of hiring decisions, the credential of Whiteness manifests itself and should be "considered a general organizational process" (p. 41). For example, when candidates for a job are equally qualified in terms of so-called "objective" criteria, hiring decisions are often made on perceived "fit," and when "perceived fit" becomes an implicit hiring criterion, discrimination is most often neutralized.

The fourth and final tenet is that the decoupling of formal rules from organizational practice is often racialized. "Organizational rules designed to protect minority classes from discrimination are routinely broken, and racialized organizations are likely to apply rules differently based on the race of the rule-breaker" (p. 42). For example, most organizations have policies against racial discrimination and policies that protect those who file allegations of racial discrimination from retaliation. But research has shown that those filing these complaints are often ostracized, which illustrates the racialization of decoupling formal organizational rules from organizational practice (Roscigno, 2007).

The Case

Frederick Douglass "Fritz" Pollard and Bobby Marshall were the first Black players to play in the National Football League in its inaugural 1920 season (Pro Football Hall of Fame, n.d., para. 2), and institutionalized racism followed soon thereafter. For more than a decade, from the mid-1930s to just after World War II, an unwritten segregation of Blacks from professional football existed that ended when four players – Kenny Washington, Woody Strode, Marion Motley, and Bill Willis – were drafted as players into the league (Martinez, 2021, para. 1). Minorities quickly gained a foothold among the player ranks but not in hierarchically superior positions such as coach, general manager, and owner. Supporting the idea that the NFL was a closed society of "good ole boys," it was not until 1989 when Art Shell became the first Black NFL head coach of the modern era in Oakland, and the NFL waited for a new millennium before Ozzie Newsome became the first Black general manager in Baltimore in 2002 (Associated Press, 2020, para. 18).

For decades, the NFL has struggled with racial diversity in its coaching and front office ranks. For an organization in which Black players now constitute nearly 70% of the on-field talent (69.4%), only a paltry 24.5% and 13.7% hold the title of vice president or above in the NFL League Office and at the team level, respectively (Lapchick, 2020, pp. 1–4). This begs the question: What type of system exists that suppresses people with elite talent and superior knowledge of the game from rising to positions of power in a multi-billion-dollar juggernaut industry like the NFL? The problem is better understood by applying the tenets of racialized organizations theory to the NFL case.

Diminishing Racial Groups

Segregation

Limiting the pool of minority candidates for promotion is a way of prioritizing one group over another without requiring those with hiring responsibilities to actively discriminate. Loy and McElvogue (1970) studied how *centrality* – the idea that the most important players occupy positions closest to the football – impacts minority representation. For example, these positions might be the quarterback and center on offense. A position farthest from the ball might be the defensive cornerback or safety. In 1970, the researchers found that White players dominated central positions around the football. In 2018, Moore and Levitt reported that more than 80% of the quarterback and center positions in the NFL were occupied by Whites. Although Black quarterbacks are increasing in the NFL, they are still the minority. Moreover, of all the players identified as playing the center position in the NFL in 2021, 80% of them were White. To further make this point, there has not been a White NFL defensive cornerback since Jason Sehorn in 2003.

While the Loy and McElvogue study of centrality dealt with the positions of players, as a racialized organization, the NFL also exhibits *decision-making central-ity*, or the idea that the most important decisions in an organization are made by those at the top of the bureaucratic hierarchy. In the NFL, owners and general managers are the key positions when hiring head coaches, and those owners and general managers are overwhelmingly White and male. This fact has not changed since the inception of the Rooney Rule, despite the fact that studies have clearly shown that diversity in group composition leads to greater satisfaction in the organization (Downey et al., 2015), better decisions in educational groups (Gurin et al., 2002), jury deliberations (Sommers, 2006), and decisions about the value of commodities in marketplace trading (Levine et al., 2014). The 2022 version of the Rooney Rule considers it a positive step if team ownership includes diverse individuals, but it does not require minority participation in the ownership struc-ture (Seifert, 2022, para. 10–11).

Regarding NFL coaches, the practice of moving minorities to defensive coaching positions but then hiring head coaches from the offensive side of the ball is now common practice (Moore & Levitt, 2018, para. 5). In 2018, "of the eight minority head coaches to start [that] season, three-quarters of them [had] predominantly defensive backgrounds. In contrast, two thirds of the rest of the league's head coaches [came] from offensive backgrounds" (Moore & Lev-itt, 2018, para. 3). The updated Rooney Rule addresses this issue by requiring every NFL team to hire "a female or a member of an ethnic or racial minority" offensive assistant coach (Seifert, 2022, para. 2) to increase the pool of minor-ity candidates for future head coaching positions. To comply with the Rooney Rule, with women now in the pool, it is entirely possible for teams to interview White women for head coaching positions and then hire a White coach without interviewing a person of color.

Edwards (1973) explains that slight maneuvers, like those given before, mar-ginalize minorities and maintain the status quo. He explains they "channel Blacks away from alternative high-prestige positions, thus lessening the pressure of competition between them and dominant group members for valued goods and services [in this case, prime coaching positions] without resort[ing] to overt repression and physical coercion" (p. 203). In other situations, like race–norming, the racial element is more overt, as is the profit-loss equation, and the minimiza-tion of a Black athlete's life.

Legitimizing Unequal Distribution of Resources

Race-Norming

Greenlaw and Jensen (1996) define race-norming as "changing or modifying employment related tests on the basis of race or ethnicity" (p. 13). The practice was originally adopted in the 1990s ostensibly to compensate for bias in test questions that resulted in higher scores for Whites over minorities. Race-norming was also controversially applied in neuropsychology, including in the NFL, in determining compensation for traumatic brain injury cases. Race-norming is an illegal act according to the Civil Rights Act of 1991 (Greenlaw & Jensen, 1996, p. 17).

The NFL allegedly implemented a policy of race-norming its Black players when evaluating the level of dementia and, in so doing, decreased the monetary compensation for which a minority player could be eligible on the basis of cognitive impairment due to football-related injuries. In an investigative piece by *The Washington Post*, neuropsychologists hired by the NFL to evaluate levels of dementia in players say they were required by the NFL to apply race-norms to their evaluations. The NFL denies this, saying the decision to factor in race was at the discretion of the physician (Hobson, 2021, para. 9).

The race-norming practice, however, brings to light the fact that the NFL is convinced that minority players are inherently less mentally equipped than Whites. It is not a far leap then to assume that since the league has actually devalued Black players' intellect and mental abilities in the past, the league may be less likely to consider minorities as top-level coaching candidates. This is especially the case of minority veteran players in the NFL whose longevity as players may also make them more prone to traumatic brain injuries.

Rationalizing a System that Creates Minority Power

It is logical to think that a talent pool of managerial candidates might exist among a group of people who have mastered their profession. Professional athletes-turned-coaches abound in many sports. In fact, in two of America's major sports – Major League Baseball and the National Hockey League – where White players outnumber minorities, former players do become top coaches. However, in America's sports leagues where Black players are the majority – the National Basketball Association and the National Football League – former players rarely become top coaches (Bacon & Paine, 2020, para. 31). In the case of the NBA and the NFL, the team owners and executives are overwhelmingly White. But, elite athletes face an additional roadblock – time.

The best professional football players' careers may extend into those athletes' thirties. In tracking a person's journey up the coaching ladder, Bacon and Paine (2020) found that considering that a first NFL head coaching position usually comes before the age of 50, a playing professional is inherently behind the coaching curve. A more typical player's career may end in their early twenties when they then become an entry-level graduate assistant coach. Their mid-twenties to mid-forties are spent working their way through various coaching positions in college (position coach and coordinator) until they ultimately may reach the NFL. Bacon and Paine found that the majority of head coaches were chosen from NFL coordinator positions (2020, para. 14). Even among all NFL coordinators, the number of people of color is extremely low. Of the 61 offensive and defensive

NFL coordinator positions in 2020, there were 2 Black offensive coordinators, 9 Black defensive coordinators, and 1 Arab American defensive coordinator (2020, para. 14). And, of those NFL coordinators, head coaches are chosen predominantly from the offensive coordinator pool.

Eric Bieniemy is an example of a standout Black former player, with impeccable NFL coaching credentials as an offensive coordinator for a successful NFL franchise, but who, as of early 2022, has never been offered a head coaching position. Many pundits posit it is because Bieniemy leads an offense where the head coach, a White man, calls the plays. In this case, the Rooney Rule may get Bieniemy a meeting but may not get him the head coaching job. Whatever the situation, Bieniemy, a prime coaching prospect, with impeccable credentials, and wide recognition as such by NFL watchers, has been routinely passed up for head coaching positions.

Whiteness as a Credential

"Researchers found that minorities still fare worse when it comes to hiring, retaining their positions, and being granted 'second chances' at NFL head coaching positions" (Johnson, 2019, para. 2). According to a 2020 Global Sport Institute study, fired White NFL head coaches found new NFL head coaching jobs at twice the rate as their fired Black head coach counterparts (Global Sport Institute, 2020, para. 23). These fired White head coaches also found offensive coordinator positions – the prime job for future head coaching job considerations – at nearly three times the rate of coaches of color, based on the Global Sport Institute data (2020, para 23).

At the time of the 2020 study, only one outgoing head coach of color had gone on to another NFL head coaching position compared to nine White coaches (2020, p. 22). According to the Global Sport Institute (2020):

> It is noteworthy that Ron Rivera, who was fired by the Carolina Panthers, was subsequently hired by the Washington Football Team [now the Washington Commanders] for the 2020–21 season. This is an atypical example of a head coach of color getting a 'second chance.' This second chance for a head coach of color was not observed in any of the ten seasons included in the original data set.
>
> *(para. 2)*

Madden (2004) studied the differences in success factors of NFL coaches by race from 1990 to 2002. Her results found that Black coaches were more successful than White coaches, winning 1.1 games more per season than their White counterparts (p. 9). The analysis considers overall season records (p. 9), records in the first year (p. 11), and records in the year of an involuntary departure (p. 12). Madden's conclusion is that since Black coaches perform better than White coaches, it appears to be more of a "pipeline" problem – not enough Black coaches to choose from. However, others blame team owners who prefer to hire White coaches who look like them and function as the "face" of their franchise.

Sports reporter Jamele Hill recounts in *The Atlantic* times when NFL owners went out of their way to give White coaches interview opportunities not offered to Blacks. In 2020, Eric Bieniemy of the Super Bowl champion Kansas City Chiefs interviewed unsuccessfully for six NFL head coaching jobs. At that same time, Nick Sirianni, a White offensive coordinator for the Indianapolis Colts, was called for a head coaching interview with the Philadelphia Eagles while he was on vacation. Sirianni indicated interest but warned the team owner he did not have business attire with him, suitable for interviewing. In response, the team owner and his staff dressed casually to make the coaching candidate more comfortable. Sirianni was offered, and he accepted the coaching position (Hill, 2021). Sirianni's accomplishments in Indianapolis were impressive, but most would agree that they were not to be compared to Bieniemy's success in Kansas City.

Even dangling carrots like compensating teams for developing minority coaches appears fruitless. The NFL recently adopted this tactic in addition to expanding its interview requirements as part of its Rooney Rule. But even these changes have had no impact (Reimer, 2021, para. 18). Thus, it may be necessary to scrap this game plan and start anew.

Racializing the Decoupling of Formal Rules from Organizational Practice

The NFL recognizes the need to change its past organizational practices in order to diversify its on-field and front office leadership. To that end, the NFL provides incentives to its teams, by way of the Rooney Rule, to enhance the candidate pool and reward the hiring of minority candidates for both head coaching and managerial positions. As examples, the league now allows teams to interview candidates from other teams in the final two weeks of the season, creating a richer candidate pool. Improved draft selections are also available for teams that hire minority team leaders. However, despite this overt attempt to racialize the decoupling of organizational practices through the passage of new rules, these new incentivization policies do not appear to work.

Bacon and Paine suggest changes the NFL can make that might lead to the hiring of Black coaches:

> (1) diversify the ranks of offensive and defensive coordinators, (2) ensure the path to coordinator or head coach is not about connections and nepotism, (3) give a real first chance – and perhaps a second chance – to Black coaches, (4) be open to older coaches, and (5) ensure that playing in the NFL is not a negative credential – and even make it a positive one.
>
> *(2021, paras. 12–34)*

For these to be implemented league-wide, though, *attitudinal* change must occur. The latest changes to the Rooney Rule may make some headway toward attitudinal change. The mandated hiring of minority offensive coaches appears to be a positive step, although if a team already has one minority person in that position, they need not hire another. The formation of an NFL Diversity Advisory Committee realizes a promise made by NFL Commissioner Roger Goodell to have outsiders evaluate the league's diversity issues (Seifert, 2022). Significant steps forward are unlikely without even more concrete and lucrative incentives offered to team management. Toothless mandates and altruistic endeavors clearly do not get the attention of team owners.

You Make the Call

ROT makes clear that administrative change is worthless without foundational philosophical change within an organization, starting at the top. Even in a "win-or-face-firing" industry like the National Football League, the selection of professional football coaches must overcome deep-seated, historically based, racial systems that invisibly cloud the decision-making process.

Moore and Levitt (2018) summarized the problem and the potential solution well:

> If the NFL sideline is ever going to look like the men who suit up every Sunday, it's going to take more than diversity initiatives from the top. These problems represent generations-old biases that have burrowed deep within the minds of players, assistants, coaches, and scouts from coast to coast and from the youth level up through the professional ranks, and fixing it will take deep reflection and conscious action from the White men who remain overrepresented in positions of power.
>
> *(2018, para. 15)*

Changing a culture like the National Football League takes time, effort, and commitment at every level. The first step for the NFL is recognizing its racist past. Then, the NFL must consciously and conspicuously atone for past and current inequities in its policies and practices – like race-norming. Next, the NFL should act quickly and decisively to scaffold the Rooney Rule with new and immediate policies that allow for greater job candidate inclusion for all races at the coaching level and above, which it appears to be doing with its recent iteration of the Rooney Rule.

Last, there needs to be action by those impacted. The coaching candidates need to bring discrimination lawsuits at either the team or league level. Brian Flores's lawsuit will force the league into introspection, at the very least. NFL players need to be more vocal about the hiring of head coaches by team owners. Players today are outspoken about myriad social issues and use their powerful social media presence to shine a light on and address social disparities. However, the racial representation in NFL head coaching positions has not been on that agenda. If players publicly spotlight this issue, and if it is formally addressed by the NFL Players Association, these key stakeholders might move the topic more prominently to the fore.

This is all in the future, of course. For now, it is a matter of the NFL changing diversity-related policies, like the Rooney Rule, so that they actually address the problem for which they were created – increasing racial representation within the upper echelon of the NFL – and for the league's stakeholders like the players, fans and, sponsors to hold the NFL accountable for making the proper call.

Discussion Questions

1. Update the head coaching situation in the NFL. How has the number of head coaches of color changed since this book's printing? Has the NFL's Rooney Rule been changed? Discuss why you believe the coaching numbers stand as they do.
2. Since the goal of any competitive professional sport is to win, how might the current NFL hiring process that appears to de-emphasize pro players and people of color hinder that goal?
3. If you were the public relations professional for an NFL team searching for a head coach, how would you address questions about the NFL's policy of "race-norming" players and how that might impact the hiring of potential head coaches?
4. What suggestions do you have for NFL owners to assist them in recruiting, hiring, and retaining a more diverse workforce in their front office?
5. Analyze other professional sports' hiring policies and practices. Is there a model from another sport the NFL could adopt to improve its diversity hires at all levels of the organization?

References

Associated Press. (2020, January 8). Only 4 NFL coaches are minorities, while 70% of players are. *Market Watch*. www.marketwatch.com/story/nfl-hiring-of-Black-coaches-remains-at-historic-low-2020-01–08

Bacon, Jr., P., & Paine, N. (2020, January 29). A 5-part plan to fix the NFL's coaching diversity problem. *FiveThirtyEight*. https://fivethirtyeight.com/features/a-5-part-plan-to-fix-the-nfls-coaching-diversity-problem/

Bazner, K. (2021). Views from the middle: Racialized experiences of midlevel student affairs *administrators. Journal of Diversity in Higher Education*. Advance online publication. http://dx.doi.org/10.1037/dhe0000384

Blunt, T.O. (2018, December 12). NFL expands Rooney Rule requirements to strengthen diversity. *NFL Communications*. https://nflcommunications.com/Pages/NFL-EXPANDS-ROONEY-RULE-REQUIREMENTS-TO-STRENGTHEN-DIVERSITY.aspx.

Celis, L.E., Hays, C., Mehrotra, A., & Vishnoi, N.K. (2020). The effect of the Rooney Rule on implicit bias in the long term. *Computers and Society*, 1–54. https://arxiv.org/abs/2010.10992

Collins, B.W. (2007). Tackling unconscious bias in hiring practices: The plight of the Rooney Rule. *New York University Law Review, 82*, 870–912.

Corapi, J. (2012). Red card: Using the National Football League's Rooney Rule to eject race discrimination from English professional soccer's managerial and executive hiring practices. *Fordham Intellectual Property, Media & Entertainment Law Journal, 23*(1), 341–395.

Dixon, S. (2020, June 14). The NFL – with or without fans this season – is on decent financial footing because of its lucrative TV contracts. *Chicago Tribune*. https://www.chicagotribune.com/sports/breaking/ct-nfl-tv-money-20200614-ghh5urtcfvawbdl-h5xv4pp3w6m-story.html

Downey, S.N., van der Werff, L., Thomas, K.M., & Plaut, V.C. (2015). The role of diversity practices and inclusion in promoting trust and employee engagement. *Journal of Applied Social Psychology, 45*(1), 35–44. http://doi/org/10.1111/jasp.12273

DuBois, C. (2015). The impact of "soft" affirmative policies on minority hiring in executive leadership: The case of the NFL's Rooney Rule. *American Law and Economics Review, 18*(1), 208–233. https://doi.org/10.1093/aler/ahv019

Duru, N.J. (2008). The Fritz Pollard Alliance, the Rooney Rule, and the quest to "level the playing field" in the National Football League. *Virginia Sports and Entertainment Law Journal, 7*(2), 179–198.

Edwards, H. (1973). *The sociology of sport.* Homewood, IL: The Dorsey Press. https://archive.org/details/SociologyOfSport/page/n209/mode/2up

Enriquez, L.E., Vazquez, D.V., & Ramakrishnan, S.K. (2019). Driver's licenses for all? Racialized illegality and the implementation of progressive immigration policy in California. *Law and Policy, 1*(41), 34–58. http://doi.org/10.1111/lapo.12121

Global Sport Institute (2020). Field studies: A 10-season snapshot of NFL coaching. *Global Sport Matters*. https://globalsportmatters.com/from-our-lab

Greenlaw, P.S., & Jensen, S.S. (1996). Race-norming and the civil rights act of 1991. *Public Personnel Management, 25*(1), 13–24. https://doi.org/10.1177/009102609602500102

Gurin, P., Dey, E.L., Hurtado, S., & Gunn, G. (2002). Diversity and higher education: Theory and impact on educational outcomes. *Harvard Educational Review, 72*, 330–366.

Hill, J. (2021, February 5). 'Some team has to want me': The NFL has pledged to address racism, but team owners still won't put Black coaches in charge. *The Atlantic*. www.theatlantic.com/ideas/archive/2021/02/Black-coaches-see-the-limits-of-the-nfls-racial-reckoning/617943/

Hobson, W. (2021, August 2). How "race-norming" was built into the concussion settlement. *The Washington Post*. www.washingtonpost.com/sports/2021/08/02/race-norming-nfl-concussion-settlement/

Johnson, M. (30, December 2019). New study: Minority coaches still fare worse during NFL hiring process. *Andscape*. https://andscape.com/features/new-study-minority-coaches-still-fare-worse-during-nfl-hiring-process/

Lapchick, R.E. (2020, December 9). *The NFL racial and gender report card.* The Institute for Diversity and Ethics in Sport. www.tidesport.org/_files/ugd/138a69_8715a573a5174 2ce95dddeb0461cfc82.pdf

Lerma, V., Hamilton, L.T., & Nielson, K. (2020). Racialized equity labor, university appropriation and student resistance. *Social Problems, 67*, 286–303. http://doi/org/10.1093/socpro/spz011

Levine, S.S., Apfelbaum, E.P., Bernard, M., Bartelt, V.L., Zajac, E.J., & Stark, D. (2014). Ethnic diversity deflates price bubbles. *Proceedings of the National Academy of Science, 111*, 18524–18529.

Loy, J.W., & McElvogue, J.F. (1970). Racial segregation in American sport. *International Review of Sport Sociology, 5*, 5–23.

Madden, J.F. (2004). Differences in the success of NFL coaches by race, 1990–2002: Evidence of last hire, first fire. *Journal of Sports Economics, 5*(1), 6–19. http://doi/org/10.1177/1527002503257245

Martinez, A. (2021, September 22). 'The forgotten first': Remembering Black players who broke the NFL's color barrier. *NPR*. www.npr.org/2021/09/22/1039565509/the-forgotten-first-remembering-Black-players-who-broke-the-nfls-color-barrier.

Moore, J., & Levitt, D. (2018, September 19). The NFL's Rooney Rule: Why football's racial divide is larger than ever. *The Guardian*. www.theguardian.com/sport/ng-interactive/2018/sep/19/nfl-rooney-rule-coaching-statistics

Nichols, M.J. (2008). Time for a Hail Mary? With bleak prospects of being aided by a college version of the NFL's Rooney Rule, should minority college football coaches turn their attention to Title VII litigation? *Virginia Sports and Entertainment Law Journal, 8*(1), 147–172.

Pro Football Hall of Fame. (n.d.). Frederick Douglass "Fritz" Pollard. www.profootball-hof.com/players/fritz-pollard/

Ray, V. (2019). A theory of racialized organizations. *American Sociological Review, 84*(1), 26-53. https://journals.sagepub.com/doi/10.1177/0003122418822335

Reimer, A. (2021, January 22). NFL teams egregiously passing on Black head coaches shows Rooney Rule can't change bias. *Forbes*. www.forbes.com/sites/alexreimer/2021/01/22/nfl-teams-egregiously-passing-on-Black-head-coaches-shows-rooney-rule-cant-change-biases/?sh=ec7e02118025

Roscigno, V. (2007). *The face of discrimination: How race and gender impact work and home lives*. Plymouth: Rowman and Littlefield.

Seifert, K. (2022, March 29). NFL says all teams must add minority offensive coach, expands Rooney Rule to include women. *ESPN*. www.espn.com/nfl/story/_/id/33617341/nfl-says-all-teams-add-minority-offensive-coach-expands-rooney-rule-include-women.

Solow, B.L., Solow, J.L., & Walker, T. (2011). Moving on up: The Rooney Rule and minority hiring practices in the NFL. *Labor Economics, 18*, 332–337. https://doi.org/10.1016/j.labeco.2010.11.010

Sommers, S.R. (2006). On racial diversity and group decision making: Identifying multiple effects of racial composition on jury deliberations. *Journal of Personality and Social Psychology, 90*, 597–612.

Tiako, M.J.N, South, E.C., & Ray, V. (2021). Medial schools as racialized organizations. *Annals of Internal Medicine, 174*(8), 1143–1145. https://doi.org/10.7326/M21-0369

3

WHEN FANDOM STAINS YOUR TEAM

Evaluating the Effectiveness of the Utah Jazz's Organizational Responses to Racist Incidents

Nicola A. Corbin and Anne Bialowas

Introduction

During a 2019 NBA game against the Utah Jazz, then-Oklahoma City Thunder star Russell Westbrook was captured on video yelling profanely at Jazz fans off-camera. The clip of the lopsided diatribe by Westbrook made the rounds in traditional and social media accompanied by heated debate. Westbrook said the fan told him to "get down on your knees like you're used to," words the fan subsequently denied (Stevens & Draper, 2019, para 2). This encounter was not the first for Westbrook. In 2018, again at the Jazz, Westbrook was called "boy" repeatedly by a fan. Two years later, three Jazz fans racially abused and sexually harassed the family of the Memphis Grizzlies' Ja Morant as they watched him play in Utah. Tee Morant, father of Ja, recounted one fan saying "I'll put a nickel in your back and watch you dance, boy" in an interview (MacMahon, 2021a, para 7).

The 2018 and 2019 Westbrook incidents touched off steady media conversation about disrespectful fan behavior. Former and current players, sports commentators, and columnists used these opportunities to relate their own experiences playing at Jazz home games. Former player Stephen Jackson[1], whose career spanned eight NBA teams, said that "Utah is probably the worst city I've played in in my career dealing with that [racism] because it's definitely not a place for the brothas" (Bayless & Sharpe, 2018 1:56) Another former player, Etan Thomas, confirmed these sentiments in an op-ed titled, "When it comes to racially abusive fans, the NBA has a Utah problem" (2019), saying that the usual fan heckling seems different with racial undertones in Utah and that this reputation is a "poorly kept secret" (para. 7) among players in the league.

Vernon Maxwell, who regularly criticized the Utah Jazz on social media, explained why he did so on *The Rex Chapman Show* podcast in 2021:

DOI: 10.4324/9781003316763-5

> The people out there, they abused me. Talk about my mama, my grandma, talk about the stillborn; they call me the N-word. You see what they did to Ja Morant and his mom and dad. I keep telling these people they've been doing this for a long time. People are acting like this shit is new.

It is clear the Utah Jazz has developed a negative reputation, both inside and outside of the NBA, connected to racial harassment by its fans that exploded in 2018 and 2019, prompting responses from the Jazz organization. This case study analyzes team management responses within the context of the theory of corporate responsibility to race (CRR) (Logan, 2021) to assess its potential efficacy in addressing deeply ingrained, socio-cultural issues.

Background

To better understand the development of the negative racial reputation regarding the Utah Jazz fans and its resonance, it is necessary to contextualize particular dynamics and conditions both within the NBA and the state of Utah. The NBA was once a predominantly White organization from players to owners; however, its composition has shifted starkly over the years. It is now a league of predominantly Black players even as the coaches, professionals, and owners remain mostly White. According to a 2020 report from The Institute of Diversity and Ethics in Sport, 74.2% of all NBA players identified as Black or African American while 16.9% identified as White (Lapchick, 2020). Roughly 83% identified as people of color (Lapchick, 2020). As of July 2020, there were 10 head coaches of color, or 33.3% of all coaches, 26% of these identified as Black or African American. According to Lapchick (2020), this percentage of people of color is the best in men's professional sport.

All in all, the current portrait of the NBA is one that is racially polarized in representation – predominantly Black players on the one hand and a predominantly White coaching, professional, and ownership circle on the other. These dynamics enable racialized power dynamics in a sport in which people are "owned" and "traded." A poignant example of this dynamic was the 2014 case of then-LA Clippers owner Donald Sterling who was recorded telling his girlfriend that he did not want her publicly associating with Black people after she posted a picture of herself and NBA Hall of Famer Magic Johnson on her social media page (Golliver, 2014). This episode created a crisis within the team with charges of a "plantation mentality" (c.f. Shelburne, 2019).

Media, Masculinity, Race, and Sport

Despite legislation that ostensibly affords equal access and opportunities in athletic pursuits, there is still racism in the arena of sport that, in general, characterizes Black males as "natural" athletes and White male athletes as harder workers, superior leaders, more mentally astute, and team orientated (Buffington, 2005). False assumptions and myths exist that, biologically, Blacks are "built for" particular sports. Characteristics usually attributed to Blacks are "quickness, strength, aggressiveness, instincts, and natural ability" (Levy & Bryant, 1993, p. 115). In addition to the stereotypical mediated portrayal of Black athletes playing particular sports is a representation of "Blackness" and Black athletic bodies in need of regulation and containment.

Within particular sports, such as professional basketball, Leonard (2006) argued that Black athletes are represented as embodying a population that "necessitates surveillance and regulation" (p. 160; also see Leonard, 2012) because the Black body can be seen as "potentially unruly and unproductive" (Hughes, 2004, p. 179). Analyzing the fallout as a result of the 2004 Detroit Pistons and Indiana Pacers brawl[2], Griffin (2012) argues that the NBA needed to commodify "the Black male body to reify Whiteness as the status quo" as the NBA needed to protect the image of the league following the fight (p. 162). While not in direct reference to the Palace brawl, Lavelle (2015) analyzed racial representations in the NBA and noted that when Black players "break rules, they are more quickly punished or vilified than their White counterparts" (p. 298). This is not to say that Black NBA players are not deserving of punishment for breaking rules, but the NBA is a place where masculinity, and Black masculinity in particular, is on display for critique and articulated into our everyday understandings of race. Within the earlier stages of the Black Lives Matter movement, Manning et al. (2021) argued NBA players were part of a discursive shift where the NBA was a contested platform for social justice issues as players took a more explicit role in activism.

Next, it is necessary to contextualize the environment from which the Utah Jazz fandom emerges. Utah's general demographics present representational barriers for NBA players who might be more used to racially mixed audiences in the stands. According to the 2020 U.S. Census (U.S. Census Bureau, n.d.), Utah's White population stood at 90% while its Black or African American population constituted only 1.5% of the state's population. For further consideration is the religious and political constitution of the state. Utah is the headquarters for the Church of Jesus Christ of Latter-day Saints (LDS) with 68.5% of the state's population identifying as members of the church (Statistics and church facts, n.d.). According to Mueller (2017), Latter-day Saints are reliably Republican, pro-life and anti-gay marriage. These statistics largely extend to its political class and government. Further, for more than a century, the LDS church banned Black men and women from entering its most sacred place, the temple, as they were deemed unworthy because of their race. Mueller (2017) cites church papers that document the religion's founders and church presidents up until 1970 asserting "in speeches and widely read theological treatises that because they were members of a divinely cursed race, people of African descent were spiritually unworthy to be full members of the church" (p. 10). Only in 2013 did the church begin to distance itself theologically from such treatises.

All of these realities impact the environment from which the Jazz's fan base emerges and the context within which the Jazz players and visiting teams operate. Originally based in New Orleans, the Jazz moved to Salt Lake City in 1979. It has been the only professional sports organization located in Utah until the recent arrival of the REAL Salt Lake soccer team. The team's prominence and what it means to the state's residents in terms of visibility and group identity contribute to the loyalty and fervor of its fan base.

Owned until 2020 by the Miller family, the Jazz is a small market team that attempts to attract and retain big market players. However, the state's racial demographics and dominant political attitudes create moments of hostility and intolerance to outsiders or those who are different from the dominant group. As an example of the balance the organization attempts to strike between church culture and the NBA's requirements is a ban on Sunday home games during the regular season. This policy is in line with the Latter-day Saints policy of observing Sunday as the Sabbath. This policy does not extend to the NBA's playoff schedule or away games. All in all, the Utah Jazz finds itself in a contextual milieu of trying to achieve success in its own local market through attracting and retaining loyal fans, while also chasing larger market attention and fans to expand its financial reach and ultimately win an NBA championship with high caliber players.

The larger U.S. racial context within which the Westbrook and Morant incidents occurred also impacted their resonance. The national conversation about race re-emerged in sharper relief with the election of Barack Obama in 2008. Soon thereafter, the murder of Trayvon Martin, a Black 17-year-old boy by a vigilante neighbor who was later acquitted, triggered the formation and rise of the Black Lives Matter movement (Herstory – Black Lives Matter, n.d.). This case was followed by a series of violent incidents that managed to garner public media attention involving Black men and boys and law enforcement, which brought increasing tension and protests nationwide. Additionally, there was an observable decline in civil public rhetoric.

The Case

On March 12, 2019, one day following the Westbrook incident at a Jazz home game, the Utah Jazz organization issued a lifetime ban to a fan for excessive and derogatory verbal abuse of a player, and the NBA fined Westbrook $25,000 for directing profanity and threatening language toward a fan (Gephardt Daily, 2019). Two days later, 75-year-old Gail Miller, owner and chair of the team, walked onto center court and delivered a three-and-half minute address to the 18,000 plus fans (Miller, 2019). The address received a standing ovation in the arena and was hailed as "simply a powerful and from-the-heart statement" by the game's sports broadcaster (Miller, n.d). Multiple news outlets reported on the story, and social media was abuzz with positive response for both Miller and the Utah Jazz. The team also sent an email to season ticket holders that reiterated Miller's main points and included a mention of the arena's code of conduct (Gephardt Daily, 2019). Were the public statement by Gail Miller, the organization's lifetime ban of the spectator, and the season ticket holder email enough to undertake the heavy psychological lift associated with addressing cultural racism? To address this question, this case study eschews more traditional academic frameworks of crisis and image restoration (e.g., Benoit, 1995; Coombs, 1995) as they fall short in explicitly addressing the deeply embedded issue of race that sits at the center of this case. To better answer the question, CRR is utilized.

Developed by Logan, the theory of CRR provides a specific analytic lens to guide and critique corporate engagement with racial issues. Logan (2021) argues that such a theory is a necessary departure from the "self-interested way that corporations typically communicate about matters of race . . . that often aim to protect reputations, augment labor resources, and ultimately enrich the corporate bottom line" (p. 1). While the pragmatism of such goals cannot be easily dismissed, it is worth noting that the moral imperative to act in particular situations supersedes an organization's bottom line. Racist acts and racism, which are bound up in power and ideological dynamics that shape social relations, fit the criteria. Additionally, Logan (2021) argues that because corporations have historically benefited from, and even perpetuated, systems of racial oppression, they now have specific moral responsibilities of redress to ensure a more racially just and equitable society. In short, CRR argues that corporations must challenge the status quo and advocate for racial justice because it is simply the right thing to do for the greater society.

CRR prescribes the following principles to which communicators should adhere: (1) Name and draw attention to the racist act, practice, structure, or system; (2) highlight the implications of the act and the complexities within which such racism operates; (3) advocate for racial justice and racial equity; (4) express a desire to improve race relations for the benefit of a more equitable and harmonious society; and (5) prioritize the needs of society over the economic needs of the corporation (Logan, 2021).

Although it was publicly a success by the standards of Jazz players, fans, and many within the NBA circuit, Miller's strong statement has room for improvement when held to CRR scrutiny. The first principle of CRR is to name and draw attention to the racist act, ensuring that it is more than a vague allusion. Miller did not directly state that the Westbrook incident was racist, even though the player called it so (Stevens & Draper, 2019). Instead, she used direct descriptors of an "unfortunate event" and a "bad incident" that was offensive (Miller, 2019). The only mention of the word racism came when she said, "We are not a racist community" (Miller, 2019, para. 2). The choice to not directly call the incident itself racist, but to make a broader defense of Jazz fans against allegations of racism was an artful rhetorical turn. Given the discrepancy of the public reports of the incident about who said what (Stevens & Draper, 2019), Miller chose instead to address the larger, reputational conversation that the incident provoked about the Jazz. This statement is an acknowledgment that the team has a problem with its fans' image around race. Jazz player Rudy Gobert echoed these sentiments when he said in a post-game interview that "It hurts to see other people calling Jazz fans racist. I think she got affected a lot by it" (Falk, 2019, para. 17).

In this instance, Miller's approach fails to connect in a direct way to the actions and thus fails to satisfy CRR's first principle. The emailed statement to season ticket holders, however, was more direct in making the connection to fan behavior in the arena. It read in part that "We do not permit hate speech, racism, sexism or homophobia. We also do not allow disruptive behavior, including bullying, foul or abusive language, or obscene gestures" (Gephardt Daily, 2019).

However, Miller did draw attention to problematic behavior that some would interpret as racist, while others might argue against. One of the many challenges with calling out racism is the difficulty in evidencing it, although present. Since it is often couched in references to historically offensive terms better known to the affected group than to the wider population, a debate as to whether a statement was racist can ensue, diluting, diverting, and detracting from the harm the statement caused. For example, in the 2018 incident, Westbrook was repeatedly called "boy." This word is a historically specific insult emanating from slavery that continues to be used to demean the manhood of Black men. However, depending on one's exposure, it is likely not well understood.

The second principle outlined in CRR is that the communicator must highlight the implications of the racist act and the complexities within which racism operates. Again, Miller's statement only partially accomplishes this principle in two places when she named the stakeholders affected by the fan's actions. First she named the people offended:

> I am extremely disappointed that one of our quote "fans" conducted himself in such a way as to offend not only a guest in our arena, but also me personally, my family, our organization, the community, our players, and you, as the best fans in the NBA.
>
> *(Miller, 2019, para. 1)*

This statement hailed the wide audiences who were affected by the actions. By including herself and her family in this group, she personalized the impact of the act, which as a wealthy, older White woman has significance. As former NBA player Steve Kerr, who is White, said:

> There is no question the reaction to me saying exactly the same thing as a black athlete is taken a different way even if the words were exact. It is looked at differently. I think it is important for everybody to speak out if they feel comfortable doing so.
>
> *(Spears, 2019, para. 12)*

In the same way, Miller's intersectional identities of race, gender, age, and socioeconomic status certainly intervened in positive ways in this instance. Additionally, her smaller physical stature, soft-spoken nature, and a known avoidance of the spotlight make her appearance on the court, and the personalization of hurt, feel even more significant. The inclusion of the community, players, and fans in this statement nodded vaguely to the overall corrosive ramifications of racism to organizations and communities. At the same time, in a negative sense, it is interesting to note that she separates "our organization" and "our players," reinforcing the distinction between owners and owned.

More specifically, she said that "When bad incidents like Monday night happen, it not only affects the player it's directed at, it also affects our players" (Miller, 2019, para. 3) This second statement is a step more specific than the first, but stops short of saying *how* it affects the Jazz players, many of whom are Black men. All in all, these statements begin to approach the implications and avoid being complicit with silence, which is commendable; however, they are not incisive enough to explain the ramifications of these actions to the players and the community, which would often lead to more audience understanding.

CRR principles also call for communications to advocate for racial justice and equity by challenging, expressing a desire to improve race relations for the benefit of a more equitable and harmonious society, and prioritizing the needs of society over the economic needs of the corporation, simply because it is the right thing to do. Although Miller's statement is more vague and less direct linguistically than CRR principles demand – requiring a more overt address to race – Miller did call on Jazz fans to:

> Support our players as citizens of our community, and treat them and their families with respect. They have chosen to be a part of our community, and they make us richer with our diversity . . . No one wins when respect goes away.
>
> *(Miller, 2019, para. 4)*

You Make the Call

From the public's perception, Gail Miller's decision to make her statement at center court on March 12, 2019 was a courageous demonstration of leadership. It was also evident that this decision emanated from her personal feelings about the incident:

> It happened in my house, which was the arena. I felt like if I didn't make my thoughts and desires known, who else could? There wasn't anybody in a position to do that better than I was because I had the right, I had the platform, and I had the opportunity, and I had the desire.
>
> *(Watkins, 2021, 1:55)*

Then-Jazz player Jae Crowder said:

> It means the world. For her to be courageous and go up in front of our fans to make that statement, we applaud her. We're behind her. We let her know that even before she made the speech. It means a lot to us players and hopefully it means a lot to our fans, to respect and listen to what she has to say.
>
> *(Falk, 2019, para. 18)*

It is worth considering further actions the Jazz organization took beyond this incident to address issues of race, as one statement alone may not meet all CRR principles. Following her 2019 statement, Miller and the Jazz organization directed the launch of *Lead Together*, an initiative involving athletic leaders that focused on respect, civility, and sportsmanship.

Former Jazz player Kyle Korver, who is White, also published a well-received introspective article, after Miller's initial speech, examining his own privilege in comparison to the observed experiences of his Black teammates (Korver, 2019). In the piece, Korver sketched a context in which racism dangerously persists not as the loud and stupid kind "that announces itself when it walks into the arena" (Korver, 2019, para. 63). For Korver, it persists in the person who does and says all the right and very polite things in public, but in private "they sort of wish that everyone would stop making everything 'about race' all the time" (para. 63). Korver's argument engages the CRR principles by first calling for identification of racism and, then, for denouncing it – "actively, and at every level" (Korver, 2019, para. 67). According to Korver, these steps constitute the bare minimum. One might assume that Miller's demonstrated leadership also provided openings for players to express themselves; Korver's essay directly aligned linguistically with stated CRR principles.

After the murder of George Floyd at the hands of police in May 2020, and the subsequent countrywide protests, Miller was one of the first Utah leaders to issue a clear and direct statement: "Hearts across America, and in Utah, are hurting following events of racism, discrimination, and injustice sparked by the recent and senseless death of George Floyd" (Miller, 2020, para. 1). Miller said that following Floyd's murder, she met with Black Jazz employees and players for a deep conversation about their experiences. Under new leadership with Ryan Smith, the Jazz's minority ownership group now includes former NBA star Dwayne Wade, who is Black and has had his own race-based experiences as a player. In 2021, Ryan Smith introduced a program offering a 4-year college scholarship to an underrepresented or minority student after each Jazz win (Wells, 2021).

Taken together, the statement by Gail Miller, the email sent to season ticket holders, and the action of permanently banning the fan were strong initial steps. Miller's statement was heartfelt and authentic, though it missed a critical opportunity to explicitly name and shame racism; instead, in a nod to Utah's cultural norms and demographics, Miller opted for language advocating civility, respect, and good manners. Within the context of the CRR framework, this decision weakened the potential for organizational redress. To wit, the racist heckling incident with Ja Morant's parents that resulted in the banning of three Jazz fans occurred in 2021. In this incident, Tee Morant, Ja Morant's father, was clear to say that other Jazz fans intervened (just as Miller had asked in her statement) and supported the family, for which Morant expressed public appreciation (MacMahon, 2021b). Miller's continued leadership within the state on the issue, and the new owner's equity-minded first steps, indicate that the Jazz is moving progressively forward to make substantive changes that will benefit society first and the team's reputation.

Discussion Questions

1. Update the chapter to identify other NBA teams that have faced similar racial incidents. Given the context of each situation, including the political and demographics of the home state, prescribe a list of action steps for each organization to take adhering to CRR principles.
2. Is a theory of corporate responsibility of race worthwhile for all sports organizations to explore? Why? If not, which sports organizations would benefit most and least from using this theory in their public relations processes?
3. What is the best way for an organization to issue an apology? Public speech? Tweet? Press conference? How can an organization appear authentic while also addressing CRR?
4. Are White male athletes characterized differently from Black athletes and/or other athletes of color? Why or why not?

Notes

1 Stephen Jackson was part of the infamous Malice at the Palace brawl in 2004 which began with a fight between players and escalated when a fan threw a beverage from the stands at a player.
2 The 2004 brawl is infamous, as noted by the 2021 Netflix Documentary *Untold: Malice at the Palace*, as both team benches cleared, and NBA players and fans were fighting with each other in the stands and on the court.

References

Bayless, S., & Sharpe, S. (2018, April 30). Skip and Shannon: UNDISPUTED. Stephen Jackson on who's to blame for Thunder's early exit in 2018 NBA playoffs. [Video] *Youtube*. www.youtube.com/watch?v=KfHsAIaq8Ds&t=154s

Benoit, W.L. (1995). *Accounts, excuses, and apologies: A theory of image restoration strategies.* Albany: SUNY Press.

Buffington, D. (2005). Contesting race on Sundays: Making meaning out of the rise in the number of Black quarterbacks. *Sociology of Sport Journal, 21*, 19–37.

Chapman, R. (2021, June 27). The Rex Chapman Show. Vernon Maxwell explains what made him hate Utah Jazz fans. *Youtube*. www.youtube.com/watch?v=PL3oVwYJtVI

Coombs, W.T. (1995). Choosing the right words: The development of guidelines for the selection of the "appropriate" crisis-response strategies. *Management communication quarterly, 8*(4), 447–476.

Falk, A. (2019, March 15). 'No one wins when respect goes away,' Utah Jazz owner Gail Miller tells fans in pregame address. *Utah Jazz.* www.nba.com/jazz/news/utah-jazz-owner-gail-miller-delivers-message-fans-vivint-smart-home-arena

Gephardt Daily Staff. (2019, March 15). Jazz owner Gail Miller issues statement on NBA code of conduct, fan behavior. *Gephardt Daily.* https://gephardtdaily.com/local/jazz-owner-gail-miller-issues-statement-regarding-nba-code-of-conduct/

Golliver, B. (2014, April 26). NBA investigating clippers owner Donald Sterling for alleged racist comments. *Sports Illustrated.* www.si.com/nba/2014/04/26/donald-sterling-nba-investigation-racist-comments-clippers

Griffin, R.A. (2012). The disgrace of commodification and shameful convenience: A critical race critique of the NBA. *Journal of Black Studies, 43*(2), 161–185.

Herstory – Black Lives Matter. (n.d.). https://blacklivesmatter.com/herstory/

Hughes, G. (2004). Managing Black guys: Representation, corporate culture, and the NBA. *Sociology of Sport Journal, 21,* 163–185.

Korver, K. (2019, April 8). Privileged. *The Players Tribune.* www.theplayerstribune.com/articles/kyle-korver-utah-jazz-nba

Lapchick, R.E. (2020). The 2020 racial and gender report card: National Basketball Association. *The Institute for Diversity and Ethics in Sport.* www.tidesport.org/_files/ugd/7d86e5_9ed7a1185cc8499196117ce9a2c0d050.pdf

Lavelle, K.L. (2015). No room for racism: Restoration of order in the NBA. *Communication & Sport.* https://doi.org/10.1177/2167479515584046

Leonard, D.J. (2006). The real color of money: Controlling Black bodies in the NBA. *Journal of Sport & Social Issues, 30,* 158–179.

Leonard, D.J. (2012). *After artest: The NBA and WNBA and the assault on blackness.* New York: State University of New York Press.

Levy, K.D., & Bryant, J.E. (1993). A content analysis of copy and advertisement photographs in *Sports Illustrated* and *Sport*: A measure of discrimination. *Physical Educator, 50,* 114–120.

Logan, N. (2021). A theory of corporate responsibility to race (CRR): Communication and racial justice in public relations. *Journal of Public Relations Research.* https://doi.org/10.1080/1062726X.2021.1881898

MacMahon, T. (2021a, May 27). Ja Morant's dad says 3 banned Jazz fans made lewd, racist remarks during Game 2 in Utah. *ESPN.* www.espn.com/nba/story/_/id/31523231/utah-jazz-ban-three-fans-verbal-altercation-game-2-vs-grizzlies

MacMahon, T. (2021b, June 3). Ja Morant's father pulling for Utah Jazz after team's response to fan incidents. *ESPN.* www.espn.com/nba/story/_/id/31560640/ja-morant-father-pulling-utah-jazz-team-response-fan-incidents

Manning, A., Suh, S.C., & Green, K. (2021). Discursive footwork on the hardwood: Players' negotiations of the NBA as a contested racial area. *European Journal for Sport and Society.* https://doi.org/10.1080/16138171.2021.1941614

Miller, G. (2019). Gail Miller addresses the home crowd. *Youtube.* www.youtube.com/watch?v=J35NmHP2aqI

Miller, G. (2020, May 31). A statement from Gail Miller, Owner of the Larry H. Miller Group of Companies and the Utah Jazz. *Lhm.com.* www.lhm.com/press-releases/working-together-for-peace-understanding-and-respect/

Mueller, M.P. (2017). *Race and the making of the Mormon people*. Chapel Hill, NC: The University of North Carolina Press.

Shelburne, R. (2019, August 20). The Donald Sterling-Clippers controversy almost made the NBA shut down. SportsCenter, ESPN. [Video] *Youtube*. www.youtube.com/watch?v=BiA4_UQSDjE

Spears, M.J. (2019, April 9). Why Kyle Korver's words on white privilege and racism matter. *The Undefeated*. https://theundefeated.com/features/why-jazz-kyle-korver-words-on-white-privilege-and-racism-matter/

Statistics and Church Facts: Total church Membership. (n.d.). Statistics and church facts: Total church membership. https://newsroom.churchofjesuschrist.org/facts-and-statistics/state/utah

Stevens, M., & Draper, K. (2019, March 12). Russell Westbrook says Utah Jazz Fan made 'Racial' Taunt that led to confrontation. *The New York Times*. www.nytimes.com/2019/03/12/sports/russell-westbrook-utah-fan.html

Thomas, E. (2019, March 15). When it comes to racially abusive fans, the NBA has a Utah problem. *The Guardian*. www.theguardian.com/sport/2019/mar/15/russell-westbrook-fan-abuse-utah-jazz-racist

U.S. Census Bureau. (n.d.). Quick facts Utah. www.census.gov/quickfacts/UT

Watkins, R. (2021, January 29). A conversation about civility with Gail Miller. *Office of the President*. https://president.utah.edu/u-rising-podcast/a-conversation-about-civility-with-gail-miller/

Wells, D. (2021, January 8). New Jazz owner Ryan Smith to offer scholarship for every jazz win. *KSTU*. www.fox13now.com/news/local-news/new-jazz-owner-ryan-smith-to-offer-scholarship-for-every-jazz-win

4

CONCUSSION SETTLEMENT AND RACIAL NORMING

The NFL Fumbles into a Crisis

Cory Young, Terry L. Rentner and Annemarie Farrell

Introduction

Imagine for a moment three professors representing different perspectives – public relations/ crisis communications, conflict, and sports management – sitting at a bar. All three have researched the National Football League (NFL) and its concussion crisis. As part of the lawsuit filed by 5,000 NFL players, a settlement of $765 million was awarded in 2013. Since August 2020, the League has been involved in court-ordered mediation with two retired NFL players Kevin Henry and Najeh Davenport, who alleged race-based benchmarks were "used by doctors to evaluate dementia-related claims . . . [and] 'explicitly and deliberately' discriminated against hundreds if not thousands of Black players" (Belson, 2021, para. 1).

According to Madden (2021a):

> The practice of adjusting test scores for race, widely known as 'race-norming,' is in use across several different medical fields as a safeguard against misdiagnosis. But because these 'norms' as used in a neuropsychology context, assume that the average Black football player starts at a lower level of cognitive functioning than the average White player at the outset of their careers, Black players need to show larger cognitive declines than White players to qualify for compensation.
>
> *(para. 15)*

Accordingly, using different scales for different races is "literally the definition of systematic racism" (Madden, 2021b, para. 19).

We were captivated by the concept of racial norming that emerged because of perceived inequities in the criteria used to allocate the 2013 lawsuit settlement

DOI: 10.4324/9781003316763-6

funds of $765 million as an outcome of the concussion crisis. We wanted to analyze the mediation process between the League and its players in real time and understand the League's crisis communication strategies, using the theoretical and conceptual framework of nesting, a paradigm that illustrates how crises (Carastathis, 2018; Mohandesi, 2020) and conflicts (Dugan, 1996) may arise from many sources and be intertwined, or nested, within one another. Combining a nesting perspective on crisis with a nested perspective on conflict allowed us to create a new theoretical paradigm – a nested model of crisis. Finally, best practices are offered for how communicators can navigate a nested crisis.

Background

The NFL as a professional sports organization has fumbled many scandals, crises, and "gates" but remains a strong viable institution embedded in the American cultural psyche. It is a complex organization that exists at the confluence of specific socio-historical contexts and political issues related to race (Black Lives Matter) and concerning organizational communication processes such as collective bargaining agreements, conflict resolution, and crisis and reputation management strategies. This phenomenon has vast implications, as almost 70 % of NFL players identify as African Americans (Lapchick, 2019).

Since the death of Mike Webster, a former Pittsburgh Steelers player, the NFL has been in the spotlight over a concussion crisis that emerged due to Chronic Traumatic Encephalopathy (CTE), a degenerative brain disease associated with repeated brain injuries or blows to the head discovered in Webster and in the brains of other deceased football players. The lawsuit filed against the NFL appeared to resolve the concussion crisis. However, Judge Anita Brody of the U.S. District Court for the Eastern District of Pennsylvania ordered the NFL and Christopher Seeger, lead lawyer for 20,000 or so retired players, into mediation to "'address the concerns relating to the race-norming issue' . . . but provided no specifics to guide the mediator . . . There is no timeline for the sides to reach any agreement" (Belson, 2021, paras. 5–6). Cyril Smith, Henry and Davenport's lawyer, questioned Seeger's ability to fairly represent Black players' interests in mediation and expressed concern "that the Court's proposed solution is to order the very parties who created this discriminatory system to negotiate a fix" (Madden, 2021a, para.7). The race-norming conflict became intertwined with the concussion crisis.

Theoretical Framework

To account for this phenomenon, we needed a theoretical framework that addressed the interconnected nature of this crisis and the conflict within. A nested crisis, according to Mohandesi (2020), refers to a situation when catastrophic autonomous events are combined and become interlocked, "each amplifying the power of the other" (p. 3). He uses COVID-19 as an exemplar of several nested crises: The pandemic itself is "a crisis of neoliberalism . . . a crisis of capitalistic social reproduction . . . and an epochal crisis of planetary life itself" (Mohandesi, 2020, p. 3). Mohandesi's purpose in identifying these overlapping or nested spheres is to reflect on how a complex nested crisis requires a complex nested response. Unfortunately, he does not offer a pathway forward on how to accomplish a nested response.

Carastathis (2018) also explores the concept of nesting within Greece's volatile political environment. Economic/financial, nationalist, and humanitarian factors created "the figure of nesting crises – a 'new' crisis in the midst of an 'ongoing' crisis, a 'humanitarian' crisis within an 'economic' crisis" (Carastathis, 2018, p. 143). These nested crises functioned to "conceal the systemic and structural underpinnings of violent processes . . . to authorize the imposition of regimes of management" (Carastathis, 2018, p. 143) and to create a territorial us versus them mentality.

In this case, player deaths, domestic violence, and CTE were catastrophic events that became crises within the larger concussion crisis. When combined and amplified over a period of two decades, these events nested together and contributed to the lawsuit settlement. The lawsuit settlement should have signaled the culmination of the concussion crisis allowing the NFL to then implement post-crisis communication strategies. However, the civil lawsuit filed by Henry and Davenport shifted the territorial dynamics of the crisis from "us" (NFL players) to "them" (The League), thus holding the League accountable and revealing structural underpinnings of systemic racism and racial norming. To settle the dispute between the National Football League and former players, the court system ordered mediation. This process of mediation created what Márie Dugan (1996) identifies as a nested conflict.

Dugan's nested theory of conflict accounts for four different types of interrelated conflicts that are layered and nested together – issue, relational, systemic, and subsystemic. The first type is issue specific: "As its name suggests, the source of an issue-specific conflict is one or more issues. The disagreement may occur over information, differing interpretations of agreed-upon information or divergent interests over the item(s) of concern" (Dugan, 1996, p. 15**)**. A relational conflict stems from problematic interaction patterns of the parties and their feelings toward each other. The third type of conflict may be structural inequities institutionalized within a system. The fourth layer includes (1) systemic conflicts, which are difficult to identify because of hidden ideologies and strategies of denial that obscure the dynamics, and (2) subsystemic structural conflicts embedded in "rules, procedures, and traditions of particular social organizations which are, perceived to be, inequitable, antiquated, or ineffectual" (Dugan, 1996, p. 16).

Combining Dugan's nested approach to conflict with Mohandesi and Carastathis' nested layers of crises provides a new framework – nested model of crisis – to identify systemic layers of this crisis and the substructural relationships and issues that are embodied within the conflict between players and the League.

The Case

Systemic/Structural Elements of the Concussion Crisis and Issue-Specific Conflict

As the concussion crisis emerged and unfolded, narratives about the tenuous link between traumatic brain injuries and violence erupted, while "passionate football fans [joined] with league administrators and coaches in denying the link's plausibility" (Brain Injury Law Center, n.d. para. 11). One set of narratives included Webster's death; the suicides of other prominent NFL stars like Andre Waters, Dave Duerson, and Junior Seau; and increasing incidents of NFL players and domestic violence in the news media (Ray Rice punching his fiancée unconscious; Jeff Gladney strangling his girlfriend; Chad Wheeler assaulting his girlfriend; and Ezekiel Elliot beating his girlfriend) spotlighting the severity of the concussion crisis. These incidents suggested a link between domestic violence and concussions. Meanwhile, counternarratives were constructed by the NFL. Denial became a consistent strategy for the League, documented in both the book *League of Denial: The NFL, Concussion, and the Battle for Truth* (Fainaru-Wada & Fainaru, 2014) and Frontline/PBS documentary *League of Denial: The NFL's Concussion Crisis*, revealing how two decades of cover ups snowballed into an endless stream of denials, despite mounting, contrary scientific evidence (Kirk et al., 2013). Former NFL Commissioner Paul Tagliabue had been downplaying the issues of concussions since 1994, claiming that instances were low.

Still, the NFL convened a Mild Traumatic Brain Injury Committee (MTBI) in 1994 and produced a report finding no link between football and traumatic brain injuries from concussions (Breslow, 2015), which supported Tagliabue's claims. Three years later, the NFL rejected the American Academy of Neurology's established guidelines for athletes to play after suffering a concussion (Coates, 2013). In 2002, Forensic Pathologist Dr. Bennet Omalu discovered a relationship between mental problems, brain diseases, and the NFL, but the following year the League said, "No NFL player has ever suffered chronic brain damage as a result of repeat[ed] concussions" (Breslow, 2016, para. 5). Instead, the NFL publicly discredited Omalu's research and rebranded the problem as "mild traumatic brain injury" as it continued to downplay the seriousness of concussions. Omalu pushed back and released additional findings published in 2005 in which he named the disease chronic traumatic encephalopathy (CTE).

In 2007, the NFL distanced itself from its own MTBI findings, disbanded the committee, and convened an NFL summit that produced a pamphlet, which was later withdrawn, stressing the inconclusiveness of concussion research. The summit was also instrumental in shaping NFL Commissioner Roger Goodell's two key messages about concussion and football over the following years: (a) The League is studying the problem and (b) much of the research is flawed (Rentner &

Campbell, 2019). In 2013, the NFL reached a surprise settlement with more than 5,000 former players who sued the NFL over concussion-related issues for more than $765 million.

From 2012 to 2014, 306 players suffered a combined 323 concussions, and it is estimated that 96% of NFL players have CTE (Pramuk, 2015). In 2017, the *Journal of the American Medical Association* (JAMA) released a study which found that 99% of the 111 NFL players' brains that were donated to scientific research had CTE (Mez et al., 2017). It was after the 2017 season that the NFL instituted rule changes that included penalties for helmet-to-helmet blows and changed kickoff rules to avoid collisions (Reyes, 2020). Prior to these changes, in preseason and regular season play, the NFL reported 271 concussions in 2015, 243 in 2016, and 281 in 2017 (NFL, 2021). The rule changes brought about a 23.8% decrease in the 2018 season, from 190 in the 2017 season to 135 in 2018 (Reyes, 2019). The 2019 season reported 224 concussions in both the preseason and regular season, up by 47% from 2018, but 20.3% lower than the 2017 season (Reyes, 2020), and the 2020 season posted 172 concussions, a 23.3.% drop from the previous year.

As more and more players came forward with medical issues, "differing interpretations of agreed-upon information, or divergent interests over" (Dugan, 1996, p. 14) inequities in health and safety standards between White and Black players were revealed within the allocation of the concussion lawsuit settlement funds, which created a specific issue conflict related to race.

Issue of Race-Norming

The concussion settlement has been under fire since players began filing claims in 2018 with criticisms ranging from delays in payouts, fraud, predatory lenders, and an overall lack in transparency (Belson, 2020; NFL Concussion Settlement, 2022), but claims by two retired players accusing the NFL of "explicitly and deliberately" discriminating against hundreds, if not thousands of Black players, has gained the most attention (Belson, 2020, para. 1). Over 2,000 former NFL players have filed dementia claims, but fewer than 600 have received compensation from the settlement (BBC News, 2021).

Racial norming, also known as race correction, is defined as the practice of adjusting test scores to account for the race or ethnicity of the person taking a test (Miller et al., 2011). It is seen as a highly discriminatory practice dating back to slavery and used in medicine for years (Trimbur, 2021). Further known as within-group score conversion and score adjustment strategy, the practice was first implemented by the federal government but later prohibited under the Civil Rights Act of 1999 (Greenlaw & Jensen, 1996).

In terms of the NFL concussion settlement, these "norms," as used in a neuropsychology context, "assumes that the average Black player starts at a lower level of cognitive functioning than the average White player at the outset of their careers" (Madden et al., 2021, para. 12). This meant that Black players had to prove more impairment than White players to receive benefits, meaning, when tested, Black players needed to show larger cognitive declines than White players to qualify for compensation (Trimbur, 2021, para. 11–12). Thus, the settlement applied two different standards, one for Blacks and one for Whites, in determining the level of cognitive impairment and the monetary reward amount, which is systemic racism (Madden et al., 2021).

In May 2019, NFL lawyers first became aware that race-norming was contributing to denials of concussion settlement payouts and that the practice was discriminatory toward Black players (Hobson, 2021). But despite this finding, the law firm hired by both sides issued rulings reinforcing race-norming practice, citing a failure to use the correct race-based norms in the denials (Hobson, 2021). In fact, the NFL defended the practice of racial norming, citing that its standards had been widely practiced, but saying that adoption of this practice was not mandatory and was left up to the doctors taking part in the concussion settlement program to decide whether to apply these standards (Steinbach, 2021). Despite claiming that the settlement decisions were left up to doctors, and calling the lawsuit entirely misguided, the NFL appealed against some of the injury claims from Black players whose cognitive scores were not adjusted for race (BBC News, 2021).

In March 2021, Judge Anita Brody dismissed the racial-norming lawsuit and ordered the NFL into mediation (Associated Press, 2021). Since then, an NFL spokesman said the League was working to "identify alternative testing techniques" (BBC News, 2021, para. 18) and pledged to halt racial norming practices in determining brain injury settlements. The decision of the courts to order mediation reveals two parallel conflicts that are connected, nested, and intertwined with the history of the NFL and within the overall concussion crisis.

Substructural and Relational Conflicts in NFL's CBA and Mediation

The origin of relational conflicts within the NFL's Collective Bargaining Agreement (CBA) can be potentially attributed to the development of the NFL and Frederick Taylor's principles of scientific management – efficiency, formalized divisions of masculine labor, and timed mechanized movements – which created mythologies of players and their bodies' capabilities (Gilbert, 2018).

These underlying assumptions create a relational conflict with the disciplinary structure of the NFL, which documents methods and appeals for disciplinary actions and, more specifically, the authority of the Commissioner (Reece, 2010). Historically, the NFL Commissioner has been perceived to be the judge, jury, and executioner of disciplinary policies (Graziano, 2020; Pannullo, 2019) allowing the person in the position unchecked discretionary power to judge, punish, and impose discipline on players for "conduct that reflects poorly on the character and integrity of the game or . . . diminishes public confidence" (p. 14) through the Personal Conduct Policy, according to Reece (2010).

This dialectical tension between players being disciplined in their mechanized performance of the game and the Commissioner imposing discipline as a form of punishment is problematic especially within dispute resolutions related to player conduct. The Commissioner's legal authority, per Pannullo (2019), and the NFL's process create inconsistencies, and "increased hostility between parties . . . [resulting in a] lack [of] legitimacy . . . [and] impartiality" (p. 139), which then can result in long-term consequences. Gill & Wilkinson (2012) assert that the problem is more endemic to the culture of football. As an example, while Commissioner Goodell lauded league efforts to reduce concussions and serious injuries, he also advocated for a cultural shift to "change the 'warrior mentality' of players unwilling to disclose when they are hurt" (Belson, 2012, p. B13, para. 1). This behavior is consistent with the deny strategy for crisis management in which blame is shifted away from the organization or individual toward someone or something else (Amaresan, 2021). In reference to Judge Brody's decision to end the practice of racial norming, Goodell responded with further deflection, blaming the courts' decision-making processes, according to Abril (2021).

The lack of legitimacy and potential for hostility stemming from the Commissioner's legal authority, coupled with the culture of football supporting dangerous conduct, have added consequences for the collective bargaining agreement as an "NFL player has no way of reversing the Commissioner's decision if it is excessive or arbitrary" (Reece, 2010, p. 2). Football players have a "finite period of time to earn by playing their sport and the rest of a lifetime . . . to figure out what to do when a CBA no longer governs their existence" (Isaac, 2013, p. 168). Furthermore, within the National Labor Relations Act, employment conditions and grievance procedures must be collectively bargained (Reece, 2010). As Graziano (2020) states, "This has been a point of contention among players who have felt the discipline and appeals process has been unfair since the people in charge of imposing the discipline have been the ones who hear the appeals" (para. 33).

Wolpert (2019) points to differences in respective interests between the Commissioner, who stands for the NFL and its profits, and the NFL Players Association (NFLPA), which advocates on the players' behalf. Having opposing interests creates an uneasy situation where a win–win scenario is unlikely.

The latest iteration of the NFL's collective bargaining agreement was approved in February 2020 as the racial norming lawsuit continued. This latest CBA, governing through 2030, however, includes language replacing the commissioner with a "neutral disciplinary officer" in most disciplinary cases (National Football League Players Association, 2020). While on the surface, it may appear that the role of commissioner is weakened, many note the new language merely allows players to appeal the decision of the Disciplinary Officer to the Commissioner. Neutral arbitration is therefore only for initial disciplinary procedures (Florio, 2020). As Andrew Brandt of SI.com notes, "Commissioner Goodell will retain his appeal power, no longer 'jury', but still 'judge and executioner'" (Brandt, 2020, para.21).

Relational Conflicts in NFL Mediation

Systems of arbitration are a common mechanism for settling disputes in industries where labor is organized into unions. The process of structured mediation, however, is not a focus of disciplinary procedures outlined in earlier CBAs. Sports law author, Jimmy McEntee, presents his case for why mediation should be embraced by both the NFL and NFLPA (McEntee, 2019). Pannullo (2019) argues in favor of mediation as well, claiming that it is an underutilized dispute resolution technique in professional sports, especially within the NFL. Bucher (2011) concurs on the value and effectiveness of mediation, despite adversities the NFL experienced after three prior failed attempts at mediation due to lack of face-to-face dialogue, lack of proper participation, presence of media coverage, lack of transparency, and imposition of deadline.

Despite failed mediation attempts in the racial norming case, Judge Brody ordered the NFL and Seeger to continue negotiations to remove racial-norming and ordered all negotiations to remain confidential (Hobson, 2021). The judge's orders have exacerbated the relational conflicts and perpetuated the already tenuous and dysfunctional relationships between the NFL and the players, resulting in many criticisms of the parties involved in the mediation.

You Make the Call

In both the first and second nest of the Nest Model, the NFL engaged in reactive communication practices, first using denial (denying links between football and brain injuries), then using deflection (citing racial norming as a widely used practice). In each of the first two nests, a lack of transparency resulted in defensive statements by the NFL. For example, the NFL-appointed MTBI committee released many statements (described earlier) and journal articles refuting scientific evidence, until it was disbanded. In the case of racial norming, both the League and Seeger created a confidential guidebook for doctors evaluating former players with no choice but to use racial norming (Hobson, 2021), clearly withholding this information from players making settlement claims.

The blame game was another tactic used in both nests to deflect responsibility from the League to others. For example, Tagliabue blamed media hysteria for stirring up a head injury issue that he insisted did not exist. Seeger blamed doctors for using race norms to decide concussion settlement payouts (Hobson, 2021). Finally, NFL mission and values statements appear to be at odds with its *Commitment to Diversity Statement*, which states in part that the NFL "is committed to building a diverse, equitable and inclusive work environment that reflects our incredibly diverse fan base" (National Football League, n.d., para. 1), and "accordingly, the NFL honors and celebrates the broad ranges of human difference among us, while also embracing the commonalities we share, and to provide each individual with the opportunity to achieve their full potential" (n.d. para. 2).

The statement includes a section titled *The Black Engagement Network*, which states as its vision "to strengthen the NFL's engagement of its Black employees as well as strengthen the NFL's commitment to diversity" (n.d. para. 5). Players, of course, are employees of the NFL. The practice of racial norming and League officials' waffling of messages related to racial injustices are incongruent with the aforementioned statement.

Lessons learned from the missteps in both crisis nests start with the NFL's need to follow mission and value statements. Organizations fall out of favor with their publics when they fail to live up to their stated values while those that adhere to their values are viewed more favorably (Guth & Marsh, 2012). Proactive communication messages are necessary to build strong relationships with key publics and strengthen an organization's reputation. Proactive messages help an organization avoid crafting messages that often come off as defensive. One way to accomplish this is by working with an organization's crisis management team to look for risk signs before they become a crisis (Coombs, 2019). In both nests, risk assessments may not have been performed, as riskier approaches like denial and casting blame were dominant tactics used. Whereas denial and blame are weak communication tactics, honesty and transparency are seen by scholars and practitioners as effective tactics. Transparency means that an organization is available to the media, is willing to disclose information, and is honest (Coombs, 2019).

As of November 2021, the court-ordered mediation between the NFL and former players ended. The 2020 CBA includes Appendix Y: Neurocognitive Benefit Release and Covenant Not to Sue in which a player and/or any personal representative

> [H]ereby waives and releases and forever discharges the NFL Releasees . . . from any and all claims . . . arising out of . . . any head and/or brain injury sustained during his employment by the Club.
> *(National Football League Players Association, 2020, p. 432)*

The intention behind mentioning these facts is not to vilify the NFL, but rather to provide up-to-date contexts in which the concussion crisis and various nested layers of conflict and mediation remain alive, and with an unknown outcome. Further, we acknowledge all the positive strides that the NFL has made to improve player safety and encourage the League to continue examining its practices.

Discussion Questions

1. Provide an update to this chapter. Specifically, what evidence, if any, indicates that the NFL has stopped its practice of racial norming?
2. Should the NFL have seen this coming? That is, should they have foreseen the practice of racial norming as being a problematic outcome of the concussion

settlement or was it an unintended consequence? Explain your reasoning. To what extent do you think other current racial injustice issues impacted public and media attention given to the NFL's racial norming crisis?

3. Touitou (2020) suggests that researchers "look at communication, conflict and crisis management with a view to reducing or resolving conflicts and crises through effective and efficient communication" (p. 7). What communication suggestions do you have for the NFL to reduce or resolve conflicts and crises?

4. We chose to use nesting as the theoretical perspective to analyze this case. What other theoretical perspectives might one use to analyze this conflict or crisis?

Acknowledgments

This project was supported by a 2021 Summer Research Grant awarded by Ithaca College's Center for Faculty Excellence.

References

Abril, D. (2021, June 9). NFL commissioner Roger Goodell on 'race norming': 'Yes, it should be changed if there are better processes'. *Fortune.* https://fortune.com/2021/06/09/nfl-commissioner-roger-goodell-race-norming-black-players/

Amaresan, S. (2021, June 30). Situational crisis communication theory and how it helps business. https://blog.hubspot.com/service/situational-crisis-communication-theory

Associated Press (2021, March 9). Judge tosses suit over 'race-norming' in NFL dementia tests. *NBC News.* www.nbcnews.com/news/latino/judge-tosses-suit- race-norming-nfl-dementia-tests-rcna376

BBC News. (2021, June 3). NFL agrees to drop race bias in concussion claims. www.bbc.com/news/world-us-canada-57336282

Belson, K. (2012, November 16). Goodell speaks of changes needed in N.F.L. culture. *New York Times.* www.nytimes.com/2012/11/16/sports/football/roger-goodell-nfl-commissioner-speaks-on-concussions.html

Belson, K. (2020, August 25). Black former NFL players say racial bias skews concussion payouts. *The New York Times.* www.nytimes.com/2020/08/25/sports/football/nfl-concussion-racial-bias.html

Belson, K. (2021, March 9). NFL asked to address race-based evaluations in concussion settlement. *The New York Times.* www.nytimes.com/021/03/09/sports/football/nfl-concussions-settlement-race.html.

Brain Injury Law Center. (n.d.). From brain trauma to violence – The long-term effects of pro football. *Brain Injury Law Center.* www.brain-injury-law-center.com/blog/from-brain-trauma-to-violence/

Brandt, A. (2020, March 19). The NFL CBA aftermath. *SI – Sports Illustrated.* www.si.com/nfl/2020/03/19/reviewing-nfls-new-collective-bargaining-agreement-17th-game-cba

Breslow, J.M. (2015, September 15). New: 87 deceased NFL players test positive for brain disease. *Frontline.* www.pbs.org/wgbh/frontline/article/new-87-deceased-nfl-players-test-positive-for-braindisease/

Breslow, J.M. (2016, March 15). NFL acknowledges a link between football, CTE. *Frontline*. www.pbs.org/wgbh/frontline/article/nfl-acknowledges-a-link-between-football-cte/

Bucher, T.J. (2011). Inside the huddle: Analyzing the mediation efforts in the NFL's Brady settlement and its effectiveness for future professional sports disputes. *Marquette Sports Law Review*, *22*(1), 211–234. http://scholarship.law.marquette.edu/sportslaw/vol22/iss1/8

Carastathis, A. (2018). Nesting crisis. *Women's Studies International Forum*, *68*, 142–148. https://doi.org/10.1016/j.wsif.2017.11.007

Coates, T. (2013, January 25). The NFL's response to brain trauma: A brief history. *The Atlantic*. www.theatlantic.com/entertainment/archive/2013/01/the-nfls-response-to-brain-trauma-a-brief-history/272520/

Coombs, W.T. (2019). *Ongoing crisis communication: Planning, managing, and responding*. (5th ed.). London: Sage Publication.

Dugan, M. (1996). A nested theory of conflict. *A Leadership Journal: Women in Leadership – Sharing the Vision*, *1*, 9–20. https://emu.edu/cjp/docs/Dugan_Maire_Nested-Model-Original.pdf

Fainaru-Wada, M., & Fainaru, S. (2014). *League of denial: The NFL, concussions, and the battle for truth*. New York: Three Rivers Press (an imprint of the Crown Publishing Group).

Florio, M. (2020, March 6). New CBA doesn't diminish Commissioner's ultimate power over personal conduct policy cases. *NBC Sports*. https://profootballtalk.nbc-sports.com/2020/03/06/new-cba-doesnt-diminish commissioners-ultimate-power-over-personal-conduct-policy-cases/

Gilbert, D.A. (2018). The gridiron and the gray flannel suit: NFL football and the modern U.S. workplace. *Journal of Sports and Social Issues*, *42*(2), 132–148. https://doi.org/10.1177/0193723518756850

Gill, S., & Wilkinson, K. (2012, September 18). How the NFL can tackle culture change. *USA Today*. https://amp.usatoday.com/amp/1566209

Graziano, D. (2020, March 15). NFL CBA approved: What players get in new deal, how expanded playoffs and schedule will work. *ESPN*. www.espn.com/nfl/story/_/id/2890 1832/nfl-cba-approved-players-get-new-deal-how-expanded-playoffs-schedule- work

Greenlaw, P.S., & Jensen, S.S. (1996, March). Race-norming and the civil rights act of 1991. *Public Personnel Management*, *25*(1), 13–24. https://doi.org/10.1177/0091026 09602500102

Guth, D.W., & Marsh, C. (2012). *Public relations: A value-driven approach* (5th ed.). Pearson Education.

Hobson, W. (2021, August 2). How 'race norming' was built into the NFL concussion settlement. *The Washington Post*. www.washingtonpost.com/sports/2021/08/02/ race-norming-nfl-concussion-settlement/

Isaac, K.D. (2013). Employment ADR and the professional athlete. *Appalachian Journal of Law*, *12*, 167–190. https://papers.ssrn.com/sol3/papers.cfm?abstract_id=225867

Kirk, M., Gilmore, J., & Wiser, M. (Producers). (2013, October 8). League of denial: The NFL's concussion crisis. *Frontline Productions*. www.pbs.org/wgbh/frontline/film/League-of-denial/

Lapchick, R. (2019, October 30). *The 2019 racial and gender report card: National Football League*. Report from the Institute for Diversity and Ethics in Sport. https://43530132-36e9-4f52-811a-182c7a91933b.filesusr.com/ugd/7d86e5_5af5faf45ba7443da733f900f54638b4.pdf

Madden, P. (2021a, March 8). Judge orders NFL, class counsel to 'address the concerns' about race-norming in concussion settlement. *ABC News*. https://abcnews.go.com/Sports/judge-orders-nfl-class-counsel-address-concerns-race/story?id=76321584

Madden, P. (2021b, March 15). Former NFL players seek to intervene in race-norming mediation, citing mistrust of class counsel. *ABC News*. https://abcnews.go.com/US/nfl-players-seek-intervene-race-norming-mediation-citing/story?id=76456781

Madden, P., Park, C., & Smith, R. (2021, June 2). Negotiator of NFL concussion settlement program on race-norming: 'I was wrong.' *ABC News*. https://abcnews.go.com/US/negotiator-nfl-concussion-settlement-program-race-norming-wrong/story?id=78031699

McEntee, J. (2019, January 1). Mediation before arbitration: Why professional sports Leagues should expand the role of mediation beyond collective bargaining negotiations to individual player grievances. www.sportslaw.org/docs/McEntee.pdf

Mez, J., Daneshvar, D., Kiernan, P.T., Abdolmohammadi, B., Alvarez, V.E., Huber, B.R., ... McKee, A.C. (2017). Clinicopathological evaluation of chronic traumatic encephalopathy in players of American football. *JAMA Network*. https://jamanetwork.com/journals/jama/fullarticle/2645104

Miller, L.A., McIntire, S.A., & Lovler, Robert L. (2011). *Foundations of psychological testing: A practical approach* (3rd ed.). Los Angeles, CA: SAGE Publications.

Mohandesi, S. (2020, May 13). Crisis of a new type. *Viewpoint Magazine*. https://viewpointmag.com/2020/05/13/crisis-of-a-new-type/

National Football League (n.d.). Commitment to diversity. *National Football League*. www.nfl.com/careers/diversity

National Football League. (2021, April 21). Injury data since 2015. *National Football League*. www.nfl.com/playerhealthandsafety/health-and-wellness/injury-data/injury-data

National Football League Players Association. (2020, March). NFL collective bargaining agreement. *National Football League Players Association*. https://nflpaweb.blob.core.windows.net/media/Default/NFLPA/CBA2020/NFL-NFLPA_CBA_March_5_2020.pdf

NFL Concussion Settlement. (2022, February 28). Past summary reports. *NFL Concussion Settlement*. www.nflconcussionsettlement.com/Reports_Statistics.aspx

Pannullo, R. (2019). Facilitating change: Addressing the underutilization of mediation in professional sports. *Harvard Negotiation Law Review*, 25(1), 103–167. www.hnlr.org/wp-content/uploads/sites/22/103-pannullo.pdf

Pramuk, J. (2015, Sept 18). 96% of NFL players studied show brain disease. *CNBC*. www.cnbc.com/2015/09/18/96-of-nfl-players-studied-show-brain-disease.html

Reece, J.A. (2010). Throwing the red flag on the commissioner: How independent arbitrators can fit into the NFL's off-field discipline procedures under the NFL collective bargaining agreement. *Valparaiso University Law Review, 359*, 1–41. https://scholar.valpo.edu/vulr/vol45/iss1/11

Rentner, T.L., & Campbell, L.C. (2019). The NFL concussion crisis: More than just a bad headache. In B.R. Brunner & C.A. Hickerson (Eds.), *Cases in public relations: Translating ethics into action*. New York, NY: Oxford University Press.

Reyes, L. (2019, January 24). NFL says player concussions dropped by 29 percent in 2018 regular season. *USA Today*. www.usatoday.com/story/sports/nfl/2019/01/24/nfl-concussions-players-2018-statistics-data/2668414002/

Reyes, L. (2020, January 23). NFL data shows concussions increased slightly in 2019, but League touts 'new benchmark.' *USA Today*. www.usatoday.com/story/sports/nfl/2020/01/23/nfl-concussions-increased-slightly-2019-season/4555094002/

Steinbach, P. (2021, June). NFL to end 'race-norming' in brain injury settlements. *Athletic Business*. www.athleticbusiness.com/governing-bodies/nfl-to-end-race-norming-in-brain-injury-settlements.html

Touitou, T.C. (2020, August). Communication, conflict, and crisis management. *EJMBR, European Journal of Business and Management Research, 5*(4), 1–7. www.ejbmr.org/index.php/ejbmr/article/view/251

Trimbur, L. (2021, June 8). The NFL's reversal on 'race norming' reveals how pervasive medical racism remains. *NBC News*. www.nbcnews.com/think/opinion/nfl-s-reversal-race-norming-reveals-how-pervasive-medical-racism-ncna1269992

Wolpert, J. (2019, December 1). Concussions and contracts: The National Football League's limitations to protecting its players from Chronic Traumatic Encephalopathy. *Journal of Law and Health, 33*(1), 1–18. https://engagedscholarship.csuohio.edu/cgi/viewcontent.cgi?article=1555&context=jlh

5

MAJOR LEAGUE SOCCER'S NAVIGATION OF THE 2019 IRON FRONT CRISIS

Caleb Bills

Introduction

Major League Soccer (MLS) completed its 26th season at the end of the 2021 calendar year. Despite rises in factors such as match attendance and TV revenue, MLS has historically struggled to compete with the other popular domestic sports in the United States like football, basketball, and baseball (SBJ, 2006; MLS, 2014; Smith, 2019). The league's tumultuous beginnings spun out of a FIFA mandate in which the United States could only host the 1994 FIFA World Cup if the United States had a centralized, professional division one league, regardless of the existence of other professional and semi-professional leagues in the country (Fraser v. Major League Soccer, 2000).

Before each season begins, both MLS and specific MLS teams release stadium policies and codes of conduct outlining what fans can and cannot do in and around the stadium grounds during game days. However, the 2019 MLS campaign was mired in an unforeseen controversy that pitted the league office, including Commissioner Don Garber, against some of the most passionate fans in MLS. These stadium policies can range from the mundane, such as prohibiting selfie sticks, to the obvious warnings that violent acts can result in stadium bans and legal action.

Leading up to the 2019 season, some MLS teams experienced a rise in far-right organizations and neo-Nazi groups that were reportedly becoming violent, distributing White supremacist propaganda, and yelling racist and homophobic chants inside stadiums (Lewis, 2015; Silverman, 2019; Evans, 2019). Frustrated by perceived inaction from the league to curtail those acts from occurring during matches, a group of fans began displaying imagery of the Iron Front on signs, flags, and T-shirts to be flown in various stadiums to counteract the rise in

DOI: 10.4324/9781003316763-7

White supremacist rhetoric. Historically, the Iron Front was a German anti-Nazi paramilitary organization in the 1930s, the iconography of which has since been co-opted in the 21st century by anti-fascists who oppose White supremacy and the neo-Nazi movements (Friedman, 2017).

The new league-wide policy that spawned the unintended uproar dealt with the types of speech that could be used within the stadium. The 2019 Fan Code of Conduct stated that action would be taken against fans if they were "using (including on any sign or other visible representation) political, threatening, abusive, insulting, offensive language and/or gestures which includes racist, homophobic, xenophobic, sexist or other inappropriate language or behaviors," at an MLS match (MLS, 2019, para. 2). While the initial sentiment seemingly has good intentions to create a welcoming atmosphere for players and fans alike, the season-long conflict stemmed from one word in the previous policy – political. The crux of the crisis for MLS is that they identified the Iron Front and the display of Iron Front iconography at matches as political speech and thus began issuing match bans to those anti-fascist fans who displayed the images (Carlisle, 2019a; Norling, 2019).

This chapter intends to provide a succinct outline of events in the lead-up to the 2019 MLS season as well as analyze the league's response to the swelling crisis. Approaching this case through Fearn-Bank's (2017) definition of a crisis and Benoit's (1997) writings on image repair can provide useful insight into what strategies the league implemented throughout the several months when this Iron Front crisis took place. Finally, this chapter allows you to evaluate MLS' response.

Background

MLS launched with just 10 teams in its inaugural 1996 season and was faced with immediate hardships. These difficulties largely stemmed from financial woes and low attendance (Stejskal, 2017). Teams from Tampa Bay and Miami folded within the first 5 years of their existence, and MLS as a whole lost over $350 million in its first decade (Eligon, 2005). From the traditional soccer fan's perspective, the "Americanized" rule changes tainted the game of soccer and turned soccer purists away (Rivera, 2014). The initial turbulent years resulted in the ousting of MLS Commissioner Doug Logan and the instatement of Don Garber, who has overseen the league since 1999.

Garber immediately implemented changes to the league in hopes of keeping it afloat. One of the most notable pushes was for the construction of soccer-specific stadiums. Most MLS teams were renting expensive NFL stadiums that could seat up to 80,000 spectators, while fewer than 20,000 seats were being filled for MLS matches. By 2008, over half of the then-14 teams in the league were playing in their own soccer-specific stadiums with seating capacities ranging between 15,000 and 30,000 fans (Rivera, 2014). Other notable initiatives throughout

Garber's tenure included aggressive expansion and lucrative television rights deals (Baxter, 2016: Henderson, 2019; Ourand & Botta, 2014; Reuters, 2015).

As the match bans for displaying Iron Front signage began to accumulate in 2019, fans dug in their heels and continued to defy the league. By the mid-season All-Star break, Commissioner Garber reiterated in an interview with ESPN that the Iron Front was a political organization and that displaying Iron Front imagery broke the Fan Code of Conduct. However, when later pressed with a hypothetical of a fan wearing a "Make America Great Again" hat into a stadium, he demurred saying, "I don't want to get engaged with that. It's very simple: We do not allow for political signage in our stadiums" (Carlisle, 2019b, para. 15).

This strife between the league and its fans continued to build until it was put on full display in a nationally televised match on ESPN between the Seattle Sounders and Portland Timbers. Arguably the fiercest rivalry in MLS, Seattle and Portland fans set aside their sporting displeasure with one another and came to an agreement to collectively fly flags with Iron Front imagery at a specific time in the game in a movement they dubbed #AUnitedFront on Twitter. With the season coming to a close and the Iron Front movement seemingly unrelenting, MLS officials met with various fan groups to deal with the Iron Front issue. On September 24, 2019, then–MLS President and Deputy Commissioner Mark Abbot rescinded the ban on Iron Front iconography and promised to revise the Fan Code of Conduct. After a year-long saga, fans flying Iron Front signage were finally allowed to do so without any threat of repercussions.

Despite the league compromising with fans to find an eventual solution, the process was slow moving and often times ineffective. MLS' unwavering stance that displaying Iron Front imagery violated the code of conduct and the Iron Front fans' continued insistence to display those images created a stalemate. As fans continued to defy the league, this Iron Front problem developed into an Iron Front crisis that MLS would have to solve.

Crisis Communication and Image Restoration Theory

In this chapter, Fearn–Banks's (2017) writings on crisis communication will be the overarching guide to examining this case. Fearn-Banks (2017) describes a crisis as a "major occurrence with a potentially negative outcome affecting the organization, company, or industry, as well as its publics, products, services, or good name" (p. 16). A crisis is more than just a mere problem or issue, and it often interrupts the normal flow of the organization. However, a crisis is not an automatic death sentence for an organization. MLS endured their crisis and continues to exist as a sports league today.

When a predicament arises, crisis communication strategies are often implemented to help the organization negotiate the said crisis. Crisis communication "is the dialog between the organization and its public(s) prior to, during, and after the negative occurrence. The dialog details strategies and tactics designed to minimize damage to the image of the organization" (Fearn-Banks, 2017, p. 16). Crisis communication aims not just to eradicate the crisis, but also to return an organization's standing to the same, or optimally, higher stature. Additionally, the definitions for what constitutes a crisis and crisis communication mention the importance of publics. Publics are essentially the individuals who are targeted by crisis communication strategies to repair or regain the trust of the organization.

Crises often have five identifiable stages. These stages include detection, prevention/preparation, containment, recovery, and learning (Fearn-Banks, 2017). The detection stage begins with the awareness of warning signs. These warning signs could be incredibly obvious or so subtle that they are difficult to identify. The prevention or preparation stage is largely centered around specific tactics to combat a potential crisis. Prevention strategies could involve engaging in communication with publics to build goodwill and lessen the severity of a crisis. If prevention is not possible, crisis preparation requires that a plan is in place that outlines roles and responsibilities for members of an organization to properly respond to the crisis. The containment stage attempts to limit the length or the spread of the crisis. The recovery stage sees that the organization attempts to return to a stage of normalcy, leaving the crisis behind. Last, the learning stage evaluates how the organization performed throughout the crisis and what improvements could be made to help avoid a similar crisis from occurring in the future.

When investigating an organization's response to a crisis, crisis communication theories can help identify and explain the specific strategies used by the organization. Most contemporary crisis communication theories grew out of the excellence theory (Grunig & Hunt, 1984; Grunig & Grunig, 1992). Image restoration theory was one approach that evolved from the initial excellence theory models as it considered what the organization determined as the threat to its reputation or image and how the publics should be addressed to restore a positive image. For this case study, image restoration strategies are applied to view how MLS addressed their publics in its attempt to restore the league's image with some of its most passionate fans.

The Case

Having defined what a crisis is, it is important to determine how this case qualified as a crisis for MLS, its teams, and its fans. Looking at the definition of a crisis, some of the most important aspects of that definition include *the potential for a negative outcome* to affect the organization alongside a detrimental impact to an organization's publics or product. MLS executives certainly found themselves in the midst of a crisis as the potential for a negative outcome became a reality from multiple fronts.

As the 2019 season transitioned from spring to summer, match bans were continuing, and news stories about what was happening were gaining traction online in various forms. ESPN interviewed Commissioner Garber during the league's summer break and questioned where the line was drawn between what was, and was not, political speech in a stadium (Carlisle, 2019b). *The Seattle Times* featured fans who threatened to cancel their season tickets if Iron Front bans continued, while other Seattle fans organized a walkout during a game (Calkins, 2019). Even *The Washington Post* found the problem newsworthy (Rosenberg, 2019).

Live sporting event organizers pride themselves on both the on-field product and the stadium atmosphere. Yet, these Iron Front bans were negatively impacting the stadium atmosphere by resulting in the aforementioned walkouts or in-game protests. A Seattle Sounders fan present at one walkout posted a picture of the empty seats and stated that it was the quietest they had ever heard the stadium (Oshan, 2019). In September 2019, team officials for Minnesota United reiterated the ban of the Iron Front symbol on flags, banners, clothing, and patches (Wonderwall, 2019). A week later, Minnesota fans took part in an anti-fascist protest during the 33rd minute of the game by flying flags and wearing T-shirts displaying the Iron Front symbol. A rivalry match between the Columbus Crew and FC Cincinnati also featured a few Iron Front banners sprinkled throughout the crowd. As a response, FC Cincinnati sent out flyers encouraging individuals attending matches to notify stadium operators if fans were brandishing Iron Front signage (Switzer, 2019). With the league and a subsection of fans facing off on opposite ends of the spectrum regarding the political speech ban, this had all the hallmarks of a full-blown MLS crisis.

By labelling this case a crisis, each stage of the crisis is explored and evaluated. As noted previously, the detection stage focuses on identifying the warning signs. Unfortunately for MLS, the warning signs had been appearing for years.

The 2015 MLS season was the New York City Football Club's (NYCFC) inaugural year. The creation of NYCFC simultaneously spawned the largest fan association for the team, the Empire State Ultras. Since their inception, the Empire State Ultras have been embroiled in controversy due to specific members being associated with neo-Nazi groups like Battalion 49 and far-right political groups such as the Proud Boys. Certain members of the Empire State Ultras were involved in street violence, and the distribution of White supremacy materials directly tied to the Ultras (Lewis, 2015; Silverman, 2019). In Seattle, verbal abuse and threats of violence were attributed to self-identified Proud Boys members who had run-ins with fans outside the stadium before a match (Evans, 2019).

In reaction to these incidents, Seattle fans hung a banner that read "Anti-fascist, anti-racist, always Seattle," which MLS forced them to take down while also removing the fans responsible for the banner. The ownership group of the Seattle Sounders released a statement the next day showing support for the ousted fans and pushing back against MLS' decision for removal (Oshan, 2017). The seeds for this crisis were planted years before it fully came to fruition, which may have been why crisis prevention was a difficult step for MLS to navigate by 2019.

One aspect of the prevention/preparedness stage was the implementation of a Fan Code of Conduct in the first place. It is far simpler to avoid a crisis involving fans when certain limitations are placed on them. There are also a legion of stadium employees who work for specific teams and the league to enforce stadium policies and take action against fans who breach the code of conduct. For example, a video was posted to YouTube of the Seattle fans who were removed from the match in 2017 for their "Anti-fascist, anti-racist, always Seattle" banner mentioned previously. The 8-minute video shows stadium or league representatives approaching the fans, confiscating the banner, and then removing the fans (Anderson, 2017). The preparedness and prevention plans fundamentally began with removing those who broke policies. Additional steps included releasing statements restating that political speech and Iron Front iconography were prohibited inside stadiums. However, these strategies were only successful when it was a small number of fans who were viewed as rule breakers. MLS' policy of "confiscate and ban" proved ineffective as the Iron Front movement grew throughout 2019.

The containment stage was perhaps the least successful stage from the league's viewpoint. While many of the more publicized instances of bans and fan pushback stemmed from the Pacific Northwest, containment failed both in terms of crisis duration and the spread of Iron Front protests into other regions of the MLS map, such as Minnesota and Ohio (Wonderwall, 2019; Switzer, 2019). In an attempt to contain or limit any further animosity, the Portland Timbers released a statement ceding some ground in the matter by allowing fans to wear shirts, pins, or badges with the Iron Front logo, while reinforcing the prohibition of flags and banners with the same imagery (Portland Timbers, 2019). By September 2019, the league seemed to realize they were in a battle that was becoming increasingly difficult to win. Their shift from the containment stage to the recovery stage began with a series of meetings which included the league president, Mark Abbott, and members of various fan organizations (Murray, 2019).

The meetings regarding the Iron Front movement resulted in MLS reversing its stance and allowing Iron Front imagery in its stadiums. Furthermore, league officials promised to revamp the MLS Fan Code of Conduct for future seasons to avoid similar issues (Carlisle, 2019c). The revocation of the Iron Front ban coincidentally occurred 3 weeks before the MLS playoffs began, which was more than likely an intentional move to bar any further controversy from transpiring and to start repairing the relationship between the league and its fans.

Demonstrating that the league had learned from the previous year's mistake, MLS released their updated Fan Code of Conduct before the 2020 season kicked off. The revised code of conduct established regulations prohibiting fans from displaying "signs, symbols, images, using language or making gestures that are threatening, abusive, or discriminatory, including on the basis of race, ethnicity, national origin, religion, gender, gender identity, ability, and/or sexual orientation" (MLS Fan Code of Conduct, 2020, para. 2), while also banning the display of "signs, symbols or images for commercial purposes or for electioneering, campaigning or advocating for or against any candidate, political party, legislative issue, or government action" (MLS, 2020, para. 2). This new policy attempted to clearly define what MLS considered as political speech by mentioning specific forms of speech as examples.

You Make the Call

Often times in a crisis, the organization involved will engage in strategies to repair their public image. Benoit (1997) outlined five major strategies that could occur. The first strategy is denial or shifting the blame. The second strategy is evading responsibility. Strategy three includes reducing the offensiveness of the event. Strategy four sees the organization take corrective action. Finally, the fifth strategy is mortification, where the organization accepts responsibility and seeks forgiveness. For the sake of this case, MLS appeared to engage in strategies two, three, and four.

Beginning with the evasion of responsibility, Benoit (1997) notes that there are four versions of this specific image repair strategy – the organization might claim provocation, defeasibility, the offense may have been accidental, or the offense was made with good intentions. Out of these four, MLS Commissioner Garber utilized the fourth strategy, by insisting that the bans for fans flying Iron Front signage were made with the best intentions. When discussing the bans with ESPN, Garber stated,

> We don't allow political signage, and it's not a question of judgement about which group is right and which group is wrong . . . Our stadiums are not environments where our fans should be expressing political views . . . the vast majority of fans do not see sports events as environments that should be driven by politics. They want to go to a game and experience it and participate in a game without having to be confronted by issues that might make them uncomfortable.
>
> *(Carlisle, 2019b, paras. 12–13)*

Garber's words make it clear that he believes the Iron Front bans benefit a larger number of people in the stadium who do not wish to see political statements while attending a match. By upholding the code of conduct and removing the signage along with the fans involved, Garber created, what he believed to be, a more positive atmosphere around the games.

Portions of the aforementioned quote from Garber, as well as a previously mentioned Portland Timbers statement, display the league's attempt to reduce the offensiveness of the bans. One subsection of this strategy is to engage in minimization. Minimization intends to paint the actions in a more positive light by making them appear less serious (Benoit, 1997). Garber insists that the majority of fans do not want politics invading their sports. In his extended statement, he mentioned, but did not cite specifically, research conducted that supported his assertion that most sports fans wanted to avoid politics when watching a sporting event. Placing those fans who violate the conduct code and receive bans in the minority helps Garber and the league minimize the problem by making it appear less serious. Similarly, the statement released by the Portland Timbers that addressed Iron Front imagery on clothing or badges also engaged in minimization. Explicitly stating in its revised code that fans can wear Iron Front imagery on T-shirts or sewn on patches acts as an attempt to find middle ground and minimizes any residual frustration some fans may feel regarding past Iron Front flag and banner confiscation. Portland was hoping that allowing the Iron Front logo on a shirt would show that the flag ban was not as serious as it appeared, yet those concessions were apparently insufficient.

The final image repair strategy – corrective action – was implemented by MLS after previous strategies lacked any sense of finality in the Iron Front saga. The changes made included allowing Iron Front imagery on flags and banners as well as the promise to rework the Fan Code of Conduct for future seasons. MLS deserves some credit for following through on its promises. Rather than making empty gestures, to this day, the Iron Front logo is seen in stadiums on match days, and the section on political speech in the updated Fan Code of Conduct has remained untouched since 2020. The corrective action taken by MLS appears to have ended the crisis and aided in avoiding any similar future crises.

Implications

MLS finally resolved their Iron Front issue by allowing the iconography to be displayed inside their stadiums. For MLS and its fans who persistently flew Iron Front flags, this decision appears successful on the surface. A vocal subsection of fans got what they wanted, and MLS was able to end the crisis by rescinding the Iron Front prohibition. Yet, there remain potential implications that stem from this decision.

First, the league succumbed to demands from a vocal minority. Commissioner Garber's mid-season interview with ESPN suggests that the league knew that the resistance swirling around the Iron Front bans was originating from a minority of fans. Despite that, by the end of the season, those fans were rewarded for their consistent disregard of stadium policies. Second, stadium policies banning specific forms of political speech still remain. To attend an MLS match, you must willingly waive some personal rights. For most fans, these issues of political speech in stadiums may never impact them personally; the average fan might prefer to wear a shirt with their team's logo on it to a match rather than one with their political affiliation. However, if they choose the latter, that fan is in violation of the code of conduct. This case only addresses one aspect of the blurring lines between politics and sport while leaving others for further study and investigation. Fans who oppose stadium speech restrictions will easily cause future crises, not just for MLS, but also for other susceptible sports leagues across the United States.

Discussion Questions

1. The updated MLS Fan Code of Conduct still prohibits several types of political speech. What is the value in a league limiting the types of speech that a fan can engage in while attending a game? What other similar incidents have occurred in sports?

2. Commissioner Garber held firm throughout the majority of the season that the Iron Front was a political organization and that fans flying Iron Front flags violated the code of conduct. If you were in Garber's position, what would your response be? How would you have addressed the Iron Front protests?

3. According to ESPN, the 2021 average viewership of an MLS game on an ESPN network was less than 300,000 viewers. Compare that to the average 2021 NFL ratings of 17.1 million viewers. How could the size of match attendance and television viewership impact the response of MLS to the Iron Front crisis?

4. MLS fans took to social media to post pictures or videos of themselves displaying Iron Front signage in defiance of the Fan Code of Conduct. What role do you think social media played in the decision to end the Iron Front ban?

References

Anderson, K. (2017, October 30). Anti-Fascist banner confiscated [Video]. *YouTube.* www.youtube.com/watch?v=4sH-n4laC4c

Baxter, K. (2016, March 7). MLS Commissioner Don Garber isn't celebrating triumphs; he's too focused on the future. *Los Angeles Times.* www.latimes.com/sports/sportsnow/la-sp-sn-mls-commissioner-don-garber-look-ahead-20160307-story.html

Benoit, W. (1997). Image repair discourse and crisis communication. *Public Relations Review, 23*(2), 177–186.

Calkins, M (2019, October 18). How MLS' ruling allowing Iron Front flag might be pushing away Sounders fans. *Seattle Times.* www.seattletimes.com/sports/sounders/i-have-no-supporters-home-how-mls-ruling-allowing-iron-front-flag-might-be-pushing-away-sounders-fans/

Carlisle, J. (2019a, September 5). MLS takes on Portland's most passionate fans over protests. What's this feud about? *ESPN.* www.espn.com/soccer/major-league-soccer/story/3935417/mls-takes-on-portlands-most-passionate-fans-over-protests-whats-this-feud-about

Carlisle, J. (2019b, July 31). Don Garber q&a: MLS commissioner talks legacy, politics, gambling, and Liga MX. *ESPN.* www.espn.com/soccer/major-league-soccer/story/3909803/don-garber-qanda-mls-commissioner-talks-legacypoliticsgambling

Carlisle, J. (2019c, September 24). MLS suspends ban on Iron Front flag for season. *ESPN.* www.espn.com/soccer/mls-all-stars/story/3951035/mls-suspends-ban-on-iron-front-flag-for-season

Eligon, J. (2005). For M.L.S., the sport's future is in the eye of the beholder. *New York Times.* www.nytimes.com/2005/11/11/sports/soccer/for-mls-the-sports-future-is-in-the-eye-of-the-beholder.html

Evans, J. (2019, August 4). Fans marching to Sounders match hear curses from people who pledge allegiance to Proud Boys. *Seattle Times.* www.seattletimes.com/sports/sounders/fans-marching-to-sounders-match-hear-curses-from-people-who-pledge-allegiance-to-proud-boys-organization/

Fearn-Banks, K. (2017). *Crisis communications: A casebook approach* (5th ed.). London: Routledge.

Fraser v. Major League Soccer, L.L.C., (2000). United States Court of Appeals, First Circuit.

Friedmann, S. (2017, August 15). This is what the antifa flag symbols mean. *Bustle.* www.bustle.com/p/what-do-the-antifa-symbols-mean-the-flags-often-feature-three-arrows-76629

Grunig, J.E., & Grunig, L.A. (1992). Models of public relations and communications. In J.E. Grunig (Ed.), *Excellence in public relations and communication management* (pp. 117–157). Mahwah, NJ: Lawrence Erlbaum Associates.

Grunig, J.E., & Hunt, T. (1984). *Managing public relations.* London: Holt.

Henderson, D. (2019, August 20). Major League Soccer awards expansion franchise to St. Louis; announcement Tuesday. *Fox 2 Now.* https://fox2now.com/sports/stl-city-sc/major-league-soccer-awards-expansion-franchise-to-st-louis-announcement-tuesday/

Lewis, B. (2015, August 9). NYCFC, Red Bulls fans have wild brawl outside Newark pub. *New York Post.* https://nypost.com/2015/08/09/nycfc-red-bulls-fans-have-wild-brawl-outside-newark-pub/

Major League Soccer. (2014, May 12). MLS, U.S. Soccer sign landmark tv and media rights partnerships with ESPN, FOX, & Univision Deportes. *MLS.* www.mlssoccer.com/news/mls-us-soccer-sign-landmark-tv-and-media-rights-partnerships-espn-fox-univision

Major League Soccer. (2019). Fan code of conduct. *Major League Soccer.* https://web.archive.org/web/20190321095831/www.mlssoccer.com/fan-code-of-conduct

Major League Soccer. (2020, February 18). Updated MLS fan code of conduct released for 2020 season. *Major League Soccer.* www.mlssoccer.com/news/updated-mls-fan-code-conduct-released-2020-season

Murray, C. (2019, September 20). As Iron Front policy protests grow, clubs want MLS to fix problem of its own making. *Yahoo! Sports.* https://sports.yahoo.com/as-iron-front-ban-protests-grow-fans-want-mls-to-fix-problem-of-its-own-making-151405875.html?guccounter=1&guce_referrer=aHR0cHM6Ly93d3cucmVkZGl0LmNvbS8&guce_referrer_sig=AQAAAMfYpN43phIkTsxJ8NvC8l7m46jkKeDTSjBncv66wv9bsPg1xsGJEYucliIwdB1JToB3JKcTO_43FlGscsmCABOM5gGmEO5ka50CJ6LlnKwqnQYglrANDJ1EuYCZz_Xorvq5-snwHI2RSdusrSFfOx0kEeDUB4u2yp-EnYWDttzV

Norling, A. (2019, September 14). Minnesota United clarifies their ban on the Iron Front symbol. *SB Nation.* www.epluribusloonum.com/2019/9/14/20862939/minnesota-united-has-clarified-their-ban-on-the-iron-front-symbol

Ourand, J., & Botta, C. (2014, May 12). MLS's big play. *Sports Business Journal.* www.sportsbusinessjournal.com/Journal/Issues/2014/05/12/Media/MLS-TV.aspx

Oshan, J. (2017, October 31). Sounders owners to fans: Inclusion and acceptance are "non-political" values. Sounder at Heart. https://www.sounderathea rt.com/2017/10/31/16588246/sounders-owners-statement-anti- fascist-anti-racist

Oshan, J. (2019, September 15). It appears ECS is walking out after a capo flying the Iron Front flag was ejected. *#AUnitedFront [Tweet].* https://twitter.com/JeremiahOshan/status/1173375143407579136

Portland Timbers. (2019, August 19). Portland Timbers front office on the iron front symbol, politics at stadiums and human rights. *Portland Timbers.* www.youtube.com/watch?v=4sH-n4laC4c

Reuters. (2015, February 25). Sky sports lands for-year deal for MLS broadcast rights. *Reuters.* www.reuters.com/article/us-soccer-mls-sky/sky-sports-lands-four-year-deal-for-mls-broadcast-rights-idUSKBN0LT27G20150225

Rivera, A. (2014). MLS 3.0 series: A history of MLS 1.0. *Last Word on Sports.* http://lastwordonsports.com/2014/07/25/mls-3-0-series-history-mls-1–0/

Rosenberg, E. (2019, August 31). There is an anti-fascist rebellion brewing in the Pacific Northwest. And soccer is at the center of it. *Washington Post.* www.washingtonpost.com/sports/2019/08/31/there-is-an-anti-fascist-rebellion-brewing-pacific-northwest-soccer-is-center-it/

Silverman, R. (2019, March 1). *How New York City soccer fans are fighting fascism in the stands.* Huffington Post. www.huffingtonpost.ca/entry/new-york-city-football-club-far-right-extremists_n_5c76d679e4b062b30eba721a

Smith, C. (2019, November 4). Major league soccer's most valuable teams 2019: Atlanta stays on top as expansion fees, sale prices surge. *Forbes.* www.forbes.com/sites/chrissmith/2019/11/04/major-league-soccers-most-valuable-teams-2019-atlanta-stays-on-top-as-expansion-fees-sale-prices-surge/?sh=622bc4cc51b5

Sports Business Journal. (2006, August 7). ESPN, MLS reach eight-year tv deal that includes rights fees. *Sports Business Journal.* www.sportsbusinessjournal.com/Daily/Issues/2006/08/07/Sports-Media/ESPN-MLS-Reach-Eight-Year-TV-Deal-That-Includes-Rights-Fees.aspx

Stejskal, S. (2017, February 28). A look back at the history of MLS expansion. *MLS Soccer.* www.mlssoccer.com/news/a-look-back-at-the-history-of-mls-expansion-321546

Switzer, D.J. (2019, August 30). A few noticed the "Iron Front" banners at Sunday's FC Cincinnati-Columbus Crew match, notable as the same symbol has. [Tweet] https://twitter.com/wrongsideofpond/status/1167459834276601858?s=21

Wonderwall (2019, September 9). Official statement: MNUFC bans iron front symbol from Allianz field. *Minnesota Wonderwall.* https://mnwonderwall.com/2019/09/10/official-statement-mnufc-bans-iron-front-symbol-from-allianz-field/

6

PROTECTING THE BREES BRAND

How Drew Brees Said "Sorry" for His National Anthem Protest Comments

Steph Doehler

Introduction

The video of George Floyd's detainment, and subsequent murder, at the hands of a Minneapolis police officer went viral in May 2020, sparking worldwide anti-racist activism. The brutality of the White officer kneeling on Floyd's neck for 9 minutes, while the Black, unarmed individual cried out until his body went limp shocked America in a manner that had not occurred since the Civil Rights Era. As the world stood to attention, numerous athletes spoke out in support of protests, and many joined them in person.

Images of both professional and amateur athletes kneeling during the American national anthem has been a consistent occurrence in sport since 2016, largely inspired by NFL's Colin Kaepernick who, some allege, sacrificed his football career as a result of protesting for the duration of the season (Jenkins, 2020). As the NFL geared up for the 2020 season amid a global pandemic, tensions across the United States seemed at a breaking point, and many sports fans expected to witness players, once again, taking the knee during the national anthem to protest authoritarian tactics by law enforcement and the violent oppression of civil freedoms, particularly toward Black citizens.

During an interview with Yahoo Finance on June 3, 2020, 9 days after Floyd's death, veteran NFL quarterback Drew Brees responded to a question about the on-field protests and his responsibility as a locker room leader during such politically fractured times. Brees, who was a vocal critic of Kaepernick in 2016, reiterated his perception that players should stand:

> I will never agree with anybody disrespecting the flag of the United States of America or our country . . . I envision my two grandfathers, who fought

DOI: 10.4324/9781003316763-8

for this country during World War II . . . both risking their lives to protect our country and to try to make our country and this world a better place.

(Rosenberg, 2020, para. 3)

The quarterback courted controversy and condemnation from every corner of sport. Fans, athletes, teammates, and the media openly took issue with Brees' stance, including NBA's Lebron James who tweeted "You literally still don't understand" (Just, 2020a), then-San Francisco 49ers player Richard Sherman called Brees "beyond lost" (Shapiro, 2020), and Brees' own teammate and long-time friend, Malcolm Jenkins, said "You're part of the problem" (Canova, 2020). Brees, a mainstay on the annual *Forbes* World's Highest Paid Athletes list, was now a controversial footballer who quickly sought to rectify his position through two public apologies posted on his social media accounts. This case study examines the steps Brees took to re-establish his views on racial inequality through Benoit's image repair theory (IRT).

Background

The Drew Brees Brand

The majority of subjective discussions on the greatest NFL quarterbacks of all time include Drew Brees in the debate. Although more obvious suggestions often point to the likes of Tom Brady, Joe Montana, or Peyton Manning, Brees' consistency at the top level is impossible to refute. Spending the majority of his 20-year professional football career with the New Orleans Saints, Brees may have been a Super Bowl champion only once; nonetheless, at the time of his retirement in 2021, he held records for most career pass completions, most career passing yards, most consecutive games with a touchdown pass, most pass completions in a single season, and tied for the most touchdown passes in a game (Swenson, 2021).

Brees' endeavors off the gridiron are equally impressive. According to *Forbes* (2020), the $15 million he accrued annually in endorsements leads all NFL players through his sponsorship deals with the likes of Nike, Verizon, and AdvoCare. Described in *Sports Illustrated* as "an athlete as adored and appreciated as any in an American city today" (King, 2010, para. 4) for his leadership within New Orleans in the aftermath of devastating Hurricane Katrina, Brees created and cultivated a brand which produced adulation among Saints' supporters. Shortly after arriving in New Orleans, his charity activity included financing a local school's weights room, helping to build the Brees Family Field, which became a symbol of restoration for the area following the hurricane, and raising $2 million, including a $250,000 personal donation, to help rebuild schools, parks, and playgrounds in his adopted hometown (Germer, 2021).

Sustained charity work led to the formation of the Brees Dream Foundation in 2013, which has contributed more than $45 million to causes globally (The Brees Dream Foundation, 2021). For many, Brees' philanthropical pursuits are more impactful than his on-field accomplishments. This was a White athlete who sat in a predominantly Black locker room and was lauded for his work within the community. Yet, an imbroglio erupted which centered around his perceived tone-deaf views related to the motivation behind national anthem protests. This put Brees at the heart of a national furore, making him a target for athletes, politicians, and sports fans across the country.

Why Was There a Need for Image Repair?

First, the timing provides an important contextual insight into the social and cultural backdrop of America. Simply put, in regard to cultural moments, 2020 was very different from 2016. Colin Kaepernick was widely condemned when he first knelt during the national anthem in 2016, and while Brees stressed he had no issue with Kaepernick's desire to speak out about racial injustice, he took umbrage with Kaepernick's method. "I wholeheartedly disagree," Brees told ESPN, describing the American flag as "sacred" (Triplett, 2016, para. 2). In 2016, Brees' view was consistent with many around the country, including, importantly, the NFL. Conversely, Kaepernick received limited support for his cause among sports writers, players, and politicians. Kaepernick's desire to bring the issue of police brutality to White America's attention was largely rejected, and subsequently the protest was twisted and co-opted into a debate around patriotism and the military (Doehler, 2021).

Fast forward four years and America was a far more splintered environment. For many, it took the murder of George Floyd, and others, to grasp the vivid reality of police officers killing defenseless Black citizens. The NFL, which had been quick to criticize those who protested during the national anthem in previous years, is now engaged in a new sentiment – unity. Demonstrating a ubiquitous attitude of solidarity and intolerance toward racism, the league and most of its teams released statements and public support to the Black Lives Matter movement. An issue the NFL had brushed away with indignation in 2016, when many team owners threatened players who knelt with disciplinary action, was considered essential to support, if not unequivocally embraced, by 2020.

Despite the intervening 4 years where Brees had several opportunities to watch other athletes, including his own teammates, support Kaepernick by kneeling themselves or read about the deaths of Philando Castile, Eric Garner, and Daunte Wright among others at the hands of police officers, it appeared as though Brees' stance remained unchanged. He was condemned as "wilfully ignorant" (Armour, 2020a, para. 1) and "dangerous" (Jacobs, 2020, para. 8) by sports columnists and journalists. The same journalists who labelled Kaepernick in 2016 as a traitor and a renegade were now tackling Brees for being out of touch.

The situation highlighted the changing political, social, and cultural environments within the United States. Politically, the country had rarely been more fractured than during Donald Trump's presidency, which saw social justice and social issues at the forefront of many conflicts. Culturally, after his comments, Brees' connection to his club and city was threatened. Brees operated on a field surrounded by Black teammates, many with personal experiences of racial discrimination and who lived in New Orleans, a city with a long history of police corruption, where over 60% of the population is Black (Jacobs, 2020).

While many White athletes carefully reflected on the systemic racism that remains prevalent across the United States, Brees doubled down on his viewpoint by perpetuating the notion that Kaepernick's action was about patriotism and not police brutality. In so doing, Brees became to many a symbol of White privilege. *Sports Illustrated* writer Michael Rosenberg suggested "Drew Brees has not learned that his American experience is not everyone's," (2020, para. 8) while Rod Walker, columnist for *The Times-Picayune*, the local newspaper for Brees' club, wrote, "Surely, he didn't say this today, I thought to myself. Surely, he gets it after watching that video of George Floyd's death" (Walker, 2020, para. 3).

The Case

Image Repair Theory

Image refers to "perceptions of the source held by the audience, shaped by the words and deeds of that source, as well as by the actions of other relevant actors" (Meng & Pan, 2016, p. 89). Benoit (1995) suggested that when a person or organization is accused of wrongdoing, the accused produces a message that attempts to repair their image. Despite being adapted and expanded upon in recent years, Benoit's IRT is consistently utilized by academics when evaluating crisis communication responses (see Frederick et al., 2014; Legg, 2009; Sanderson, 2008).

In professional sport, image plays a vital role in determining an athlete's worth, social and community standing, financial status, and performance and promotional prospects (Allison et al., 2020). Consequently, the risks associated with a damaged image are vast, and, therefore, when an athlete faces a perceived negative response to an event, they engage in image restoration work to repair their public persona.

Benoit's (2015) typology of image repair is broadly organized into five primary strategies, with each subcategorized into numerous communication tactics – denial (a disavowal or shifting of blame), evading responsibility (provocation, defeasibility, excuse making and justification through good intentions), reducing offensiveness (bolstering, minimization, differentiation, transcendence, attacking their accuser, and offering compensation), corrective action (vowing to fix the problem), and mortification (admitting the wrongful act and asking for forgiveness). This typology has been used by scholars to examine the image repair of elite athletes such as Abby Wambach and Maria Sharapova (Allison et al., 2020), Lance Armstrong (Hambrick et al., 2013), Ryan Lochte (Hull & Boling, 2018), Tiger Woods, Kobe Bryant, and Ben Roethlisberger (Meng & Pan, 2016). Within these seven examples, all five strategies were present in some capacity – denial (Armstrong), evading responsibility (Sharapova, Bryant), reducing offensiveness (Bryant and Roethlisberger), corrective action (Wambach, Woods, Bryant, and Roethlisberger), and mortification (all athletes except Sharapova). This case study lends support to research into athlete image repair strategies by examining the communication strategies employed by Brees following his comments which generated an "all-out blitz of criticism" (Rhoden, 2020, para. 1).

Social Media Apologies

On June 4, 2020, the day following his interview, a short apology was posted on Brees' social media accounts, accompanied by a stock image of an interlinked Black and White hand (the statement's text can be found in Appendix A). Shortly after his written apology, Brees issued one in video form (the transcript of which can be found in Appendix B), although the video itself has since been deleted from his social media pages.

Initially, a deductive approach was utilized for both statements by the author in order to determine whether the individual apologies could be categorized according to Benoit's typology. Although neither statement was overly long, each individual sentence was examined, and there were occasions when multiple image repair strategies were used within one sentence. Both statements were initially read to familiarize the author with the data and coded into one of Benoit's five typologies. Further scrutiny placed each unit of analysis into one of the 14 tactics outlined within the IRT and supplemented by the introduction of an additional tactic, "shared accountability." This tactic is a concept derived from the author as opposed to Benoit's typology and highlights how an individual might draw others' actions into their apology as a means to deflect ill feeling toward the individual and encourage others to reflect on their own culpability within the subject.

For the written statement, a total of 336 words were analyzed, and all but 8 words were coded to a strategy and subsequent tactic. Within this apology, Brees primarily used the strategy of reducing offensiveness, in which the accused attempts to reduce the degree of ill feeling experienced by the audience. Almost one-third (32.7%) of Brees' apology fell into this category, with several tactics being employed. Brees used bolstering throughout the apology with statements such as "I stand with the Black community," "I have ALWAYS been an ally," and "I recognize that I am part of the solution and can be a leader for the Black community in this movement." Here, Brees reinforces his positive attributes in an attempt to offset negative feelings toward his initial claims. The tactic of transcendence was also present within this strategy whereby Brees would refer to the broader context of racial inequality (e.g., "I condemn the years of oppression that have taken place throughout our Black communities and still exists today"). This approach directs attention away from the accused's wrongdoing and directs the audience's attention to a higher issue.

The second-most frequently demonstrated strategy was Brees' mortification (24.7%). This is generally used when the accused admits a wrongful act and seeks forgiveness. "It breaks my heart to know the pain I have caused" and "I am very sorry and I ask your forgiveness" are two examples of this strategy. However, in this apology, much of Brees' mortification centers around the perception of his comments, rather than apologizing for the comments themselves. This is clearly highlighted when he states that "I am sick about the way my comments were perceived yesterday." Evading responsibility was present within 13.4% of his statement as Brees attempted to reduce his culpability for offending the audience. When Brees wrote "In an attempt to talk about respect, unity, and solidarity centered around the American flag and the national anthem," he suggested his comments were based on good intentions. Elements of defeasibility were also present within this strategy when Brees pleaded a lack of information over important factors in the situation (e.g., "I will never know what it's like to be a Black man or raise Black children in America"). Brees used corrective action strategies more sparingly (11%) by declaring that he would "work every day to put myself in those shoes and fight for what is right." Benoit (2015) suggests it is wise to couple corrective action with mortification, which Brees does toward the end of his apology when he writes "I take full responsibility and accountability [mortification]. I recognize that I should do less talking and more listening [corrective action]."

Brees employed an interesting and unique approach in his apology, which constituted 10.1% of his overall message. This approach failed to situate itself into one of Benoit's tactics, and, thus, the author proposes an additional tactic be added to the evading responsibility strategy, *shared accountability*. Shared accountability is present when the accused evades sole responsibility for their actions, preferring instead to focus attention on where they and others have collective accountability for the situation or wider context. In Brees' case, this was present in the statements "I acknowledge that we as Americans, including myself, have not done enough to fight for that equality or to truly understand the struggles and plight of the Black community" and "We all need to listen." This proposed tactic differs from a variant within the denial strategy, shifting the blame. In Brees' case, he did not directly deny the act, and, therefore, this newly suggested tactic feels more appropriate due to his inclusive use of "we." The remaining strategy, denial, was used by Brees in just 5.7% of his apology. However, this strategy was not utilized to deny the statements he made within the interview. Rather, he denied the perception his words had "misled people into believing that somehow, I am an enemy. This could not be further from the truth."

Later the same day, Brees uploaded a video apology to his Instagram account, totalling 147 words and only 3 words were not coded to a strategy. As with the written apology, reducing offensiveness (39.5%) and mortification (35.4%) were the primary strategies employed. The transcendence tactic was once again present as Brees placed his apology in the wider context of racial inequality, name-checking both George Floyd and Ahmaud Arbery and stating that "The years and years of social injustice, police brutality, and the need for so much reform and change in regards to legislation. So many other things to bring equality to our Black communities." In repetition from his written apology, Brees reinforced his status as an ally to bolster his reputation through offering support to the marginalized demographic. Within the mortification strategy, Brees reiterated that he was sorry, explaining that he wanted people "to see in my eyes." In a departure from his written apology where he appeared contrite for the perception of his remarks, Brees directly apologized for making them in the video version – "how sorry I am for comments that I made yesterday." Evading responsibility was present to a similar extent as in the previous apology accounting for 11.6%, as evidenced by saying that "I know there's not much that I can say that would make things any better right now." Here Brees enacts the tactic of defeasibility by pleading a lack of control over the situation. Paradoxically, he used this statement to begin the video and yet spends the remainder of his apology attempting to "make things better."

The two remaining strategies used by Brees appeared in less than 10% of the video apology. In the video, he echoes the written apology that he must play a role in the solution (corrective action, 8.2%), "I will do better and I will be part of the solution," and continues using denial as a tool to highlight how his words are incorrectly perceived, "That was never my intention" (to hurt others). Where the video apology clearly differs from his earlier one is that there is no evidence of shared accountability; the general tone of Brees' video apology appears more personal regarding the impact of his comments.

You Make the Call

Like *The Times*, Americans' reactions to Drew Brees' two apologies were polarized. The messages were derided by some, deemed not "good enough" (Armour, 2020b, para. 14), and "hollow" by others (Florio, 2020, para. 7), while ESPN commentator Michael Wilbon suggested that Brees failed to properly address the wider issue of White Americans who question the patriotism of players who kneel in protest of racial injustice (ESPN, 2020). Meanwhile, for others, including Brees' teammate Michael Thomas, who had criticized Brees following the initial interview, Brees' recompense was enough. "He apologized & I accept it because that's what we are taught to do as Christians," Thomas tweeted (Thomas, 2020). Another teammate, Demario Davis, suggested that "For him to admit he was wrong, that is leadership at its finest" (Whitfield, 2020, para. 2). It is, perhaps, predictable that Brees' own New Orleans Saints' teammates would display a more forgiving tone. Publicly, at least.

In the days that followed his apologies, Brees displayed a changed stance, directing a clear message to President Trump after the president criticized Brees for apologizing. He tweeted:

> To Donald Trump, through my ongoing conversations with friends, team-mates, and leaders in the Black community, I realize this is not an issue about the American flag. It has never been. We can no longer use the flag to turn people away or distract them from the real issues that face our Black communities.
>
> *(Brees, 2020a)*

In the wake of this image restoration challenge, Brees went from "alienating nearly every Black professional athlete in America to being hailed as a hero for calling out the president of the United States" (Rhoden, 2020, para. 4). However, this sparked anger from conservative pundits who were upset that Brees had back-tracked from his original stance (Bernstein, 2020). The national anthem protests have long provided fuel for conservative media outlets that believe a culture war exists in the United States between political correctness and traditions. Widely described as providing conservative political positions, Fox News spent the week decrying Brees' about-turn as caving to a liberal agenda. Host Laura Ingraham, who had famously once told LeBron James to "shut up and dribble," defended Brees' initial views from the Yahoo Finance interview, claiming that critical responses to the quarterback were "totalitarian conduct" and "Stalinist" (Bieler, 2020). Brees stayed true to his primary image repair strategies of mortification and reducing offensiveness two months later during a training camp conference call with reporters, stating that "To think for a second that New Orleans or the state of Louisiana or the Black community would think I was not standing with them for social justice, that completely broke my heart. It was crushing. Never ever would I feel that way" (Just, 2020b).

Ultimately, Brees' image repair strategies appear to have been successful and support an assertion from Hambrick et al. (2013) who suggest that athletes who exhibit multifaceted image repair strategies can embolden identification and attachment with their followers. Brees did not lose any sponsorship deals, nor did the controversy appear to inhibit what turned out to be his final season with the New Orleans Saints. Teammate Cam Jordan later recalled that the open dialogue resulting from Brees' interview led to a positive impact in the locker room:

> The moment we heard it, it was instant text messages. Instant calls to Drew. Being your brother's keeper: *This is what I've gone through, what I've seen, what I've been through, how are you not able to relate?* It's that uncomfortable conversation that really led to our locker room being that much closer.
>
> *(Tynes, 2021, para. 36)*

Following his retirement, Brees remains in the football realm, joining NBC Sports as an analyst and continues his charitable endeavors through the Brees Dream Foundation.

Brees' status as a footballing icon remained largely unharmed following the initial controversy. However, a wider issue which focuses on the contrasting political and societal views between elite athletes and their supporters remains a challenging domain for everyone to navigate. Perhaps one reporter from *The New York Times*, and a New Orleans Saints fan, summarized it most eloquently, "I both hold unreserved joy over Brees's career and clearly understand the lingering ambivalence about his conservatism among progressive fans" (Smith, 2021, para. 6). Whether his teammates, Saints' fans, and others would have been so forgiving of Brees' stance had the level of his on-field performances not been so unbelievably high for a player approaching the end of his career remains hypothetical, but it nonetheless highlights the conundrum many sport consumers face when their heroes require image repair. Thus proving that, ultimately, compartmentalization needs to occasionally co-exist in fandom, even when all parties are uncomfortable with that accommodation.

Discussion Questions

1. How has the perception of national anthem protests changed between 2016 and today, and why might this be the case?
2. Take a look at the two apologies Brees published on June 4, 2020:
   a. Why did he make a second statement (video) so soon after his first (written)?
   b. Compare the consistency between the messages.
   c. In what ways did they differ, if at all?
3. What socio-cultural factors may have impacted both how Brees responded to criticism following his interview and how his apologies were received?
4. Since Brees' statements, national anthem protests have continued within American sport. How have other star athletes navigated the challenging debate surrounding this action? What might they have learnt from the Brees situation?
5. Discuss any new developments in the ongoing issue relating to athlete activism itself and the response to such activism. What has occurred lately to impact the conversation?

References

Allison, R., Pegoraro, A., Frederick, E., & Thompson, A.-J. (2020). When women athletes transgress: An exploratory study of image repair and social media response. *Sport in Society*, *23*(6), 1023–1041. https://doi.org/10.1080/17430437.2019.1580266

Armour, N. (2020a, June 5). Opinion: As protests rage over racial inequality, Drew Brees' tone-deaf comments show Saints QB is willfully ignorant. *USA Today*. https://eu.usatoday.com/story/sports/columnist/nancy-armour/2020/06/03/drew-brees-saints-willfully-ignorant-flag-national-anthem-george-floyd/3137613001

Armour, N. (2020b, June 5). Opinion: Drew Brees needs to do more than apologize for comments on protests. *USA Today*. https://eu.usatoday.com/story/sports/columnist/nancy-armour/2020/06/04/george-floyd-drew-brees-needs-do-more-than-apologize-comments/3144320001

Benoit, W.L. (1995). *Accounts, excuses, and apologies: A theory of image restoration strategies*. Albany, NY: State University of New York Press.

Benoit, W.L. (2015). *Accounts, excuses, and apologies: Image repair theory and research* (2nd ed.). Albany, NY: State University of New York Press.

Bernstein, D. (2020, September 13). Drew Brees and the national anthem: Revisiting the Saints QB's controversial anti-kneeling comments. *Sporting News*. www.sportingnews.com/us/nfl/news/drew-brees-national-anthem-kneeling-controversy/wmpdn843dhyn1hh5598pbavo3

Bieler, D. (2020, June 4). LeBron James calls out Fox News host Laura Ingraham over Drew Brees. *The Washington Post*. www.washingtonpost.com/sports/2020/06/04/lebron-james-calls-out-laura-ingraham-over-drew-brees

Brees, D. [@drewbrees]. (2020a, June 6). To @realdonaldtrump Through my ongoing conversations with friends, teammates, and leaders in the black community, I realize this is not [Tweet]. *Twitter*. https://twitter.com/drewbrees/status/1269089165972471814

Canova, D. (2020, June 3). Malcolm Jenkins responds to Drew Brees: "You're a part of the problem." *Fox News*. www.foxnews.com/sports/malcolm-jenkins-drew-brees-youre-a-part-of-the-problem

Doehler, S. (2021). Taking the star-spangled knee: The media framing of Colin Kaepernick. *Sport in Society*. https://doi.org/10.1080/17430437.2021.1970138

ESPN. (2020, June 5). Drew Brees' apology never addressed the issue – Michael Wilbon [Video]. *YouTube*. www.youtube.com/watch?v=QyJxycozusw

Florio, M. (2020, June 4). Drew Brees' apology leaves one specific question unanswered. *NBC Sports*. https://profootballtalk.nbcsports.com/2020/06/04/drew-brees-apology-leaves-one-specific-question-unanswered

Forbes. (2020). #67 Drew Brees. *Forbes*. www.forbes.com/profile/drew-brees/?sh=96da7d4722dc

Frederick, E.L., Burch, L.M., Sanderson, J., & Hambrick, M.E. (2014). To invest in the invisible: A case study of Manti Te'o's image repair strategies during the Katie Couric interview. *Public Relations Review, 40*(5), 780–788. https://doi.org/10.1016/J.PUBREV.2014.05.003

Germer, S. (2021, March 26). For many, Drew Brees' dedication to New Orleans meant as much as his work in a Saints jersey. *The Times-Picayune*. www.nola.com/sports/saints/drew_brees/article_a5b50378-8b5b-11eb-8a44-e398d0025bc1.html

Hambrick, M.E., Frederick, E.L., & Sanderson, J. (2013). From yellow to blue: Exploring Lance Armstrong's image repair strategies across traditional and social media. *Communication & Sport, 3*(2), 196–218. https://doi.org/10.1177/2167479513506982

Hull, K., & Boling, K.S. (2018). I was very intoxicated: An examination of the image repair discourse of Ryan Lochte following the 2016 Olympics. In T.L. Rentner & D.P. Burns (Eds.), *Case studies in sport communication* (pp. 202–210). London: Routledge. https://doi.org/10.4324/9781315189833-20

Jacobs, M. (2020, June 4). Drew Brees's tone-deaf comments on protests are both ignorant and dangerous. *The Guardian*. www.theguardian.com/sport/2020/jun/04/drew-brees-protest-comments-ignorant-saints

Jenkins, S. (2020, May 30). This is why Colin Kaepernick took a knee. *The Washington Post*. www.washingtonpost.com/sports/2020/05/30/this-is-why-colin-kaepernick-took-knee/

Just, A. (2020a, June 3). Drew Brees slammed after he says "he'll never agree with" protests during anthem. *The Times-Picayune.* www.nola.com/sports/saints/article_e279b606-a5be-11ea-8ee5-fbc0090fa50d.html

Just, A. (2020b, August 1). Saints' team "in good shape" after Drew Brees reconciles with teammates after protest comments. *The Times-Picayune.* www.nola.com/sports/saints/article_0ed8e29e-d404-11ea-9382-6fb45474e48b.html

King, P. (2010, January 18). The heart of New Orleans. *Sports Illustrated.* https://web.archive.org/web/20100116052045/http:/sportsillustrated.cnn.com/vault/article/magazine/MAG1164811/3/index.htm

Legg, K.L. (2009). Religious celebrity: An analysis of image repair discourse. *Journal of Public Relations Research, 21*(2), 240–250. https://doi.org/10.1080/10627260802557621

Meng, J., & Pan, P-L. (2016). Revisiting image-restoration strategies: An integrated case study of three athlete sex scandals in sports news. *International Journal of Sport Communication, 6*(1), 87–100. https://doi.org/10.1123/IJSC.6.1.87

Rhoden, W. (2020, June 9). Saints' Demario Davis says Drew Brees' sudden change of heart is for real. *The Undefeated.* https://theundefeated.com/features/saints-demario-davis-says-drew-brees-sudden-change-of-heart-is-for-real/

Rosenberg, M. (2020, June 4). Drew Brees still hasn't learned four years after Kaepernick took a knee. *Sports Illustrated.* www.si.com/nfl/2020/06/04/drew-brees-american-flag-kneeling-comments-colin-kaepernick

Sanderson, J. (2008). "How do you prove a negative?" Roger Clemens's image-repair strategies in response to the Mitchell report. *International Journal of Sport Communication, 1*(2), 246–262. https://doi.org/10.1123/IJSC.1.2.246

Shapiro, M. (2020, June 4). Drew Brees apologizes for kneeling comments: "I have always been an ally." *Sports Illustrated.* www.si.com/nfl/2020/06/04/drew-brees-apologizes-kneeling-comments

Smith, T.J. (2021, March 16). On loving Drew Brees, and deciding not to cancel him. *The New York Times.* www.nytimes.com/2021/03/16/sports/football/drew-brees-kneeling-protest-anthem.html

Swenson, D. (2021, March 26). How many NFL and Saints records did Drew Brees retire with? Here's the full breakdown. *The Times-Picayune.* www.nola.com/sports/saints/drew_brees/article_902415b2-85a7-11eb-9c65-1b97f0dbb064.html

The Brees Dream Foundation. (2021). *Our mission.* The Brees Dream Foundation. https://drewbrees.com

Thomas, M. [@cantguardmike] (2020, June 4). One of my brothers made a public statement yesterday that I disagreed with. He apologized & I accept it because [Tweet]. *Twitter.* https://twitter.com/Cantguardmike/status/1268592412454248454

Triplett, M. (2016, August 29). New Orleans Saints QB Drew Brees on 49ers Colin Kaepernick protest. *ESPN.* www.espn.com/blog/new-orleans-saints/post/_/id/23063/drew-brees-wholeheartedly-disagrees-with-colin-kaepernicks-method-of-protest

Tynes, T. (2021, August 5). Cam Jordan wants a super bowl – And maybe for Jameis Winston start at QB. *GQ Magazine.* www.gq.com/story/cam-jordan-saints-interview

Walker, R. (2020, June 3). Walker: Drew Brees, known for his accuracy, misses the mark again with his anthem comments. *The Times-Picayune.* www.nola.com/sports/saints/article_726a1a52-a5f2-11ea-8aba-6b2975de0833.html

Whitfield, K. (2020, June 4). Saints teammates, others react to Drew Brees' apology: "He apologized and I accept it." *The Times-Picayune.* www.nola.com/sports/saints/article_1b8d64f0-a665-11ea-bb22-13a366ea863e.html

7

"KICKING HATE OUT OF OUR GAME"

San Diego Loyal Soccer Club's Stand against Racism and Homophobia

Jeffrey W. Kassing, Isaiah D. Utley and Steffanie M. Kiourkas

Introduction

San Diego Loyal (SDL), a professional U.S. men's soccer team, began operations in June 2019 as the newest member of the United Soccer League (USL) Championship (i.e., U.S. soccer's second tier). They played their first full season in the league during 2020. Toward the end of that season, the club confronted bigotry in two consecutive matches. The first involved a racial slur targeting an SDL player during a match on September 23 against LA Galaxy II, the second team for the LA Galaxy franchise of Major League Soccer (MLS). The second occurred a week later on September 30th and involved a homophobic slur directed at SDL's Collin Martin, the only openly gay player in the league, during a match against conference-leading Phoenix Rising FC. While both incidents resulted in initial denials, the league investigated each incident and levelled punitive sanctions against the offending players, which left little question about the validity of the cases. The events set in motion a club-wide response designed to address bigotry in sport. This case examines the SDL response and fan reactions to it.

Background

Stakeholder theory asserts that organizations consider an array of interests beyond profitability, taking into account how corporate actions influence diverse audiences – those that maintain a stake in the actions of the organization (Freeman, 1984). For sport organizations, franchises, and clubs, stakeholders encompass supporter groups, fans, players, club employees and staff, club administrators, local government officials, local residents, competing teams, sport governing

DOI: 10.4324/9781003316763-9

bodies, and professional leagues. These stakeholders monitor the actions of, and hold expectations for, specific sport organizations.

Organizations vary in the degree to which they recognize and count stakeholders as being consequential. Key stakeholders tend to influence the organization, relate to it legitimately, and require vital attention from the sport organization (Mitchell et al., 1997). Moreover, the relationship between stakeholders and organizations is reciprocal because stakeholders can exert pressure against, and impact, organizations by protesting, boycotting, or withholding resources and support (Seeger, 1997). Sport organizations operate in an interesting environment as they need to balance stakeholders focused on the economic viability of the operation with fans who expect and desire sporting success, while also representing a geographic place and identity (Clark, 2006). Fans, however, vary in their affiliation with soccer clubs, ranging from those whose lives are highly intertwined with their respective teams to those who provide support intermittently (Giulianotti, 2002). Thus, when confronted with crisis, sport organizations must account for a cohort of stakeholders that will fluctuate in their commitment and expectations.

Crisis involves events that produce high degrees of uncertainty and direct threats to organizational goals (Seeger et al., 1998). In times of crisis, organizations attempt to remain responsive to numerous stakeholders, but, in reality, act decisively to address the crisis, tending to favor internal over external stakeholders (Crable & Vibbert, 1985; Ulmer & Sellnow, 2000). This tendency to look inward can prove particularly challenging for sport organizations that prioritize protecting sporting success over social issues deemed significant to the organization and the community at large. This dynamic played out in professional European soccer (Kassing, 2019a).

Football Club Barcelona (FCB) maintains a long-standing association with, and has become representative of, Catalan culture and nationalism (Kassing, 2021; Shobe, 2008). This association has been emphasized to varying degrees over the club's history, increasing in relevance during periods of Catalan cultural repression enacted by Spain. Most recently, FCB's association with Catalan nationalism has become conflated with the region's push to secede from Spain. Against this backdrop, FCB was confronted with the decision to play or forfeit a match on October 1, 2017, when the semi-autonomous Catalan government conducted an independence referendum vote.

Deemed illegal by the Spanish government, the vote resulted in violence between voters and national police leaving several hundred injured. Footage of police firing rubber bullets into crowds, hitting protesters with batons, and forcibly removing would-be voters from polling stations quickly appeared on international news.

In the wake of the violence, FCB requested the league to postpone the match. The league refused and warned the club that forfeiting that afternoon's match would also incur an additional 3-point deduction (i.e., an overall penalty equivalent to two losses). With such high competitive stakes on the line, FCB decided, just 24 minutes before kickoff, to play the game behind closed doors, locking thousands of fans out of the stadium. Whereas matches in empty stadiums became commonplace due to the COVID-19 pandemic, voluntarily doing so was highly unusual. The club argued in subsequent publicity materials that the actions were meant to show solidarity with the Catalan people. Yet, when confronted with the choice of taking a strong stand in support of Catalan nationalism or losing points, the club opted for a solution that proved disappointing to many stakeholders. Indeed, board members, current and former players and coaches, and global fans roundly criticized the decision (Kassing, 2019a). FCB found itself in an unenviable position, faced with the paradoxical choice of either competing or addressing an important social issue.

Paradox is an applicable analytical tool for sport case studies because of the potential conflict between pursuit of social issues relevant to sport (e.g., gender equality, bigotry) and the underlying ethos of competition. Paradox in social context concerns tensions that result from a clash of ideas, principles, or actions that need to be addressed in interaction and everyday practices (Stohl & Cheney, 2001). Accordingly, paradox necessitates reconciling two apparently contrasting and conflicting views that require actions that are antithetical to the pursuit of a specific objective. Paradoxes, therefore, emerge in social interactions and relationships, are context dependent, and take shape over time. The recognition and productive handling of social paradoxes can lead to advancement and empowerment.

Sport scholars have considered paradox in a variety of studies. For example, Stahley and Boyd (2006) asserted that displays in the National Collegiate Athletic Association's (NCAA's) Hall of Champions museum implied a paradox centered on excellence. Excellence paradoxically manifested as representations of athletic success defined predominantly by winning versus associations with self-improvement and doing one's best. An examination of the One World Fútbol organization, which provides ultra-durable soccer balls to underserved communities, revealed that its efforts addressed the paradox of outfitting the global game. That is, providing equipment to the large majority of soccer players who reside outside of the more affluent league structures existing elsewhere (Kassing, 2019b).

In other work, Gorsevski and Butterworth (2011) uncovered the paradox evident in the violent threats used by Muhammad Ali to advocate for nonviolent change, whereas Shea (2001) discovered that female bodybuilding simultaneously blurred and delineated lines between masculinity and femininity – when judges paradoxically expected competitors to focus on their hair and makeup as well as their muscular physique. Similarly, recent work revealed that female college soccer players in the United States confronted the female athlete paradox of embracing athleticism while exaggerating femininity (Festle, 1996). They did so by constructing provocative, humorous, and ironic social media content that cleverly integrated themes of physique and fashion, competitiveness and aggression, and dedication and commitment (Kassing, 2018).

Organizations engage social issues through corporate social responsibility (CSR) efforts. But the public has grown increasingly skeptical of CSR because such efforts may not be genuinely targeting social issues but rather primarily increasing organizational reputations and brands. Thus, CSR can be symbolic and self-servingly pursued or it can be genuine and substantive, with the differentiation fundamentally manifesting in terms of the beneficiary of such efforts (Donia & Tetrault Sirsly, 2016). Symbolic CSR tends to benefit organizations directly whereas substantive CSR addresses actual causes and benefits non-organizational audiences. Relatedly, symbolic CSR stems from strategic motives, whereas substantive CSR entails determination to address pressing social issues. In an empirical examination, researchers found that substantive, but not symbolic, CSR related favorably to the level of organizational commitment employees reported, the degree to which employees felt connected to their organizations' values, how well employees felt they fit in with their organizations, and the quality of relationships they maintained within those organizations (Donia et al., 2017). In short, the approach taken to address social issues matters to the public and directly affects stakeholders.

Sport organizations must be responsive to a variety of stakeholders ranging from corporate sponsors to local fans. Additionally, when social issues surface that warrant attention, sport organizations must confront and navigate the paradox of effectively addressing the social issue while risking their competitive standing. How the sport organization responds in these paradoxical crisis situations will be evaluated by stakeholders as being substantive or merely symbolic responses. SDL's response to the incidents of bigotry experienced at the end of the 2020 season provides an interesting case to examine such a paradox.

The Case

In SDL's penultimate game of the 2020 season, played in an empty stadium due to the COVID-19 pandemic, the team experienced its first incident of bigotry when an opposing player from LA Galaxy II directed a racial slur at Elijah Martin. Given the absence of a crowd, the players, field officials, and the opposing coaches heard the slur. However, no discernable action was taken at the time. The SDL coach, Landon Donovan, and club officials did not learn of the affront until after the match. Two days later, the club officially announced it would forfeit the point earned for the match that ended in a draw. As part of the official statement SDL's Chairman, Andrew Vassiliadis, said that "We don't even want to recognize being a part of a match where these types of actions take place. The Loyal in our name is symbolic of the diversity in our community and as a club we will not stand for this" (San Diego Loyal, 2020a, para. 2).

Referencing the fact the player was not disciplined by either the LA Galaxy II coaching staff or the game officials, the official statement continued that "The team believes they should've walked off the field with the lack of discipline for this action. As a team, they have decided to forfeit the match" (San Diego Loyal, 2020a, para. 5). The team statement served to both stridently condemn the incident and forecast to stakeholders what they could expect from the club if a similar situation occurred. Coach Landon Donovan retweeted the official statement, adding on his personal Twitter account:

> I couldn't be more proud to be part of this club. What's the point of the BLM [Black Lives Matter] jerseys/armbands, the kneeling before every game and the commitment to ending racism if we don't address it when it happens right before our eyes? This is NEVER acceptable and we will not stand for it.
>
> *(Donovan, 2020)*

Donovan's comment reaffirmed the club's stance and its intent for future action (i.e., substantive versus symbolic responses).

Remarkably, the club's resolve was tested shortly thereafter. Only a week later, in their next league match, a member of Phoenix Rising FC directed a Jamaican homophobic slur at SDL player Collin Martin, who is openly gay. The first-half incident resulted in a heated exchange between both head coaches – Landon Donovan and Rick Schantz – captured on video and widely disseminated via social media as stakeholders learned of the incident. The exchange was transcribed and featured on a nationally televised morning show segment that included both Martin and Donovan, who commented on the incident a few days later (Good Morning America, 2020). The coaches' transcribed exchange appears here:

Donovan: This is beyond soccer.
Schantz: Come on man, don't make a big scene.
Donovan: What do you mean not a big deal? We have to get this out of our game.
Schantz: It's got nothing to do with racism.
Donovan: Calling a player gay?
Schantz: They're competing.
Donovan: It's not racism, they're calling him gay. It's homophobia.
Schantz: How long have you been playing soccer?
Donovan: (exasperatedly putting his hands on his head) You're better than that.

Reportedly, Donovan requested that either the official or Schantz should remove the offending player from the squad for the second half. The player remained. The official argued that he did not understand the offensive comment and therefore could not in good conscience discipline the player. Coach Schantz simply refused Donovan's request to pull the player for the second half. Subsequently, SDL players discussed the situation at halftime and decided if the player remained in the game, they would not take the field for the second half. Thus, after halftime, the SDL squad stepped onto the pitch, saw the offending player was still present, and waited for the whistle to sound. Once it did, the team collectively walked off the field, forfeiting the game.

The coordinated reaction by the SDL team and coaches was clearly dramatic, but it also was noteworthy as the team was winning the game 3–1, and a victory would put the franchise in playoff contention in its inaugural season. SDL's unusual response, combined with the competitive repercussions of the decision, garnered broad media coverage. The team's response prompted attention from general news programs and networks including *Good Morning America* and CNN (Church & Klosok, 2020; Good Morning America, 2020), as well as sporting news outlets like ESPN and *Sports Illustrated* (ESPN, 2020; Selbe, 2020).

In a recorded message posted on SDL's official Twitter account, Donovan defended his team's actions in response to the incident (San Diego Loyal, 2020b). He asserted that the organization "made a vow to ourselves, to our community, to our players, to the club, to USL, that we would not stand for bigotry, homophobic slurs, things that don't belong in our game." He added that because the players and coaches regretted not doing something in the moment with the previous incident, they had embraced the refrain "I will speak, I will act" – even adding it to their stadium sign boards. Donovan also shared that, perhaps ironically, players from SDL and Phoenix Rising had agreed, before the game, to coordinate a public statement incorporating the need to speak up and confront instances of bigotry in soccer. Apparently, the players arranged to stop the game in the 71st minute (the same time in which the racial abuse incident had occurred in the previous match) and "hold a banner together that said 'I will speak, I will act'." Donovan stressed that the anticipated action was necessary "because we don't want to just talk about it, we actually want to do it. And we want to send a message" (San Diego Loyal, 2020b).

In the same recorded statement appearing on Twitter, addressing the incident that actually occurred (i.e., the homophobic slur), Donovan reiterated his team's desire to continue play, particularly since they were winning, but conceded that "if we wanted to be true to who we are as a club – we have to speak and we have to act" (San Diego Loyal, 2020b). Donovan confirmed the walk-off and forfeiture was a team decision made at halftime and praised their choice saying "Our guys, to their immense credit, just said we're not going to stand for this" and that "they were very clear in that moment that they were giving up all hopes of making the playoffs," reasoning that "It doesn't matter, there's [sic] things more important in life and we have to stick up for what we believe in" (San Diego Loyal, 2020b).

Collin Martin, in turn, posted an official statement on his Twitter account acknowledging it was "not the first time I've heard this homophobic slur" but adding it was the "first time in my eight-year playing career that a slur has been directed at me during a game" (Martin, 2020). Martin complimented the response of his teammates, coaches, and organization declaring that "Their collective decision to walk off the field in solidarity and forfeit the match speaks volumes of their support for me and what this organization is standing up to" and said the action did much in regard to "kicking hate out of our game." Fellow teammates echoed their support of Martin and the club via their respective Twitter accounts including, but not limited to, Captain Sal Zizzo ("We stand by what we believe in"), defender Tarek Morad (. . . "Proud to be a part of this club – been an honor and privilege to wear the @ SanDiegoLoyal kit this season . . ."), midfielder Alejandro Guido ("I will speak. I will act"), and forward Irvin Parra ("I love you my brother I stand with you").

You Make the Call

Fans generally reacted favorably to SDL's anti-bigotry actions. Evidence of this was widely available on social media in response to the club's posting of an official statement about forfeiting the point earned in the match sullied by the racial slur. SDL fans, for example, shared: "I love this. My club forever and ever" (@ericdwilke), "I honestly, truly, didn't think I could love this team more" (@McAwesomeOC), and "Extremely proud to cheer on these players and this organization" (@Jigglyduffy). Fans of other USL clubs offered equally compelling reactions. A Las Vegas Lights fan commented that "I respect the SD [San Diego] decision to really put your money where your mouth is" (@ozzel1138), whereas a Pittsburgh Riverhounds supporter similarly suggested that "That's putting your figurative balls on the table right der [sic]" (@European_Red_Fox). A supporter of MLS's Seattle Sounders appreciated that the club took decisive action, submitting that putting "up anti-racism signs or whatever" was only a start because "it's way better when they [people, teams or organizations] start acting on it" (@Squirrels_Gone_Wild).

People reacted similarly to SDL's walk-off forfeiture in response to the homophobic slur. Club supporters expressed team pride in how well it represented the local community, particularly given the stakes. For example, "Extremely proud of my team for standing up for what's right. Local. Loyal. PROUD" (@Singin4TheTaste), "I'm proud of my team. We had so much on the line in a big game we were winning, it's sending a big message" (@robozomb), and "Loyal fan who was looking forward to t.he playoffs here – fully support their stance and proud of their support for their teammate and equality" (@hushnicely). Likewise, fans of other clubs joined the chorus of approval. An MLS fan, who supports Orlando City, admitted that "San Diego has gained another fan today" (@sault9), whereas a supporter of the Portland Timbers confessed that "I am not a Loyal fan but this action in two straight games, this desire and drive to stand up for what's right made me buy a jersey" (@tanquinho). The unequivocal anti-bigotry response of SDL seemingly drew new fans to the club and to the sport. For instance, a local resident announced: "Proud to be a San Diegan today. I don't even like soccer but I'm happy to support a team that does things right" (@grants_your_wishes).

The club's actions also gave rise to important conversations about bigotry in sport on the Reddit platform after it posted a statement about forfeiting the match on September 30th (San Diego Loyal, 2020c). Some contributors expressed disappointment, such as "It's amazing people still use slurs like this in this culture we live in this country" (@Sctvman), whereas others stridently condemned the behavior by claiming "No place for that type of shit on the field" (@Heil-Heimskr) and "This kind of behavior and treatment of other players has no place in soccer, let alone any other sports" (@PerfectLogic). Despite the expressions of disappointment and disgust, people found solace not only in the definitive actions of the club, but also in the pervasive support the club garnered and in the widespread condemnation of the offenses. One particularly popular and highly-rated comment in the Reddit discussion captured this sentiment well; it read in part: "Yea this situation is bad, but the response from the fans (Phoenix, San Diego and fans of other teams) has been a reassuring sign that society IS changing. We will no longer allow or condone these types of behavior [sic]" (@RetakingAnatomy).

The positive outlook underscored the nearly unanimous opinions by social media users that homophobia needed to be removed from sport. This sentiment, however, belies another sporting paradox – that is, the use of racial and homophobic slurs as a form of trash talk during athletic competition voiced by both athletes and fans (Magrath, 2018; Rainey, 2012; Rainey & Granito, 2010). Because people commonly conflate sport with hyper-masculinity, derogating opponents with racial or homophobic slurs often gets excused as part of competition (Cleland, 2014; Magrath, 2018; Millward, 2008).

Phoenix Rising Coach Schantz's comments during his exchange with Landon Donovan revealed this tendency to dismiss such language, which drew the ire of stakeholders associated with SDL, Phoenix Rising, and other clubs. Contributors to the aforementioned Redditt thread used profanity and vulgarity to express their disgust posting comments like "WOW. Fuck that piece of shit coach" (@Helvetimusic), "What a fucking moron" (@NextDoorNeighbrrs), and "Fuck this guy" (@powerfulndn). Whereas these contributors impugned Schantz's character, others called for his resignation (e.g., @PersonnelFowl commented "Schantz needs to be gone. Now") and questioned his conduct (e.g., @notmacdemarco stated "Honestly disgusting behavior from him. It sounded like he didn't think it was a big deal."). For some stakeholders, Schantz represents the distasteful and outdated attitudes about homophobia that are no longer accepted by fans and supporters (Cashmore & Cleland, 2012; Magrath, 2018), yet remain persistent within sport culture generally (Schallhorn & Hempel, 2017).

The events that concluded the 2020 season and SDL's first year of competition presented the nascent franchise with a crisis that compelled an unambiguous organizational response directed to its various stakeholders. Confronted with tackling important social issues, specifically racism and homophobia in sport, warranted navigating the paradox of facing social issues substantively (versus merely symbolically) at the risk of conceding competitive success.

The racist and homophobic assaults directed at members of SDL tested the organization's adherence to its core pillars – independence, authenticity, inclusivity, and optimism. This value system helped ground the organization, frame its relationship both within the sport itself and the community where it resides, and helped focus its actions accordingly. Although most organizations, sports franchises included, have clear guiding principles underscoring their operations, it is clear SDL lived by these guiding principles when confronted with an issue rather than have them serve as merely window dressing. The organization's forfeiture of points, when it really mattered in sporting terms, proved noteworthy to stakeholders (i.e., club personnel, coaches, players, supporters, opposing fans, general spectators, and community residents). The events that transpired moved the club to act on its promise of practicing and supporting inclusivity. Consequently, SDL responded independent of the traditional sporting pressures that might comprise the club's ability and willingness to take a strong stand regarding social issues. The specific actions taken enlivened the speaking/acting orientation it embraced, revealing it to be authentic. And, the organization's responses apparently generated optimism within the stakeholder community both internally (i.e., team pride) and externally (i.e., as social justice activists). Interestingly, the "I Will Speak, I Will Act" refrain became a part of the club's brand. Fans could now order stickers that feature the slogan, club crest, and team colors from the SDL website. Merely focusing on the sticker might infer that SDL performs symbolic CSR, but this case suggests that the team's early activist history, as represented by the sticker, implicates the club's willingness to substantively engage in social issues.

Discussion Questions

1. In your view, how and why did SDL's decision to forfeit points and the possibility of making the playoffs resonate with various stakeholders?
2. Coach Landon Donovan revealed that players intended to display an anti-bigotry banner during the Phoenix Rising match. If the homophobic slur had not preempted this, what effect would it have had among stakeholders? Would potential reactions differ from the forfeiture of the match?
3. Due to COVID-19, there were no fans in attendance when SDL decided to walk off the field and forfeit the match. How might that same decision play out differently if fans were present?
4. At the time of these incidents, SDL was a new club in the U.S. second tier of competitive soccer. Would better known and more established clubs that operate at higher levels and with larger fan bases be able to act similarly?
5. Are there comparable situations in sport that have occurred since the SDL case unfolded? What aspects differ from this case?

References

Cashmore, E., & Cleland, J. (2012). Fans, homophobia and masculinities in association football. *British Journal of Sociology, 63*(2), 370–387.

Church, B., & Klosok, A. (2020, October 1). US soccer team walks off pitch after alleged homophobic abuse of gay player. www.cnn.com/2020/10/01/football/san-diego-loyal-homophobia-protest-spt-intl/index.html

Clark, T. (2006). 'I'm Scunthorpe 'til I die': Constructing and (re)negotiating identity through the terrace chant. *Soccer and Society, 7*, 494–507.

Cleland, J. (2014). Racism, football fans, and online message boards: How social media has added a new dimension to racist discourse in English football. *Journal of Sport and Social Issues, 38*(5), 415–431.

Crable, R.E., & Vibbert, S.L. (1985). Managing issues and influencing public policy. *Public Relations Review, 11*, 3–16.

Donia, M., & Tetrault Sirsly, C.A. (2016). Determinants and consequences of employee attributions of corporate social responsibility as substantive or symbolic. *European Management Journal, 34*, 232–242.

Donia, M., Tetrault Sirsly, C.A., & Ronen, S. (2017). Employee attributes of corporate social responsibility as substantive or symbolic: Validation of a measure. *Applied Psychology, 66*(1), 103–142.

Donovan, L. (2020, September 25). I couldn't be more proud to be part of this club [Tweet]. https://twitter.com/landondonovan/status/1309676025773662208

ESPN. (2020, September 30). USL's San Diego Loyal forfeit in protest, alleging ant-gay slur. www.espn.com/sports/soccer/story/_/id/30013159/usl-san-diego-loyal-forfeit-protest-alleging-anti-gay-slur

Festle, M.J. (1996). *Playing nice: Politics and apologies in women's sports.* New York: Columbia University Press.

Freeman, R.E. (1984). *Strategic management: A stakeholder approach.* London: Pitman Publishing.

Good Morning America. (2020, October 2). Soccer player and coach speak out on forfeiting match over Gay Slur. [Video File]. www.youtube.com/watch?v=2oH3Cixi0d4

Gorsevski, E.W., & Butterworth, M.L. (2011). Muhammad Ali's fighting words: The paradox of violence in nonviolent rhetoric. *Quarterly Journal of Speech, 97*(1), 50–73.

Giulianotti, R. (2002). Supporters, followers, fans, and flaneurs: A taxonomy of spectator identities in football. *Journal of Sport & Social Issues, 26*(1), 25–46.

Kassing, J.W. (2018). Confronting the female athlete paradox with humor and irony: A thematic analysis of SoccerGrlProbs YouTube video content. *Sport in Society, 21*(7), 1096–1111.

Kassing, J.W. (2019a). 'Mes que un club' and an empty Camp Nou: A case study of strategic ambiguity and Catalan nationalism at Football Club Barcelona. *International Journal of Sport Communication, 12*, 260–274.

Kassing, J.W. (2019b). Paradox and the gift of an indestructible ball: A case study of the One World Fútbol Project. *Soccer & Society, 20, 569–583.*

Kassing, J.W. (2021). Connecting global and local audiences: Communication in, around and about Football Club Barcelona. In M.L. Butterworth (Ed.), *Handbook of communication and sport* (pp. 235–252). London: De Gruyter Mouton.

Magrath, R. (2018). 'To try and gain an advantage for my team': Homophobic and homosexually themed chanting among English football fans. *Sociology, 52*(4), 709–726.

Martin, C. (2020, October 1). My statement on what happened in last night's match [Tweet]. https://twitter.com/martcw12/status/1311756841647443968

Millward, P. (2008). Rivalries and racism: 'Closed' and 'open' Islamophobic dispositions. amongst football supporters. *Sociological Research Online, 13*(6). https://doi.org/10.5153/sro.1816.

Mitchell, R.K., Agle, B.R., & Wood, D.J. (1997). Toward a theory of stakeholder identification. and salience: Defining the principle of who and what really counts. *Academy of Management Review, 22*, 853–886.

Rainey, D.W. (2012). Sport's officials' reports of hearing trash talk and their responses to trash talk. *Journal of Sport Behavior, 35*, 78–93.

Rainey, D.W., & Granito, V. (2010). Normative rules for trash talk among college athletes: An exploratory study. *Journal of Sport Behavior, 33*, 276–294.

San Diego Loyal. (2020a, September 25). "We don't even want to recognize being part of a match where these types of actions take place" [Tweet]. https://twitter.com/SanDiegoLoyal/status/1309641373268680704

San Diego Loyal. (2020b, September 30). Landon Donovan on why the team decided to forfeit tonight's match against Phoenix Rising FC [Tweet]. https://twitter.com/SanDiegoLoyal/status/1311553192711184385

San Diego Loyal. (2020c, September 30). San Diego loyal walk off field with a 3–1 lead after player was called a homophobic slur [Online forum]. www.reddit.com/r/USLPRO/comments/j30wyr/san_diego_loyal_walk_off_field_with_a_31_lead/

Schallhorn, C., & Hempel, A. (2017). Media coverage of Thomas Hitzlsperger's coming-out in German newspapers. *Journalism Studies, 18*(9), 1187–1205.

Seeger, M.W. (1997). *Ethics and organizational communication.* London: Hampton Press.

Seeger, M.W., Sellnow, T.L., & Ulmer, R.R. (1998). Communication, organization and crisis. In M. E Roloff (Ed.), *Communication yearbook, 21* (pp. 231–275). London: Sage.

Selbe, N. (2020, October 1). USL's San Diego Loyal walk off pitch after anti-LGBTQ slur from opposing player. www.si.com/soccer/2020/10/01/san-diego-loyal-leave-field-following-anti-lgbtq-slur-from-opponent

Shea, B.C. (2001). The paradox of pumping iron: Female bodybuilding as resistance and compliance. *Women and Language, 24*(2), 42–46.

Shobe, H. (2008). Place, identity and football: Catalonia, Catalanisme and Football Club Barcelona, 1899–1975. *National Identities, 10*, 329–343.

Stohl, C., & Cheney, G. (2001). Participatory processes/paradoxical practices: Communication and the dilemmas of organizational democracy. *Management Communication Quarterly, 14*, 349–407.

Stahley, M.B., & Boyd, J. (2006). Winning is(n't) everything: The paradox of excellence and the challenge of organizational epideictic. *Journal of Applied Communication Research, 34*(4), 311–330.

Ulmer, R.R., & Sellnow, T.L. (2000). Ambiguity in organizational crisis communication: Jack in the Box as a case study. *Journal of Business Ethics, 25*, 143–155.

8

ISSUES AND CRISIS MANAGEMENT IN ATHLETE ACTIVISM

Colin Kaepernick and the Take a Knee Movement

Lillian Feder

Introduction

NFL player Colin Kaepernick started the Take a Knee movement in August of 2016 as a silent protest denouncing police brutality in the United States. The protest took place within the competition space (i.e., on the football field) and in the form of a silent disruption to one of the most sacred ritualistic performances in sport (Billings et al., 2015). By first sitting and then taking a knee, during the United States' national anthem, Kaepernick ensured that media and fans would take note. And they did. His silent protest was met with overwhelming outrage and eventually led to the abrupt ending of his NFL career. This public outrage, while grounded to an extent in the disruption of ritual and escape provided by sport as a form of entertainment, was fueled by an ignorance to Kaepernick's intention behind the action of taking a knee and overall message of the movement.

With any silent protest, the careful crafting and intentional maintenance of the movement's narrative are paramount. Kaepernick's failure to specifically, clearly, and consistently communicate the intention behind the Take a Knee movement led to the re-framing of the movement's narrative by conservative politicians and media. Kaepernick's opposition distorted the genuine intention behind his kneeling by diverting the publics' collective attention away from what Kaepernick hoped to achieve by kneeling and redirecting it to *when* and *how* he knelt (Coombs et al., 2020); in this sense, the nonverbal nature of this movement enabled agenda-setters' critique of his silent protest. Thus, the meaning of Take a Knee shifted away from a denouncement of police brutality and morphed into a blatant display of antimilitarism and anti-Americanism, situating both Colin Kaepernick and the NFL in crisis.

DOI: 10.4324/9781003316763-10

Background

By kneeling on the football field in 2016, Colin Kaepernick brought societal issues into the realm of sport. Shortly before he knelt, Philando Castile and Alton Sterling were murdered by police officers, adding to a long list of fatal instances of police brutality targeting unarmed Black men (Karlis, 2019). By this time, the Black Lives Matter movement had dedicated 3 years to fighting White supremacy and raising societal awareness to the continued racial inequity in the United States and abroad (Blacklivesmatter.com, 2022). Simultaneously, Donald Trump used his 2016 presidential campaign platform to spread divisive rhetoric, pitting Americans against one another on the basis of nationality, sex, religion, and race (McCammon, 2016). In such tumultuous times, many fans depended on sport as a vehicle to escape the realities of life (Feder & Smith, forthcoming). In this way, sport fans consumed competition similar to other avenues of entertainment (e.g., movies, novels). With the juxtaposition between the increasing visibility of police brutality and the popularity of then-presidential candidate Donald Trump's call to "make America great again," leading to frequent protests and national discussions of racial inequity, sport fans had plenty to escape from in 2016. The ritual of tuning out existing inequities while tuning into the alternate utopian reality provided by football, where fair play and vicarious achievement rule, was interrupted in August 2016 when Colin Kaepernick initially sat, and then repeatedly knelt, during the U.S. national anthem (Karlis, 2019). As the season progressed, tensions between Kaepernick's supporters and critics grew. The more Kaepernick knelt, the more difficult it was for fans to continue to compartmentalize sport and society.

With this collision between sport and society, came the recognition of racial inequity within professional football. Inequity that, in many ways, mirrored the racial injustices playing out in society. As the Take a Knee movement gained traction and other NFL stars joined Kaepernick in kneeling before games, tensions between owners and athletes grew. With the majority of NFL athletes identifying as Black (Karlis, 2019) and all but two NFL owners identifying as Caucasian (Garcia, 2018), the power imbalance in the NFL paralleled the power imbalance in society. Some NFL owners attempted to enforce their own anthem policies to combat the narrative that their players were unpatriotic. For example, Jerry Jones, the owner of the Dallas Cowboys, publicly promised to bench any athlete who knelt during the anthem at the start of the 2017 NFL season. However, the official NFL anthem policy at the time merely stated that players "should" stand during the anthem (Reid, 2017). In unilaterally converting a suggestion to a mandate and threatening the livelihood of athletes who did not comply, NFL owners like Jerry Jones attempted to use their power to stifle the First Amendment rights of their players.

Further blurring the line between sport and society was the support Kaepernick received from the Black Lives Matter movement juxtaposed with the hatred he received from conservative politicians, fans, and media. For example, in September 2016, then-presidential candidate Donald Trump inserted himself into the conversation, urging those kneeling during the national anthem to find another country of residence (Haislop, 2020). Two weeks later, *Time* magazine featured Kaepernick on the cover of their October issue, signaling support for him and the cause (Haislop, 2020). These charged reactions brought discussions of Take a Knee to televisions, newspapers, barbershops, kitchen tables, classrooms, water coolers, and perhaps most significantly, social media. The hashtag #TakeAKnee turned Kaepernick's movement into a trending topic (Lacy, 2017), which sustained the polarizing conversations regarding his decision to kneel well beyond NFL game days.

Kaepernick missed the opportunity to solidify the purpose of his protest through proactively engaging the media and public. Rather than drawing attention to the parallel power imbalances present in sport and society through a variety of media, he discussed his intentions for the silent protest during pre- and post-game press conferences and interviews, disregarding traditional news outlets and social media. As a result, the narrative of the Take a Knee movement was quickly co-opted and distorted by conservative media and social media users. Understandably, traditional news media became the opinion leaders with respect to Take a Knee (McCombs & Shaw, 1972), minimizing Kaepernick's voice and instead framing his protest as anti-American (Entman, 1993; Goffman, 1974).

In media reports, news outlets neglected to mention how Kaepernick arrived at the decision to kneel (rather than sit) and instead emphasized the American expectation of standing at attention during the national anthem. News outlets framed Kaepernick's protest as taking a critical aim at American soldiers, failing to report that Kaepernick consulted with former U.S. Army Green Beret Nate Boyer to ensure his protest would not disrespect the American military (Karlis, 2019). Thus, in the absence of Kaepernick's voice, conservative news media set the agenda for the publics' consumption of the Take a Knee movement, framing it as anti-American and unrelated to police brutality.

The combination of interrupting sport fans' abilities to consume football for escape and the media's framing of Take a Knee situated both Colin Kaepernick and the NFL in crisis. Supplementing Karlis' (2019) discussion in *Case Studies in Sport Communication* (1st ed.), which focuses on the NFL's delayed and inadequate response to this crisis, this chapter examines Kaepernick's enactment of the Take a Knee movement from a crisis perspective. Particular attention is placed on Kaepernick's missteps in terms of the management of the issues, which led to the athlete reputational crisis (ARC) that ended his football career (Coombs, 2018). In recognizing the role effective issues management plays in crisis prevention (Page & Parnell, 2018), this chapter suggests issues management strategies for athlete activists. Additionally, this chapter connects agenda-setting and media framing to issues management by arguing that Kaepernick should have set the agenda for his own movement and better framed its narrative to support his goals. Ultimately, questions will be raised regarding the effectiveness of Kaepernick's silent protest and the fate of his athletic career.

The Case

Colin Kaepernick provides a ripe case study to explore contemporary social justice issues in sport communication as one of the first key actors in the post-digital wave of athlete activism. Before Kaepernick knelt, Derrick Rose successfully initiated and carried out a silent protest in response to a grand jury's decision not to try the police officer responsible for the death of Eric Garner. This took shape as groups of NBA athletes across a variety of teams wore T-shirts adorned with the slogan "I Can't Breathe" while warming up for games in December of the 2014–2015 NBA season. With athletes like Kobe Bryant and LeBron James endorsing this campaign and the NBA's commissioner, Adam Silver, reluctantly accepting it, focus quickly shifted from the athlete who started the campaign to its messaging. Kaepernick's case is distinct from this one, as his effort to protest police brutality did not catch on within the NFL quite as quickly, nor was it accepted by NFL leadership. Rather, Kaepernick remained the sole face of the Take a Knee movement for a sustained period of time and was the subject of negative response via traditional and social media channels.

Importantly, as one of the first to engage in athlete activism in the social media era, Kaepernick had little way of knowing how much attention his actions might get. This is evident by his lack of preparation in executing issues management. Issues management is an integral public relations practice, as it emphasizes proactively identifying and mitigating issues that could potentially evolve into crises (Page & Parnell, 2018). Had Kaepernick anticipated potential issues with taking a knee, such as the sociopolitical climate of the time and likelihood that his kneeling could be misinterpreted, he may have had a much better chance to control the movement's narrative. However, without seeing more athletes navigate activist efforts via social media, Kaepernick lacked the foresight to include a social media strategy in his plan of action. Further, Kaepernick might not have considered publics would even use social media to respond to his activism. Still, had Kaepernick engaged in issues management, he might have recognized social media as an important arena of discourse at the time of his protest and might have altered his communication strategy to include a social media component. For example, in the same year Kaepernick began kneeling, Zignal Labs (2016) published research demonstrating the importance of social media in anticipating, preventing, and navigating crises. Thus, in failing to engage issues management and neglecting social media while initially enacting the Take a Knee movement, Kaepernick relinquished his power as the agenda-setter and framer for his own movement, leaving its narrative vulnerable to co-optation.

The vulnerability of the movement's narrative was exacerbated by the silent nature of Kaepernick's on-field protest. Silent protest requires explicit, clear, and consistent discussion about the movement's purpose, ideally through a variety of media outlets. Kaepernick clearly explained the intention behind his kneeling action in pre- and post-game press conferences and interviews. However, not all fans who tune into the game also watch or listen to press conferences and interviews. Additionally, social media coverage of the NFL and commentary on Kaepernick's protest negate the need for fans to watch games live to know what happened and to form opinions. Therefore, press conferences and interviews alone cannot effectively reach all publics exposed to the protest, or news of the protest, and should not be relied on exclusively to communicate the purpose of the movement.

Opportunities for competing narratives regarding the Take a Knee movement were born out of Kaepernick's decision to enact the movement through nonverbal communication. Kaepernick stood by his intent to assert his constitutional right to speak freely and express discontent with injustice (Branch, 2017). However, this narrative was drowned out by conservative media who argued Kaepernick's failure to stand during the national anthem represented a blatant disrespect of the American military, positioning Kaepernick as anti-American (Lewis, 2017). This alternate narrative was adopted widely and reinforced by Donald Trump's repeated denouncements of the Take a Knee movement (Haislop, 2020). The danger of Kaepernick allowing the conservative media to become the dominant opinion and thought leader surrounding his movement is reflected in the trajectory of his athletic career following the Take a Knee movement. In line with the NFL's partnership with the American military, sport fans have come to expect athletes to express love and appreciation for their nation (Summers & Morgan, 2008). Thus, the narrative that Kaepernick disrespected the military by kneeling rather than standing during the national anthem served as a trigger for fans, violating their expectation of athletes' patriotism (Summers & Morgan, 2008). As a result, Kaepernick's presence on the football field became a distraction from the sport, irritating fans and owners alike.

Kaepernick's enactment of the Take a Knee movement simultaneously embodied a new wave of athlete activism and a self-inflicted, career-ending ARC (Coombs, 2018). An ARC is embodied by an athlete's on or off-field conduct holding potentially negative implications on their reputation and can be either intentional or unintentional (Coombs, 2018; Sato et al., 2015). The ARC brought on by Kaepernick's protest posed a value threat to sports fans, as the act of kneeling during the national anthem was perceived by fans to be disrespectful to the American military. Additionally, news media framed the early coverage of Colin Kaepernick and the Take a Knee movement as anti-American, thus reinforcing fan perception (Park et al., 2019). This also impacted the NFL, as viewership decreased drastically through the 2016 season (Ozanian, 2016), and fans were divisively polarized by the competing narratives of the Take a Knee movement.

After the 2016 NFL season, Kaepernick opted out of his contract with the San Francisco 49ers and became a free agent (Haislop, 2020). Fans were shocked when the free agency period closed, and Kaepernick remained unsigned. Although Kaepernick was not on an NFL roster for the 2017 season, national anthem protests continued nonetheless. Additionally, then-President Donald Trump continued to denounce athletes who knelt during the anthem during speaking engagements and on Twitter, further polarizing discussions surrounding the movement (Haislop, 2020).

While out of the league, Kaepernick began to engage in a variety of media appearances to clarify his position. Without the platform of NFL game day, Kaepernick had to rely on popular press interviews, speaking engagements, and social media to continue his protest message. While it may have been too late in the game to sway publics who were convinced that his original protest disrespected the military, over time, Kaepernick's consistent messaging mobilized supporters to advocate for racial equity. For example, in 2020, Megan Rapinoe, Sue Bird, and Russell Wilson wore Black Lives Matter T-shirts as they hosted the ESPY Awards and delivered an opening segment centering a call to action for publics to stand against racial injustice and police brutality.

In October 2017, Kaepernick filed a grievance against NFL owners for collusion, citing retaliation for his enactment of the Take a Knee movement as their motivation for pushing him out of the league (Haislop, 2020). Kaepernick reached a settlement with the NFL in 2019 for the grievance filed 2 years prior. With the settlement came a confidentiality agreement preventing either party from publicly addressing the grievance moving forward (Haislop, 2020). In November 2019, the NFL held a workout for Kaepernick, but nothing came of it. Athletes in the league questioned the intentions of the NFL in arranging this workout, regarding it as a performative measure to save face (Haislop, 2020). At the time of this writing, Kaepernick remains unsigned by an NFL franchise.

Since leaving the league, Kaepernick has continued to work out regularly and is hopeful for an opportunity to work his way back onto an NFL roster. Additionally, he has leaned into his role as an activist and continues to be a voice for racial equity. Specifically, Kaepernick has sought to address systemic inequity by educating both local and global audiences through speaking engagements, content creation, and philanthropic campaigning. Most notably, Kaepernick developed a Know Your Rights camp, which now engages over 1,400 participants across seven U.S. cities in education, self-empowerment, and empowering Black and Brown communities with a full understanding of their constitutional rights (Know Your Rights Camp, n.d.). He also launched Kaepernick Publishing in 2019 as a means of affording Black and Brown writers the opportunity to take back the narratives of their cultures and tell their own stories (Kaepernick Publishing, n.d.).

Kaepernick's dedication to the mission of the Take a Knee movement has inspired others to speak out for racial justice as well. For example, in addition to kneeling, athletes have continued the mission of the Take a Knee movement by engaging a variety of protest efforts in support of Black Lives Matter. During the NBA's 2020 Bubble season, the Milwaukee Bucks refused to take the court in protest of the police shooting of Jacob Blake. Additionally, in 2021, the NFL amended league regulations to allow Black Lives Matter decals calling for racial equity to be placed on athletes' helmets. Further, athletes of all ages across many sports both within and outside of the United States continue to kneel during the national anthem. Importantly, kneeling is no longer reserved for athletics alone. For example, beginning in 2017, many actors (e.g., Michael Moore, Olivia Wilde) and musicians (e.g., John Legend, Stevie Wonder) knelt in solidarity with Kaepernick at the conclusion of their onstage performances. Additionally, in 2020, hospital staff across the United States knelt for 9 minutes in memory of George Floyd who was killed by a police officer in Minneapolis, MN (Williams, 2020). As these examples show, the Take a Knee movement has transcended the arena of sport and evolved into an iconic and globalized symbol of anti-racism. While the social justice benefits of his protest are undisputable, Kaepernick paid the ultimate price at the individual level, sacrificing his athletic career to be a martyr for the cause of racial equity in police reform.

You Make the Call

Ultimately, the nonverbal nature of Kaepernick's protest coupled with his reluctance to consistently discuss its purpose through a variety of media initially left his narrative vulnerable to co-opting and essentially ensured his athletic demise. The amount of time between the movement's inception and when publics started positively responding to the movement can also be explained by Kaepernick's missteps in messaging. In particular, the silent, symbolic action of Kaepernick's kneeling complicated his ability to establish and maintain control of his protest narrative. Without explicitly communicating his narrative while publicly protesting through the NFL's game day platform, Kaepernick could not effectively explain the mission of the movement himself, which worked to his detriment (Pines, 1985). Additionally, Kaepernick did not actively respond to the negative publicity regarding the Take a Knee movement while enacting the protest. These missteps, illustrating Kaepernick's failure to sufficiently engage the "golden hour" of crisis, further fueled the severity of the crisis brought on by his protest (Pines, 1985; Seitel, 2011).

Kaepernick contributed to his own reputational demise by not addressing the media and key publics who then misinterpreted his intentions and were upset by his actions (Zhou & Ki, 2018). By neglecting these key stakeholders, conservative politicians and the media were able to co-opt the narrative of the Take a Knee movement and politicize Kaepernick's protest, which resulted in fans blaming the quarterback for the tension between sport entertainment and social justice (Harker, 2019). Had Kaepernick had the foresight to effectively anticipate and manage the issues surrounding his protest before they evolved into a crisis, he could still be playing in the NFL today (Lopez, 2021).

Additionally, the co-opting and politicization of the narrative of the Take a Knee movement thwarted Kaepernick's ability to reach publics, which lacked an awareness and understanding of the systemic racial inequities existing in America. As a result, the movement's capacity to inspire attitudinal change was stunted, as publics were already polarized before Kaepernick was able to effectively communicate the purpose of his protest. Kaepernick initially may have reached a wider audience and thus continued his NFL career had he employed the following tactics in his enactment of the Take a Knee movement:

- Evaluate the potential implications of his protest on his athletic career and reputation before kneeling
- Evaluate the potential success of his efforts in relation to the potential drawbacks of engaging the protest before kneeling
- Evaluate the NFL's mission, policies, and values to anticipate how the organization would respond to his protest
- Consider potential responses from fans (private and mediated) before kneeling
- Engage in issues management to minimize the potential for a crisis to develop while kneeling
- Clearly establish the narrative of the movement himself and consistently and systematically communicate it through a variety of media at the beginning of the movement and continue through every stage
- Engage social media as a public relations resource for himself and the movement while kneeling
- Quickly address negative publicity regarding the movement through a variety of media while kneeling

Despite Kaepernick's initial missteps, the movement has lasted for over 5 years and is likely to continue to grow. The longevity of the movement may be due, in part, to Kaepernick's ability to focus on further developing the movement while being unemployed by the NFL. While Kaepernick initially endured an onslaught of negativity, he is now recognized as a leader of social justice, having received multiple humanitarian awards including *Sports Illustrated*'s Muhammad Ali Legacy Award in 2017 and Amnesty International's Ambassador of Conscience Award in 2018 (Amnesty International, 2020; Rosenberg, 2017). The overall cost–benefit analysis of the Take a Knee movement with respect to society skews benefit; only Kaepernick can speak to whether that holds true with respect to his personal life as well.

Discussion Questions

1. Discuss the Take a Knee movement's success had Colin Kaepernick followed the suggestions presented in this chapter. How might prioritizing his NFL career have sacrificed the potency and enduring nature of the Take a Knee movement?

2. What suggestions, beyond those presented in this chapter, would you offer an athlete looking to engage in activism within the competition and entertainment space?

3. Discuss whether Take a Knee truly embodied a "self-inflicted athlete reputational crisis." How might this form of crisis be viewed as avoidable or manageable in the context of athlete activism? How can athletes best avoid and/or manage these crises in their activist efforts?

4. What instances of athlete activism have you witnessed since this chapter was published? How do they differ from Kaepernick's protest? To what degree have the maintenance of athletes' reputations and/or careers been considered in strategizing issues and crisis management in these contexts?

5. Considering the entertainment value of sport, how can athletes best engage in activism within this context?

Acknowledgments

The author is grateful for the insightful, supportive, and constructive feedback provided by Dr. Diana Zulli (Purdue University) on earlier iterations of this chapter.

References

Amnesty International. (2020). *Colin Kaepernick: Ambassador of conscience.* www.amnesty. org/en/latest/news/2018/04/colin-kaepernick-ambassador-of-conscience/

Billings, A.C., Butterworth, M.L., & Turman, P.D. (2015). *Communication and sport: Surveying the field.* Thousand Oaks, CA: SAGE.

Blacklivesmatter.com. (2022). About BLM. https://blacklivesmatter.com/about/

Branch, J. (2017). The awakening of Colin Kaepernick. *The New York Times.* www. nytimes.com/2017/09/07/sports/colin-kaepernick-nfl-protests.html

Coombs, D.S., Lambert, C.A., Cassilo, D., & Humphries, Z. (2020). Flag on the play: Colin Kaepernick and the protest paradigm. *Howard Journal of Communication, 31*(4), 317–336. doi:10.1080/10646175.2019.1567408

Coombs, W.T., (2018). Athlete reputational crises: One point for liking. *Reputational challenges in sport: Theory and application,* 13–24.

Entman, R.M. (1993). Framing: Toward a clarification of a fractured paradigm. *Journal of Communication, 43*(4), 51–58.

Feder, L., & Smith, B. (forthcoming). Athlete activism online: An examination of subsequent fan engagement. In M.L. Anderson (Ed.), *Social justice and the modern athlete: Exploring the role of athlete activism in social change.* London: Lexington Books.

Garcia, A. (2018). These are the only two owners of color in the NFL. *CNNMoney Sport.* https://money.cnn.com/2018/05/18/news/nfl-nba-mlb-owners-diversity/index.html

Goffman, E. (1974). *Frame analysis: An essay on the organization of experience.* Cambridge, MA: Harvard University Press.

Haislop, T. (2020). Colin Kaepernick kneeling timeline: How protests during the national anthem started a movement in the NFL. *Sporting News.* www.sportingnews.com/us/ nfl/news/colin-kaepernick-kneeling-protest-timeline/xktu6ka4diva1s5jxaylrcsse

Harker, J. (2019). Let's talk sports: An egocentric discussion network analysis regarding NFL crisis perceptions. *Communication and Sport, 9*(4), 576–602. doi:10.1177/2167479519875970

Kaepernick Publishing. (n.d.). *About.* Kaepernick Publishing. www.kaepernickpublishing.com/about

Karlis, J. (2019). Taking a knee or not taking a stand. In T.L. Rentner & D.P. Burns (Eds.), *Case studies in sport communication: You make the call* (pp. 223–232). New York, NY: Routledge.

Know Your Rights Camp. (n.d.). Mission. *Know Your Rights Camp.* www.knowyourrightscamp.com

Lacy, L. (2017). #TakeAKnee generates plenty of conversation, but not from brands. *The Drum.* www.thedrum.com/news/2017/09/26/takeaknee-generates-plenty-conversation-not-brands

Lewis, N. (2017). The NFL and the first amendment: A guide to the debate. *The Washington Post.* www.washingtonpost.com/news/fact-checker/wp/2017/10/05/the-nfl-and-the-first-amendment-a-guide-to-the-debate/

Lopez, J.K. (2021). Rewriting activism: The NFL takes a knee. *Critical Studies in Media Communication, 38*(2), 183–196. doi:10.1080/15295036.2021.1884275

McCammon, S. (2016). Donald Trump has brought on countless controversies in an unlikely campaign. *NPR.* www.npr.org/2016/11/05/500782887/donald-trumps-road-to-election-day

McCombs, M., & Shaw, D. (1972). The agenda-setting function of mass media. *Public Opinion Quarterly, 36,* 176–187.

Ozanian, M. (2016). Confirmed: NFL losing millions of TV viewers because of national anthem protests. *Forbes.* www.forbes.com/sites/mikeozanian/2016/10/05/confirmed-nfl-losing-millions-of-tv-viewers-because-of-national-anthem-protests/?sh=11fd0568226c

Page, J.T., & Parnell, L.J. (2018). Issues management and crisis communication. In *Introduction to strategic public relations* (pp. 300–324). Thousand Oaks, CA: Sage

Park, B., Park, S., & Billings, A. (2019). Separating perceptions of Kaepernick from perceptions of his protest: An analysis of athlete activism, endorsed brand, and media effects. *Communication and Sport, 8*(4–5), 629–650. doi:10.1177/2167479519894691

Pines, W.L. (1985). How to handle a PR crisis: Five dos and five dont's. *Public Relations Quarterly, 30*(2).

Reid, J. (2017). NFL owners' pushback against protests could inch players closer to the positive change they seek. *The Undefeated.* https://theundefeated.com/features/nfl-owners-pushback-against-protests-could-inch-players-closer-to-the-positive-change-they-seek/

Rosenberg, M. (2017). Colin Kaepernick is recipient of 2017 sports illustrated Muhammad Ali legacy award. *Sports Illustrated.* www.si.com/sportsperson/2017/11/30/colin-kaepernick-muhammad-ali-legacy-award

Sato, S., Ko, Y.J., Park, C., & Tao, W. (2015). Athlete reputational crises and consumer evaluation. *European Sport Management Quarterly, 15*(4), 434–453.

Seitel, F.P. (2011). Crisis management. In *The practice of public relations* (pp. 355–374). London: Pearson.

Summers, J., & Morgan, M. (2008). More than just the media: Considering the role of public relations in the creation of sporting celebrity and the management of fan expectations. *Public Relations Review, 34,* 176–182. doi:10.1016/j.pubrev.2008.03.014

Williams, D. (2020). They spent months helping patients breathe. Now health care workers are kneeling for George Floyd. *CNN.* www.cnn.com/2020/06/05/us/george-floyd-hospital-protest-trnd/index.html

Zhou, Z., & Ki, E.-J. (2018). Does severity matter?: An investigation of crisis severity from defensive attribution theory perspective. *Public Relations Review, 44*(4), 610–618.

Zignal Labs. (2016). 10 ways big data will modernize your crisis communication plan. http://go.zignallabs.com/crisis-communications-ebook

9

REPUTATION MANAGEMENT STRATEGIES AT ESPN

Kevin Hull and Denetra Walker

Introduction

In sports broadcasting, one of the most prominent jobs is that of a studio host during a major sporting event. This person is reporting live from the arena or stadium and is often the first voice viewers hear when tuning in, leading the halftime show roundtable, and interviewing the star athletes during postgame wrap-up. At a major network such as ESPN, competition to get one of those elite hosting jobs can be as serious as the action in the games themselves. The network spends about $1.4 billion per year to broadcast the NBA (Ourand & Lombardo, 2014), making the studio host of the NBA Finals perhaps the biggest job available.

When ESPN announced in 2020 that Maria Taylor would lead their coverage of the NBA Finals, another ESPN anchor, Rachel Nichols, was not pleased. Nichols, who is White, complained to a friend in a phone call that Taylor only got the job because she is Black. Nichols also cited her own experience with ESPN's poor hiring practices with women in her comments, saying,

> If you need to give her more things to do because you are feeling pressure about your crappy longtime record on diversity – which, by the way, I know personally from the female side of it – like, go for it. Just find it somewhere else.
>
> *(Draper, 2021a)*

However, Nichols was unaware that her phone conversation was being recorded back at ESPN through the video camera on her computer. That recording was then passed around ESPN, causing the network to address the issue internally among those involved. While the tension simmered behind the scenes at the sports television

DOI: 10.4324/9781003316763-11

network for months, it became public in July 2021 when *The New York Times* printed a story that contained all the salacious details (Draper, 2021a). What was once an open secret among ESPN employees was now public knowledge. Nichols and ESPN both issued statements, while Nichols' cohosts on a basketball-centric show defended her, causing them to have to issue follow-up statements after online backlash toward them. The next days resulted in Nichols being removed from NBA Finals coverage completely; Taylor leaving ESPN following the expiration of her contract; and increased attention on the network's treatment of Black, Indigenous, and people of color (BIPOC) employees (Draper, 2021b, 2021c). The purpose of this study is to examine, compare, and contrast the reputation management strategies used by the various parties involved in this story, with an additional focus on how the story fits into the decades of racial inequalities in sports broadcasting.

Background

Racial Inequalities in Sports Broadcasting

In 2020, as much of the world acknowledged deficiencies with their previous hiring practices regarding race, the sports media was no exception. The Associated Press Sports Editors' (APSE) *2018 Racial and Gender Report Card* found that the numbers for newsroom diversity had been practically unchanged in 12 years (McCreary, 2018). White males dominate sports journalism jobs including 85% of sports editors, 80% of columnists, and 82% of reporters (McCreary, 2018). Some Black sports broadcasters reported that if a television station already had one Black sportscaster, they believed that would be the limit. One wrote that "If another Black sports journalist is at the station, some of us don't even bother in applying to that job" (Hull et al., 2022).

However, the Institute for Diversity and Ethics in Sports stated that one of the few media organizations that did have a good history in diversity was ESPN. The network was cited as being an industry leader in hiring of BIPOC editors, writers, and columnists for ESPN.com (Lapchick, 2018). One of the highest paid on-air personalities at ESPN is Stephen A. Smith, a Black man who reportedly makes $12 million annually (Marchand, 2021a). Despite this, some behind-the-scenes employees at ESPN claimed that racism was still prevalent at the television station. In an article from *The New York Times*, more than two dozen current and former ESPN employees said the company had limited career paths for Black personnel (Draper, 2020).

Gender Inequalities in Sports Broadcasting

Another element to this case is the acknowledgment of poor gender hiring practices in the sports media. Both Maria Taylor and Rachel Nichols held prominent on-air roles for their work at ESPN, which is a rarity for women in the industry.

For many years, the most visible jobs in sports broadcasting went almost exclusively to men (Schmidt, 2018). Therefore, when executives did make the decision that a woman could do a high-profile job, the few women on staff were all seemingly pitted against each other to get it.

A study of television news directors found they were more likely to perceive females as unqualified to be sportscasters (Sheffer & Schultz, 2007). This has led to a struggle to feel accepted in the male-dominated industry of the sports media. A survey of women sports journalists found that they felt there was a general lack of respect from male colleagues, with the women feeling like "second-class" employees (Hardin & Shain, 2006) and a lack of upward career mobility based on their gender (Hardin & Shain, 2005, 2006). Additionally, female sportscasters often feel an intense pressure to perform well due to the rarity of positions. That then leads to burnout, which adds to the disparity between the number of male and female sportscasters (Hardin & Whiteside, 2009).

Intersectionality: Race and Gender

There are intersectional qualities to factor in surrounding the fact that Taylor was Black and a woman. Intersectionality (Crenshaw, 1991) means her identity of race and gender were an additional layer to explain her experiences of additional pressure and barriers as an on-air talent at ESPN. This is especially true in this case as Nichols' comments spoke of her own experiences as a White woman in sports but were noticeably dismissive of Taylor's experience as a Black woman, alluding to her earning a spot because of "diversity" and not her talent. This was a point further explained in *The New York Times* article which initially broke the story. Taylor's experiences in two underrepresented group categories (female and Black) in sports journalism adds an additional layer to this conversation about this case study.

Reputation Management

ESPN and its on-air employees are viewed by millions of people daily throughout the world. As with almost any business, there are occasions in which employees do something unseemly outside of their time at work. While the employees are individuals, scandalous headlines will often identify the person as an ESPN employee, lumping the network into the crisis somewhat unwillingly. For example, "ESPN's Britt McHenry caught on camera going nuts on parking lot attendant" (Yoder, 2015) and "Curt Schilling, ESPN analyst, is fired over offensive social media post" (Sandomir, 2016) both identify ESPN in the headline despite neither action having anything to do with the network beyond the fact that the person works there.

Therefore, when an incident involving ESPN and one of its employees arises, the parties involved typically engage in some type of reputation management.

This is the practice of attempting to influence how stakeholders evaluate the organization or individual (Fombrun, 1996; Smith, 2013). Simply put, if public opinion has become negative regarding ESPN or the broadcasters, those involved will attempt to sway that perception back to the positive. The concept of image restoration theory (IRT) explains how people and organizations attempt to repair the public's opinion of that entity following a crisis. The developer of this theory stated that people used denial, evading responsibility and reducing offensiveness, corrective action, and mortification to repair their public image (Benoit, 1995).

In the world of broadcast media, a negative perception can directly influence viewership. Sports fans may not want to watch the network or a specific broadcaster if those viewers have an unfavorable opinion of them. This lower viewership can directly impact the financial bottom line of the company, as having fewer viewers means that the network will likely get less money from advertisers. For the individual employee, a negative perception can lead to fewer prominent assignments or perhaps even their release from the company. Therefore, it is important for both the network and the individual broadcasters to use reputation management to keep viewers from changing the channel.

The Case

Following publication of the article in *The New York Times*, Nichols read a statement on her ESPN show, which then led to a discussion among her cohosts about the situation. That conversation led to another on-air personality needing to clarify his position after his comments were not received positively online. ESPN management attempted to increase positive public sentiment by issuing a statement and doing some personnel shuffling for the remainder of the NBA Playoffs. Meanwhile, a prominent member of this story remained silent.

Rachel Nichols

The story in *The New York Times* was published on a Sunday, so when the show Nichols hosted, *The Jump*, returned to the air on Monday, the journalist wasted little time addressing the issue. In fact, the show began with Nichols reading a statement that lasted about 25 seconds:

> The first thing they teach you in journalism school is, "Don't be the story." And I don't plan to break that rule today or distract from a fantastic Finals. But I also don't want to let this moment pass without saying how much I respect, how much I value our colleagues here at ESPN. How deeply, deeply sorry I am for disappointing those I hurt, particularly Maria Taylor. And how grateful I am to be a part of this outstanding team.
>
> *(Mangan, 2021)*

Nichols' statement is a straightforward apology, which means it falls under the concept of mortification within image restoration theory. She does not deny saying the words, does not pass blame to anyone else, and does not attempt to minimize the impact of what she said. When it comes to attempting to repair her image, Nichols is accepting responsibility by apologizing to Taylor directly, apologizing to her other colleagues, and acknowledging how fortunate she believes she is to be a part of ESPN.

Nichols could have taken an entirely different route and chosen to evade responsibility. Her private conversation with another person was recorded without her knowledge back at ESPN headquarters in Bristol, Connecticut. Both Connecticut and Florida (where Nichols was at the time of the recording) are two-party consent states, meaning that, legally, Nichols would have to be told that her comments were being recorded (Marchand, 2021b). Therefore, the ESPN host could have started her show that day discussing how her privacy was violated, how the conversation was illegally recorded, and how she felt about this recording being given to a reporter from *The New York Times*. In that case, she would have been evading responsibility for her actions and instead focusing on how the recording was acquired in the first place.

However, this tactic likely would not have garnered much sympathy or repaired her image. The public is more likely to remember the words on the recording and not how that recording was acquired. This is especially true with prominence of the conversation in *The New York Times* which spread on social media. Even though Nichols' privacy was legally violated, the words she said about Taylor carried much more weight in the public. Therefore, her plan to apologize, accept responsibility, and attempt to move forward did appear to be the correct decision in her first step toward repairing her image.

Kendrick Perkins

On Monday's episode of *The Jump*, Nichols' 25-second statement was followed immediately by comments from ESPN basketball analyst Kendrick Perkins. Perkins, who is Black, played in the NBA and was now a frequent contributor to ESPN following his retirement. He said:

> Rachel, I want to say thank you. Thank you for accepting responsibility for your actions.
>
> You know, as someone who has known you for a long time, being around you, you have treated me with the upmost respect. And you always make me feel comfortable in your presence. I know your heart, you know. Great person, great individual.

Perkins followed up those comments with similar support for Maria Taylor. While Perkins' attempt to support both Nichols and Taylor appeared to be genuine, the online reaction from many focused on his support for Nichols. Several questioned why a Black man would support Nichols in this situation, and, perhaps more importantly, why ESPN would put Perkins in that situation (Shropshire, 2021). The feedback was so harsh that Perkins would go on Spaces, Twitter's audio app, later that night to defend his comments:

> I'm saying that you can be mad with whoever else but at the end of the day Kendrick Perkins didn't have anything to do with none of this conversation. Kendrick Perkins was scheduled to be on "The Jump" regardless before this even came out yesterday. Now I had to address it and I thought I addressed it appropriately, I thought I handled it appropriately. I spoke and acknowledged Rachel for however you want to say her apology was, she apologized and I also said that she had never done anything towards me because she didn't . . . and I gave Maria her flowers . . . At the end of the day I can't go out there and go off and go crazy and risk losing my job because some people want me to go on there and speak for how they feel.
>
> *(Alonso, 2021)*

Perkins used the strategy of reducing offensiveness to try to improve his public image. He was bolstering his own appearance on the show by saying he was already scheduled to be there and that he was not going to say things that would get him fired. Additionally, he revealed that he sent flowers to Taylor, another way to demonstrate that he was not only supporting Nichols. While Perkins had nothing to do with the initial controversy, he found himself having to defend his reputation, following his appearance on the show.

ESPN

While ESPN's leadership did not directly address the comments made by Nichols in *The New York Times* article, they employed the strategy of utilizing corrective actions to try to repair the network's image. Two days after the article was published, ESPN announced that Nichols would no longer be the sideline reporter during the NBA Finals. In a brief statement, the network said that "We believe this is best decision for all concerned in order to keep the focus on the NBA Finals. Rachel will continue to host The Jump." Nichols would be replaced by Malika Andrews – who is a Black woman (The Athletic Staff, 2021). Hours after that statement, Tuesday's episode of *The Jump* did not air, but was back in its normal timeslot the following day (Mangan, 2021).

ESPN determined that the best way to curb the controversy regarding Taylor and Nichols during the NBA Finals was to remove Nichols from the situation. By making this move, the network was able to demonstrate that it was taking this corrective action, but not completely dismissing Nichols, as she was able to still host her show *The Jump*. Meanwhile, Taylor remained the host of the NBA Finals, appearing on the pregame and halftime shows during the series.

Maria Taylor

While Nichols, ESPN, and Perkins all made public comments and statements, the other key person in this story, Maria Taylor, did not. In the days following the publication of the article, Taylor stayed silent. She did not make any direct statements about the article, or the issues discussed in it. It should also be noted that Taylor was not quoted directly in the article either. It appears as if her public relations strategy was to let the material in the article speak for her and let others come to her defense. Her only comments came from a tweet that did not directly address the controversy, but did appear to allude to it:

> During the dark times I always remember that I am in this position to open doors and light the path that others walk down. I've taken some punches but that just means I'm still in the fight. Remember to lift as you climb and always KEEP RISING.
>
> *(Taylor, 2021)*

While Taylor's image did not need repairing, she chose to stay silent in the days and weeks following the article, seemingly believing that saying nothing was the best strategy for her.

You Make the Call

Despite dealing with this issue internally, ESPN had to take corrective actions in a short period of time as the controversy came to light during a key part of the NBA season. As the NBA Finals were in full swing, the network kept Taylor in the host position for the Finals, while quickly removing Nichols from the sideline reporter position, but keeping her daily show on the air. Instead of making drastic changes, the network kept most positions status-quo, while only removing Nichols from the position of a sideline reporter. This was likely the correct decision at the time as ESPN did not want to take the focus away from the basketball games and instead chose to make further changes in the future. Making widespread changes, or addressing the situation with multiple statements, would have likely dominated the conversation around the first few games of the NBA Finals.

However, the challenges faced by the network during this time period came to a head shortly after the NBA Finals were finished. The day after the clinching game, ESPN announced that Maria Taylor was leaving the network after the two sides could not agree on a contract extension (ESPN Press Room, 2021). Less than two months later, Rachel Nichols was out at ESPN, too. In this case, ESPN removed her from all NBA programming and cancelled her show *The Jump*. Despite the fact that there was still a year left on her ESPN contract, speculation was that she would not appear on the network again (Ourand, 2021). While

ESPN can state that Taylor had reportedly received a larger salary offer from NBC (McCarthy, 2021), it is still likely not ESPN's preferred public outcome. Less than a month after one of its prominent BIPOC on-air talents was revealed to have faced discriminatory comments from a co-worker, that person decided she was better off leaving the network. With Nichols, the prospect of putting her back on NBA coverage, especially after Taylor's departure, was likely not something the public would have embraced.

Ultimately, a clean break from both might have been the best solution to repair the network's image. Instead, an entirely different NBA pregame and halftime crew was selected, and a new basketball-centric show was placed in the time slot formally occupied by *The Jump* (Marchand, 2021c). In this case, ESPN seemed to ultimately decide that starting over from scratch was the best way to move past this incident.

One of the issues that, as of this writing, has not been fully addressed is the legality of the recording of Nichols. While her comments were understandably the main part of the story, some have speculated that the former ESPN host has a legal case against her employer (Fleming, 2021; Mariotti, 2021). As stated previously in this chapter, due to the two-party consent laws in both Connecticut and Florida, Nichols would have to be informed that she was being recorded. The initial articles from *The New York Times* stated that ESPN feared a lawsuit from Nichols regarding the recording (Draper, 2021), and others have speculated that ESPN reached a financial settlement with their former anchor after her show was cancelled (Fleming, 2021). For the reputation of both Nichols and ESPN, it would probably be best for that possible conflict to be settled privately. Neither party would benefit from that as it would look as if the legal battle was perhaps making Nichols' disparaging comments seem less important than how they were gathered.

There were likely no winners in how the situation played out at ESPN. Taylor had to stay silent publicly about the situation for over a year, while ESPN, Rachel Nichols, and Kendrick Perkins all had to issue what were certainly embarrassing apologies in the first few days after the article was published. In the end, as of the writing of this chapter, all parties have seemingly moved on from the situation with their careers moving in different directions.

Discussion Questions

1. Discuss any updates to this situation. In the months following the article, both Taylor and Nichols left ESPN. Taylor landed at NBC Sports, while, at the time of this writing, Nichols had not surfaced at a new place. What, if anything, is the latest?
2. The article from *The New York Times* stated that ESPN had attempted to address this situation internally but was unsuccessful. What other avenues could they have taken to avoid how the situation ultimately played out?

3. An article in the *New York Post* placed some of the blame on Maria Taylor for not working with Rachel Nichols after her recorded comments to come to a satisfactory resolution. What do you think? Should Taylor have done more to help ESPN and Nichols avoid the negative publicity?
4. ESPN ultimately decided that having Nichols still appear on the network following the NBA Finals was not acceptable. Was this too harsh? Should Nichols have been punished much earlier? Discuss ESPN's handling of Nichols' employment status throughout the saga.

References

Alonso, J. (2021, July 6). ESPN's Kendrick Perkins defends his appearance on 'The Jump' during Rachel Nichols apology after receiving backlash. *Brobible*. https://brobible. com/sports/article/espns-kendrick-perkins-the-jump-rachel-nichols/

Benoit, W.L. (1995). Accounts, excuses, and apologies: A theory of image restoration strategies. Albany, NY: State University of New York Press.

Crenshaw, K. (1991). Mapping the margins: intersectionality, identity politics, and violence against women of color. *Stanford Law Review, 43*(6), 1241–1299.

Draper, K. (2020, July 13). ESPN employees say racism endures behind the camera. *The New York Times*. www.nytimes.com/2020/07/13/sports/espn-racism-black-employees.html

Draper, K. (2021a, July 4). A disparaging video prompts explosive fallout within ESPN. *The New York Times*. www.nytimes.com/2021/07/04/sports/basketball/espn-rachel-nichols-maria-taylor.html

Draper, K. (2021b, July 6). Rachel Nichols out for N.B.A. Finals coverage on ABC. *The New York Times*. www.nytimes.com/2021/07/06/sports/basketball/rachel-nichols-espn-malika-andrews.html

Draper, K. (2021c, July 21). With the N.B.A. Finals complete, Maria Taylor leaves ESPN. *The New York Times*. www.nytimes.com/2021/07/21/sports/basketball/maria-taylor-espn.html

ESPN Press Room. (2021, July 21). Statements from ESPN and Maria Taylor. *ESPN Press Room*. https://espnpressroom.com/us/press-releases/2021/07/statements-from-espn-and-maria-taylor/

Fleming, K. (2021, August 31). What's next for Rachel Nichols after her controversial split from ESPN? *New York Post*. https://nypost.com/2021/08/31/whats-next-for-rachel-nichols-after-her-split-from-espn/

Fombrun, C.J. (1996). *Reputation: Realizing value from the corporate image.* Watertown, MA: Harvard Business School Press.

Hardin, M., & Shain, S. (2005). Strength in numbers? The experiences and attitudes of women in sports media careers. *Journalism & Mass Communication Quarterly, 82*(4), 804–819.

Hardin, M., & Shain, S. (2006). "Feeling much smaller than you know you are": The fragmented professional identity of female sports journalists. *Critical Studies in Media Communication, 23*(4), 322–338.

Hardin, M., & Whiteside, E. (2009). Token responses to gendered newsrooms: Factors in the career-related decisions of female newspaper sports journalists. *Journalism, 10*(5), 627–646.

Hull, K., Walker, D., Romney, M., & Pellizzaro, K. (2022). "Through our prism": Black television sports journalists' work experiences and interactions with Black athletes. *Journalism Practice.* https://www.tandfonline.com/doi/pdf/10.1080/17512786.2022.20 50468?needAccess=true

Lapchick, R. (2018, May 2). The 2018 associated press sports editors racial and gender report card. *ESPN.com.* www.espn.com/espn/story/_/id/23382605/espn-leads-way-hiring-practices-sports-media

Mangan, D. (2021, July 7). NBA reporter Rachel Nichols back on ESPN after one-day rest following Maria Taylor race furor. *CNBC.* www.cnbc.com/2021/07/07/nba-reporter-rachel-nichols-returns-to-espn-amid-maria-taylor-furor-.html

Marchand, A. (2021b, August 25). ESPN embarrassed itself during the Rachel Nichols saga. *New York Post.* https://nypost.com/2021/08/25/espn-embarrassed-itself-during-the-rachel-nichols-saga/

Marchand, A. (2021a, July 9). The $12 million truth about Stephen A. Smith's ESPN deal. *New York Post.* https://nypost.com/2021/07/09/stephen-a-smiths-espn-contract-pays-him-12-million-per-year/

Marchand, A. (2021c, October 5). Mike Greenberg, Stephen A. Smith are the winners in ESPN's drama-filled NBA shakeup. *New York Post.* https://nypost.com/2021/10/05/mike-greenberg-stephen-a-smith-get-what-they-want-in-espns-nba-shakeup/

Mariotti, J. (2021, August 26). Time for Rachel Nichols to sue the pants off Mickey Mouse. *BSM Media.* https://barrettsportsmedia.com/2021/08/26/rachel-nichols-sue-mickey-mouse/

McCarthy, M. (2021, July 14). ESPN's Maria Taylor at 'half-yard line' of deal with rival NBC. *Front Office Sports.* https://frontofficesports.com/nbc-sports-maria-taylor-espn-football-night-in-america-mike-tirico/

McCreary, J. (2018, May 2). APNews: Study diversity remains in sports news departments. https://apnews.com/a45d1d2abc7746aaa4dbeaa7f7987923/Study:-Diversity-remains-low-in-sports-news-departments

Ourand, J. (2021, August 25). ESPN takes Rachel Nichols off NBA programming. *Sports Business Journal.* www.sportsbusinessjournal.com/Daily/Closing-Bell/2021/08/25/Rachel-Nichols.aspx

Ourand, J., & Lombardo, J. (2014, October 6). NBA's nine-year media rights deal with ESPN, Turner worth $24b. *Sports Business Journal.* www.sportsbusinessjournal.com/Daily/Morning-Buzz/2014/10/06/NBA-media-deals.aspx

Sandomir, R. (2016, April 20). Curt Schilling, ESPN analyst, is fired over offensive social media post. *The New York Times.* www.nytimes.com/2016/04/21/sports/baseball/curt-schilling-is-fired-by-espn.html

Schmidt, H.C. (2018). Forgotten athletes and token reporters: Analyzing the gender bias in sports journalism. *Atlantic Journal of Communication, 26*(1), 59–74.

Sheffer, M.L., & Schultz, B. (2007). Double standard: Why women have trouble getting jobs in local television. *Journal of Sports Media, 2*(1), 77–101.

Shropshire, T. (2021, July 6). Kendrick Perkins ripped for defending ESPN's Rachel Nichols. *Rolling Out.* https://rollingout.com/2021/07/06/kendrick-perkins-ripped-for-defending-espns-rachel-nichols/

Smith, R.D. (2013). *Strategic planning for public relations* (4th ed.). Abington: Routledge.

Taylor, M. [@MariaTaylor]. (2021, July 7). During the dark times I always remember that I am in this position to open doors and light the path that others walk down. I've taken some punches but that just means I'm still in the fight. Remember to lift as you climb and always KEEP RISING [Tweet]. *Twitter.* https://twitter.com/mariataylor/status/14 12904620167286787?lang=en

The Athletic Staff. (2021, July 6). ESPN removes Rachel Nichols from NBA Finals sideline coverage. *The Athletic.* https://theathletic.com/news/espn-removes-rachel-nichols-from-nba-finals-sideline-coverage/WY2dP9HujgA3/

Yoder, M. (2015, April 16). Video: ESPN's Britt McHenry caught on camera going nuts on parking lot attendant (updated). *Awful Announcing.* https://awfulannouncing.com/2015/espns-britt-mchenry-caught-on-camera-going-nuts-on-parking-lot-attendant.html

10

FROM *LES ESQUIMAUX* TO THE ELKS

Addressing Social Responsibility in the Canadian Football League

David J. Jackson and Lori Liggett

Introduction

For several decades, teams from across the spectrum of athletics have been challenged to confront their role in perpetuating ethnic stereotypes, racist attitudes, and behavior. In both the United States and Canada, the polarizing issue has plagued youth teams to professional leagues representing various sporting traditions. Recently, several major sport franchises have concluded that rebranding is necessary in order to acknowledge historical and ongoing social injustices and to move their teams and fans into a more enlightened present. After several years of increasingly harsh criticism over the long-time use of a mascot name that symbolizes racially insensitive and destructive colonial policies toward Indigenous Peoples, one of the most successful teams in the Canadian Football League, the Edmonton Eskimos, made the decision in 2021 to rebrand, becoming the Edmonton Elks.

Rebranding is a complex, challenging process that must take into consideration a multitude of perspectives. For athletics, central to the process are fan preferences, team histories, community values, brand image, and sponsor buy-in. To provide a manageable structure in which to understand the intricacies of the subject matter, this study refers to Grunig's excellence theory to examine the effectiveness of the Edmonton football team's public relations strategies throughout the years-long process before rebranding. One particularly useful principle of excellence theory is how institutional communication should convey a commitment to social responsibility.

Often, brand evolution is initiated after current public perception of a brand is irrevocably tarnished, and reinvention is necessary to save it. Or, sometimes, a brand becomes outdated, and seemingly fresher brands are successfully usurping

DOI: 10.4324/9781003316763-12

it in the marketplace. But neither of these scenarios accurately describes the Edmonton team's situation. Since its founding in 1949, it has been a popular, successful franchise winning 14 Grey Cup contests, second only to the record-holding Toronto Argonauts. It proudly represents what is affectionately known as the "City of Champions" (Jones, 2020c). Instead, an identity transformation became necessary because the brand collided with erupting social justice movements in Canada, the United States, and other countries.

In all rebranding campaigns, internal adoption, such as fan acceptance, is key to its ultimate success. Rebrand resistance, especially on social media, can be relentlessly brutal and sometimes even fatal to a brand. Public relations professionals must understand how consumers construct and connect their own identities with that of the brand. And in this case, national and regional identities are deeply embedded throughout Canadian sporting culture. Thus, to undertake a campaign of such unique sensitivities, excellence theory requires an understanding of all stakeholder groups in order to avoid confusing or contradictory messaging. It is imperative that corporate communication weaves a new story about brand value and how it authentically creates deep meaning for multiple publics. During all steps, the process is multifaceted and requires an understanding of the intricate intersection of business, culture, and politics.

Background

The Canadian Football League (CFL) has existed since 1958, although teams actually competed for football's highest honor, the Grey Cup, since 1909. The nine-team league has two divisional brackets – East and West – that represent distinct histories and cultures of Canada's vast geography, spanning from Montreal in the east to Vancouver in the west. (By comparison, the National Football League in the United States currently has 32 teams.) Individual teams are deeply rooted in their respective regions, like the Toronto Argonauts, which began playing in 1873 and purport to be the oldest, continually operating North American professional sports franchise operating under the same name in the same city. The western region of Canada was settled more recently than the east, and thus professional football began there later.

Football clubs existed in Edmonton as far back as the 1890s, and the team name "Eskimos" has been associated with Edmonton athletics since the earliest club formations. According to journalist Tim Querengesser, "The Edmonton Eskimos name outdates all other sports team names now under fire [for their problematic names] in North America" (2013, para. 15). Early sports promoter William Deacon White exalted the moniker "Eskimos," using it to name the Edmonton Eskimos baseball team (1909), the Edmonton Eskimos football team (1910), and the Edmonton Eskimos hockey team (1911) (Kirkup, 2020). Originally, the football club was called the Edmonton

Esquimaux (French for "Eskimo"), and, according to columnist Terry Jones (2020a), the city liked the name because it represented the rugged climate of northern Canada and the toughness of its people, and it found the "EE" alliteration appealing.

Over the decades, the CFL has grappled with how to retain and build fan loyalty. Andrews and Greenham (2020) detail the CFL's economic instability in the 1980s as it struggled to maintain relevance against a more media-dominant U.S. National Football League (NFL). In order to procure government subsidies and public funding to stay afloat, the CFL created marketing that relied on a rhetoric of nostalgic nationalism to portray the league as essential to unified Canadian identity (Andrews & Greenham, 2020). From the CFL's perspective, at stake in the financial drama was the survival of Canadian football and, thus, national Canadian identity. Losing the CFL would mean the domination of Americanized sport culture in Canada.

In 2013, politics collided with sport branding when Querengesser posed the question in the *Edmonton Journal: What does an Eskimo think of the Edmonton Eskimos?* The legacy of naming First Nations, Native American, and Aboriginal peoples across the North American continent is complex and layered with both distinct and overlapping sociopolitical histories that are nearly always determined or strongly influenced by a colonial past. Native studies researcher Jordan Koe, who identifies as Inuit and Dene, framed it this way: "In a way you could almost say the Edmonton Eskimos is representing the American idea of who the northern people are" (Querengesser, 2013, para. 3).

Of course, issues related to offensive athletic branding are not limited to Canada. In 2014, perhaps the most publicized incrimination occurred when the U.S. Patent and Trademark Office canceled the Washington Redskins' trademarks, deeming them to be "disparaging to Native Americans" (Kwong, 2014). Although the U.S. Supreme Court later overturned an unrelated case that led to the reinstatement of Washington's trademarks, the initial case brought the naming issue to the social consciousness. Allan Watt, then Vice President of Communications for the Edmonton Eskimos, claimed that his team had no plans to change its name, saying that "We have no backlash from our fans or politicians or any other sort. The only people we ever hear from with regard to the name 'Edmonton Eskimos Football Club' is with people like you reporters" (Kwong, 2014, para. 10).

This communication misstep was not unique. Many sports teams including the Washington Redskins, the Cleveland Indians, the Atlanta Braves, and the Chicago Blackhawks have reacted similarly. Initially, each franchise chose a defensive stance that privileged team legacy above the serious concerns of opposing stakeholders, such as Indigenous communities and their allies. Excellence theory highlights the value of elevating social responsibility in institutional decision-making and the necessity of developing long-term, quality relationships with diverse publics.

> For an organization to be effective . . . it must behave in ways that solve the problems and satisfy the goals of stakeholders as well as of management. If it does not, stakeholders will either pressure the organization to change or oppose it in ways that add cost and risk to organizational policies and decisions.
>
> *(J. E. Grunig, 2013, p. 9)*

Popular sport teams when faced with this type of scrutiny tend to present a self-protective posture that positions their irrefutable knowledge of fan devotion as the only legitimate stakeholder voice. Time and again, this has proven to be an imprudent corporate strategy.

To understand the Edmonton situation, one must recognize that the CFL positions itself as uniquely Canadian and highly differentiated from American football. There is an underlying subtext of anti-Americanism that becomes manifest, at least in CFL marketing, as nationalism. Canada and the United States share the longest, unbroken national border in the world, and U.S. influence on Canadian life via media, popular culture, business, trade, and travel is undeniable. Andrews and Greenham (2020) write that Canada's apprehension of U.S. economic domination leading to cultural domination – or a loss of Canadian national unity – is played out on the field of sport as resistance against American cultural imperialism. Unlike the NFL, the CFL views itself to be competing in an international arena in which American teams, players and coaches dominate (Cantelon, 2001). If sport is a significant expression of culture, then the behemoth size of the NFL fan base, broadcast media deals, and salaries of players and coaches loom largely over its neighbor to the north.

The origin of this competitiveness began in the late 1960s when sport became the focus of Prime Minister Pierre Trudeau's doctrine of nationalism that called for "programmes and policies which would 'strengthen our capacity to advance basic Canadian goals and develop a more confident sense of national identity'" (Franks et al., 1988, p. 672). Thirty years later, the Canadian government commissioned a sub-committee on Canadian Heritage to study "sport's impact on national unity and how this might be enhanced" (Cantelon, 2001, p. 1). Canada's federal multiculturalism policy also plays a major role in shaping perceptions of national identity within sporting culture. Since the late 1960s, the Royal Commission on Bilingualism and Biculturalism has promoted multiculturalism within a bilingual framework, formally recognizing its unique cultural mosaic of regional and multicultural differences (Laing & Cooper, 2019). Official bilingualism, English and French, is a significant symbol of Canadianness that demonstrates difference from the United States. Unlike its founders' melting pot ideology of assimilation in America, Canada views diversity as key to national identity, bringing together its four main establishing groups, English, French, First Nations, and immigrants from all over the globe (Cantelon, 2001). Imagine then, when the Edmonton franchise was charged with racial insensitivities – it was an affront to the very ideals of Canadianness.

There are a number of aspects that mark the CFL to be identifiably distinct from the NFL. Valentine (2019) provides useful details on several efforts by the Canadian government to preserve Canadianness within professional football – first by "prevent[ing] Canadian-based football teams from joining an American professional football league, and second, [by preventing] American-based teams from joining the CFL" (Valentine, 2019, p. 376). Today, the CFL regulates policies that ensure the majority of players are Canadian. This is done through a citizenship quota that limits the number of Americans who can be on a CFL roster. The protection of both roster spots and starting positions accomplishes a number of goals – some reinforce cultural identity while others are economic. Simply put, if the ratio for Canadian players in the CFL did not exist, it is likely that nearly all roster spots would go to Americans.

Canadian national identity, as a unifying principle of the CFL, is communicated primarily through its marketing campaigns and what Andrews and Greenham (2020) refer to as "willful nostalgia" constructed as a response to the perceived threat of American domination of professional football. As a marketing strategy, willful nostalgia emerged in the 1980s when the league faced serious financial jeopardy from the encroaching popularity of the NFL. Thus, the CFL has long relied on a rhetoric of willful nostalgia to arouse favorable public sentiment and even to coercively threaten when financial circumstances call for additional public funding (Andrews & Greenham, 2020). Using recognizable national symbols, Canadiana references, and patriotic sentiments, the league forefronts its product as something inimitably Canadian (Cantelon, 2001). Slogans such as "The Canadian Football League: Radically Canadian" and "What We're Made Of" have been central to the "Us vs. Them" mindset. While the American league's marketing typically pits NFL team against NFL team, fans versus fans, Canadian league marketing pits the CFL against the NFL.

A four-minute CFL promotional video released in 2008 called "This is Our League" exemplifies the essential ways in which national identity is constructed through nostalgia discourse. The introduction begins with dramatic music and historical imagery including massively attended Grey Cup parades, aerial views of stadiums, military jet flyovers, and spectacular plays made by each team. The dramatic narration intones:

> This is a league with two official languages and many unofficial languages. It's east versus west, prairie versus city, wheat versus iron, latte versus Tim's . . . It's a league where you do more than cheer. You belong . . . This is a league as diverse as the country . . . A league of Jacksons, Kwongs, Johnsons and Moscas; Verchevals, Campbells, and Conachers; Stegalls, Ziambiasis, O'Sheas, and Haji-Rasoulis . . . *This is Our League.*
>
> *(CFL, 2008)*

The list of famous players with diverse surnames links CFL symbolism to Canada's official policy of multiculturalism and reinforces the narrative of the league's centrality to national unity.

A similarly powerful and evocative video entitled "It Reflects Us All" was revived several years later to promote the upcoming Grey Cup championship game (CFL, 2012). The geographic and cultural references reinforce a national story of people from vastly different regions and cities who skirmish on the field of competition but unite as league supporters. Clearly, the CFL views itself as more than just a facilitator of sport competition, but rather as an institution that significantly aids in the maintenance of a multiethnic Canadian identity. However, while the CFL's nostalgic marketing campaigns are credited with reinvigorating football's image among Canadian sports journalists, politicians, and fans during times of economic threat, those same tactics were not capable of overcoming serious opposition to Edmonton's team name in the wake of allegations of racial insensitivity.

The Case

By 2017, the Edmonton football team was beginning to feel the accusatory sting of cultural appropriation, and there were those who felt its name was no longer justifiable.

> Painful and abusive rhetoric has both emotional and financial costs. From where I stand, "The Edmonton Eskimos" have done very well financially off of the word *Eskimo*. However, I do not see where the team or the CFL has given back to Inuit Canadians as a whole.
>
> *(Dunning, 2017, para. 12)*

Public criticism escalated as the team was ready to battle the East Division champion Ottawa Redblacks in the 103rd Grey Cup. Natan Obed, then-newly elected President of Inuit Tapiriit Kanatami, the national organization representing more than 60,000 Inuit in Canada, condemned the team's name as a racial slur, saying, "The colonial legacy of naming is about power and control. The issue of Inuit being used as a sports team mascot matters, because this is the way this legacy continues to play out in popular culture" (Dunning, 2017, para. 3).

At that time, most high-profile public attention was focused on American teams, primarily the Washington Redskins, although social media continued to agitate Edmonton. Publicly, the franchise claimed it was taking the allegations seriously and conducting an internal review. But journalist Simons wrote:

> With each passing year, the patronizing moniker starts to feel more and more like a relic of an age that was both more innocent and more thoughtless. There's only so long we can go on saying, "Well, but it's not as bad as Redskins."
>
> *(Simons, 2017, para.14)*

Some Eskimos fans were becoming concerned about public appeals to change the team's branding. In 2017, a Facebook group called "Edmonton Eskimos

Fans" described itself as, "An ode to the old name, the old years of great football! The ultimate group on Facebook for those who wish to pay homage to the glory that is the Edmonton Eskimos" (Edmonton Eskimos Fans, 2017). A clear signal that the CFL's nostalgia marketing strategies continued to resonate with some segment of fans.

That same year, several prominent public figures called on the team to begin the process of name change. Brian Bowman, the mayor of Winnipeg and member of the Métis Federation, which represents the indigenous people of Canada, weighed in saying: "I think there's an opportunity to have a more inclusive name . . ." (Kives, 2017, para. 4). The Edmonton Eskimos Football Club issued a retort saying,

> If the mayor of Winnipeg has an opinion he'd like to share with us, he should do so. At this point in time, we are actively engaged in listening to the conversation that people are having around our name . . . we are keenly listening to all input including from our loyal season seat holders and fans . . . . We use the Edmonton Eskimos name with pride and respect.
> *(Rollason & Sanders, 2017, paras. 13–15)*

Edmonton mayor Don Iveson publicly advised the team to act quickly in determining a new name (*Edmonton mayor urges Eskimos to move quickly*, 2017).

Most notably, Prime Minister Justin Trudeau strongly advised the team to seek public input. "This is a discussion and a reflection that the City of Edmonton certainly needs to undertake. Reconciliation is not just about Indigenous People and the government. It's about all of us Canadians" ("*A really important discussion*," 2017, para. 4). As public pressure continued to mount against Edmonton, the CFL turned to tried-and-true marketing tactics and rebooted the "This is Our League" campaign, renaming it "Diversity Is Strength" and highlighting diverse trailblazers from each team (CFL, 2017). But the franchise continued to stall regarding its name change decision and was supported by the league. CFL commissioner Randy Ambrosie said that "pride, respect and honour" were all that came to mind when he thought of the team's name – seemingly a romanticized mirroring of the league's principal marketing strategy, willful nostalgia in the wake of adversity (Ross, 2018).

As the cultural climate became more volatile in 2018, the team surveyed 5,000 season ticket holders but made it clear there were no plans to engage more broadly. Responding to open comments, one season ticket holder (not Indigenous) said the name was not offensive, and he did not understand catering to a "vocal minority." He feared change would erase the team's history and hoped the survey results would end the debate (Ross, 2018). His sentiments loudly echoed the majority of anti-name-changers. While it had become clear that societal attitudes were transforming and some stakeholders were demanding accountability, only the voices of the most ardent fans were being heard by the franchise.

Eventually, the Edmonton corporate office announced the formation of the Northern Engagement Community Program, an initiative intended to increase engagement with Inuit communities and evaluate their views on its name. Throughout the year, in-person interviews and other forms of polling were conducted, and team representatives and players visited schools, participated in youth gatherings, and attended community festivals. Then on February 14, 2020, the team made an official announcement on its website:

> The Edmonton Eskimo Football Club will be increasing its engagement in Canada's north following an extensive year-long formal research and engagement program with Inuit leaders and community members across Canada . . . There were a range of views regarding the Club's name but no consensus emerged to support a name change. The Club has therefore decided to retain its name.
>
> *(Edmonton Eskimos, 2020)*

Many resoundingly criticized the decision to keep the name, declaring it inauthentic and charging that the program gave only an appearance of including Inuit viewpoints. The franchise refused to make public any details or statistics contained in the study by invoking the Freedom of Information and Personal Privacy Act (Caldwell, 2020).

One month after the announcement was made, the COVID-19 virus struck, sending the world economy into a spiral of uncertainty. The 2020 CFL season, which should have begun in July, was canceled due to the pandemic, threatening to cripple all teams in the already financially tenuous CFL. During the previous season, Edmonton had lost more than $1 million dollars and stood to lose much more during a canceled season. The team's troubles continued as sponsors next began to threaten withdrawal if the team continued with its current name. *AdWeek* reported:

> Of the team's 13 major sponsors, at least four have raised concerns about the name, calling for reengagement with Inuit communities to reach a consensus over the name or flat-out threatening to divest from the organization. These companies included car and home insurance company belairdirect, Coca-Cola Canada, Jiffy Lube and British menthol lozenge brand Fisherman's Friend.
>
> *(Zorrilla, 2020, para. 6)*

The world of sport felt a shockwave in July 2020 when the Washington Redskins announced that it would change its 87-year-old franchise name. "The nail in the coffin was when the Washington Redskins came out and retired their name and logo . . . . I don't see how there is any way we can continue on using [our] name," an anonymous source within the Eskimos organization told the *Edmonton Sun*

(Moddejonge, 2020, para. 3). In addition, the team drew unnecessary negative attention when its "official Twitter feed painted a hypocritical target on its back in calling for an end to racial inequality following the killing of George Floyd at the hands of police in Minnesota" (Moddejonge, 2020, para. 9).

With tensions mounting amid a global pandemic and a terminated season, on July 21, 2020, the Edmonton front office finally announced that it would reverse its previous decision and retire the Eskimos name, seeking public input into the selection of a new one:

> Our Board of Directors has made the decision to discontinue use of the word 'Eskimo' in the team name. We'll be known as the Edmonton Football Team or the EE Football Team while we go through the process of determining a new name befitting our storied team.
>
> *(Rosvoglou, 2021, para. 3)*

Reaction was swift and represented a wide spectrum of viewpoints especially on social media. *Edmonton Sun* columnist Terry Jones, who had long opposed the name change due to the cost to rebrand, suggested that rebranding costs should be picked up by the sponsors who supported the name change. Echoing what had been heard throughout the dispute, Jones lamented, "The trouble with most of the people, other than the sponsors, [who] have been leading the cry for the Eskimos to change their name is that very few are members of the ticket-buying public" (Jones, 2020b, para. 18).

Immediately after the announcement, the Edmonton football team invited online suggestions for a new name, stipulating only that it should honor the "EE" alliteration brand tradition. The discussion board received 13,000 suggestions. In what became a national contest, communities across Canada participated in rebranding one of the league's most influential teams. On June 1, 2021, just ahead of the upcoming season, the announcement came on Twitter with this simple directive (Sportsnet.ca., 2021):

@elks
New Name. Same Game.
Let's play some football. #Elks#Charge

You Make the Call

It will take time to assess what the long-term effects of rebranding will have on the newly named Edmonton Elks. Throughout the nearly 8-year ordeal, the franchise struggled as it tried to manage obligations to multiple publics, including Indigenous Canadians, diehard gridiron fans, and corporate sponsors. Notably, the CFL's long-time reliance on marketing nostalgic unity and Canadian exceptionalism could not withstand external accusations of racism that demanded accountability and heightened social responsibility.

Amid years of sustained public and economic pressures, the team finally committed to on-the-ground research and the inclusion of diverse stakeholder voices. It was only after the franchise dropped its reactionary, oppositional stance and began listening to sociopolitical soundwaves demanding reconciliation in all aspects of life, including sport, that more authentic communication took place. The extended process by which the Edmonton football organization's decision to rename/rebrand finally became a reality will likely become a cautionary blueprint for sport teams facing similar challenges now and in the future.

Discussion Questions

1. Update the chapter by discussing how the name change of Edmonton Elks has or has not been accepted by its various publics (its fans, Indigenous Peoples, and other Canadians). In what ways have the team's PR practitioners attempted to reconnect the Elks with Canadian national identity and its Canadianness? Compare this to how the NFL's Washington Commanders has or has not been accepted.
2. After considering the lengthy time it took for the Edmonton team to rename and rebrand, how could the process have been streamlined by more effective communication and engagement?
3. Why was nostalgia marketing alone not sufficient to address evolving cultural concerns?
4. What responsibility do professional sport teams have in social and political debates? Does the same apply to collegiate and youth teams?
5. How might Edmonton's experience provide guidance for other athletic organizations experiencing similar situations?

References

Andrews, B., & Greenham, C. (2020). National responsibility: A history of willful Nostalgia in the Canadian Football League. *Journal of Sport History*, 47(3), 226–242.

Caldwell, D. (2020, March 10). 'Slanderous and outdated': Should the Edmonton Eskimos change their name? *The Guardian*. www.theguardian.com/sport/2020/mar/10/slanderous-and-outdated-should-the-edmonton-eskimos-change-their-name

Cantelon, M. (2001). *The Canadian Football League: Radically Canadian?* [Unpublished M.A. Thesis]. University of Ottawa, Ottawa.

CBC News. (2017, November 22). A really important discussion': Trudeau weighs in on name of Edmonton's CFL team. *CBC News*. www.cbc.ca/news/canada/edmonton/edmonton-eskimos-name-change-justin-trudeau-rachel-notley-1.4414960

CBC News. (2017, November 9). Edmonton mayor urges Eskimos to move quickly on name change. *CBC News*. www.cbc.ca/news/canada/edmonton/edmonton-eskimos-name-change-don-iveson-1.4395218

CFL. (2008, June 27). This is our league [Video]. *YouTube*. www.youtube.com/watch?v=BS1jCfg7Qxc

CFL. (2012, July 1). It reflects us all [Video]. *YouTube*. www.youtube.com/watch?v=QRKtgNW42xU

CFL. (2017, August 18). Diversity is strength [Video]. *YouTube*. www.youtube.com/watch?v=0OrmB9ewVtY

Dunning, N. (2017, November 29). Edmonton Eskimos is a racial slur and it's time to stop using it. *Nunatsiaq News*. https://nunatsiaq.com/stories/article/65674edmonton_eskimos_is_a_racial_slur_and_its_time_to_stop_using_it/

Edmonton Eskimos. (2020, February 14). Edmonton Eskimos announce expanded engagement with inuit communities and name decision. www.goelks.com/2020/02/14/edmonton-eskimos-announce-expanded-engagement-inuit-communities-name-decision/

Edmonton Eskimos Fans. (2017). Home [Facebook page]. *Facebook*. www.facebook.com/groups/196562654168061/?ref=share

Franks, C.E.S., Hawes, M., & Macintosh, D. (1988). Sport and Canadian diplomacy. *International Journal, 43*(4), 665–682.

Grunig, J.E. (2013). Furnishing the edifice: Ongoing Research on public relations as a strategic management function. In K. Sriramesh, A. Zerfass, & J. Kim (Eds.), *Public relations and communication management: Current trends and emerging topics* (pp. 1–26). New York: Taylor & Francis.

Jones, T. (2020a, July 17). They will always be the Edmonton Eskimos to me. *Edmonton Sun*. https://edmontonsun.com/sports/football/cfl/edmonton-eskimos/jones-they-will-always-be-the-edmonton-eskimos-to-me

Jones, T. (2020b, July 18). Price of Edmonton Eskimos' name change would be sky high. *Edmonton Sun*. https://edmontonsun.com/sports/football/cfl/edmonton-eskimos/jones-price-of-edmonton-eskimos-name-change-would-be-sky-high

Jones, T. (2020c, July 21). Name change leaves long-time Eskimos fans feeling loss. *Edmonton Sun*. https://edmontonsun.com/sports/football/cfl/edmonton-eskimos/jones-name-change-leaves-long-time-eskimos-fans-feeling-loss

Kirkup, K. (2020, July 14). Amid racism allegations, Edmonton CFL team says name invokes pride in cold weather toughness. *The Globe and Mail*. www.theglobeandmail.com/sports/article-amid-racism-allegations-edmonton-cfl-team-says-name-invokes-pride-in/

Kives, B. (2017, November 8). Winnipeg mayor raises name of CFL Eskimos with Edmonton counterpart. *CBC Press*. www.cbc.ca/news/canada/manitoba/winnipeg-mayor-edmonton-eskimos-name-1.4393494

Kwong, M. (2014, June 19). Washington Redskins fight could put pressure on Edmonton Eskimos. *CBC News*. www.cbc.ca/news/business/washington-redskins-fightcould-put-pressure-on-edmonton-eskimos-1.2680161

Laing, G., & Cooper, C. (2019). Royal commission on bilingualism and biculturalism. *The Canadian Encyclopedia*. www.thecanadianencyclopedia.ca/en/article/royal-commission-on-bilingualism-and-biculturalism

Moddejonge, G. (2020, July 16). Reports say Edmonton Eskimos ready to make name change. *Edmonton Sun*. https://edmontonsun.com/sports/football/cfl/edmonton-eskimos/reports-say-eskimos-ready-to-announce-name-change

Querengesser, T. (2013, September 27). Time to revisit the Eskimos name. *Edmonton Journal*. www.pressreader.com/canada/edmonton-journal/20130927/281801396665304

Rollason, K., & Sanders, C. (2017, November 8), Edmonton Eskimos' name insensitive, Bowman says. *Winnipeg Free Press*. www.winnipegfreepress.com/sports/football/cfl/bowman-says-eskimos-nickname-should-be-changed-because-its-insensitive-to-indigenous-people-456161833.html

‌‍‍

‌‌‍

‌‌‍‍

Ross, A. (2018, February 13). Edmonton Eskimos survey ponders future of football team's name. *CBC News*. www.cbc.ca/news/canada/edmonton/edmonton-eskimos-team-name-2018-survey-1.4534123

Rosvoglou, C. (2021, June 1). Canadian football league team officially changes name. *The Spun by Sports Illustrated*. https://thespun.com/more/top-stories/canadian-football-league-team-officially-changes-name#

Simons, P. (2017, August 11). Time to hear Tanya Tagaq's Eskimos challenge. *Edmonton Journal*. https://edmontonjournal.com/news/local-news/paula-simons-time-to-hear-tanya-tagaqs-eskimos-challenge

Sportsnet.ca. (2021, June 1). Edmonton's CFL franchise changes team name to 'Elks'. *Sportsnet.ca*. www.sportsnet.ca/cfl/article/edmontons-cfl-franchise-changes-team-name-elks/

Valentine, J. (2019). Cultural nationalism, Anti-Americanism, and the federal defense of the Canadian football league. *American Review of Canadian Studies*, *49*(3), 376–393.

Zorrilla, M.M. (2020, July 13). Edmonton Eskimos consider name change after backlash and sponsor pushback. *AdWeek*. www.adweek.com/brand-marketing/edmonton-eskimos-consider-name-change-after-backlash-and-sponsor-pushback/

11

IN THE SPACE OF INDECISION

Social and Cultural Challenges Facing Major League Soccer NEXT Academies

Saleema Mustafa Campbell and Erin E. Gilles

Introduction

Undeniably, soccer is one of the most popular sports in the world, and in recent years, professional soccer has risen in prominence in the United States as well. As of 2020, 6.2% of youth aged between 6 and 12 years and 5.7% of youth aged between 13 and 17 years participate regularly in soccer activities, according to The Aspen Institute (2021). Participation in youth sports has many benefits, including building social development, teamwork, and other life skills (Anderson-Butcher, 2019). While some youth play soccer via school affiliations or local organizations, Major League Soccer (MLS) developed a nationwide network of youth soccer academies called MLS NEXT to capitalize on the sport's growing popularity.

Image Repair Theory

This chapter applies image repair theory (IRT), a sub-theory under the public relations field's reputation management theory (Billings et al., 2020), to evaluate how MLS/MLS NEXT has addressed several organizational issues. IRT refers to:

> A common form of rhetoric [that] is designed to restore image, face, or reputation after alleged or suspected wrong-doing. By "image" we mean the perceptions of the source held by the audience, shaped by the words and deeds of that source, as well as by the actions of other relevant actors.
>
> *(Benoit & Hanczor, 1994, p. 3)*

This theory has been applied often in sports communication, such as LeBron James's decision to leave the Cleveland Cavaliers (Brown et al., 2012), the New

DOI: 10.4324/9781003316763-13

England Patriot's #deflategate scandal (Sheffer et al., 2018), and the NFL's Ray Rice domestic violence case (Smith & Keeven, 2019).

IRT has five components that are denial, evading responsibility, reducing offensiveness, corrective action, and mortification (Benoit & Hanczor, 1994). This chapter evaluates three of these components that are evasion of responsibility, reducing offensiveness, and corrective action. When an organization evades responsibility for an act, such as by not taking blame or failing to address it, they have used this tactic. Reducing offensiveness involves several tactics, and in this chapter we will look at one called transcendence, which reminds the audience of prior good behavior. Corrective action refers to the organization's intention to address the problem, and this action can come with or without an apology by the transgressor (Benoit & Hanczor, 1994). Specifically, three primary topics will be appraised within the context of these three IRT strategies for MLS NEXT, which are (1) meeting the needs of diverse players, (2) addressing the role of trash talking in perpetuating racism (both on the field and on social media), and (3) avoiding the pitfall of so-called "cause-washing."

Background

MLS Academies

In the United States, soccer registration in recreational and club sports programs is increasing, and new professional teams are popping up in cities around the country. MLS NEXT was launched in 2020 after the U.S. Soccer Development Academy ceased operations that same year (USSDA, 2022).

MLS NEXT is operated by Major League Soccer, the professional men's soccer league sanctioned by the U.S. Soccer Federation. Ideally, MLS NEXT was created to be a recruiting and training pipeline for future MLS players. Similar to Division I, II, and III university sports, there are hierarchies in these U.S.-based soccer academies. With the speed at which many of these new community affiliations and networks are expanding, inconsistencies in leadership style, brand identity, and club policies can affect how well these local academies function and support their players.

In North America, MLS NEXT comprises 133 clubs, 590 teams, and more than 11,000 players (MLS NEXT, 2022). However, among those American soccer clubs, racial and ethnic diversities do not match the face of soccer globally (Bushnell, 2020). A recent report from MLS stated that among players, diversity is improving in MLS with 61.7% of players being persons of color, which is up from 35% in 2000 (Lapchick, 2022). However, diversity is far less prevalent within the organizational hierarchy of MLS. Team ownership is 90.6% White, and just 13.8% of team CEO/presidents are women. At the youth level, there is still a poverty and race gap in soccer (Bushnell, 2020). Teams are largely situated in the suburbs, where wealthier families reside, making it challenging for urban children to participate without any access to reliable transportation. In addition, their parents may be hourly workers without the schedule flexibility of parents with greater economic privilege.

Challenges to Diversity and Misrepresentation in Elite Youth Soccer

In the United States, the average annual cost of a year of soccer is $1,472 (Barone, 2017). Less than a quarter of MLS NEXT club academies are fully funded, but in the academies that are, players' fees are subsidized by their clubs. The rest of the clubs operate on a pay-to-play model in which dues are paid by parents for their child's team membership (Ellis & Sharma, 2013). For those who cannot afford to commute, or do not live in the proximity of their MLS NEXT club's location, many clubs offer homestay programs, where local families accommodate their housing needs (Boehm, 2020). Also, these homestay players enroll in local schools in their host families' school districts. This is clearly a problem of accessibility; the median household income for the zip codes in which the elite youth soccer clubs are located is more than 60% higher than the national average (Bushnell, 2020). As a result, communities from which MLS NEXT recruits are less diverse and more suburban than the national average (Allison & Barranco, 2020).

MLS-sponsored youth academies appeal to young players from underserved communities because these programs have the potential to increase their college recruitment options and strengthen their training regimens (Bushnell, 2020). Special considerations and opportunities should be leveraged to design supportive training environments to better accommodate these traditionally underserved players. Without the right kind of support for disadvantaged players, these programs can stunt their potential at best and have deleterious effects at worst. MLS NEXT frequently spotlights exceptional players on their social media. It is common to find their Twitter feed highlighting a diverse group of overachieving young athletes. These player images and anecdotes are aspirational; however, they also promote a narrative that is more marketable than it is accurate. With these stories of exceptional players, MLS sanitizes the academy experience in a way that suggests that this high-achieving level of play is the norm. Success stories are one component of the MLS NEXT academy reality, but these academies are still largely competitive and pressure-driven environments where young people must make tremendous sacrifices in time and effort. Strategically choosing to highlight a strongly diverse cast of star players may not only market MLS NEXT as an organization that puts diversity and inclusion at the forefront, but it also misrepresents American soccer itself, which is still a sport of privilege.

Trash Talk and Racism in Soccer Culture

"Trash talk" refers to the verbal competitive exchanges between athletes during a game. Some scholars consider this to be an unsportsmanlike tactic (N. Dixon, 2008), while others contend that, in certain instances, trash talking can advantageously break opponent concentration and disrupt their strategy (Summers, 2007). Yet, Summers suggests that trash talking should occur among evenly matched players and at strategic moments, such as when a player is at bat; otherwise, it is simply considered rude. Omine (2017) calls trash talking between players verbal assault and reminds us that the penalty for trash talking may be punishable by fines or suspension by the Fédération Internationale de Football Association (FIFA). Athletes reported that motives for trash talking were to increase their own motivation and erode competitor motivation, which was accomplished most often through name-calling, maligning, or cussing at opponents (Rainey & Granito, 2010). In a study of video game players, Ortiz (2019) found that racist and sexist language was pervasive in trash talk.

However, beyond player-on-player aggression via trash talk, a culture of racism is pervasive in global soccer culture (Back et al., 1999). "Racism . . . insidiously structures the interactions and decisions in soccer culture from the terraces, locker rooms and playing fields up to the boardrooms, soccer media and patterns of financial endorsement" (Müller et al., 2007, p. 336). Back et al. (2001) write of the fans who threw bananas or shouted racist chants at professional Black players as the FIFA leagues in Europe began to become more integrated. Fields et al. (2010) suggest that the normalization of violence in sports leads to the condoning of hazing, brawling, and foul play in youth sports as part of the game, but they propose that these issues be taken seriously as a public health concern.

Cause Marketing and Cause-Washing

Many organizations undertake pro-social marketing, also called cause marketing, in which a company creates messaging that takes a stance on a particular social cause. Research indicates that cause marketing can lead to an increase in revenue and consumer satisfaction (Ballings et al., 2018) and that consumers do, whether consciously or subconsciously, assess the amount of effort that they determine organizations apply to their cause marketing efforts (De Vries & Duque, 2018).

However, when organizations are considered to be presenting a social stance, but do not reinforce it with authentic efforts, consumers may accuse the organization of cause-washing. Derisively called woke-washing, cause-washing may target particular social issues, such as environmentalism (green-washing), LGBTQ+ issues (rainbow-washing), feminism (purple-washing), and breast cancer (pink-washing), among others. Woke-washing has been studied in the context of sport, in particular Colin Kaepernick's "Dream Crazy" Nike campaign (Herbert, 2020), which polarized audiences by leading to both a boycott of Nike products *and* a 31% increase in sales (Beer, 2019). Aside from perceptions of insincerity, brands sometimes make poor decisions in their messaging around social issues. In these cases, brands may face swift and vocal criticism from audiences when brands miss the mark or cause offense. After all, audiences may vary in how they perceive particular social issues.

The Case

An Examination of MLS and MLS NEXT's DEI Initiatives as Image Repair

Corporate communication has the potential to improve or damage community relations. In response to recent social movements, many organizations are increasing attention to their diversity, equity, and inclusion (DEI) practices to recalibrate and prioritize the critical roles of workplace culture and corporate reputation. MLS and its subsidiaries are no exception.

In March 2021, MLS NEXT announced DEI initiatives to help decrease discrimination and racism in soccer. These initiatives included the addition of an Equity Action Committee (EAC) to its governance structure. The EAC consists of MLS NEXT coaches and directors, an MLS player and member of Black Players for Change (BPC), a Girls Academy representative, and the Girls Academy commissioner. With the EAC, MLS NEXT is underscoring its commitment "to creating and enacting policies and programs that protect and educate its youth soccer culture of players, coaches, and staff through a series of initiatives including educational sessions, guided discussions, and shared experiences" (MLS, 2021a, para. 2).

Fred Lipka, MLS NEXT technical director, described this campaign as an effort to reduce racial intolerance and discriminatory behavior in youth soccer (MLS, 2021a). Furthermore, Lipka explains that MLS NEXT is a unique opportunity to reach youth soccer players at a "critical time" in their lives when lessons about diversity and inclusion are important in the struggle for change (MLS, 2021a, para. 4). Specifically, the initiatives include (1) a series of instructional discussions that support MLS NEXT leaders in the development of antiracist environments; (2) an exchange of best practices with the BPC organization and The Girls Academy; (3) an increase in diversity in hiring recruitment in leadership positions and coaches by utilizing the Elite Formation Coaching License as a recruitment incentive; (4) an EAC-led policy review process to streamline incident reporting and a new disciplinary process; and (5) providing coaches, players, and parents with access to training materials which focus on minority experiences (MLS, 2021a). These initiatives indicate a managerial top-down approach with policies for MLS NEXT stemming from MLS.

Correspondingly, a 2021 report on MLS DEI initiatives conducted by the University of Central Florida's non-profit organization The Institute for Diversity and Ethics in Sport (TIDES) highlights the organization's efforts to support ethnic groups and other minorities impacted by the league (Lapchick, 2022). In some instances, there are clear examples of improvement in hiring – for example, hiring the league's first chief diversity officer in 2021 and forming its first DEI committee in 2020. Player activity may have spurred these changes, with a 170-member-strong group of players, coaches, and BPC staff forming on Juneteenth in 2020 to tackle the uneven playing field of racial representation in the sport of soccer.

Although BPC is a new organization, its strong momentum has led to it being called "a force" by Nashville's *The Tennessean* (Hills, 2021). In its first year, BPC's resume included on-field protests by members lasting 8 minutes and 46 seconds (the time it took for George Floyd to be murdered by police), transforming MLS stadiums into voting polls, pledging to establish a dozen new soccer pitches in Black communities, and helping to establish MLS's new DEI committee (Hills, 2021). MLS owners donated $1 million to the BPC through 2024 (Hart, 2020).

MLS is active in acknowledging and supporting Black players and their efforts to create change through initiatives that include a league-wide Juneteenth Program and support of the 100 Black Men of America, which are overseen by Pitch Black, a resource group of MLS employees. The TIDES report also mentions other MLS-supported initiatives such as Autism Speaks, Street Soccer USA (an organization that aspires to use soccer to reduce homelessness), Women in Tech, and others (Lapchick, 2021). These actions demonstrate the IRT principle of reducing offensiveness through transcendence. For, when allegations of racial insensitivity abound about the academy, these specialty jerseys or programs for autism can remind audiences that MLS, and by extension MLS NEXT, cares about diversity.

The TIDES report, however, mentions little about how Latinx or Asian players and employees are supported by MLS, outside of the support of the non-profit Hispanic Star coalition during Hispanic Heritage Month (Lapchick, 2022). While MLS has made certain strides, such as offering a specially designed logo for Pride Month, more consistent efforts to include more groups would help avoid accusations of cause-washing.

MLS NEXT Incidents of Racism and the Response as Image Repair

The announcement of MLS NEXT's DEI campaign on March 18, 2021 appears to coincide with several reports of racist incidents during MLS NEXT Academy competitions. One incident occurred on March 2, 2021 when players from the Real Colorado's MLS NEXT Academy club team allegedly used racist language against players from FC Dallas's MLS NEXT Academy club team during a match (Eskilson, 2021). The referee allowed the game to play on. In response, the FC Dallas Academy director instructed his team to stage a walk off. Also, this same report noted the occurrence of other racist incidents involving other MLS NEXT teams during the previous year's MLS NEXT playoff season (Eskilson,

2021). MLS NEXT was tested again publicly on September 24, 2021 when U15 (under 15 league) players for FC Dallas walked off the pitch after one of its players was the target of racist language, allegedly used by an opposing player for the Colorado Rapids (another MLS NEXT Academy team) (Eskilson, 2021). This exchange occurred during an MLS NEXT Academy Showcase series game. Later during this showcase series, FC Dallas's U14 (under 14 league) players staged a walk off during their match against another Colorado Rapids Academy team in solidarity with their club's U15 team. According to this report, there was already an open investigation into the March incident of racism between FC Dallas and Real Colorado (Eskilson, 2021). At the time of the 2Eskilson report, neither MLS NEXT nor The Colorado Rapids had commented on the incidents.

The lack of response from MLS NEXT demonstrates the IRT principle of evasion of responsibility. In the days following these incidents, MLS NEXT made no reference to these incidents and chose to forgo issuing any formal social media statement. However, parents and fans quickly criticized the organization on Twitter for its lack of response and failure to take disciplinary action. A lengthy Twitter exchange began after someone commented on the unsettling behaviors demonstrated during this incident by players, parents, and the referees involved. The tweet alleged that the referees should have stopped the game to address the incident and that some parents felt that these racist slurs were just part of the game. Many Twitter respondents tagged MLS NEXT, FC Dallas, and the Real Colorado Twitter accounts. Via the Real Colorado official Twitter account, team representatives pledged to investigate the incident and reaffirmed the team's zero-tolerance policy regarding racism. Another person, claiming to be a witness, tweeted that parents need to acknowledge that racism should be avoided in MLS NEXT, and those who saw the racist discourse should step forward and share the players' names.

Problematically, only one of the academies (Real Colorado Soccer) directly addressed the racism. This lack of coordinated messaging undermines image repair efforts. Although MLS NEXT did not acknowledge these incidents, they did enact the IRT corrective action approach via MLS, its parent organization.

In December 2021, MLS revisited elements of its DEI campaign and announced enhancements to its diversity and hiring policy. The policy changes represented an effort to reaffirm MLS' desire to diversify its organization, including its affiliates. In addition, they expressed a desire to increase minority hiring (MLS, 2021b). These updated policy changes applied to both MLS clubs and MLS NEXT academies.

MLS Organizational Responses to Public Acts of Racism as Image Repair

Often professional sports communities operate as a microcosm of their larger societies, and thus racial tensions exist within MLS as well. Most recently in November 2021, the MLS club Real Salt Lake announced that it had released its goalie,

Andrew Putna, after he directed racist language at his teammate, David Ochoa (Muller, 2021). However, Putna was still eligible to join another team once his suspension ended either through draft entry or by signing a new contract with a different team.

In June 2021, MLS launched an investigation into racist language directed at Portland Timbers player, Diego Chara. Following that incident, MLS issued a statement:

> MLS has zero tolerance for abusive and offensive language, and we take these allegations very seriously. An investigation into this matter has already begun. Further information will be provided upon the completion of that investigation.
>
> *(ESPN, 2021, para 13)*

During a 2008 game, New England Revolution player Kheli Dube was subjected to racial epithets from several fans of the Columbus Crew (A. Dixon, 2008). Steve Ralston, a midfielder on Dube's team, claimed that bananas were thrown as well. Following the incident, MLS officials issued a statement in which they vowed to ban the perpetrator from MLS properties and events for life. The organization also stated:

> MLS takes enormous pride in our commitment to racial and ethnic diversity and inclusiveness – in our stadiums, on our fields, and in our administrative, coaching and ownership ranks. We categorically will not tolerate this language in any context or setting and are working with all of our clubs and stadiums to ensure that this isolated incident is not repeated.
>
> *("From the Commish . . .," 2008, Para 2)*

In 2018, a story in *The Athletic* detailed a troubling and widely known connection between MLS's New York City Football Club (NYCFC) and fringe hate-groups (Araos, 2018). There is a history of aggressive behavior before and after NYCFC games, including offensive chants, salutes, and violent altercations. Suspicion for inciting these acts has been cast on a group of regular spectators at league games, who were also members of the hate groups the Proud Boys, 211 Bootboys, and Battalion 49 (Araos, 2018).

You Make the Call

As MLS NEXT demonstrates, youth sports organizations can be incredibly challenging from an operational perspective. Organizations dedicated to children and adolescents deserve the best efforts, recognition, and support from the adults involved. Thus, maintaining a positive public image requires effective strategies and partnerships. To this end, several recommendations for managing and developing healthy sporting experiences for young athletes are offered here:

1. **Design Player-Centered Models**. When youth players join MLS NEXT, they are making a significant time commitment, whether they live near their clubs or must commute. These academies require long hours and days of training and competition over the course of a full calendar year. To avoid accusations of *cause-washing*, MLS NEXT must plan for the total development of players who live outside predominantly White, suburban communities. An effective diversity campaign should address the unique needs of players who commute long distances to play or live in homestay locations. Successful image repair initiatives put policy into practice with clear follow through on said initiatives (Benoit, 2000).

Additionally, racism exists and can manifest in all facets of professional sports, including online. The ease of use of social media means that fans and players can effortlessly taunt opposing teams, and soccer parents can keep the feud going long after they have left the bleachers. For the players' best interests, MLS social media must directly address the need for a sea change in terms of American soccer culture.

2. **Promote Diversity in Recruitment.** It appears MLS recognizes that a more diverse community may preempt some racist incidents from occurring. Thus, increased efforts to recruit and hire a diverse workforce may result in staff with a greater sense of investment in the organization's vision for inclusivity and cultural acceptance; inclusivity requires a diversity of perspectives.
3. **Be Consistent and Clear in Rejecting Racism.** Clear, consistent, and firm messaging is required to address racism. MLS has recognized its past shortcomings, but there is still work needed to advance inclusivity. Soccer remains the most diverse and accessible sport globally, but not in the United States. Potentially, this truth undersc   ores the dilemmas central to MLS and, more importantly, MLS NEXT's sports culture. Regardless, it is important to be very direct and clear in all capacities by demonstrating a zero tolerance with acts of racism. The youth deserve these positive examples.

MLS and MLS NEXT have made notable strides in launching DEI initiatives; however, these organizations could do more to foster more inclusive on-field and online environments. The narrative can be hard to referee once missteps go public on social media. Benoit (2000) reminds us that the audience is a varied group with the potential to respond differently to IRT efforts. And, this audience – a large, varied, and vocal soccer community comprising various stakeholders – will be closely watching to see whether the organization backs up its intentions with action.

Discussion Questions

1. What kinds of responsibilities do sports organizations have regarding diversity, equity, and inclusion? How do these responsibilities differ for youth leagues versus adult leagues?

2. If you oversaw the corporate communication for MLS NEXT, what communication strategies would you implement for your different stakeholders (coaches, players, parents, community members, etc.)?
3. What kinds of examples of cause-washing do you see with MLS NEXT? What about in other brands or organizations that you support?
4. Some scholars argue that sport is an inherently aggressive environment, and trash talking is a natural part of the competitive landscape. Where do you stand on this issue? Does your stance differ when considering individual versus team sports? Youth versus adult leagues? Male versus female leagues?
5. Visit MLS NEXT's social media accounts to assess how they are continuing to manage their communication with various stakeholders. Do you see current examples of IRT?

References

Allison, R., & Barranco, R. (2021). 'A rich White kid sport?' Hometown socioeconomic, racial, and geographic composition among US women's professional soccer players. *Soccer & Society*, *22*(5), 457–469. https://doi.org/10.1080/14660970.2020.1827231

Anderson-Butcher, D. (2019). Youth sport as a vehicle for social development. *Kinesiology Review*, *8*(3), 180–187. https://doi.org/10.1123/kr.2019-0029

Araos, C. (2018, November 1). NYCFC fans troubled by a violent, far-right fringe attending matches. *The Athletic*. https://theathletic.com/627781/2018/11/01/nycfc-fans-troubled-by-a-violent-far-right-fringe-attending-matches/

Back, L., Crabbe, T., & Solomos, J. (1999). Beyond the racist/hooligan couplet: Race, social theory and football culture. *The British Journal of Sociology*, *50*(3), 419–442. https://doi-org.univsouthin.idm.oclc.org/10.1111/j.1468-4446.1999.00419.x

Back, L., Crabbe, T., & Solomos, J. (2001). "Lions and black skins": Race, nation and local patriotism in football. In B. Carrington & I. McDonald (Eds.), *Race, sport and British society*. London: Routledge.

Ballings, M., McCullough, H., & Bharadwaj, N. (2018). Cause marketing and customer profitability. *Journal of the Academy of Marketing Science*, *46*(2), 234–251. https://doi10.1007/s11747-017-0571-4

Barone, E. (2017, August 24). The astronomical cost of kids' sports. *Time Magazine*. https://time.com/4913284/kids-sports-cost/

Benoit, W.L. (2000). Another visit to the theory of image restoration strategies. *Communication Quarterly*, *48*(1), 40–43. http://dx.doi.org.univsouthin.idm.oclc.org/10.1080/01463370009385578

Benoit, W.L., & Hanczor, R.S. (1994). The Tonya harding controversy: An analysis of image restoration strategies. *Communication Quarterly*, *42*(4), 416. http://dx.doi.org.univsouthin.idm.oclc.org/10.1080/01463379409369947

Beer, J. (2019, September). One year later, what did we learn from Nike's blockbuster Colin Kaepernick ad. *Fast Company*. www.fastcompany.com/90399316/one-year-later-what-did-we-learnfrom-nikes-blockbuster-colin-kaepernick-ad.

Billings, A.C., Coombs, W.T., & Brown, K.A. (2020). Navigating brands of sport-based big business: Exploring reputation management in an evolving sport context. *Journal of Global Sport Management*, *5*(2), 121–127. https://doi.org/10.1080/24704067.2019.1604079

Boehm, C. (2020, June). Audi 1v1: Residency programs broaden the scope, depth of MLS academies. *MLS News.* www.mlssoccer.com/news/audi-1v1-residency-programs-broaden-scope-depth-mls-academies

Brown, K.A., Dickhaus, J., & Long, M.C. (2012). LeBron James and" The Decision": An empirical examination of image repair in sports. *Journal of Sports Media, 7*(1), 149–175. https://doi.org/10.1353/jsm.2012.0010

Bushnell, H. (2020, September 22). The privilege of play: Why the world's game is a white game in the U.S. *Yahoo Sports.* www.yahoo.com/now/the-privilege-of-play-why-the-worlds-game-is-a-white-game-in-the-us-150024228.html

De Vries, E.L., & Duque, L.C. (2018). Small but sincere: How firm size and gratitude determine the effectiveness of cause marketing campaigns. *Journal of Retailing, 94*(4), 352–363. https://doi.org/10.1016/j.jretai.2018.08.002

Dixon, A. (2008, June 3). Racism and MLS. *US Soccer Players.* https://ussoccerplayers.com/2008/06/racism-and-mls.html

Dixon, N. (2008). Trash talking as irrelevant to athletic excellence: Response to Summers. *Journal of the Philosophy of Sport, 35*(1), 90–96. https://doi.org/10.1080/00948705.2008.9714729

Ellis, J.M., & Sharma, H. (2013). Can't play here: The decline of pick-up soccer and social capital in the USA. *Soccer & Society, 14*(3), 364–385. https://doi.org/10.1080/14660970.2013.801266

Eskilson, J.R. (2021, September). FC Dallas walk off due to racist language. *Topdrawersoccer.com.* www.topdrawersoccer.com/club-soccer-articles/fc-dallas-walks-off-due-to-racist-language_aid49944

ESPN. (2021, June 27). Portland Timbers coach Savarese blasts alleged racist comment to Diego Chara during MLS game. *ESPN.* www.espn.com/soccer/portland-timbers/story/4421077/portland-timbers-coach-savarese-blasts-racial-abuse-of-diego-chara-during-mls-game

Fields, S.K., Collins, C.L., & Comstock, R.D. (2010). Violence in youth sports: Hazing, brawling and foul play. *British Journal of Sports Medicine, 44*(1), 32–37. http://dx.doi.org/10.1136/bjsm.2009.068320

From the Commish . . . (2008, June 4). The Columbus dispatch. www.dispatch.com/story/news/2008/06/04/from-commish/23874499007/

Hart, T. (2020, October 19). MLS launches series of social justice initiatives. *Front Office Sports.* https://frontofficesports.com/mls-social-justice-initiatives/

Herbert, N. (2020). "Woke-washing" a brand: Socially progressive marketing by Nike on Twitter and the user response to it. *Tidskrift för ABM, 5*(1), 54–70. www.divaportal.org/smash/record.jsf?pid=diva2:1438652

Hills, D. (2021, June 18). A soccer brotherhood: The story behind black players for change. www.tennessean.com/in-depth/sports/nashvillesc/2021/06/18/black-players-change-american-soccer-mls-juneteenth/5136452001/

Lapchick, R. (2022). The 2021 racial and gender report card: Major League Soccer. *The Institute for Diversity and Ethics in Sport.* www.tidesport.org/mls

Major League Soccer [MLS]. (2021a, March 18). MLS NEXT announces steps to combat racism, hate and discrimination. [Press Release]. www.mlssoccer.com/news/mls-NEXT-announces-steps-combat-racism-hate-and-discrimination

Major League Soccer [MLS]. (2021b, December 7). MLS announces updates and enhancements to diversity hiring policy. [Press Release]. www.mlssoccer.com/news/mls-announces-updates-and-enhancements-to-diversity-hiring-policy

MLS NEXT. (2022). *The NEXT Generation*. www.mlssoccer.com/mlsNEXT/about

Müller, F., Van Zoonen, L., & de Roode, L. (2007). Accidental racists: Experiences and contradictions of racism in local Amsterdam soccer fan culture. *Soccer & Society*, *8*(2–3), 335–350. https://doi.org/10.1080/14660970701224608

Muller, L. (2021, November 11). RSL GK Putna removed from team activities after alleged racist comments. *SBnation.com*. www.rslsoapbox.com/2021/11/11/22757470/rsl-gk-putna-removed-from-team-activities-after-alleged-racist-comments

Omine, M. (2017). Ethics of trash talking in soccer. *International Journal of Sport and Health Science*, *15*, 120–125. https://doi.org/10.5432/ijshs.201718

Ortiz, S.M. (2019). The meanings of racist and sexist trash talk for men of color: A cultural sociological approach to studying gaming culture. *New Media & Society*, *21*(4), 879–894. https://doi.org/10.1177/1461444818814252

Rainey, D.W., & Granito, V. (2010). Normative rules for trash talk among college athletes: An exploratory study. *Journal of Sport Behavior*, *33*(3), 276.

Sheffer, M.L., Schultz, B., & Tubbs, W. (2018). #deflategate: Sports journalism and the use of image repair strategy on Twitter. *Newspaper Research Journal*, *39*(1), 69–82. https://doi.org/10.1177/0739532918761067

Smith, J.S., & Keeven, D. (2019). Creating separation from the on-field product: Roger Goodell's image repair discourse during the Ray Rice domestic violence case. *Communication & Sport*, *7*(3), 292–309. https://doi.org/10.1177/2167479518769896

Summers, C. (2007). Ouch . . . . you just dropped the ashes. *Journal of the Philosophy of Sport*, *34*(1), 68–76. https://doi.org/10.1080/00948705.2007.9714710

The Aspen Institute Project Play. (2021). The state of play 2020: Trends and developments in youth sports. www.aspenprojectplay.org/state-of-play-2021/ages-13-17

USSDA. (2022). U.S. soccer development academy. www.ussoccerda.com/home.php

12

#WEAREALLMONKEYS

Eating Bananas as the Intersection of Hashtag Activism and Anti-Racist Solidarity

Pratik Nyaupane

Introduction

Arenas of sport are usually presented as venues of athletic prowess and entertainment for the masses; however, they also serve as a microcosm of the historical systemic inequities that pervade the larger society. The spotlight is even brighter when the most popular sport in the world, soccer – as it is called in the United States – or Fútbol – as it is called in many other parts of the world – transcends borders, languages, cultures, and religions. While many soccer supporters, pundits, and governing bodies strive to separate soccer and politics, for non-White footballers, racism is an inevitable part of the game. One of the most visible moments of racial abuse in soccer occurred when an in-stadium spectator in Spain hurled a banana at Dani Alves da Silva, a non-White Brazilian footballer during a match, degrading Alves's existence to that of a primate. Although some players fail to acknowledge racism within the game, Alves refused to let this particular incident go unanswered, and what followed became an unprecedented anti-racist social media movement.

This case study highlights an example of one athlete's protest against racial violence, how social media catalyzed a solidarity-driven movement, and how the global soccer world responded following the hashtags #SomosTodosMacacos (Portuguese) and #WeAreAllMonkeys. This case study, drawing on the insights of participatory culture and civic engagement, underscores social justice protests within sport while illuminating the role of social media and the social movements propelled by hashtag activism. In contrast with many social justice protests in sport, this movement introduced a playful participatory element to a serious issue, inviting a more diverse coalition to join, while possibly depoliticizing the issue, which led to certain elements of a "good cause" being capitalized by some organizations

DOI: 10.4324/9781003316763-14

and institutions for a public relations spectacle. As social media extend the bounds of mass communication and accessibility for voice and action, this particular movement of solidarity provides a unique instance of communication practices among players, clubs, fans, and their intersection with institutional power.

Applying a cultural approach to sport, this case study dissects ideas of narrative, specifically in the role of hashtag activism, and how the hashtag, as a tool within social media, propels the reach and popularity of a social movement (Campbell, 2005; Yang, 2016). Often, victims of racism turn to humor to cope with the trauma, which Dani Alves and his teammate, Neymar da Silva Santos Junior, or simply Neymar, sought to do (Outley et al., 2021). The act of posting a picture of oneself with a banana on social media became a game-like experience and a light-hearted act of resistance. Intentionally or not, Alves and Neymar incorporated elements of play and resistance in social impact (Gordon & Mihailidis, 2016)

Background

On April 27, 2014, Fútbol Club Barcelona player Dani Alves prepared to take a corner kick during a La Liga match between Barcelona and Villareal Club de Fútbol. Alves, like many Black and Brown players, was no stranger to acts of racism on the pitch and often encountered aggressive incidents of racial abuse consisting of monkey chants and other tactics of racialized dehumanization. During the 75th minute of the match, 26-year-old Villareal supporter David Campaya Lleo hurled a banana at Alves, which caught worldwide attention (BBC, 2014).

Monkey chants are a common form of racist fan behavior, especially in European soccer. The construction of fandom within soccer is significant in that the community is made up of the fans, the corporate front office staff, and the players who are employed as labor for the sport. The soccer club is an imagined community in which all of these actors share an identity – that of passionate "members" of a team. More often than not, supporters of a club will share some sort of geographic affiliation with a team; however, in most circumstances, the players – since they may be traded by management or willfully move from team to team – do not necessarily share that place-based identity. This allows for the "othering" of players as individuals who are outsiders.

Even at the level of national team competition, racism and xenophobia are prevalent. For instance, the French men's national football team comprises many players who are from or have parents from African countries, but whenever their performance lacks or fans deem their play unsuccessful, racism is a convenient and well-frequented scapegoat. Karim Benzema, a French footballer with Algerian heritage, famously pronounced that "If I score, I'm French. If I don't, I'm Arab" (Beydoun, 2018, p. 24).

Saeed and Kilvington write that during the 1970s, particularly in English football, racist chants were normalized, whereas now they still exist albeit in a manner that is socially less acceptable (2011). Nonetheless, racist actions by fans are still an apparent and present issue. For example, Mario Balotelli, who was born in Italy to Ghanaian parents, has made his experience of racism in soccer well known. Balotelli, who is Black and has represented the Italian national team at the highest level, was playing for Brescia in Seria A in 2019. During a match, a group of opposing fans vocalized discriminatory behaviors toward him leading Balotelli to threaten to walk off the pitch mid-match. Following the game, the manager and president of the opposing club, Hellas Verona Football Club, denied that any sort of racial abuse had occurred and insisted that Balotelli was overreacting to the passionate chants of Verona fans. The club president, Maurizio Setti, mentioned that racism does not exist in Verona because many Black players have donned the team kit (uniform) in the past. One of the fans, from an ultra-supporter group of Verona, claimed that Balotelli "is [only] Italian because he has Italian citizenship but he will never be completely Italian," implying that his Blackness prevents him from being a *true* Italian (Ubha & Mezzofiore, 2019, para. 12). Consequently, the supporter was later banned from attending any Verona match for the next 10 years. This is one of numerous instances in which Black players have faced racism from the stands while playing, supporting Alves' claim that racism is a problem that pervades Spain as well (Guardian Sport, 2019).

In response, minoritized players often vary in their tactics to combat these forms of racial abuse, and Alves decided to handle this situation with a unique approach. As he set ready to take the corner kick, the Brazilian right-back picked up the banana that was thrown at him, peeled it, and took a bite before tossing it to the side and proceeding with the corner kick undeterred. This was broadcast live on the channels showing the match all across the world, and the pictures of this event, were widely distributed via social media and news media platforms. Later on, Alves said that "You have to take it with a dose of humour. We aren't going to change things easily. If you don't give it importance, they don't achieve their objective" (Associated Press, 2014, para. 3).

Immediately following the match, Alves' fellow Brazilian and FC Barcelona teammate, Neymar da Silva Santos Junior, took to Instagram and Facebook. Neymar posted, with the hashtag #SomosTodosMacacos (translation: #WeAreAllMonkeys), a picture of himself and his son, David Lucca de Silva Santos, holding up peeled bananas, sparking a social media spectacle of solidarity against racial abuse in soccer (Neymar, 2014). Posted on April 27, 2014, the picture garnered over 705,000 likes on Instagram and over 1 million on Facebook as of January 2022.

The Case

After the worldwide banana meme campaign ignited social media, the Spanish newspaper *Diario AS* reported that, weeks earlier, Neymar and Alves had consulted with the Brazilian advertising agency, Loducca, after Neymar was the target of monkey chants from opposing fans (Manfred, 2014). Thus, a seemingly random act turned out to be a carefully crafted, social media campaign that spread globally and included even world leaders posing with bananas in their hands. This use of public relations strategy in sport and social justice illuminates the core ethos behind the reactions of Alves and Neymar, while showing the effectiveness of communication in sport and media during a high-exposure incident (Goffman, 1974; Hopwood et al., 2010).

While the public discourse largely seemed to credit Alves for his unique response in resistance against the racist act and Neymar for his prompt and seemingly creative initial post and hashtags, Loducca, in conjunction with the collaborative brainstorming of Neymar and his management team, were revealed to be the masterminds behind this creative campaign (Manfred, 2014). Loducca, as a private firm, adopted this campaign as a form of corporate social advocacy in response to overwhelming racism faced by others but particularly Neymar as a Loducca client in Spanish football (Dodd & Supa, 2014).

Additionally, many news publications reported the role of Loducca in orchestrating the planned campaign, as invalidating the original impact of the anti-racist messaging (Berger, 2014). Due to the spontaneous nature of Alves' actions, which were indeed true and unplanned, the public had tremendous respect for his creative, yet resistant act. Coupled with that, Neymar's Instagram post of himself and his son smiling added yet another overlapping element of creativity, which was perceived as real-time authenticity. While Neymar and Alves were involved in the conceptualization process of the initial idea, the corporate involvement in this anti-racist campaign thus became a letdown to many as some interpreted it as a phony public relations stunt.

Focusing on this incident, which provoked an international online anti-racism movement, we must contextualize social justice protests in sport, especially in the 21st century – the Internet age. It is imperative to understand how sport – specifically soccer – has paradoxically accommodated racism and other forms of inequities, while also providing a unique platform for racialized athletes to voice their concerns and stage protests through various means (Wagner-Egger et al., 2012; de Vlieger, 2016).

Social media as a platform has changed the way athletes perform, on and off the pitch. With a global reach, soccer, the most popular sport in the world, reaches billions around the world, and the players' impact and presence rival that of other celebrities (Ruihley et al, 2010). For context, Neymar (as of December 2021) has 166 million followers on Instagram (@NeymarJr), making him the eighteenth most followed profile in the world, the fifth most followed person from outside the United States, and the third most followed footballer, exemplifying his global impact on social media. Neymar Jr, as a brand, carries tremendous weight; anything he posts or says is heavily analyzed and scrutinized.

As mentioned previously, the globalization of soccer intersects with the dynamics of race and power and presents a fascinating way in which to uncover and understand the infamous banana incident. The racialization of soccer has been significant throughout its existence; however, its importance is often downplayed with either a color-blind approach or one that depoliticizes racism as an issue related to violence. In many parts of the world, such as South Africa or the United States, there is a historical segregation among participants in the sport. Soccer around the world has a connotation of being the game of the working-class (although it is the inverse, in the United States) and has perpetuated racial divides. In South Africa, many attribute the power of soccer's unifying capabilities to playing a role in race relations; however, there is a distinct racial difference among those who play soccer, rugby, and cricket. The Bafana Bafana – the nickname for the South African national football team for the 2010 FIFA Men's World Cup – had only one White player, while the victorious 1995 Springbok – the nickname for the South African men's rugby team as depicted in the film *Invictus* – featured all White players and only one Black player (Griffin, 2010). The racialization of the sport is deeply embedded in politics, history, economics, and cultural contexts. In Europe, where the pinnacle of club soccer exists, there is a diversity of race, but it is also met with prejudice and violence from some.

The significance of this case study is the sheer reach and popularity of soccer around the world. Its context and passion transcends simply sports or games and is deeply rooted within social and political structures. Many soccer clubs, soccer stadiums, and fans possess deeply held political identities that shape their culture, politics, and values (Guschwan, 2016; Kassing & Nyaupane, 2019; Williams, 2007; Dogliani, 2000; Llopis-Goig, 2013; Kassimeris, 2012). This case analyzes the crossroads of politics, power, and racism in soccer with modern movements and explores how the Internet and social media intersect with these traditions.

Many of the world's best athletes are non-White, yet, are put on pedestals despite obvious tensions of racism deeply rooted throughout the sporting world and woven into society at large. Scholars have investigated the labor and exploitation of the Black and Brown body in sport, and how, with many White owners and managers, sports teams emulate colonial and slavery-like logics as part of the sport and its economic models (Jarvie, 2000; Hargreaves, 1985). In European soccer, with many players of color and a majority of White fans, incidents of racial abuse are common, and players find their own ways of dealing with them. Dani Alves' response to the banana being thrown at him is a prime example. Coupled with Neymar's professionally choreographed social media reaction, the banana incident garnered international attention and resulted in significant implications about how racism is viewed within the sport.

You Make the Call

Communication scholars have studied the ways in which the Internet has changed how individuals engage in political issues, especially as young people have taken agency in organizing and participating (Jenkins et al., 2016; Freelon,

2018; Poell & van Dijck, 2018). Given that the role of social media has revolutionized the way in which movements span the globe, this case study permits a unique opportunity to gain insight into the intersection of sport and social justice protests. Additionally, the act of taking a bite out of a banana and posting supportive messages on social media add elements of resistance and play that empower people of all ages, backgrounds, and countries to participate in a charged issue such as racism (Gordon & Mihailidis, 2016).

Some of the most notable movements of hashtag activism include the #BlackOutTuesday and #SayHerName campaigns, which stem from the larger #BlackLivesMatter and #MeToo movements. #WeAreAllMonkeys as a movement and #TakeAKnee or #ImWithKap – hashtag campaigns in support of former NFL quarterback Colin Kaepernick's protest against police brutality in the United States by kneeling during the national anthem – share similarities due to their proximities to sport, but the #WeAreAllMonkeys movement differs significantly in the way that it was received by the public as well as its elements of participatory behaviors.

The #MeToo movement, similar to the #WeAreAllMonkeys movement, spanned the globe but had a much higher reach. The participatory element of the #MeToo movement invoked a seriousness that encouraged survivors of sexual harassment and sexual assault to come forward and share their stories. The #MeToo posts were graphic and detailed, whereas #WeAreAllMonkeys often did not embody a "coming forward" element but rather an allyship.

Additionally, the social media engagement with the #WeAreAllMonkeys hashtag usually had a visual component to it and integrated elements of playfulness and *memeification*, as many of the people in the pictures are often smiling and attempting to promote a positive message, rather than negatively critiquing a form of oppression (Williams, 2020; Kassing, 2020). In contrast, the #ImWithKap hashtag was not necessarily a movement but rather a declaration of support for Colin Kaepernick. Although both hashtags were similar in that they represented statements of anti-racism in sport, the commonality of engagement through participation of an individual posting a picture with a banana made the #WeAreAllMonkeys hashtag unique.

Unlike many other political statements in sport, the anti-racist rallying call for the #WeAreAllMonkeys crusade was met with little collective opposition. There was only one clear perpetrator here and that was David Campaya Lleo, the Villareal fan who threw the banana. In contrast, beer and ice cream companies were not eager to support Kaepernick nor similar cases of injustice in sport, like in the case of the U.S. women's national soccer team and their fight for equal pay. However, the #WeAreAllMonkeys social media firestorm was an excellent public relations opportunity. After all, Loducca, the successful Brazilian marketing firm whose job it was to maintain and promote the image of Neymar and Alves, were the creative artists behind this entire plan. Situating the Internet as a space for mobilization, this campaign effectively capitalized off the incident and gained global traction (Taylor & Das, 2010). This differed from other exemplifying instances of corporate social advocacy, such as Nike's sponsorship of Colin

Kaepernick or its production and marketing of an athletic hijab, both of which ultimately were aimed at maximizing profit by tapping a social justice-oriented audience (Waymer & Logan, 2020).

Joining the effort to support the anti-racist cause, which was portrayed as a humanitarian feel-good moment, private companies such as Carlsberg, the Danish beermaker, and Ben and Jerry's, the American creamery, used the banana meme to showcase their products to the consumer market. In this way, these companies simultaneously aligned themselves with Alves and the anti-racism effort, while engaging in corporate social advocacy, thus employing a social justice tool to anticipate a financially positive result (Dodd & Supa, 2014). Even the U.S. Embassy in Dhaka, Bangladesh, published a post with the hashtag denouncing racism in soccer.

From the initial racially motivated throwing of the banana to the ensuing hashtag and social media movement vilifying that action, this case presents how existing frameworks in sport communication, coupled with scholarship in areas of new media and communication, allow deeper insight into the intersection of sport and social justice protests ignited through social media. The incident involving Dani Alves was neither the first, nor will it be the last of its kind. However, the way in which it sparked a conversation, a reaction, and a newfound awareness in an unsuspecting manner is what makes it significant.

Sport media potentially provides a unifying space. However, with the exponentially rapid connectivity that social media and communication provide, it is up to the consumers and supporters of the sport to be conscientious and intentional about the equitability and justice within that space. Certainly, connectivity has the power to exert that paradigm shift. In summary, we have explored the successes and shortcomings of the hashtag campaign, highlighting the rapidly changing online world and how sport and social justice intersect with new adaptations of technology and media.

Discussion Questions

1. This incident occurred in 2014, and social media has increased in size and expanded its reach. How have players utilized social media since then, and what effects has it had on other situations of injustice within sport?
2. What are the shortcomings of social media when used as a key medium to spread social awareness about an issue?
3. When the news came out that there was a public relations firm behind the players' actions, it may have made their initial actions seem less authentic. Discuss the ways in which this could be the case and the role of public relations in social awareness.
4. What other sport-related social movements have transpired through social media? How have their elements been similar to and different from the #WeAreAllMonkeys case?

Acknowledgments

This work would not have been possible without Diego Ramos Aguilera and Kai Nham, my colleagues, but most importantly my friends who provided constant support and motivation through the beginning of our Ph.D. journeys.

References

Associated Press. (2014, April 28). *Dani Alves eats banana in response to racist taunt.* Associated Press. https://apnews.com/article/13d135f687ca4c369962569975197b03

BBC. (2014, April 30). Spanish police arrest Dani Alves Banana Thrower suspect. *BBC News.* www.bbc.com/news/world-europe-27222240.

Berger, M. (2014, April 30). The Banana selfie campaign against racism was actually a planned marketing stunt. *Buzzfeed News.* www.buzzfeednews.com/article/miriamberger/the-banana-selfie-campaign-against-racism-was-actually-a-pla

Beydoun, K. (2018). Les Bleus and black: A football elegy to french colorblindness. *Minnesota Law Review,* 103, 20. https://ssrn.com/abstract=3501260.

Campbell, K.K. (2005). Agency: Promiscuous and protean. *Communication and Critical/Cultural Studies,* 2(1), 1–19.

de Vlieger, M.A. (2016). Racism in European football: Going bananas? An analysis of how to establish racist behaviour by football supporters under the UEFA disciplinary regulations in light of the inflatable banana-case against Feyenoord. *International Sports Law Journal,* 15, 226–232. https://doi.org/10.1007/s40318-015-0078-4.

Dodd, M.D., & Supa, D.W. (2014). Conceptualizing and measuring "corporate social advocacy" communication: Examining the impact on corporate financial performance. *Public Relations Journal,* 8(3), 1–23. www.prsa.org/publications-and-news/Vol8/No3.

Dogliani, P. (2000). Sport and fascism. *Journal of Modern Italian Studies,* 5(3), 326–348. https://doi.org/10.1080/1354571X.2000.9728258

Freelon, D., McIlwain, C., & Clark, M. (2018). Quantifying the power and consequences of social media protest. *New Media & Society,* 20(3), 990–1011. https://doi.org/10.1177/1461444816676646

Goffman, E. (1974). Frame analysis: An essay on the organization of experience. Cambridge, MA: Harvard University Press.

Gordon, E., & Mihailidis, P. (2016). *Civic media: Technology, design, and practice.* Cambridge, MA: MIT Press

Griffin, N. (2010, June 7). How soccer defeated apartheid. *Foreign Policy.* https://foreignpolicy.com/2010/06/07/how-soccer-defeated-apartheid/

Guardian Sport. (2019, September 4). Inter fans tell Romelu Lukaku monkey chants in Italy are not racist. *The Guardian.* www.theguardian.com/football/2019/sep/04/inter-fans-tell-romelu-lukaku-monkey-chants-in-italy-are-not-racist

Guschwan, M. (2016). Fan politics: Dissent and control at the stadium. *Soccer & Society,* 17(3), 388–402. https://doi.org/10.1080/14660970.2015.1082763.

Hargreaves, J. (1985). The body, sport and power relations. *The Sociological Review,* 33(1), 139–159. https://doi.org/10.1111/j.1467-954X.1985.tb03304.x

Hopwood, M., Kitchin, P., & Skinner, J. (2010). *Sport public relations and communication.* London: Routledge.

Jarvie, G. (2000). Sport, racism and ethnicity. In J. Coakley & E. Dunning (Eds.), *Handbook or sport studies* (pp. 334–343). London: Sage.

Jenkins, H., Shresthova, S., Gamber-Thompson, L., Kligler-Vilenchik, N., & Zimmerman, A. M. (2016). *By any media necessary: The new youth activism.* New York: New York University Press.

Kassimeris, C. (2012). Franco, the popular game and ethnocentric conduct in modern Spanish football. *Soccer & Society, 13*(4), 555–569. https://doi.org/10.1080/1466097 0.2012.677228.

Kassing, J.W. (2020). Messi hanging laundry at the Bernabéu: The production and consumption of internet sports memes as trash talk. *Discourse, Context & Media.* https://doi.org/10.1016/j.dcm.2019.100320.

Kassing, J.W., & Nyaupane, P. (2019)."I just couldn't believe I was there": An exploration of soccer pilgrimage. *International Journal of Sport Communication, 12*(2), 167–184. https://doi.org/10.1123/ijsc.2018-0165.

Llopis-Goig, R. (2013). Racism, xenophobia and intolerance in Spanish football: Evolution and responses from the government and the civil society. *Soccer & Society, 14*(2), 262–276. https://doi.org/10.1080/14660970.2013.776461

Manfred, T. (2014, April 29). Monkeys and bananas campaign fruit of Neymar PR firm. *Yahoo News.* https://sg.news.yahoo.com/monkeys-bananas-campaign-fruit-neymar-pr-firm-171318496 – sow.html

Neymar Jr. [@neymarjr]. (2014, April 27). #somostodosmacacos #weareallmonkeys #somostodosmonos #totssommonos [Instagram photo]. www.instagram.com/p/nT115JRtuI/?hl=en.

Outley, C., Bowen, S., & Pinckney, H. (2021). Laughing while black: Resistance, coping and the use of humor as a pandemic pastime among blacks. *Leisure Sciences, 43*(1–2), 305–314. https://doi.org/10.1080/01490400.2020.1774449.

Poell, T., & van Dijck, J. (2018). Social Media and new protest movements. In J. Burgess, A. Marwick, & T. Poell (Eds.), *The SAGE handbook of social media* (pp. 546–561). London: Sage.

Ruihley, B.J., Runyan, R.C., & Lear, K.E. (2010). The use of sport celebrities in advertising: A replication and extension. *Sport Marketing Quarterly, 19*(3), 132–142.

Saeed, A., & Kilvington, D. (2011). British-Asians and racism within contemporary English football, *Soccer & Society, 12*(5), 602–612. https://doi.org/10.1080/14660970.2011.599581.

Taylor, M., & Das, S.S. (2010). Public relations in advocacy: Stem cell research organizations' use of the internet in resource mobilization. *Public Relations Journal, 4*(4), 1–22. https://prjournal.instituteforpr.org/wp-content/uploads/2011TaylorDas.pdf.

Ubha, R., & Mezzofiore, G. (2019, November 8). Balotelli suffers racist abuse as incidents continue in Serie A. *CNN.* www.cnn.com/2019/11/04/football/balotelli-racist-chants-football-serie-a-intl-spt/index.html

Wagner-Egger, P., Gygax, P., & Ribordy, F. (2012). Racism in soccer? Perception of challenges of black and white players by white referees, soccer players, and fans. *Perceptual and Motor Skills, 114*(1), 275–289. https://doi.org/10.2466/05.07.17. PMS.114.1.275-289.

Waymer, D., & Logan, N. (2020). Corporate social advocacy as engagement: Nike's social justice communication. *Public Relations Review, 27*(1), 1–9. https://doi.org/10.1016/j.pubrev.2020.102005.

Williams, A. (2020). Black memes matter: #LivingWhileBlack with Becky and Karen. *Social Media + Society.* https://doi.org/10.1177/2056305120981047.

Williams, J. (2007). Rethinking sports fandom: The case of European soccer. *Leisure Studies, 26*(2), 127–146. https://doi.org/10.1080/02614360500503414.

Yang, G. (2016). Narrative agency in hashtag activism: The case of #BlackLivesMatter. *Media and Communication, 4*(4), 13–17. https://doi.org/10.17645/mac.v4i4.692.

13

THE MILWAUKEE BUCKS

Professional Athletic Labor's Position in Racist Late-Stage Capitalism

Kevin G. Thompson

Introduction

On August 23, 2020, Jacob Blake was shot and paralyzed by police officers in Kenosha, Wisconsin. At the same time of the shooting, the Milwaukee Bucks were scheduled to play the Orlando Magic in Orlando's COVID-19 "safe" NBA bubble 1,224 miles away to start the NBA playoffs. It was the shooting of Blake, and other traumatic examples of racist police violence, which caused the Milwaukee Bucks to initiate a labor strike and stop their game from being played. The Bucks, a team that had not won a championship in nearly 50 years, but now was considered one of the best teams in the league, still stopped their game not knowing if their strike would result in a forfeit, jeopardizing their chances of winning the NBA championship.

The strike initiated a lot of commotion and solidarity among other NBA players and media figures (Hamilton, 2020), just weeks after the NBA administration and the NBA Players Association (NBPA) came to agreements about how to proceed with the season during the COVID-19 pandemic and in the wake of omnipresent police brutality against Black Americans. The strike's intersections of race, labor, class, and political resistance highlight the power of constitutive rhetoric and the need to examine the powers of Black athlete discourse in sport.

The Bucks' strike is one of several forms of Black activism portrayed in sport history (Martin, 2018). However, the Bucks' strike can be considered one of the most significant sport protests because of the strike's timeliness, attention, success of met demands, and solidarity among other sport figures. This case study addresses the question, "How does critical discourse analysis and constitutive rhetoric make the Bucks' activism effective?" There are two artifacts this essay will analyze: The Bucks' labor strike and the written statement of the Bucks' players.

DOI: 10.4324/9781003316763-15

Background

Bubble Basketball and Summer 2020

Summer 2020 marked the most significant, widespread civil rights activism in the United States since the 1960s, especially given the growing publicity and popularity of the Black Lives Matter movement. Mass demonstrations supporting the Black Lives Matter movement happened in many major cities in the United States and across the world (McFadden, 2020). After police officers killed Breonna Taylor in March 2020 and George Floyd in May 2020, conversations about police brutality and systematic, discriminatory violence dominated news headlines. Despite the newsworthy summer, though, the murders of Taylor and Floyd were just the most recent examples that year of police brutality that put the professional basketball world on notice.

Since the murder of Trayvon Martin in 2012, basketball stars like LeBron James, Kyrie Irving, Steph Curry, and many others have all spoken publicly about policing, and NBA stars have even worn attire on the court paying homage to murdered Black Americans at the hands of police (Spears, 2020). In 2013, 17 months after George Zimmerman shot and killed Martin, the #BlackLivesMatter movement began and routinely became part of contemporary civil rights discourse surrounding the need for police abolition or reform (Black Lives Matter, n.d.). In 2020, congressional legislation was introduced to reform police practices as many protestors called to defund the police. Thousands of protestors in the United States were jailed in the summer of 2020, escalating tensions among government, police, and protestors. To add to America's growing powder keg of tension, COVID-19 continued to ravage the country, killing over 150,000 people by summer's end (Sullivan, 2020). The struggle to keep communities of color safe in the United States reached a tipping point, alerting many in the NBA to act after abruptly stopping play in March.

The NBA resumed play in its "bubble" after the COVID-19 pandemic on July 22nd, the first NBA-sanctioned play since March 11th. The "NBA bubble" was the designated isolation zone at Walt Disney World in Orlando, Florida, where NBA officials resumed league play (Mannix, 2020). Twenty-two of the league's 30 teams played in the bubble, and only key team personnel were originally allowed entry. The isolated nature of the bubble was intended to contain the spread of COVID-19 so that players, coaches, and Disney workers were at less risk of exposure. Those who left the bubble campus or interacted with individuals outside of the bubble, including family, food delivery servers, and anyone else not approved by NBA administration, were subject to fines, suspensions, and even expulsion from the bubble (Baer, 2020). The NBA even instituted an anonymous tip phone line so players could tell league administrators who was not abiding by bubble codes of conduct (Baer, 2020). As NBA administration set guidelines for return to play, league personnel questioned whether they should have a season at all. Some of the most fundamental laborers in the NBA disagreed with some league administration rules, while some players debated whether resuming play would distract from ongoing protests affecting the players' communities.

After the Blake shooting, the NBPA and players competing in the "NBA Bubble" in Orlando met to discuss the future of the NBA playoffs (Li et al., 2020). Players competing in the playoffs debated if playing would be seen as disrespectful or a distraction to the Black Lives Matter movement, and some players reportedly left the meeting frustrated and in emotional distress. Kyrie Irving, the NBPA's vice president and one of the league's most outspoken players, publicly called for players to develop their own league to functionally rid the NBA of wealthy White ownership. Irving's remarks are the first time in modern NBA history that a player directly advocated for a boycott of the league in favor of a player-run league. CBS Sport Analyst Sam Quinn (2020) said:

> The NBA is unique among sports in the power individual players have. While many sports owe their success to long term loyalty from fans to teams, interest in basketball is largely owed to a small collection of individual superstars. The idea behind players starting their own league, presumably, would be separating the talent and potential wealth generation of those superstars, who are largely African American, from the institutions that typically profit off that talent, which would specifically be the mostly White team owners.
>
> *(para. 2)*

Irving's call for a new, player-run league initiated several contentious, behind-closed-door-meetings among NBPA personnel. Ultimately, the meetings resulted in teams democratically voting in favor of continuing play.

The players returned to the court under the NBPA's and NBA's agreement that messaging of an NBA return had to be centered around issues of social justice. Every televised basketball court was painted with "Black Lives Matter" at each end, and players were given the option to substitute their names on their jerseys with social justice messages like "Say Her Name" and "Freedom" (Jones & Danner, 2020). NBA owners also agreed to turn every NBA arena in the United States into a COVID-safe voting area to encourage voter turnout. Additionally, commercials during NBA game breaks regularly showed major NBA superstars like LeBron James, Jamal Murray, and Giannis Antetokounmpo discussing how police brutality and voting impact communities of color.

After a series of playoff-seeding games, the NBA playoffs continued until August 26th when police officers shot Jacob Blake, a Black resident, seven times, in Kenosha, Wisconsin. Blake survived the shooting but was left paralyzed and unable to walk (McLaughlin, 2020). News of the shooting broke just hours before the tip off between the Milwaukee Bucks and Orlando Magic's playoff game, and as game time approached, it was announced that the game was postponed indefinitely (Khan, 2020). Other NBA teams also postponed their games in solidarity with the Bucks' strike, and many other professional sport leagues including the WNBA and MLB postponed games as well. With the sport world on pause, basketball fans stood by waiting to hear why playoff basketball had come to an abrupt halt. The Bucks' players issued a statement clarifying the reason for their strike. The following is the transcript of the Bucks' statement:

> As you can see, we all thank you guys for taking part of your time and stay here with us. We're sorry that it took a little bit more time, but we thought it would be best for us as a team to brainstorm a little bit, educate ourselves and not rushing to having raw emotion, giving you guys things like that. On the behalf of ourselves and our team, we were going to place a statement as a team today and go back and continue to educate ourselves and get better awareness of what's going on. And then, we [are] going to speak to you guys later. The past four months have shed a light on the ongoing racial injustice facing our African American community. Citizens around the country have used their voices and platforms to speak out against these wrongdoings. Over the last few days in our home state of Wisconsin, we've seen the horrendous video of Jacob Blake being shot in the back seven times by a police officer in Kenosha and the additional shooting of protestors. Despite the overwhelming plea for change, there has been no action, so our focus today cannot be on basketball. When we take the court and represent Milwaukee and Wisconsin, we are expected to play at a high level, give maximum effort and hold each other accountable. We hold ourselves to that standard and in this moment, we are demanding the same from lawmakers and law enforcement. We're calling for justice for Jacob Blake and demand the officers be held accountable. For this to occur, it is imperative for the Wisconsin state legislature to reconvene after months of inaction and take up meaningful measures to address issues of police accountability, brutality, and criminal justice reform. We encourage all citizens to educate themselves, take peaceful and responsible action, and remember to vote on November 3rd on behalf of the Milwaukee Bucks.
>
> *(Helin, 2020, para 4–7)*

The 320-word statement, read by Milwaukee Bucks players Sterling Brown and George Hill, with their teammates behind them, spoke about the painful summer endured by Black Americans, the need for police accountability, and the need to focus on "change" instead of basketball. The statement, which only lasted about 2 minutes, was spoken about by sport television analysts for weeks (Khan, 2020). The message was clear: Black players are tired of being a center of consumable, profitable entertainment, while other Black people are being shot and killed by police.

Critical Discourse Analysis and Constitutive Rhetoric

The Bucks' strike and statement highlight two communication principles to explore. Critical discourse analysis (CDA) and constitutive rhetorical analysis can unveil dominant ideologies from the Bucks' strike and written statement. While rhetorical analysis can uncover the motives or persuasive nature of messages, it is difficult, if not impossible, to separate the Bucks' strike and written statement from the Bucks' Blackness and the discourse of the civil rights movement in which the players were actively participating.

Critical discourse analysis (CDA) commits to exposing power inequities through language by critically describing, interpreting, and explaining the ways in which discourses construct, maintain, or legitimize those inequities (Mullet, 2018). Fairclough's (1995) model for CDA requires three things that are objects of analysis (like verbal or visual transcripts), the means of which the artifact is produced by people (like listening, reading, speaking, or viewing), and the socio-historical conditions of the artifact(s).

Constitutive rhetoric posits that language can create collective identity for an audience and that actions ought to be taken to reinforce beliefs of that identity (White, 1985). Developed by Charland (1987), constitutive rhetoric relies heavily on Kenneth Burke's concept of identification that must happen for persuasion to occur. Identification, by definition, is the spontaneous or unconscious process of consubstantiating or "identifying" with another person –similarities in personality, ethics, message, identity, etc. to make a message seem more receptive (Burke, 1969). Similarly, constitutive rhetoric accounts for identities which "form beyond the realm of rational or even free choice, beyond the realm of persuasion" (Charland, 1987, p. 134).

To make constitutive rhetoric possible, three stages, or ideological effects, must be analyzed in an artifact. First, according to Charland (1987), constitutive rhetoric must constitute a collective subject or use language to identify a specific group of people. Second, constitutive rhetoric must posit a transhistorical subject, where an identity has existed across time even if those people did not see themselves as part of the collective identity. Third is the illusion of freedom, or the constrained "ask" or follow-through of a speech where subjects believe they are free to take an action but are actually limited to the identities that have been constituted to them.

CDA and constitutive rhetorical analysis are useful to analyze the Bucks' strike and statement because each method's limitations are addressed by the other, which is needed to posit Blackness as intelligible. One of the key limitations of CDA is the emphasis that meaning comes "*into* rather than *out of* texts" (Haig, 2004, p. 144). In other words, CDA is concerned with how texts or artifacts are informed, shaped, or otherwise impacted by hegemonic systems or structures outside of the artifact. While CDA does often engage in textual analysis, it is more concerned with the hegemonic structures in and around an analyzable artifact rather than how speeches function for a speaker, audience, or for the speech itself like rhetoricians typically analyze. On the other hand, rhetorical criticism is frequently concerned with the textual analysis of an artifact without much consideration to the hegemonic systems or histories surrounding the text (Wilson, 2015). What constitutive rhetorical criticism does offer as a method is an examination into the personability of a speaker or audience and calls for an understanding that texts can persuasively alter actions by humanizing speakers and instilling shared values or beliefs into an audience.

Thus, while the action of a labor strike would be very hard to rhetorically analyze because the action of a strike is not a text, it is impossible to divorce the act of striking from the Bucks' statement. The combination of both methods can convey the impact of overarching hegemonic structures that inform the Bucks' strike while also explaining how the Bucks' Blackness is made intelligible through their speech. The Bucks' speech explains the act of striking, while the speech itself is devoid of larger hegemonic contexts with a closed text rhetorical criticism methodology. Police brutality, a summer of civil rights protests, and fears of basketball players being an entertaining distraction to Black Lives Matter protests all inform the strike, and so does the Bucks' written statement. CDA and constitutive rhetorical analysis complement each other in ways so that each method by itself may not comprehensively address the effectiveness or ineffectiveness of the strike.

The Case

The Bucks' Strike and CDA

Using CDA, the Bucks' strike reveals two themes: Black antagonism and class struggle. The act of striking itself, by a predominantly Black team in a predominantly Black sport surrounded by predominantly Black culture and icons, is an antagonism against the hegemonic assumption that Black athletic labor is simply or exclusively in service of capitalist entertainment industries. The strike serves as an act of rejection, a rejection that entertaining labor is less important than the cultural and psychological anguish Black people endure from state-sanctioned police violence.

Furthermore, the Bucks' strike ruptures hegemonic assumptions of Black athletes as entertainers when the NBA is one of the few sources of American live sport entertainment during a deadly pandemic.

The significance of playing in a bubble when few other sports were being televised is twofold. First, sport media and social media hyped the return of basketball despite the dramatic health risks associated with players returning to play because of COVID-19 (Andrews, 2020). Messaging that the NBA's return was imminent after abruptly stopping in March 2020 dominated ESPN headlines for months. Second, fans and sport media calling for basketball's return emphasized the accepted disposability of predominantly Black athletic labor. In other words, one could argue that calling for basketball's return emphasized how little people cared about the NBA's Black laborers and how much they cared about being entertained by that Black labor. The combination of these two issues relays the importance and significance of the Bucks' strike. Since so many people were calling for a return of basketball amid a pandemic, the Bucks stopping play from happening again to demand justice for Blake challenges the assumed control fans, owners, and media have over athletes. Just as NBA consumers felt power was restored to them, the Bucks rescinded that power and asserted their own as Black laborers into a call for action.

Put differently, the Bucks' strike emphasizes Blackness to be more important than their labor. Though the actions of a strike are typically rooted in class struggle, this strike signified a racialized labor struggle. The Bucks performed the strike not because of poor labor conditions, wage disputes, or collective bargaining disagreements. The strike was a direct response to the police shooting of Blake and the fear their athletic labor would distract from a more important event affecting their own communities (Helin, 2020). A strike of this nature highlights the interwoven nature of race and class in capitalism today.

The Bucks' Written Statement and Constitutive Rhetoric

Charland's template of constitutive rhetorical analysis can also apply to the Bucks' written statement. Not only does the Bucks' statement identify a specific group of people and a transhistorical subject – Black people, and the pain they have endured for centuries and especially during summer 2020 – but it also asks for changes in policing. Specifically, the Bucks ask to meet with the Wisconsin governor and attorney general to discuss what can be done to address Blake's shooting and police violence against Black people. To make these steps understandable to the audience, speakers must consubstantiate with an audience according to Charland (1987), and the Bucks do that in the speech by claiming they "represent Milwaukee and Wisconsin", "our African American community," and stand in solidarity with those taking "meaningful measures to address issues of police accountability, brutality, and criminal justice reform" (Helin, 2020, para. 4–7).

Is the constitutive rhetoric effective? One could argue that the recognition and acceptance of the Bucks' terms – demanding an investigation into Blake's shooting and instituting more police reform in Wisconsin – show that the strike was effective and that the players were successful in getting their demands met. In fact, the Wisconsin governor and attorney general called for an investigation into Blake's shooting the same day as the Bucks' statement and publicly called for more police accountability legislation the following day (Maurer, 2020). Not only are the players using their power and privilege as wealthy, well connected-and-known elites to demand change, but they are positing their Blackness as their most important and recognizable asset as well. By making their voices heard and having their demands met under the conditions they sanctioned, the players show the rhetorical possibilities of constitutive speech.

On the other hand, police violence continues to ravage Black communities in the United States. And, while the players' specific demands were met, NBA play quickly resumed, and the sport itself was heavily criticized for engaging in "communicative capitalism," or the notion that anti-racist messages got warped for the profit of big business without systematically challenging racism (Khan, 2016). The NBA's and NBPA's quick agreement to resume play also highlights the prevailing nature of exploitative capitalism, as to convey "the show must go on" even when NBA players are concerned that their labor could be considered distracting to the cause of the Black Lives Matter protests happening across the globe. While these external forces are not necessarily direct reasons why the Bucks' speech was constitutively effective or ineffective, it does highlight the limitations of constitutive rhetoric in racist, late-stage capitalism.

You Make the Call

Overall, it seems the Bucks' strike and statement were successful in opening investigations from government and justice departments in Wisconsin. While the NBA resumed play within 24 hours, the players' actions and rhetorical choices undoubtedly challenged, or at the very least spotlighted, normative assumptions of Black athletic labor being constantly in service of capitalist entertainment industries. Additionally, the strike signaled to people inside and outside the NBA that many players self-identified as Black people first and foremost and less as athletes, entertainers, or more generally laborers.

However, by October 2021, Officer Rusten Sheskey, the White Kenosha Police Department officer who shot Blake, was not charged after "video showed Blake was armed with a knife" (Richmond, 2021). One can argue that the lack of justice for Blake means that the strike failed. At the very least, the quick return to play after the strike ended highlights how capitalism and the desire for profit by big businesses, like the NBA, challenge the very nature of rhetorical possibilities, especially considering American capitalism's long history of controlling Black labor.

It is important to consider whether the Bucks' strike and statement were more effective rhetorically for the NBA's social justice initiatives, which primarily consisted of profit-driven messaging, the protestors and Blake and his family, or the players themselves. While it is hard to say Blake, his family, and protestors benefited at all due to the fact that many forms of media vilified these parties and justice ultimately was not served for them, having high-profile athletes perform a once-in-a-generation strike in support is undeniably noteworthy and important. It is worth considering if additional tactics could have been implemented by the players to rhetorically change the shape of their strike, or if it is a moot point.

Discussion Questions

1. Discuss any new developments in the ongoing issue of athlete labor activism to contextualize the changing tenor of athlete-led strikes. Since there have been other examples of athletes withholding labor for social causes in recent years, how does the Bucks' strike compare to other more contemporary forms of athlete strikes?
2. Take a position on the success or failure of the Bucks' strike. What are the parameters by which you determined the success or failure of the strike?
3. The Bucks stressed that they could not focus on playing because of the anguish their Black and Wisconsin communities were facing. Are there other forms of identification or constitutive rhetoric the players should have used?
4. While some heralded the Bucks for striking and the athletes using their wealth and notoriety in solidarity of Blake and protestors, others criticized the strike because of how quickly it ended and it being in service of the profit-driven social justice messaging the NBA implemented in the Orlando NBA "bubble." How do you feel about the strike? Do you agree or disagree with the Bucks' choice to strike? Have any other teams attempted similar actions as the Bucks lately? If so, what was the outcome? If not, why do you suppose?
5. While the Bucks players later clarified their action was indeed a strike, there have been disagreements about what to call the Bucks' strike. Some media figures and other NBA players have referred to the strike as a "boycott," while others have called it a "walkout", "postponement," or more generally a "protest." What are the rhetorical implications for calling the strike something different? Does the discourse of striking differ from the discourse of other names used to identify the Bucks' strike like boycott, walkout, postponement, or protest?

References

Andrews, M. (2020). How close are we to live sports? Where the world's biggest leagues stand right now. *ESPN*. www.espn.com/nba/story/_/id/29200286/how-close-nfl-ncaa-nba-nhl-mlb-restarts-bundesliga-ufc-coronavirus-delays

Baer, J. (2020). Rocket's Danuel House exits bubble after NBA determines he had unauthorized guest in hotel room." *Yahoo! Sports*. www.yahoo.com/video/rockets danuel-house-exits-bubble-nba-unauthorized-guest-hotel-room-215432202.html#:~:text=Houston%20Rockets%20forward%20Danuel%20House,the%20NBA%20announced%20on%20Friday

Black Lives Matter. (n.d.). "HerStory." *Black Lives Matter Official Website*. https://blacklivesmatter.com/herstory/

Burke, K. (1969). *A rhetoric of motives*. Berkeley, CA and Los Angeles, CA: University of California Press.

Charland, M. (1987). Constitutive rhetoric: The case of the people Québécois. *Quarterly Journal of Speech, 73*(2), 133–150. https://doi.org/10.1080/00335638709383799

Fairclough, N. (1995). *Critical discourse analysis.* London: Longman Press.

Haig, E. (2004). Some observations on the critique of critical discourse analysis. *Personal Essays on Sociology,* 129–249.

Hamilton, J. (2020). The NBA strike will reverberate for years to come. *Slate.* https://slate.com/culture/2020/08/nba-strike-milwaukee-bucks-significance-jacob-blake.html

Helin, K. (2020). Milwaukee Bucks players make statement on boycott. *NBC Sports.* https://nba.nbcsports.com/2020/08/26/milwaukee-bucks-players-make-statement-on-boycott/

Jones, S., & Danner, C. (2020). NBA playoffs will resume, league and players announce new social justice initiatives. *New York Magazine.* https://nymag.com/intelligencer/2020/08/nba-teams-strike-for-black-lives.html

Khan, A. (2016). A rant good for business: Communicative capitalism and the capture of anti-racist resistance. *Popular Communication, 14*(1), 39–48. https://doi.org/10.1080/15405702.2015.1084629

Khan, A. (2020). Let's call athletes 'workers' and let's call these NBA protests what they are –strikes. *The Conversation.* https://theconversation.com/lets-call-athletes-workers-and-lets-call-these-nba-protests-what-they-were-strikes-145234

Li, D.K., Bhojwani, J., & Garcia-Hodges, A. (2020). NBA to restart playoffs Saturday, ending player walkout after Jacob Blake shooting. *NBC News.* www.nbcnews.com/news/us-news/nba-restart-playoffs-saturday-ending-player-walkout-after-jacob-blake-n1238699

Mannix, C. (2020). Free from quarantine: The NBA bubble is a unique experience. *Sports Illustrated.* www.si.com/nba/2020/07/21/nba-bubble-unique-experience-disney

Martin, L.L., (2018). The politics of sports and protest: Colin Kaepernick and the practice of leadership. *American Studies Journal, 64*(6). https://doi.org/10.18422/64-06

Maurer, M. (2020). The Bucks called, will the legislature answer? *SB Nation.* www.brewhoop.com/2020/8/29/21406810/on-wisconsin-the-milwaukee-bucks-called-how-will-the-assembly-answer-nba-strike-blm-police-reform

McFadden, S (2020). Black lives matter just entered its next phase. *The Atlantic.* www.theatlantic.com/culture/archive/2020/09/black-lives-matter-just-entered-its-next-phase/615952/

McLaughlin, E. (2020). Jacob Blake is out of the hospital, but how long he'll be in rehab remains a question. *CNN.* www.cnn.com/2020/10/07/us/jacob-blake-leaves-hospital/index.html

Mullet, D. (2018). A general critical discourse analysis framework for educational research. *Journal of Advanced Academics, 29*(2), 116–142. https://doi.org/10.1177/1932202X18758260

Quinn, S. (2020). Kyrie Irving proposed players starting their own league in call urging boycott of NBA season. *CBS Sports.* www.cbssports.com/nba/news/kyrie-irving-proposed-players-starting-their-own-league-in-call-urging-boycott-of-nba-season-per/

Richmond, T. (2021). Feds won't seek charges against cop in Jacob Blake shooting. *AP News.* https://apnews.com/article/us-news-us-department-of-justice-rusten-sheskey-jacob-blake-kenosha-4f8493dd0776ef6046e052a538cd1460?utm_medium=AP&utm_source=Twitter&utm_campaign=SocialFlow

Spears, M. (2020). Black lives matter, people: How the NBA's social justice efforts dominated the season. *The Undefeated.* https://andscape.com/features/how-the-nba-social-justice-efforts-dominated-the-season/

Sullivan, P. (2020). US records deadliest COVID-19 day of summer with over 1,500 deaths. *The Hill.* https://thehill.com/policy/healthcare/511839-us-records-deadliest-covid-19-day-of-summer-with-over-1500-deaths

White, J.B. (1985). Law as rhetoric, rhetoric as law: The arts of cultural and communal life. *The University of Chicago Law Review, 52*(3), 684–702.

Wilson, K. (2015). What do we mean by rhetorical criticism? Theories and practices of textual analysis: A seminar blog for college of arts and sciences. https://sites.psu.edu/textualanalysis/2015/10/09/what-do-we-mean-by-rhetorical-criticism/

PART III

Gender Equity, Identity, and Sexual Misconduct

14

CONQUERING A BOY'S CLUB USING AN ISSUES MANAGEMENT APPROACH

How Women's Soccer May Pioneer a Path to Pay Equity

Terry L. Rentner and David P. Burns

Introduction

Never was the support greater for women in sports than the 2019 FIFA Women's World Cup where tickets for the opening match, semi-finals, and finals sold out in just 48 hours, and about 1 billion people watched the matches on television (Wagtendonk, 2019). The U.S. Women's National Soccer Team (USWNT) won back-to-back championships, and their 2019 team jersey became the best-selling soccer jersey, male or female, ever sold on Nike.com in one season (Bachman, 2019). This tremendous accomplishment brought the tally to four championship titles – the most by any nation – but did little to close the pay equity gap in soccer. Instead, it led to 28 female players on the national team suing the U.S. Soccer Federation – their governing body and their employer – for gender discrimination. What followed was a 6 year odyssey of legal wins and losses for the women of that 2019 U.S. national soccer team, one seemingly game-ending legal loss at the hands of a federal district court judge, but ultimately leading to those players winning their back pay and, maybe most importantly, a historic agreement by U.S. Soccer for gender equity for all time (Das, 2022c).

Using a critical inquiry approach, this case study examines the gender pay gap in professional sports using the 2019 Women's World Cup (the 2020 and 2021 tournament did not take place due to COIVD-19) as the lens to investigate what impact, if any, their win and their lawsuit may have on pay equity in all sports. Some economists argue that the women's and men's sports' pay structures are too dissimilar to compare. This case study addresses this issue along with tackling other hackneyed arguments made in the past regarding market forces dictating sports coverage and exposing a noticeable silence of disparity that exists concerning women's sports.

DOI: 10.4324/9781003316763-17

Issues management, a tool in the strategic communication toolbox, serves as the foundation for how governing sport organizations address gender pay issues to their stakeholders. An understanding of issues management helps communicators strategically plan for how the pay gap may affect their organization's credibility and reputation among stakeholders and impact their bottom line dollar. Contextualizing the inequalities in gender pay is paramount to understanding how to manage the problem.

Background

The enactment of Title IX in 1972, a law prohibiting discrimination based on sex at higher education institutions, resulted in a 900% increase in women's participation in sports (Women's Sports Foundation, 2012). Although this appears to be significant progress, a closer look 50 years later indicates that equal *participation* in sports did not result in equal *compensation*.

A look at the 2021 *Forbes* list for the highest-paid athletes shows just how male-dominated the sports world is when it comes to pay. The list accounts for salaries, prize money, bonuses, endorsements, and appearance fees between May 1, 2020 and May 1, 2021. Tennis player Naomi Osaka is the first female to appear on the list at number 12, with Serena Williams at number 28, the only other female ranked among the 45 top-earning athletes (Knight & Birnbaum, n.d.).

Professional tennis is one sport where the pay gap is among the narrowest, thanks to pioneers like Billie Jean King who in the early 1970s demanded equal pay to play. Thus, the U.S. Open was the first tournament to offer equal prize money in male and female divisions in 1973 and still pays equally in all Grand Slam events. Not surprisingly then, in 2018, 9 of the 10 highest paid female athletes were tennis players, tennis being the sport where gender pay is most equitable (Abrams, 2019).

With the exception of tennis, even when women are at the top of their sport, especially traditionally male-dominated sports, their salaries and endorsements are significantly lower. The news is just as bleak, if not worse, for women who play team sports. Soccer player Carli Lloyd is the highest paid women's soccer player in 2022 earning $518,000, with her endorsements bringing her earnings to $3.3 million (Das, 2022a). Her male counterpart, Lionel Messi, has earned $97 million in salary and bonuses in 2022 and another $33 million in endorsements (Das, 2022b). Just as disparaging, FIFA has increased the 2022 men's World Cup purse to $440 million and proposes doubling the women's prize money to a mere $60 million for the 2023 World Cup (Associated Press, 2021, para. 12).

In the Women's National Basketball Association (WNBA) 2020 Collective Bargaining Agreement (CBA), the 2022 base salary is set at $60,471(202) compared with just over $925,000 in the National Basketball League (NBA) despite modest victories such as increases in minimum prize money for special competitions, better travel arrangements, motherhood/family planning, and a 50–50 revenue sharing (Gough, 2022).

Prior to the U.S. Soccer settlement, women's professional hockey also made significant strides on the team sport salary front that could serve as models for emulation. In spring 2017, the U.S. women's hockey team, a dominant force within its sport, successfully threatened a walkout (Rentner & Burns, 2019) and won a wage dispute against its employer, U.S. Hockey (Allen & Perez, 2017). Similarly, in May 2019, hundreds of professional female hockey players promised to sit out the 2019–2020 hockey season over their labor dispute. It was only thanks to a few sponsors and financial support from tennis legend Billie Jean King and the National Women's Hockey League that salaries increased and players received a 50–50 split of league-wide sponsorship revenue (Bachman, 2019).

Theoretical Approaches to Issues Management

While issues management is not itself a theory, scholars often offer theoretical approaches, informed by research and practice that provide a framework through which organizations manage issues (see Jacques, 2009; Taylor et al., 2003). The framework was originally developed to focus on an organization's participation in the public policy realm but has evolved to include non-governmental organizations and community groups (Kitchin & Purcell, 2017). Bridges (2006) offers six theories associated with issues management. They are systems theory, social exchange theory, rhetorical analysis, issues life-cycle theory, legitimacy gap theory, and stakeholder theory. Collectively, these theories serve as the foundation for understanding and applying issues management concepts.

In the sports management field, in particular, Friedman et al., (2004) offer stakeholder theory as a framework with both descriptive and prescriptive values for sport public relations practitioners and academics. Its basic tenets are concepts borrowed from institutional theory and organizational effectiveness and posit that an organization must consider the interests of "any group or individual who can affect or is affected by the achievement of an organization's purpose" (Freeman, 1984, p. 53).

In this case study, issues management is the foundation for exploring gender pay disparities in sports, particularly how sport organizations address the gender pay equity gap and whether these disparities contribute to faulty market forces theories and perpetuate the silence of disparity in discussing the gender inequity in women's sports.

The Case

As mentioned earlier, the pay gap between professional male and female athletes is staggering. In soccer, women earned a minimum of $6,842 in 2015 compared to the men who earned at least $50,000 (Harwell, 2015). This was the year the U.S. women's team won its second World Cup championship, with the final match becoming what was then the most-watched soccer game in American TV history with 25.4 million American viewers on ESPN (Block, 2015). To put this viewership number in perspective, the NBA finals averaged 19.9 million viewers that year (Block, 2015). These blockbuster numbers, however, were at odds with what was going on behind the scenes. For one, the Women's World Cup lacked the marketing, mega-deals, and corporate support as were seen in men's soccer (Harwell, 2015). Nike began selling female players' soccer jerseys that year, but only in men's sizes, whereas male players' soccer jerseys have been sold in women's sizes for years. On the field, the women played on artificial turf while the men played on grass. Artificial turf surfaces have a higher incidence of injuries than grass, according to a 2013 study by a Stanford University researcher (Mishra, 2013). Furthermore, the women's training conditions were considered inferior to their male counterparts. They shared accommodations, not so their male colleagues. They flew commercial while the men enjoy charter flights (Daniels, 2019). In November 2021, the women's team and U.S. Soccer settled the women's unequal working conditions claim (Das, 2022), but the pay issue remained unresolved.

The public outcry for pay equity simmered for years but reached a fevered pitch immediately after the U.S. Women's National Soccer Team (USWNT) won the FIFA Women's World Cup for the fourth time in 2019. FIFA President Gianni Infantio took to the field to present the championship medals and was greeted to the crowd chanting, "Equal Pay."

The women's soccer team's fight for equal pay began long before the chants. It began with a 2016 complaint to the U.S. Equal Employment Opportunity Commission. This allowed the team to then sue the U.S. Soccer Federation (USSF) which they did on March 28, 2019, for $66 million in damages under the Equal Pay Act, months before their world championship victory. In the lawsuit, the 28 team members claimed they were considerably underpaid compared to their male counterparts stating that if female players played 20 non-tournament games and won all matches, the females would be paid a maximum of $99,000 or $4,950 per game as opposed to the male players who would pocket about $263,320 or $13,166 per game (Piacenza, 2019).

What makes this pay gap even more perplexing is the way it was distributed. FIFA's prize money for the men's 2018 World Cup was $400 million which it distributed among its male players; the organization allotted only $30 million for the women's World Cup players, despite the women turning a $6.6 million profit versus the men making less than $2 million in profits. In addition, whereas the women won the World Cup that year, the men did not even qualify. Furthermore, the USSF pocketed over $5 million in profits from the women's team in 2019, while they lost $1 million from the men's team (Daniels, 2019). In 2019, when the U.S. women's team made it to the quarter-finals, they earned $90,000 in bonuses, yet if the U.S. men's team had reached the quarter-finals (they did not), they would have earned six times that amount (Murray & Morris, 2019).

Although the prize money of $30 million for the 2019 women's World Cup was twice of what it was in 2015, it is only 7.5% of the $400 million in prize money for the 2018 men's World Cup (Locker, 2019). Even more alarming is that the total prize money for the 2022 men's World Cup is expected to be $440 million, which will take women until the year 2039 to achieve pay equity (Locker, 2019).

You Make the Call

The gender pay gap in soccer, and in professional sports in general, exists partly as a management issue by the professional teams, their governing bodies, and media organizations. This became clear when the USSF and FIFA argued that men's soccer was more popular and produced more revenue than women's soccer (Daniels, 2019). FIFA defended its stance by pointing to the men's tourney's history and earning power arguing that the World Cup brought in $4.5 billion in direct revenue and had been played 20 times, compared to the seven Women's World Cups (Harwell, 2015).

Other factors include cultural influences and arguments about the physicality of males and females, rather than performance. Detractors argue male and female soccer players play entirely different games, yet both compete under the same rules, same conditions, same length of match, and same size of field. And, as Daniels points out, the more successful women "work just as hard, and sometimes harder (more games, more training, more time traveling and in media sessions) than the men, at the exact same job" (2019, para. 8) yet under poorer conditions, as described earlier.

The legal action against USSF has even sparked lawmakers to become involved. For example, during the 2019 World Cup celebratory parade, the then New York Governor Andrew Cuomo signed equal pay legislation. This was followed by a bill introduced by U.S. Senator Joe Manchin to block federal funding for the 2026 men's World Cup unless the women received equal pay (Moritz-Rabson, 2019).

In 2020, the players' pay claim was thrown out of court by the U.S. District Court of California ruling that the women had no claim because their total compensation was higher than men (Tennery, 2021), but the judge let their discrimination claim go forward. In December 2021, the U.S. women's soccer team filed their final brief to overturn the pay dismissal stating that oral compensation is not the standard under Title VII of the Civil Rights Act and the Equal Pay Act which compares "rates of pay, not total compensation" (Tennery, 2021, para.5).

In February 2022, U.S. Soccer permanently settled the matter by quietly admitting its own gender pay disparity – by agreeing to pay out $24 million to several dozen current and former women's national team players in mostly back pay compensation. Then, in May 2022, U.S. Soccer made good on its pledge to negotiate a unified collective bargaining agreement (CBA). The historic agreement equalizes on-field base and performance pay and World Cup prize money and guarantees commercial revenue sharing. In addition, the unified CBA also provides to both men's and women's teams equal access to childcare, retirement packages, identical travel and hotel accommodations, and promising the same practice and game facilities (U.S. Soccer, 2022). A select group of women players will be offered health insurance, parental leave, and short-term disability benefits (U.S. Soccer, 2022). U.S. Soccer President Cindy Parlow Cone said the long-term impact of the agreement is historic. "These agreements have changed the game forever here in the United States and have the potential to change the game around the world," (U.S. Soccer, 2022, para.5) and will "funnel millions of dollars to a new generation of women's national team players" (Das, 2022, para. 4.) The new settlement, however, requires the men's national team players to give up millions of dollars of its previously lopsided FIFA moneys to the women to level the salary playing field (Das, 2022, para. 13).

The following sections critically analyze how sports organizations, their governing bodies, and the media managed – or mismanaged – the pay disparity issue in terms of anticipating and responding to emerging trends and changes in the sociopolitical environment – key components of effective issues management.

Market Forces Myth

The "Market Forces" concept in regard to wage inequity in women's sports is a simple supply and demand equation: Pay comes with increased revenue. Interestingly, female athletes used to rank more prominently among top-earning athletes, but the last 25 years has seen an explosion of TV deals for live sports content, prompting higher salaries in men's sports (Abrams, 2019). This, coupled with the argument that television networks do not carry women's sports programming because there is a proven lack of demand for women's sports, contributes to this market forces myth. A logical conclusion, therefore, is that it would be a horrible business decision to spend money programming *women's* sports that no one watches. Advocates for women's sports say that the complaint centers more on the *women's* part of the equation than the sports part. To back up that argument, they have the viewer-averse 2022 Winter Olympics and the "*Thursday Night Football* folly."

NBC paid $7.75 billion for the rights to exclusively air the 2022 Winter Olympics in the United States. Traditionally, the rights to broadcast the Olympics have proven fruitful. However, in 2022, that proven profitability became less certain. Although NBC is mum on whether it made money, the statistics are glum. Prime-time viewership was down by 42% from the 2018 Winter Olympics in South Korea and that includes over-the-air, cable, or on the streaming service Peacock (Associated Press, 2022, para. 10). Nielsen reported a 47% drop in viewership in NBC alone, and that includes a single-night 24 million viewer bump after following the Super Bowl (Associated Press, 2022, para. 10–11). Despite astronomical investment yielding poor viewership (high supply, no demand), Comcast, NBC's parent company, shows no indication of backing out of its contractual agreement to carry the Olympics through 2032, a business action that opposes the market forces concept.

The television contract for the NFL's *Thursday Night Football* program routinely loses money for the television network or networks that own the rights to air that program. Despite having no comparable sports program competitors that evening, when considering overall revenue versus total costs, the network or networks that own the rights to *Thursday Night Football* lose hundreds of millions of dollars over the course of the season by broadcasting the games (Bryan, 2016). If the same market forces rule were applied in this case, *Thursday Night Football* would never be programmed let alone garner competitive contracts worth hundreds of millions of dollars.

In regard to women's athletics the blame has often been placed on the athlete or on the sport – *why can't women's sports fill a stadium? Why can't women's sports deliver a TV audience?* However, between 2016 and 2018, the U.S. Women's Soccer Team generated about $1 million more in revenue than their male counterparts (Tulshyan, 2019). With successful women's sports like women's soccer proving it can fill stadiums and deliver a television audience, a better question might be, *why can't television executives market a blockbuster female sports product?* Thus, the Market Forces concept becomes more mythical than matter-of-fact. However, what is very evident is the willful practice of underpaying women at the expense of all others – a practiced silence of disparity.

Silence of Disparity

In a 2017 *Forbes* (2019) article, Berri estimates that the NBA pays out about half of the league's total revenue to its male players. In comparison, the WNBA shells out less, about 23% of its total revenue to its female players (Berri, 2017). These players are doing the same job, and, for their respective professional sports association, their star power is the same, yet there is a distinct, purposeful, and significant difference in the way the WNBA's management prefers to share the wealth.

In a similar fashion, until recently, the USSF willfully ignored efforts to pay its female champions an equal wage compared to their also-ran male counterparts. Since USSF holds complete discretion over how it allocates FIFA bonus money, it even recognized that the pay disparity was so vast between the prize money of its male and female teams that it was "not reasonable or fiscally sound for U.S. Soccer to make up the gap" (Das, 2020, para. 11), thus in past years it, chose to use the bonus money to fund things like youth development, as well as coach and referee programs. In regard to using some of these funds to compensate its female players more equitably, the USSF had said that "It would seriously impair our ability to support our mission and invest in these other critical development areas" (Associated Press, 2020, para. 8).

The USSF initially refused to release the details of the men's collective bargaining agreement that expired in 2018; however, the U.S. Women's Soccer Team lawsuit forced the details to be made public. In a bold move over the summer of 2019, the USSF claimed they paid the women's team more than the men's team from 2010 to 2018. Lawyers for the women's team quickly charged the USSF with creative accounting, but the USSF stood its ground. That was until the men's team also took issue with the claim. In a released statement, the U.S. National Soccer Team Players Association said:

> The women's national team players deserve equal pay and are right to pursue a legal remedy from the courts or Congress. The Federation correctly points to the different payment systems with USWNT players on contracts, but we do not believe that justifies discrediting the work they do or the real value of their profound impact on the American sports landscape.
>
> *(Peterson, 2019, para. 4).*

The men's union also took exception with the USSF's statement that the women generated less gross revenue from 2009 to 2019 and that the women's games resulted in a net loss for the federation in the tens of millions of dollars, saying those points lacked context (Peterson, 2019). The 2022 settlement will force the men's national team to literally "put their money where their mouths are" as they will need to cede some of their FIFA funds to the women's team to balance the pay ledger.

The silence of disparity may have been the loudest in the way the details of the prior collective bargaining agreements were described and framed. The men's pay structure was often described as "pay for games played" and with "performance bonuses." Both terms sound like a fair wage for work performed and a reward structure for success. In describing the women's agreement, "dog whistle" terms were used that might belie a sense of extravagance. In more than one report, the article mentions that the women's agreement covers things like child care and parental leave (Associated Press, 2020). However, in this Post-#MeToo moment, these perks are actually things both males and females expect from their employer and are promised in the new, unified CBA. Thus, in the future, it is possible that these types of descriptions will have less traction in all corporate boardrooms.

Recommended Communication Strategies

The foundations justifying pay inequities based on sex are being eroded, and the sports arena is helping in tangible ways. Just as the playing fields, courts, and arenas are used to make political points, those same venues are staging grounds for women everywhere to visualize a world of financial parity.

Female Athletes as Advocates

Female athletes are taking the ownership of framing their narratives as a way to evoke the gender pay discussion. In particular, female athletes are using social media platforms as a way to fuel the discussion. Probably the most recent and most vocal of female athletes is Megan Rapinoe, who has taken to social media to advocate for pay inequity with such tweets as "Someday, a woman's goal will be worth as much as a man's" (Rapinoe, 2019).

Female athletes also are creating new marketing opportunities for themselves. As Dan Levy, who heads the Olympics and female divisions at Wasserman, explains, "Pro athletes now have a way to connect with their fans that doesn't rely on network TV to build a fan base and connectivity to consumers that brands want to reach" (Badenhausen, 2019, para. 13). Levy further explains how Wasserman, which counts Alex Morgan, Megan Rapinoe, and Katie Ledecky among its 2,000 clients, launched Athlete Exchange in July 2019 to help match athletes with brands and target audiences (Badenhausen, 2019). Going one step further, Bruce and Bruce (2016) suggest that agencies include women's own voices, meaning that female athletes should define and describe their own experiences.

Corporate Advocates

The World Cup win in women's soccer prompted some corporate sponsors to stand up and advocate for pay equality in sports. Advocates such as Clif Bar & Co.'s LUNA Bars and Adidas AG both pledged to donate money directly to team athletes. Procter & Gamble's Secret deodorant also joined in by donating $529,000 to the U.S. Women's Team Players Association ($23,000 for each of its 23 players) after they won the World Cup (Daniels & DeVault, 2019). In the same tweet as given before, Rapinoe thanked LUNA bar for "closing the roster bonus gap and standing alongside us in our fight for #Equalpay" (Rapinoe, 2019). To promote this discussion, Secret deodorant took out a full-page ad in the *New York Times* that read, "We urge US Soccer Federation to be a beacon of strength and end gender pay inequality once and for all" and further urged the organization to "be on the right side of history" (Trafecante, 2019, para. 2 & 3).

Shortly after winning the 2019 World Cup, Nike released a 60-second spot with its key message that the USWNT's win was about more than just winning a soccer title (Trafecante, 2019). At the same time, Nike received pushback from two professional women runners who spoke about Nike's threat of reduced pay after they became pregnant. Nike has since drafted new language to players' contracts that protect rather than punish pregnant athletes.

Organizational Strategies

As stated earlier, Hallahan describes issues management as a public relations administrative specialization that focuses on how an organization monitors its environment, analyzes potential threats and opportunities, and communicates with its publics about disputes or matters of contention (Hallahan, 2001). In addition, The Institute for Public Relations defines issues management as "an anticipatory, strategic management process that helps organizations detect and respond appropriately to emerging trends or changes in the socio-political environment" (Dougall, 2008, para. 5). Applying these definitions to inevitable wage parity disputes on the horizon makes good precautionary sense for any business. The concepts of monitoring the environment, analyzing potential threats, and anticipating emerging trends and changes are good practices for any business but become crucial when a problem is on the immediate horizon. The lessons to be learned from the U.S. Women's Soccer case and others discussed in this chapter are legion and should serve as a cautionary tale for any business. Our recommended communication strategies follow.

Organizations should prepare for a classic management versus labor dispute that includes female boycotts, strikes, and lawsuits. Dougall (2008) describes how an issue moves through five stages that are early, emergent, current, crisis, and dormant, and as the issue moves through the first four stages, the number of stakeholders, publics, and influencers increases while the number of strategic options for the organization decreases making the issue less manageable. Thus, as an issue moves through the five stages, it becomes imperative that organizations adopt these eight key strategies – align, accumulate, analyze, appoint, ally, account, accept, and adapt. Both sides will likely follow this model, thus the team that can do the better job will win the day. These principles emerged from the six theories that contribute to the issues management framework described earlier. As an issue enters the early and emergent stages, it is important for an organization to align, accumulate, and appoint. When the issue enters the current stage, the organization should be actively allying and accounting. If the issue reaches the crisis stage, the organization must accept and adapt to its new environment because by the time the issue becomes dormant, the organization is out of strategic options for controlling the situation.

Prudence dictates that any organization should proactively engage its personnel and resources to examine its policies, procedures, and pay structures, and then create a plan to address similar lawsuits that *are* likely on the horizon. Women's soccer is not the first women's sport to demand and win equal pay, nor will it be the last.

Discussion Questions

1. Update this chapter, focusing on any impact the U.S. Soccer settlement has had on national soccer and professional women's sport.
2. Bridges (2006) offers six theories associated with issues management that are systems theory, social exchange theory, rhetorical analysis, issues life-cycle theory, legitimacy gap theory, and stakeholder theory. Explore each theory and describe how each assists in understanding and applying issues management concepts.
3. Beside the ones described here, what other strategies do you recommend for a professional women's sport to achieve equal pay?

4. Find other professional sports where viewers prefer the women's version of the sport over the men's version. Compare the salaries of the male and female athletes in those sports and discuss your results on the basis of the silence of disparity issue discussed in this chapter. Compare the television coverage of those sports based on their TV ratings and then apply the market forces rule discussed in this chapter.

References

Abrams, O. (2019, June 23). Why female athletes earn less than men across most sports. *Forbes.* www.forbes.com/sites/oliviaabrams/2019/06/23/why-female-athletes-earn-less-than-men-across-most-sports/#2808ab1240fb

Allen, K., & Perez, A.J. (2017, March 28). U.S. women agree to new deal with USA Hockey; will play at world championships. *USA Today.* www.usatoday.com/story/sports/hockey/2017/03/28/usa-hockey-women-dispute- world-championships/99538056/

Associated Press. (2020, March 7). U.S. Soccer offers women same pay as men for matches it controls. *Sports Illustrated.* www.si.com/soccer/2020/03/08/us-soccer-women-equal-pay-matches-control

Associated Press. (2021, September 10). U.S. Soccer eyes USMNT, USWNT joint negotiations over World Cup prize money. *Sports Illustrated.* www.si.com/soccer/2021/09/10/us-soccer-usmnt-uswnt-world-cup-prize-money-equal-pay

Associated Press. (2022, February 20). Why NBC's nearly $8 billion investment in Olympics may have been a bad bet. *Market Watch.* www.marketwatch.com/story/why-nbcs-nearly-8-billion-investment-in-olympics-may-have-been-a-bad-bet-01645404252

Bachman, R. (2019, December 27). In 2019, women insisted that sports pay up. *The Wall Street Journal.* www.wsj.com/articles/in-2019-women-insisted-that-sports-pay-up-11577448001

Badenhausen, K. (2019, August 6). The highest-paid female athletes 2019: Serena and Osaka dominate. *Forbes.* www.forbes.com/sites/kurtbadenhausen/2019/08/06/the-highest-paid-female-athletes-2019-serena-and-osaka-dominate/#526668f82fcc

Berri, D. (2017, September 20). Basketball's growing gender wage gap: The evidence the WNBA is underpaying its players. *Forbes.* www.forbes.com/sites/davidberri/2017/09/20/there-is-a-growing-gender-wage-gap-in-professional-basketball/#753e1ed836e0

Block, J. (2015, July 6). Women's world cup final was the most watched soccer match in U.S. history – for women of me. *HuffPost.* www.huffpost.com/entry/most-watched-us-soccer-game_n_7736438

Bridges, J.A. (2006). Corporate issues campaigns: Six theoretical approaches. *Communication Theory, 14*(1), 51–77. doi: https://doi.org/10.1111/j.1468-2885.2004.tb00303.x

Bruce, T., & Bruce, T. (2016). New rules for new times: Sportswomen and media representation in the third wave. *Sex Roles, 74*(7), 361–376. doi:10.1007/s11199-015-0497-6

Bryan, B. (2016, February 1). CBS and NBC are almost guaranteed to lose money on the NFL's new 'Thursday Night Football' package. *Business Insider.* www.businessinsider.com/networks-lose-money-on-thursday-night-football-2016-2

Daniels, D., & DeVault, K. (2019, August 9). U.S. women's soccer team treated unfairly. *Indianapolis Business Journal, 40*(24). www.ibj.com/articles/u-s-womens-soccer-team-treated-unfairly

Das, A. (2020, March 8). For U.S women, a narrow victory and a growing divide. *The New York Times.* www.nytimes.com/2020/03/08/sports/soccer/uswnt-equal-pay-letter.html

Das, A. (2022a, February 18). Top 10 richest female soccer players in2022/football money list. *Sports Browser*. https://sportsbrowser.net/richest-female-soccer-players/

Das, A. (2022b, January 20). Top 10 highest paid soccer players 2022/football rich list. *Sports Browser*. https://sportsbrowser.net/highest-paid-soccer-players/

Das, A. (2022c, February 22). U.S. Soccer and women's players agree to settle equal pay lawsuit. *The New York Times*. www.nytimes.com/2022/02/22/sports/soccer/us-womens-soccer-equal-pay.html

Dougall, E. (2008, December 12). Issues management. *Institute for Public Relations*. https://instituteforpr.org/issues-management/

Freeman, R.E. (1984). *Strategic management: A stakeholder approach*. Boston, MA: Pitman.

Friedman, M.T., Parent, M.M., & Mason, D.S. (2004). Building a framework for issues Management in sport through stakeholder theory. *European Sport Management Quarterly*, *4*(3), 170–190.

Gough, C. (2022, March 15). Minimum player salary per year in NBA 2017–2024. *Statista*. www.statista.com/statistics/1009569/minimum-nba-salary/

Hallahan, K. (2001). The dynamics of issues activation and response: An issues processes model. *Journal of Public Relations Research*, *13*(1), 27–59

Harwell, D. (2015, July 6). Why hardly anyone sponsored the most-watched soccer match in U.S. history. *The Washington Post*. www.washingtonpost.com/news/wonk/wp/2015/07/06/the-sad-gender-economics-of-the-womens-world-cup/

Jacques, T. (2009). Issues and crisis management: quicksand in the definitional landscape. *Public Relations Review*, *35*, 280–286. http://dx.doi.org/10.1016/j.pubrev.

Kitchin, P.J., & Purcell, P.A. (2017). Examining sport communications practitioners' approaches to issues management and crisis response in Northern Ireland. *Public Relations Review*, *43*, 661–670.

Knight, B., & Birnbaum, J. (eds). (n.d). Highest-paid athletes: The top 50 sports stars combined to make nearly $2.8 billion in a year of records. *Forbes*. www.forbes.com/athletes/

Locker, M. (2019 June 7). Here's how much women's world cup soccer players are paid compared to men. *Fast Company*. www.fastcompany.com/90360375/womens-world-cup-soccer-gender-pay-gap-women-salaries-vs-men

Mishra, D.K. (2013, March 28). Study reveals higher ACL tear rates on artificial turf vs. grass fields. *Sideline Sports Doc*. www.sidelinesportsdoc.com/study-reveals-higher-acl-tear-rates-on-artificial-turf-vs-grass-fields/

Moritz-Rabson, D. (2019, July 26). Gender pay gap in sports is more of an issue after women's world cup win. *Newsweek*. www.newsweek.com/gender-pay-gap-sports-more-issue-after-womens-world-cup-win-1451335

Murray, C., & Morris, S. (2019, June 28). Revealed: the $730,000 gender pay gap in US world cup bonuses. *The Guardian*. www.theguardian.com/football/ng-interactive/2019/jun/28/revealed-the-731003-gender-pay-gap-in-us-world-cup-bonuses

Peterson, A.M. (2019, July 30). U.S. men's national team union takes issue with Carlos Cordeiro for release of women's pay: 'The women's national team players deserve equal pay and are right to pursue a legal remedy.' *Chicago Tribune*. www.chicagotribune.com/sports/soccer/ct-usmnt-equal-pay-carlos-cordeiro-20190730-2zyqnplvcrdqtj33jfp2lusive-story.html

Piacenza, J. (2019, July 22). After women's world cup, over a third say sports' gender pay gap is bigger concern. *Morning Consult*. https://morningconsult.com/2019/07/22/after-womens-world-cup-over-a-third-say-sports-gender-pay-gap-is-bigger-concern/

Rapinoe, M. [@mPinoe]. (2019, April 2). Someday, a woman's goal will be worth as much as a man's. [Tweet]. https://twitter.com/mpinoe/status/111312506494423449 6?lang=en

Rentner, T.L., & Burns, D. (2019). Challenging a Boy's Club: Reputation management and the case of pay inequity in professional women's sport. In T.L. Rentner & D. Burns (Eds.), *Case studies in sport communication: You make the call* (pp. 139–148). London: Routledge.

Taylor, M., Vasquez, G., & Doorley, J. (2003). Merck and AIDS activists: Engagement as a framework for extending issue management. *Public Relations Review, 29*, 257–270.

Tennery, A. (2021 Dec. 13). U.S. women's national team files final brief in equal pay appeal. *Reuters.* www.reuters.com/lifestyle/sports/us-womens-national-team-files-final-brief-equal-pay-appeal-2021-12-13/

Trafecante, K. (2019, July 14). Secret deodorant to contribute $529,000 to US women's soccer to address pay gap. *CNN Business.* https://www.cnn.com/2019/07/14/business/secret-campaign-soccer-pay-equity/index.html

Tulshyan, R. (2019, September 25). 7 lessons from the U.S. women's soccer team's fight for *equal pay. Harvard Business Review.* https://hbr.org/2019/09/7-lessons-from-the-u-s-womens-soccer-teams-fight-for-equal-pay

U.S. Soccer. (2022, May 18). U.S. Soccer Federation, women's and men's national team unions agree to historic collective bargaining agreements [press release]. www.ussoccer.com/stories/2022/05/ussf-womens-and-mens-national-team-unions-agree-to-historic-collective-bargaining-agreements.

Wagtendonk, A. (2019, July 7). US women's soccer team wins its fourth world cup. *Vox.* www.vox.com/2019/7/7/20685183/us-womens-soccer-team-fifa-world-cup-title-2019-france-vs-netherlands

Women's National Basketball Association Collective Bargaining Agreement. (2022). https://wnbpa.com/wp-content/uploads/2020/01/WNBA-WNBPA-CBA-2020-2027.pdf

Women's Sports Foundation. (2012). A Title IX primer. www.womenssportsfoundation.org/home/advocate/title-ix-and-issues/what-is-title-ix/title-ix-primer

15

COMMUNICATING IN CRISIS WITHOUT THE POWER TO ACT

Bradley J. Baker

Introduction

Crisis can strike a sport organization at any time and without warning. How organizations – and the individuals within them – respond to crisis and communicate with stakeholders is critical to organizational reputation (Coombs, 2007). Failing to communicate effectively and mitigate fallout from a crisis can have long-reaching financial and reputational consequences. While every crisis is unique, reviewing past scenarios, in the light of established crisis communications theory and principles, provides invaluable insight and planning that can improve future outcomes. This case examines the public communications by USA Fencing in response to allegations of sexual misconduct against Alen Hadzic, an alternate on the 2020 U.S. Olympic team.

Shortly following the announcement of Hadzic's qualification as the replacement athlete for the U.S. men's épée team for the 2020 Olympic Games in Tokyo, at least three women reportedly filed formal complaints with the U.S. Center for SafeSport (USCSS) against Hadzic alleging sexual misconduct dating back to 2013[1] (Davis, 2021b). The USCSS is an independent nonprofit organization formally designated under U.S. federal law as having jurisdiction over the United States Olympic & Paralympic Committee (USOPC) and individual sport National Governing Bodies (NGBs) to enact and enforce policies to prevent the emotional, physical, and sexual abuse of amateur athletes in the United States. Thus, NGBs such as USA Fencing have limited power to act once the USCSS asserts jurisdiction over a particular case. In the lead up to, during, and in the immediate aftermath of the 2020 Olympic Games, the allegations against Hadzic generated media attention on a sport that normally operates outside the spotlight. USA Fencing was harshly criticized for not taking action – action largely beyond its power to take – and for a lack of effective communication.

DOI: 10.4324/9781003316763-18

The current case highlights the double bind confronting sport organizations that are simultaneously called upon by key stakeholders to take decisive action and demonstrate leadership, while often being powerless to act at all due to resource or legal constraints. This lack of agency or power to act adds a layer of complexity and nuance that is typically present but often overlooked in crisis planning, creating an environment where sport managers may not have any acceptable options yet cannot decline to act. Crises confront organizational leaders with time-critical decisions that require immediate and appropriate response to minimize reputational damage. Situational crisis communication theory (SCCT) provides a framework that can guide organizations in determining the best strategic response. Working in a case study setting allows readers to reflect on a realistic dilemma facing sport managers and practice the skills necessary to navigating a treacherous communication and leadership decision.

Background

USA Fencing organizes and oversees competitive fencing in the United States, as recognized by the USOPC. USA Fencing provides local, regional, and national competition opportunities; selects and supports individuals and teams representing the United States in international competitions; and promotes the sport of fencing (USA Fencing, 2021b). The organizational mission statement reads, "To grow and promote the sport of fencing in the United States, honor its rich traditions, and achieve sustained competitive international excellence" (USA Fencing, n.d., para. 5). While USA Fencing members range from novices to established international competitors, as with many sport NGBs, the selection of the national team for world championships and the Olympic Games is one of the most high-profile organizational activities. At the same time, USA Fencing also has legal and ethical responsibilities to create and foster a safe and positive sporting environment for all participants (USA Fencing, 2021e). This duty of care to sport participants has become known as Safe Sport.

Following a series of high-profile athlete abuse cases, the USOPC and NGBs developed and began implementing formal measures designed to protect athletes. Initially led by USA Swimming in 2010, policies were rapidly adopted across sports as governing bodies rushed to put protective schemes into place (USA Swimming, 2021). The inadequacy of a piecemeal approach and conflicts of interest inherent to athlete protection systems overseen by the same organizations that employed many of the abusers came to a head with the widely publicized Larry Nassar scandal. Nassar was convicted of a series of crimes stemming from charges of sexual abuse of at least 265 victims while serving as the team doctor for the U.S. women's national gymnastics team (Friess, 2018). This resulted in the U.S. Congress establishing an independent body to oversee athlete protection.

The *Protecting Young Victims from Sexual Abuse and Safe Sport Authorization Act of 2017* (2017) established the U.S. Center for SafeSport (USCSS) and delegated to it exclusive jurisdiction to enact and enforce policies to prevent the emotional, physical, and sexual abuse of amateur athletes in the United States. While sport NGBs retain responsibility for investigating and resolving allegations of emotional or physical abuse of athletes under their aegis, the USCSS asserts exclusive authority over alleged violations that involve sexual misconduct. When an NGB receives a report alleging sexual misconduct, the case is immediately forwarded to the USCSS, and the NGB loses its authority to further investigate or sanction individuals.

The Case

The Olympic Games are the highest profile competition in many sports, including fencing. Selection to an Olympic team is a career-crowning achievement that represents years of hard work, phenomenal skill, and a fair amount of good luck, and it is typically highly celebrated. For USA Fencing, the final team selection event for the 2020 Olympic Games in Tokyo[2] was the North American Cup held from May 6 to 9, 2021, in Richmond, VA (USA Fencing, 2021c). In men's épée, one of three disciplines in the sport, the final Olympic berth, as a team alternate, came down to the gold medal match between Adam Rodney and Alen Hadzic, with the winner securing a coveted place in Tokyo. Hadzic triumphed by a 15–12 score and became the replacement athlete (alternate) for the U.S. Olympic team.

In the weeks that followed, at least three women reportedly filed formal complaints with the USCSS against Hadzic alleging sexual misconduct dating back to 2013 (Davis, 2021b). On June 2, 2021, the USCSS temporarily suspended Hadzic, barring him from participating in any capacity in events, programs, activities, or competitions under the auspices of the USOPC or USA Fencing, subject to appeal. On June 28, Hadzic won an appeal in arbitration, lifting his suspension, permitting him to resume training at USA Fencing member clubs, and restoring his eligibility to participate in the 2020 Olympic Games. In response, USA Fencing implemented a *safety plan* designed to physically separate Hadzic from other Olympic team members during travel to and from Tokyo and while on location at the Olympic Games (Davis, 2021b). Among other provisions, the safety plan required Hadzic to travel on different flights than his teammates, be housed in an off-site hotel rather than in the Olympic Athlete Village, and follow a staggered practice schedule to avoid his training at the same time as female athletes on the U.S. team. Ultimately, the U.S. men's épée team lost to Japan (the eventual Olympic Champions) in the opening round of the team competition on July 30 and was placed ninth (IOC, 2021). Hadzic never entered the match, thereby failing to gain official recognition as an Olympic athlete. A summary of the timeline of key events in the case is provided in Table 15.1.

TABLE 15.1 Timeline of Key Events in the Case

Date	Event
May 7, 2021	Alen Hadzic wins the gold medal at the North American Cup to move into fourth place in the USA Fencing National Team Point Standings and qualifies for the 2020 Olympic Games as a replacement (alternate) athlete.
May 2021	At least three women file formal complaints of sexual misconduct by Hadzic with the U.S. Center for SafeSport.
June 2, 2021	The U.S. Center for SafeSport temporarily suspends Hadzic from sport participation pending the final resolution of their investigation. The suspension would preclude Hadzic from traveling to or participating in the 2020 Olympic Games.
June 28, 2021	Hadzic wins an appeal lifting the U.S. Center for SafeSport suspension through a formal arbitration hearing.
July 13, 2021	USA Fencing puts into place a safety plan designed to physically separate Hadzic from Olympic teammates, particularly female teammates, during travel to and from Tokyo and during the Olympic Games, including separate housing at an off-site hotel rather than in the Olympic Athlete Village.
July 22, 2021	Hadzic loses an appeal via arbitration hearing to lift restrictions imposed as part of the USA Fencing safety plan.
July 30, 2021	The USA men's épée team loses its opening match to Japan and is eliminated. Hadzic does not enter the match, thereby failing to officially become an Olympic athlete.

As these events played out, USA Fencing received considerably more publicity and attention than is typical for a niche sport unaccustomed to the spotlight. The case was carefully followed among both the domestic and international fencing communities. Further, the story attracted general media attention from outlets including the financial news website, Business Insider (Davis, 2021a, 2021b), BuzzFeed News (Nashrulla & Sacks, 2021; Sacks & Segura, 2021), *The New York Times* (Longman, 2021a, 2021b), and *USA Today* (Peter & Brennan, 2021). The reputational crisis for USA Fencing continued after the conclusion of the Olympic Games at a time when USA Fencing hoped instead to celebrate a historical achievement by Olympic Champion Lee Keifer, the first American to win an Olympic gold medal in individual foil.

In light of continued media attention and calls from USA Fencing members to take action, USA Fencing President Peter Burchard called an emergency meeting of the USA Fencing board of directors on August 13. The single item of business on the agenda was a connected set of motions to establish a task force to study measures to protect USA Fencing members, request additional information from the USCSS, implement an organizational communications platform for items related to SafeSport, and mandate additional SafeSport training for all

USA Fencing members (USA Fencing, 2021a). Based on objections from other board members, the emergency meeting was procedurally halted by a vote of 7–2 prior to consideration of Burchard's motions (Meyer, 2021). Two weeks later, Burchard brought identical motions before the board at its regularly scheduled meeting on August 31; they failed when no one seconded the motions (USA Fencing, 2021d).

Sport organizations frequently face ethical and reputational challenges precipitated by actions taken by athletes, such as the sexual misconduct allegations against Hadzic. Managing public perception in the aftermath of such reputational crises is imperative to continued success and ability to pursue organizational objectives. Faced with crisis, sport organizations have a wide range of communications responses available, including denial of the crisis, diminishing the magnitude of the crisis, or assuming responsibility for the crisis and rebuilding organizational reputation (Coombs, 2006). Situational crisis communication theory (SCCT) is a "comprehensive, prescriptive, situational approach for responding to crises and protecting the organizational reputation" (Coombs & Holladay, 2002, p. 167). Based on attribution theory, SCCT provides a framework for understanding how crises impact organizational reputation and crisis response strategies, and how stakeholders respond to crisis and organizational communications (Coombs, 2007).

According to SCCT, stakeholder perceptions define whether an event is a crisis and determine the efficacy of organizational communications responses (Coombs, 2021). Three factors play a role in shaping the reputational threat from a crisis and the best communications strategy for an organization – crisis responsibility, crisis history, and prior relational reputation (Coombs, 2007). Crisis responsibility is determined by the degree to which stakeholders believe the organization is responsible for the crisis (Coombs, 1995). Crisis responsibility is characterized by crisis type, ranging from low responsibility when stakeholders view the organization as a *victim* (e.g., of a natural disaster), to minimal responsibility due to *accident* (e.g., technical errors), to strong attribution of responsibility due to *intentional* crises (e.g., human error or organizational misdeed) when stakeholders perceive purposeful (in)action (Coombs & Holladay, 2002). Crisis history is the extent to which the organization has faced similar crises in the past, with a history of crisis indicative of an ongoing problem (Coombs, 2007). Prior relational reputation captures perceptions of how the organization in crisis has treated stakeholders in the past (Coombs, 2007), as existing reputation influences how new events are interpreted by stakeholders (Porritt, 2005). Crisis type determines the degree of reputational threat, while crisis history and prior relational reputation mitigate or intensify the degree of responsibility stakeholders attribute to the organization. A history of similar crises and poor established relationships can lead to greater blame attaching to the organization, while a first-time crisis that could not be anticipated or a positive prior relationship can reduce blame and buffer an organization from reputational damage (Coombs, 1995, 2007).

When developing a crisis communication strategy, organizations must consider the extent to which stakeholders attribute the crisis to the organization and anticipate stakeholder response to the chosen communication strategy. Organizations can respond to crisis through *deny* strategies that seek to avoid responsibility, *diminish* strategies that minimize the seriousness of the crisis, or *rebuild* strategies whereby the organization accepts responsibility and redresses failings (Coombs, 2006). While a successful denial strategy results in minimal reputational damage, denial may not be convincing or sufficient when responsibility attribution is high (Elsbach, 2006). Stronger responses that explicitly accept responsibility and shift the focus to rebuilding are, however, more costly (Coombs, 2007). Inappropriate communication responses to crisis can lead to escalation, whereby reputational damage among stakeholders is increased due to the initially inadequate actions taken by organizational leaders (Kellison et al., 2015). The original crisis is thus compounded by negative response to the organization's inability to resolve the crisis event (Elsbach, 2006).

Correctly identifying the crisis type is the most important step in mitigating reputational damage as the crisis response strategy must match the responsibility attribution from stakeholders (Coombs & Holladay, 2002). For a crisis in the victim cluster, stakeholders make weak attribution of crisis responsibility, and denial strategies can be effective (Coombs, 2007). However, when stakeholders strongly attribute responsibility, denials or excuses are unlikely to be credible (Elsbach, 2006) and stronger responses accepting responsibility, asking for forgiveness, and seeking to compensate victims and rebuild are more appropriate (Coombs, 2007).

USA Fencing opted for a crisis response strategy of denial. The organization and its leaders made few public statements regarding the allegations against Hadzic or USA Fencing's role in the investigation. The statements that were made were designed to distance USA Fencing from the case. USA Fencing referred media questions about the investigation to USCSS, while media reports quoted a member of USA Fencing's board of directors as saying the matter would "all blow over" in what appears to be a private meeting held in executive session (Davis, 2021a). While crisis denial is the strategy organizations most often adopt in practice (Kim et al., 2009), this approach runs counter to recommendations based on SCCT when stakeholders attribute high levels of responsibility to the organization (Coombs, 2021).

Arguably, stakeholders should have attributed relatively low responsibility to USA Fencing. The actions at the heart of the crisis – Hadzic's alleged behavior and the allegations against him – were not made directly by the organization. Under U.S. federal law, once the USCSS asserts jurisdiction over a case alleging athlete abuse, no further steps are necessary or possible to be taken by the sport NGB until the case is resolved. Lacking authority to take any action on the case, USA Fencing attempted to position itself as a peripheral party. Yet, stakeholders such as organizational members clearly did attribute a high level of responsibility to USA Fencing. This may be due to the influence of crisis history and prior relational reputation.

As with many sport NGBs, USA Fencing has experienced numerous cases of athlete abuse, including physical, emotional, and sexual abuse. In 2021 alone, at least four former fencing coaches received permanent bans from the USCSS resulting from allegations of sexual misconduct, while two others faced temporary suspensions or restrictions pending further investigation (USCSS, n.d.). Other reported cases have not resulted in bans or lesser sanctions, leaving perceptions both of an unreasonably high volume of cases and poor resolution of those cases that are filed (Davis, 2021a; Sacks & Segura, 2021). The sheer quantity of alleged sexual misconduct cases within the fencing community establishes a crisis history that precludes USA Fencing from dismissing the Hadzic incident as a one-off occurrence. Widespread perceptions of ineffective systems in place to investigate allegations and punish perpetrators led to a poor prior relational reputation between USA Fencing and key stakeholders within the fencing community. These factors act to intensify attributions of responsibility when a new sexual misconduct crisis arises.

While the media spotlight has largely moved on, USA Fencing's response to the Hadzic allegations continues to roil the fencing community, with negative reactions posted across social media and blogging sites. Communication strategies that are poorly received by stakeholders and the public can generate backlash that exacerbates the crisis (Kellison et al., 2015). Vociferous negative outcry from USA Fencing members may have contributed to the departure of multiple key USA Fencing staff members, including the CEO, Director of Communications, and General Counsel in the months following the Tokyo Olympics (Davis, 2021a). Recovery after a crisis escalates, due to perceptions of a mishandled or inadequate response, can require pacification measures, such as key decision makers leaving the organization (Kellison et al., 2015).

You Make the Call

USA Fencing leadership faced an intractable dilemma when news of the allegations against Hadzic became public. Without authority to take action to investigate the allegations or sanction Hadzic, USA Fencing was bound by the decisions and timeline imposed by the USCSS process. Lacking power, USA Fencing opted primarily to do nothing, abrogating responsibility to others. This inaction was viewed as being insufficient, drawing harsh critiques from Olympic athletes, USA Fencing members, and the public, resulting in substantial reputational damage to USA Fencing among key stakeholders. Further, negative perceptions around the organization in the period following the Olympic Games limited opportunity to capitalize on competitive success in Tokyo and may have contributed to the departure of multiple high level staff members.

While USA Fencing legitimately lacked power to take direct action in response to the allegations, the organization retained the ability to communicate with stakeholders, shaping perception of the crisis and USA Fencing's role and responsibility. By focusing on what actions U.S. federal law barred the organization from taking, USA Fencing lost sight of its core responsibility toward its members. As a result, USA Fencing's lack of active response to the Hadzic crisis reminded stakeholders of USA Fencing's history of mishandling similar crises, which resulted in poor prior reputation and failures to address allegations of sexual misconduct or appropriately protect fencing participants. Instead, USA Fencing needed to implement an appropriate crisis communication strategy that addressed the situation and mitigated reputational damage.

Adopting a denial strategy in communications responding to the Hadzic crisis represented a missed opportunity. With strong attributions of responsibility, SCCT suggests that USA Fencing should have taken a proactive position acknowledging responsibility and immediately embarking on a series of meaningful changes to rebuild organizational reputation and standing. Such an approach could also restore USA Fencing to a position of leadership, fulfilling its legal and ethical responsibilities to maintain a safe sporting environment for participants (USA Fencing, 2021e). By contrast, the inadequate response of USA Fencing's chosen communication strategy opened the organization to criticism by outsiders focused on attacking the organization's perceived lack of genuine commitment to safe sport principles. Confronted by a situation where the organization was severely circumscribed in its ability to take meaningful action, USA Fencing was ultimately unsuccessful in their outward communications and public relations efforts, leading to substantial reputational harm and missed opportunities to rebuild tattered relationships with stakeholders.

Discussion Questions

1. While USA Fencing's approach is criticized in the case presentation and described as being inadequate, this assumes that some other approach may have been more successful. What might suggest that a denial strategy was the "least bad" of a set of unacceptable options available to USA Fencing leadership, and thus the appropriate choice?

2. The communication strategy adopted by USA Fencing was widely deemed inadequate by USA Fencing members and other stakeholders. Following the SCCT precepts, what is a better approach and why would your solution lead to more desirable outcomes?

3. Beyond communication, USA Fencing officials were highly constrained in their ability to act by legal limits to their authority to investigate the allegations against Hadzic or impose sanctions. What else could USA Fencing do, as demanded by USA Fencing members, without the power to act?

4. How has USA Fencing modified or maintained their initial crisis communication strategy in light of developments with the Hadzic scandal since the events described in the case?

Notes

1 Hadzic has denied these allegations.
2 Due to postponement related to the global COVID-19 pandemic, the 2020 Olympic Games took place in 2021.

References

Coombs, W.T. (1995). Choosing the right words: The development of guidelines for the selection of the "appropriate" crisis-response strategies. *Management Communication Quarterly*, *8*(4), 447–476. https://doi.org/10.1177/0893318995008004003

Coombs, W.T. (2006). The protective powers of crisis response strategies: Managing reputational assets during a crisis. *Journal of Promotion Management*, *12*(3–4), 241–260. https://doi.org/10.1300/J057v12n03_13

Coombs, W.T. (2007). Protecting organization reputations during a crisis: The development and application of situational crisis communication theory. *Corporate Reputation Review*, *10*(3), 163–176. https://doi.org/10.1057/palgrave.crr.1550049

Coombs, W.T. (2021). *Ongoing crisis communication: Planning, managing, and responding* (6th ed.). London: Sage publications.

Coombs, W.T., & Holladay, S.J. (2002). Helping crisis managers protect reputational assets: Initial tests of the situational crisis communication theory. *Management Communication Quarterly*, *16*(2), 165–186. https://doi.org/10.1177/089331802237233

Davis, B.W. (2021a). After sexual assault allegations rocked US fencing's Olympic team, one executive said the scandal would 'blow over.' Instead, the sport's top officials are resigning. *Business Insider*. www.businessinsider.com/us-fencing-executives-resign-in-the-wake-of-an-olympic-sexual-assault-scandal-2021-9

Davis, B.W. (2021b). The US Olympic fencing team is in uproar over the handling of sexual-assault claims against one of its members. *Business Insider*. www.businessinsider.com/us-olympic-fencers-object-alen-hadzic-tokyo-2021-7

Elsbach, K. (2006). *Organizational perception management*. Mahwah, NJ: Lawrence Erlbaum Associates. https://doi.org/10.4324/9781315740379

Friess, S. (2018). Prosecutors say more than 265 victims have accused USA Gymnastics doctor Larry Nassar of sexual misconduct. *Business Insider*. www.businessinsider.com/265-victims-accuse-us-olympic-doctor-larry-nassar-of-sexual-misconduct-2018-2

International Olympic Committee [IOC]. (2021). Tokyo 2020 fencing men's épée team results. *IOC*. https://olympics.com/en/olympic-games/tokyo-2020/results/fencing/men-s-epee-team

Kellison, T.B., Bass, J.R., Lovich, J., & Bunds, K.S. (2015). Compounding crisis events and the organizational response. *International Journal of Sport Management*, *16*(4), 573–600.

Kim, S., Avery, E.J., & Lariscy, R.W. (2009). Are crisis communicators practicing what we preach?: An evaluation of crisis response strategy analyzed in public relations research from 1991 to 2009. *Public Relations Review*, *35*(4), 446–448. https://doi.org/10.1016/j.pubrev.2009.08.002

Longman, J. (2021a, August 1). Fencers silently protest an accused teammate. *New York Times*, SP5. www.nytimes.com/2021/07/31/sports/olympics/us-fencing-pink-masks.html

Longman, J. (2021b, July 23). Sexual misconduct accusations make U.S. Olympic fencer an outcast. *New York Times*, B8. www.nytimes.com/2021/07/22/sports/olympics/olympic-fencer-alec-hadzic-misconduct.html

Meyer, D. (2021). What happened at the US Fencing emergency board meeting on sexual assault. *Fencing Parents*. www.fencingparents.org/whats-new-in-fencing/2021/8/13/what-happened-at-the-us-fencing-emergency-board-meeting-on-sexual-assaults

Nashrulla, T., & Sacks, B. (2021). US Olympic fencers wore pink masks to protest against their teammate accused of sexual assault. *BuzzFeed News*. www.buzzfeednews.com/article/tasneemnashrulla/fencers-pink-masks-alen-hadzic

Peter, J., & Brennan, C. (2021). US fencer accused of sexual misconduct unhappy with treatment at Tokyo Olympics. *USA Today*. www.usatoday.com/story/sports/olympics/2021/07/21/2021-olympics-us-fencer-accused-sexual-misconduct-reaches-tokyo/8038132002/

Porritt, D. (2005). The reputational failure of financial success: The 'bottom line backlash' effect. *Corporate Reputation Review*, *8*(3), 198–213. https://doi.org/10.1057/palgrave.crr.1540250

Protecting young victims from sexual abuse and safe sport authorization act of 2017, 36 U.S.C. § 220541 et seq. (2017). https://uscode.house.gov/view.xhtml?path=/prelim@title36/subtitle2/partB/chapter2205/1&edition=prelim

Sacks, B., & Segura, M. (2021). "Protected again and again": How a fencer made it to the Tokyo Olympics despite sexual assault allegations. *BuzzFeed News*. www.buzzfeednews.com/article/briannasacks/olympics-fencers-safesport-abuse

US Center for SafeSport [USCSS]. (n.d.). Centralized disciplinary database. *USCSS*. https://uscenterforsafesport.org/response-and-resolution/centralized-disciplinary-database/

USA Fencing. (n.d.). Mission statement. *USA Fencing*. www.usafencing.org/about

USA Fencing. (2021a). Agenda: Emergency meeting of the USA Fencing Board of Directors. *USA Fencing*. https://cdn1.sportngin.com/attachments/document/e17a-2498263/BOD_Meeting_Agenda_August_13.pdf

USA Fencing. (2021b). Bylaws United States Fencing Association. *USA Fencing*. https://cdn3.sportngin.com/attachments/document/0050/9062/Fencing_Bylaws_Final_08_31_2021.pdf

USA Fencing. (2021c). Khalil Thompson and Alen Hadzic quality as replacement athletes for Tokyo Games. *USA Fencing*. www.usafencing.org/news_article/show/1162905

USA Fencing. (2021d). Minutes: Special meeting of the USA Fencing Board of Directors. *USA Fencing*. https://cdn4.sportngin.com/attachments/document/f0ff-2558107/BOD_Meeting_Approved_Minutes_Aug_31_2021.1.pdf

USA Fencing. (2021e). USA Fencing fencesafe handbook. *USA Fencing*. https://cdn4.sportngin.com/attachments/document/8e05-2577344/SS_Policy_revised_Fence_Safe_12022021.pdf

USA Swimming. (2021). USA Swimming looks back on 10 years of safe sport initiatives. *USA Swimming*. www.usaswimming.org/news/2021/02/10/usa-swimming-looks-back-on-10-years-of-safe-sport-initiatives

16

STRATEGIC RESISTANCE THROUGH COMMUNICATION CAPITAL

Rapinoe's Reframing of Women-Identified Athletes through Mind–Body Performance for Social Change

Elesha L. Ruminski and Dorene Ciletti

Introduction

Sport has played a significant role in leading social change, and, in particular, women in sport have contributed to our nation's collective consciousness concerning democracy, from suffrage to social justice. Of interest here is how women–identified athletes (WIAs)[1] in the United States support social change through mind–body performance, strategic use of accumulated communication capital, and mindful media reframing. This case provides historical context for how WIAs engage civically and politically, with an emphasis on professional soccer player and U.S. Olympian Megan Rapinoe's recent social justice efforts and the risks and rewards of reframing perceptions of WIAs through her mind–body performance as a global sport leader.

As history reveals, athletes can generate social change through intentional acts that begin on, yet extend beyond, the field or court. Rapinoe is a significant model athlete and mindful strategic communicator and connector who earned respect through team building and advocating for herself and others through media. Rapinoe is vocal in her support for equity for the Lesbian, Gay, Bisexual, Transgender (LGBTQ) and Black, Indigenous, and People of Color (BIPOC) communities and other contemporary social justice issues. Her participation in the U.S. Women's Soccer team's fourth World Cup win in 2019 provided an international platform as she knelt in solidarity with former-NFL player Colin Kaepernick and rallied students to vote (McInerney, 2020). Recognized by Wingard (2019) as a "lateral leader," Rapinoe demonstrates horizontal leadership while maintaining focus on expertise and athletic skill, relationship building, and publicly communicating her values, including empathy, as evident by being the first athlete outside of American football to kneel in solidarity with Black Lives

DOI: 10.4324/9781003316763-19

Matter efforts (NBC Sports, 2020). With her mind–body performance in the spotlight, Rapinoe engages her communication capital to facilitate resistance, taking risks to illuminate social injustices with the goal of changing perceptions and realities for WIAs and others to level the playing field in sport and life.

Background

Richelieu and Boulaire (2005) argue that "[w]ith the exception of music, cinema, and religion . . . no other field of activity . . . generates such passion among its customers as sport" (p. 24). PricewaterhouseCoopers (2019) projects the North American sport market alone to grow more than 3.2%, from $71.1 billion in 2018 to $83.1 billion in 2023. Sport's impact stretches beyond the economy into the sociocultural realm, what Standeven and DeKnop (1999) refer to as the "sportification of society." Sport, still viewed by many as competitive, passive spectator entertainment, gives us "a sense of history . . . tradition, and . . . identity" (Schultz, 2018, p. 1). In the West, sport has favored "former colonial powers" and "wealthy nations" as "activities invented by and for men" focused on "'masculine' attributes, such as strength, power, and aggression" (pp. 6–7). After WWII, sport was recognized as contributing to civic identity and pride through men's leagues (Schultz, 2018), which fostered community spirit and even national unity (Staurowsky, 2016, p. xvi). However, organizations like the National Organization for Women and Girls in Sport contrast this competitive, masculine framework with inclusive missions (Ladda, 2009), though Daniels recognizes "the lack of visibility of . . . [women's] sporting involvement in the greater population" (2016, p. xxii). Differences in athletic opportunities led to the 1972 U.S. Title IX legislation as a legally mandated structural mechanism for addressing parity, recognized by some as "nearly as important to our nation's history as the 19th amendment," but unfortunately without the same impact as civil rights legislation (Staurowsky, 2016, p. 27).

Today, sport is seen as a

> [M]outhpiece for the modern age, . . . a prominent backdrop for diplomacy. Whether it is an athlete protesting for social justice, or a politician rallying public support, the sporting arena presents a stage to express one's own personal outlooks.
>
> *(Impey, 2020, para. 1)*

Globally recognized as a human right by the Olympic Charter and the United Nations Educational, Scientific, and Cultural Organization (UNESCO) (Schultz, 2018), sport can affect social change since it is "a means to promote education, health, development, and peace," as noted in the U.N. General Assembly's special resolution (Goss & Alexandrova, 2005; U.N. General Assembly, 2015, para. 37).

Despite such international recognition of sport as a right for *all* humans, control of women has been at the root of constraints for WIAs, leading first-wave feminists to advocate for physical fitness to support mindful activism. Charlotte Perkins Gilman's "The Yellow Wallpaper" (1892/1999) chronicled the effects of the Victorian rest cure therapy, a common medical establishment solution to women's "nervousness." Women who exerted themselves physically or mentally were said to diminish their functions of fertility, pregnancy, and birthing, so were forbidden to go outdoors or use their minds creatively. They were meant to rest themselves to wellness.

Within this context, Vertinsky (1989) argued, Gilman supported women's physical fitness as a "strategy for emancipation" by examining how "notions of mind–body relationships illustrate dominant modes of thought about female health and autonomy in the late nineteenth century" (1892/1999, pp. 6–7). Gilman was driven toward self-dependence and strength, including physical fitness (Vertinksky, 1989), relying on William Blaikie's *How to Get Strong and How to Stay So* (1879/2011), even identifying herself as "I, the budding athlete" (1892/1999, p. 9). She explored the link between mind and body fitness when her husband sought medical treatment for her (Vertinsky, 1989). However, the "rest cure" focused on mothering rather than fitness, indicating a disjointed connection between mind and body. The prescription "was a behavior modification treatment designed to make nervous, over-active, and dissatisfied women more passive, feminine, and healthy, and to help them learn that domesticity was the cure, not the cause, of their problems" (p. 15); in contrast, Gilman felt, "Mental and physical health . . . were so intimately connected that true growth could only occur when both aspects were allowed to develop" (1892/1999, p. 16). Gilman's writing reflected her mind–body struggle to resist the rest cure, with her later novel *Herland* (1915) projecting a utopian view of mind–body balanced "healthfulness" for women (1892/1999, p. 25).

Resistance to gendered physical restrictions was linked with women's efforts toward suffrage. For example, women's desire to bicycle in the late 20th century signaled that the physical limitations imposed upon them were correlated to limiting their other contributions as full human beings:

> Out of necessity, they [women] started dressing in a less-restrictive fashion . . . They were getting a taste of freedom and an entrée into citizenship; they began to view themselves as having the right and responsibility to advocate for things like better roads. Why shouldn't they get to cast a ballot too?
>
> *(Shapely, 2020, para. 4)*

Frances E. Willard of the Women's Christian Temperance Union, an advocate of bicycling, recognized it as a catalyst for women's empowerment: "I began to feel that myself plus the bicycle equaled myself plus the world, upon whose spinning-wheel we must all learn to ride" (p. 27). Similarly, the suffrage hikes Schultz (2010) researched focused on "physical activism" with political aims to raise women's consciousness about their voice. As Staurowsky (2016) suggests, "sport has often served as the site where social struggles around race, ethnicity, religion, sexuality, and gender have played out in both overtly public and subtly private ways" (p. xi).

Yet, early efforts with women's sport were not intersectional. Parks Pieper (2020) recognizes, as our history of suffrage reflects, that race was a contested issue amid these feminist efforts: "Thus, in many ways, participation in physical activities embodied the spirit of the women's suffrage movement, as well as its racialized dynamics" (p. 103). In her analysis of how suffragettes used men's baseball to promote suffrage by hosting "Suffrage Days" at games, she cites research that indicates how women used "physical activities as a way to support their right to vote" (p. 101), using the community around sport and the attention it garnered as a way to raise suffrage awareness – but primarily for White women at the time. More intersectional support came later.

Building awareness through physical activism helped women generate communication capital to further suffrage efforts. Ray (2007) recognizes the public performance of U.S. suffragists when they registered to vote and then voted, in this way "performing a participatory argument in an ongoing public controversy about the parameters of the polity" in a post-Civil War context when voting was "a visibly public and communal activity" (p. 1). Women showed up at polling places, "representing themselves as physical examples of the category 'citizen' and invoking the political power of a recognizable ritual of citizenship, they performed a reverential commitment to the sacredness of the form and the political institutions that it upheld" (p. 2). Mind and body were at the center of these performances of natural rights and expressions of citizenship.

Such mind–body reframing represents "individual action emerging from personal networks and collective decision-making," or *social capital* (Ray, p. 6). Social capital "consists of the stock of active connections among people, the trust, and shared values that bind people into networks and make cooperative action possible" (Jeffres et al., 2013, p. 542). *Communication capital* expands from this concept to recognize "the impact of communication phenomena in a changing environment" (p. 539) and that communication skills cannot be practiced in isolation or segregation. Instead, communicators must be competent at interacting, messaging, and listening in multifaceted ways to navigate the full spectrum of communication needed to lift their voices within a society that is media-driven yet in need of strategy and civility. According to Jeffres et al., (2013), *communication capital* includes:

1. Interpersonal discussion of social problems and programs among family and friends, in the workplace, and in the neighborhood and community
2. Discussion of social problems and programs in the non-work organizational context

3. Attention to public issues and business in the media
4. Using media for civic engagement. (p. 556)

Communication capital leads to capacity for *civic capital*, which means one has the resources, norms, practices, and processes needed for enhanced civic capacity to create and sustain social change that is informed by intersectional distributive understandings of justice and deliberative inquiry (Carcasson & Sprain, 2016).

Trailblazers transformed the performance of suffrage and initiated constitutional change; today, WIAs are publicly raising their collective voice through voter engagement campaigns that are intricately tied to raising awareness and combating misinformation on social media, often coordinated as team or through broader league efforts. And it is not only those in positional leadership roles who are taking communicative risks; WIA grassroots efforts are supporting women's broader democratic engagement. A greater range of social, communication, and civic capital is being demonstrated by WIAs like Rapinoe, a leading mind–body performance risk-taker and media reframer.

The Case

Rapinoe, an American professional soccer winger and co-captain of the National Women's Soccer League team OL Reign, is recognized for playing on the U.S. women's soccer team that won gold in the 2012 Olympics and won the 2019 World Cup championship. She unapologetically shows up in mind and body as "an activist-athlete icon," noting that she "would like to use this platform to unify people" (Morchese, 2019, para. 1, 3). Her social justice efforts and the risk and rewards of her mind–body performance and use of accumulated communication capital are important to examine, particularly the way she reframes through communicative resistance, whether kneeling for racial justice or standing up for WIA pay equity.

Athletes hold credibility and trust within society, enabling them to magnify their voices for advocacy. Sport has a history of breaking down barriers, suggesting that athletes serve as change agents and risk-takers, as mind–body mobilizers for social change. Initially, mainstream society recognized men of color breaking down barriers; later, women became barrier-breakers. First, it was playing the game, embodying the opportunity to be an equal on the playing field; now athletes interact with the team, fan base, and even the broader public through civic and democratic engagement. However, WIAs have faced unique challenges related to perception, especially mass-mediated perception. Media can influence the framing of sport culture, impacting societal perspectives of athletes, functioning as a gatekeeper and agenda-setter, making choices related to coverage of sport events and athletes, including the amount and type of coverage, and can perpetuate bias and stereotypes (Pedersen, 2002; Tuggle, 1997; Tuggle et al., 2002).

Historically, WIAs have often faced constraints through media coverage, which often discounts their athleticism (Fink & Kensicki, 2002; UNESCO, n.d.).

Carty (2005) states that "corporate interests have a hand in promoting certain gender representations" (p. 139) desiring physical attractiveness and femininity in media-placed advertising and other messaging. Therefore, women were less likely to have their sport accomplishments connected to their athletic skill and commitment. When mainstream media provides the frame of reference, argues Billings and Eastman (2002), "the identity stereotypes embedded within coverage can readily become [the audience's] perception of reality, setting expectations about gender, ethnicity, and national similarities and differences" (p. 368).

Women's presence in sport has also been framed through the metaphor of the glass ceiling. Several examples of WIAs who have "broken" that ceiling exist; in 2020 alone, Emily Zaler became the first female coach for the National Football League's Denver Broncos (Legwold, 2020), and Kim Ng was hired as the first female general manager for Major League Baseball's Miami Marlins (Connor, 2020). But the glass ceiling can be a limiting metaphor to represent systemic or structural change since it often focuses on individual achievement, like making it through the pipeline or up the hierarchy. It is linked to the concept of the double-bind for women, who are seen more negatively for applying their leadership (Eagly & Carli, 2007; Ruminski & Holba, 2012).

Gertrude Ederle and Serena Williams, nearly a century apart, both broke barriers and shifted norms in performance, fashion, and society in ways that did more than break glass ceilings. Ederle demonstrated the ability of women to excel in sport performance, breaking swimming records held by men, and becoming the first woman to successfully swim the English Channel in 1926, demonstrating both the mental and physical capability to overcome women's perceived inferiority, while claiming agency over her appearance and identity. Prior to her successful swim across the English Channel, a few years after ratification of the 19th amendment, Ederle resisted the traditional swimsuit which, at that time, modestly covered the body but took on water. Ederle claimed agency over her appearance, designing and wearing a two-piece swimsuit that would not detract from her ability to swim (Severo, 2003), which was considered "nearly scandalous" (Stout, 2009).

Similarly, Williams competed in attire outside the norm. The full-body catsuit she wore to the French Open in 2018 served a functional purpose: After giving birth, the catsuit would help prevent blood clots. Williams said the suit made her feel "like a superhero" (Guardian Staff, 2018, para. 11); yet, French Open President Bernard Giudicelli suggested that her apparel had "gone too far" and instituted a new dress code (Associated Press Staff, 2018). Regardless, Williams continues to support women, speaking out against systemic prejudice, both in tennis and society, and promoting those who are marginalized through her venture capital firm and fashion line (Maitland, 2020).

Agency for WIAs has expanded beyond self-empowerment through attire. As mentioned earlier, WIAs like Rapinoe advocate for equal pay, voting rights, and social justice, representing the fourth wave of feminism and its leveraging of communication capital, particularly with the proliferation of social media, to advocate for social change by engaging fellow athletes and fans alike. Rapinoe, whose calls for social justice for the LGBTQ and BIPOC communities have been magnified since the team's fourth World Cup win in 2019, also called on students to vote (McInerney, 2020). Rapinoe suggests that women should form a voting plan, calling for intersectional solidarity: "We need more focus on Black women, working moms, immigrants, essential workers, domestic workers, and service workers. Lifting them up eventually lifts everyone up. We *know* that" (ctd. in Singer, 2020, para. 5). She also recognizes the importance of education, reading, and paying attention to current events and other athletes' challenges, when using her platform:

> After reading everything I could about social and racial injustice, it became clear to me not only how deep the roots of white supremacy went, but also that it was the system from which all other inequalities came. This was a huge lightbulb moment: realizing we are not free until we're all free.
>
> *(Rapinoe & Brockes, 2020, p. 161)*

These examples demonstrate the ongoing ability of WIAs to impact social change. Rather than managing the tension between athleticism and hegemonic femininity by reinforcing gender hierarchies, Ederle, Williams, and Rapinoe resisted, demonstrating agency over appearance and identity, showing up in mind and body publicly, in contrast with the "feminine apologetic" of an earlier era when women compensated for their involvement in male domain matters by enhancing their feminine or even (false) heterosexual qualities (Schultz, 2018, p. 48). When Rapinoe was asked if sport should be a "nonpolitical oasis," she responded:

> I don't understand that argument at all. You want us to be role models for your kids. You want us to endorse your products. You parade us around. It's like, we're not just here to sit in the glass case for you to look at. That's not how this is going to go. Yeah, I don't [expletive] with that concept at all.
>
> *(Morchese, 2019, para. 11)*

Rapinoe resists traditional media framing by enhancing her communication capital through social media and by authoring op-eds, appearing for interviews and in documentaries, protesting on the field, collaborating with teammates, and sparring publicly with politicians. As a champion athlete[2], she gets featured, so she voices her resistance. She openly acknowledges that celebrity status has been key, as well as looking at how all team members (not just the team hierarchy) can contribute: [B]y looking at people's skills off the field, we essentially developed a business within a business. We developed clear goals and strategies. We put systems in place to handle media interest. Younger players were encouraged to speak up and get involved.

> *(Rapinoe & Brockes, 2020, p. 139)*

In an op-ed, Rapinoe (2021) asserted that the "threats to women's and girls' sports are lack of funding, resources, and media coverage; sexual harassment; and unequal pay," and she continues to call out racism, suggesting stronger sanctions in athletics because "it really is everybody's issue" (Roper, 2019, para. 21). She advocates for gender pay equity[3], voting rights, LGBTQ issues, and transgender athletes. We know this because she communicates this publicly. In a testimonial in *The Players' Tribune*[4] titled "Why I am Kneeling" (2016), Rapinoe acknowledges that an athlete's role is not just relegated to the field:

> I haven't experienced over-policing, racial profiling, police brutality or the sight of a family member's body lying dead in the street. But I cannot stand idly by while there are people in this country who have had to deal with that kind of heartache . . . I am choosing to do something. I am choosing to care.
>
> *(para. 3, 13)*

In 2019, she called out then-President Donald Trump through Twitter and media interviews for being exclusionary (TMZ Sports, 2019) and rejected the idea of visiting the White House if the team won the FIFA World Cup (North, 2019), which they won. And they did not go.

You Make the Call

As this case illustrates, WIAs have strived to play well and advocate well, demonstrating capability through their mind–body performance as well as their strategic communication and savvy reframing. WIAs increasingly embrace opportunities from a collective rather than narcissistic perspective, pushing the boundaries of their role *on* the field to impact social justice *off* the field. Sport, as a cultural and political construct, gives WIAs an opportunity to intersect their mind–body performance with their position in the marketplace. WIAs have contributed to our nation's collective consciousness for at least a century and have kept the focus on how sport contributes to societal expectations that are not just economic, but also equitable.

WIAs can unite others by mobilizing teams, leagues, and even fans into action. While sport may have missed its live audience in the pandemic era, the fans are still there, streaming live games and interacting through social media. WIAs and those who support them work hard to use media to keep the sport community connected (The Social Intelligence Lab, 2021). Often, WIAs face risks due to harsh media perceptions and interactions, including trolling – yet social media provides a tool to reframe and a means to build communication capital and solidarity together.

WIAs communicate nonverbal resistance by showing up as fit athletes, focusing on performance-enhancing attire, and simply being themselves, all working to present representations that resist typical media framing. They assertively discuss issues that matter to them while in the mediated public spotlight. Zheng (2020) claims employees and customers alike are looking for more in their organizational and consumer experiences of corporate products and services – stakeholders expect more *corporate social justice*, which highlights increasing interest in a collective consciousness around common ethical standards. Organizations and individuals can choose to leverage their influence to reflect and support the communities in which these companies and, in this case, sport teams and leagues, including WIAs, are embedded.

Social justice's more pronounced emergence in sport through WIAs' mind–body performance reveals a culture that is beginning to shift through opportunities to engage in shaping that culture. The culture that is emerging resists *over*emphasis of the economic impact of sport that has favored certain (male) teams because they are consumed or valued more economically. The trend in sport leadership through these examples is that WIAs, not just industry leaders, are moving away from self-important narcissistic communication focused on personal, or even team, status, toward the collective interests of society. This helps to shift the overall culture of both sport and society.

Balance, commitment, and resilience have become priorities, shifting from a focus on economic demands and control. This is what mind–body performance is about – assessing and maintaining the mind's and body's abilities to perform. In the past, women faced restrictions that limited control of their bodies and minds; today, many have sought autonomy and raised collective consciousness so they are more often viewed as *whole* persons with a significant and equal role to play in society. Corporate culture must continue to raise the bar with its social justice efforts to correspond with equitable treatment of WIAs and all athletes.

Women's empowerment and equity will rely on local and global, governmental and non-governmental, fan and athlete, and cross-gendered partnerships. By highlighting pioneers like Rapinoe and their efforts, sport offers an empowered future for girls, but only with continued support for WIAs and their mind–body performance on the field and in the media. Rapinoe repeatedly challenges stereotypical framing by showing up in mind and body, using her accumulated capital and the public platform afforded her through her athleticism to model and advocate for full participation in democracy. From kneeling individually on the field to standing with others through litigation, she and other WIAs are engaged agents of social change.

Discussion Questions

1. What challenges did Rapinoe face as an athlete coming from her intersectional standpoint, and how did she overcome them? Since this publication, how have other WIAs pioneered strategies to overcome similar challenges?
2. How does public solidarity with a movement like Black Lives Matter communicate resistance, as when Rapinoe knelt to support Kaepernick? What would you consider if you were an athlete contemplating a comparable act of solidarity?

3. Is society changing to support WIAs in their efforts to shape social justice and voting rights? What changes will support women's public participation as equal athletes and citizens?
4. What risks would you take in the public eye utilizing media to support social justice?

Acknowledgments

The co-authors would like to thank the *Pennsylvania Communication Annual* for granting permission to draw from the article referenced here to develop this case study. The article is available through Communication Source.

Ruminski, E.L., & Ciletti, D. (2020). From suffrage to social justice: The mind–body performative role of women athletes in social change in the United States. *Pennsylvania Communication Annual, 76*(2), 83–108.

Notes

1 While recognizing that rules for sport competition concerning gender designation vary and are in flux (Elsesser, 2021), we use the term "women-identified athlete" (WIA) to reference cis-gender and transgender athletes who identify as female biologically or otherwise.
2 The importance of women being supported as athletes (as through Title IX) cannot be understated, as it provides a means for athletic performance, the platform of which supports communication capital. As Rapinoe (2021) herself acknowledged, "Being able to play sports as a child shaped my life's path."
3 The U.S. Women's National Team's (USWNT's) pay discrimination case against the U.S. Soccer Federation was chronicled in the 2021 documentary *LFG* (Nix & Fine, 2021). After a lawsuit dismissal in May 2020, a settlement was reached in February 2022. Rapinoe has advocated, both individually and with the team, to address systemic issues of sexism, homophobia, and racism (see Murray, 2021; Treisman, 2022).
4 *The Players' Tribune* (www.theplayerstribune.com/about), founded by Derek Jeter, is "a new media company that provides athletes with a platform to connect directly with their fans, in their own words" (para. 1).

References

Associated Press Staff. (2018, August 24). French open says 'Non!' to Serena's black catsuit. *Associated Press.* https://apnews.com/article/a5acc142672642aba7976d0fd0a9e3b6

Billings, A.C., & Eastman, S.T. (2002). Selective representation of gender, ethnicity, and nationality in American television coverage of the 2000 summer Olympics. *International Review for the Sociology of Sport, 37*(3/4), 351–371.

Blaikie, W. (1879/2011). How to get strong and how to stay so. *Project Gutenberg.* www.gutenberg.org/files/36557/36557-h/36557-h.htm

Carcasson, M., & Sprain, L. (2016). Beyond problem solving: Reconceptualizing the work of public deliberation as deliberative inquiry. *Communication Theory, 26*, 41–63. https://doi.org/10.1111/comt.12055

Carty, V. (2005). Textual portrayals of female athletes. *Frontiers: A Journal of Women Studies, 26*, 132–155.

Connor, C. (2020, November 16). The long-overdue hire of Kim Ng shows what women in sports are up against. *The Guardian*. www.theguardian.com/sport/2020/nov/16/kim-ng-miami-marlins-gm-groundbreaking

Daniels, D.B. (2016). Introduction: Becoming a female athlete. In E. J. Staurowsky (Ed.), *Women and sport: Continuing a journey of liberation and celebration* (pp. xv–xxvii). Champaign, IL: Human Kinetics.

Eagly, A.H., & Carli, L.L. (2007). *Through the labyrinth: The truth about how women become leaders*. Cambridge, MA: Harvard Business School Press.

Elsesser, K. (2021, July 27). What makes an athlete female? Here's how the Olympics decide. Forbes. www.forbes.com/sites/kimelsesser/2021/07/27/what-makes-an-athlete-female-heres-how-the-olympics-decide/?sh=55b4941e4f9c

Fink, J.S., & Kensicki, L.J. (2002). An imperceptible difference: Visual and textual constructions of femininity in Sports Illustrated and Sports Illustrated for Women. *Mass Communication & Society*, *5*(3), 317–340.

Gilman, C.P. (1892/1999). The Yellow Wallpaper. *Project Gutenberg*. www.gutenberg.org/files/1952/1952-h/1952-h.htm

Goss, J., & Alexandrova, A. (2005). HIV/AIDS Prevention and peace through sport. *Lancet*, *366*, S3-S4.

Guardian Staff. (2018, May 29). Serena Williams on her 'Black Panther' catsuit: 'It's my way of being a superhero'. *The Guardian*. www.theguardian.com/sport/2018/may/30/serena-williams-wakanda-catsuit-superhero-roland-garros

Impey, S. (2020, October 30). 'Sport should reflect the society we live in': Social justice and the case for adapting the field. *SportsPro*. www.sportspromedia.com/from-the-magazine/social-justice-racial-gender-equality-black-lives-matter-diversity-sport

Jeffres, L.W., Jian, G., & Yoon, S. (2013). Conceptualizing communication capital for a changing environment. *Communication Quarterly*, *61*(5), 539–563.

Ladda, S. (2009). The National Association for Girls and Women in Sport: 110 years of promoting social justice and change. *Journal of Physical Education, Recreation & Dance*, *80*(7), 48–51.

Legwold, J. (2020, September 5). Denver Broncos make Emily Zaler first female coach in franchise history. *ESPN*. www.espn.com/nfl/story/_/id/29820680/denver-broncos-make-emily-zaler-first-female-coach-franchise-history

Maitland, H. (2020, October 5). "Tennis is a small play in the whole scheme of things": Serena Williams is just getting started. *British Vogue*. www.vogue.co.uk/arts-and-lifestyle/article/serena-williams-interview

McInerney, M. (2020, October 14). Soccer star Megan Rapinoe calls on USF students to vote. *USF News*. www.usfca.edu/news/rapinoe-calls-on-students

Morchese, D. (2019, July 29). Megan Rapinoe is in celebration mode. And she's got some things to say. *New York Times*. www.nytimes.com/interactive/2019/07/29/magazine/megan-rapinoe-sports-politics.html

Murray, C. (2021, December 13). USWNT makes final plea in equal pay lawsuit appeal, calls dismissal 'flatly wrong'. *ESPN*. www.espn.com/soccer/united-states-usaw/story/4546856/uswnt-makes-final-plea-in-equal-pay-lawsuit-appealcalls-dismissal-flatly-wrong

NBC Sports. (2020, July 30). Sports Northwest. www.nbcsports.com/northwest/more/us-womens-soccer-star-megan-rapinoe-mission-make-politics-cool

Nix, A. (Director and Writer), & Fine, S. (Writer). (2021). LFG. HBO Max. www.hbomax.com/a/grw-lfg?utm_id=sa%7c71700000084305879%7c58700007147538106-%7cp64270085140&gclid=Cj0KCQjwr-SSBhC9ARIsANhzu17-6zqv1TTt3-wZ85dzKjqCh8HHnl6bCp3sl2wH4f2Wn95wyo96dRYaAjFxEALw_wcB&gclsrc=aw.ds

North, A. (2019, July 3). Why the president is feuding with Megan Rapinoe, star of the US women's soccer team. *Vox*. www.vox.com/identities/2019/7/3/20680073/megan-rapinoe-trump-world-cup-soccer

Parks Pieper, L. (2020). "Make a home run for suffrage": Promoting women's emancipation through baseball. *Women in Sport and Physical Activity Journal, 28*, 101–110. https://doi.org/10.1123/wspaj.2020-0017

Pedersen, P.M. (2002). Investigating interscholastic equity on the sports page: A content analysis of high school athletics newspaper articles. *Sociology of Sport Journal, 19*, 419–432.

PricewaterhouseCoopers. (2019). At the gate and beyond: PwC outlook for the sports market in North America through 2023. www.pwc.com/us/en/industries/tmt/assets/pwc-sports-outlook-2019.pdf

Rapinoe, M. (2016, October 6). Why I am kneeling. *The Players' Tribune*. www.theplayerstribune.com/articles/megan-rapinoe-why-i-am-kneeling

Rapinoe, M. (2021, March 28). Opinion: Megan Rapinoe: Bills to ban transgender kids from sports try to solve a problem that doesn't exist. *The Washington Post*. www.washingtonpost.com/opinions/2021/03/28/megan-rapinoe-transgender-kids-sports-ban/

Rapinoe, M., & Brockes, E. (2020). *One life*. London: Penguin Press.

Ray, A.G. (2007, May 8). The rhetorical ritual of citizenship: Women's voting as public performance. *Quarterly Journal of Speech, 93*, 1–26. www.tandfonline.com/doi/abs/10.1080/00335630701326845

Richelieu, A., & Boulaire, C. (2005). A post-modern conception of the product and its application to professional sport. *International Journal of Sports Marketing and Sponsorship, 7*(1), 23–34.

Roper, E. (2019, November 8). Megan Rapinoe's fight for equality. *BBC News*. www.bbc.com/news/newsbeat-50290213

Ruminski, E.L., & Holba, A.M. (2012). Introduction and Afterword. In E.L. Ruminski & A.M. Holba (Eds.), *Communicative understandings of women's leadership development: From ceilings of glass to labyrinth paths*. London: Lexington Books, a division of Rowman & Littlefield.

Schultz, J. (2010). The physical is political: Women's suffrage, pilgrim hikes and the public sphere. *The International Journal of the History of Sport, 27*(7), 1133–1153.

Schultz, J. (2018). *Women's sports: What everyone needs to know*. Oxford: Oxford University Press.

Severo, R. (2003, December 1). Gertrude Ederle, the first woman to swim across the English Channel, dies at 98. *New York Times*. www.nytimes.com/2003/12/01/sports/gertrude-ederle-the-first-woman-to-swim-across-the-english-channel-dies-at-98.html

Shapely, H. (2020, September 18). The surprising role sports played in women's suffrage. *Teen Vogue*. www.teenvogue.com/story/womens-suffrage-sports-history

Singer, J. (2020, August 21). 'Make a plan and don't get discouraged': Megan Rapinoe and Jennifer Siebel Newsom on staying sane in 2020. *Glamour*. www.glamour.com/story/megan-rapinoe-and-jennifer-siebel-newsom-on-staying-sane-in-2020

Standeven, J., & DeKnop, P. (1999), *Sport tourism*. London: Human Kinetics.

Staurowsky, E.J. (2016). *Women and sport: Continuing a journey of liberation and celebration*. London: Human Kinetics.

Stout, G. (2009). *Young woman and the sea: How Trudy Ederle conquered the English Channel and inspired the world*. London: Houghton Mifflin Harcourt.

The Social Intelligence Lab. (2021). The female playing field: How brands and social media can be a driving force behind change and sports equality. https://thesilab.

com/the-female-playing-field-how-brands-and-social-media-can-be-a-driving-force-behind-change-and-sports-equality/

TMZ Sports. (2019, July 10). Megan Rapinoe to president Trump: 'You're excluding people like me.' www.tmz.com/2019/07/10/megan-rapinoe-donald-trump-white-house-cnn/

Treisman, R. (2022, February 22). The U.S. national women's soccer team wins $24 million in equal pay settlement. *NPR Sports*. www.npr.org/2022/02/22/1082272202/women-soccer-contracts-equal-pay-settlement-uswnt

Tuggle, C.A. (1997). Differences in television sports reporting of men's and women's athletics: ESPN, SportsCenter and CNN Sport3 Tonight. *Journal of Broadcasting & Electronic Media, 41*(1), 14–25.

Tuggle, C.A., Huffman, S., & Rosengard, D.S. (2002). A descriptive analysis of NBC's coverage of the 2000 summer Olympics. *Mass Communication & Society, 5*(3), 361–376.

U.N. General Assembly. (2015). Transforming our world: The 2030 agenda for sustainable development. www.un.org/ga/search/view_doc.asp?symbol=A/RES/70/1&Lang=E

United Nations Educational, Scientific and Cultural Organization (UNESCO). (n.d.). Gender equality in sports media. https://en.unesco.org/themes/gender-equality-sports-media#:~:text=Coverage%20of%20women%20in%20sports,dominating%2C%20and%20valued%20as%20athletes.&text=In%20recent%20times%2C%20sports%20broadcasting,is%20still%20a%20noticeable%20gap

Vertinsky, P. (1989, Spring). Feminist Charlotte Perkins Gilman's pursuit of health and physical fitness as a strategy for emancipation. *Journal of Sport History, 16*(1), 5–26.

Wingard, J. (2019, July 19). Megan Rapinoe: How a 'radical individualist' led the U.S. women's soccer team. *Forbes*. www.forbes.com/sites/jasonwingard/2019/07/19/megan-rapinoe-how-a-radical-individualist-led-the-us-womens-soccer-team/?sh=7d87306a604f

Zheng, J.L. (2020, June 15). We're entering the age of corporate social justice. *Harvard Business Review*. https://hbr.org/2020/06/were-entering-the-age-of-corporate-social-justice

17

ALYSIA, ALLYSON, AND NIKE'S "BAND OF BROTHERS"

Exposing the Hypocrisy between Corporate Marketing and Internal Practices

Amy Aldridge Sanford, Nikola Grafnetterova and RJ Loa

Introduction

On Mother's Day 2019, Nike – the largest sports apparel and footwear company in the world – was publicly called out by mother-athletes who were currently and formerly sponsored by the corporation. The women – all champion runners – claimed that Nike showed a lack of support for their decisions to have babies. Additionally, they accused the organization of being hypocritical in a social justice advertising campaign that featured activist-athletes Colin Kaepernick and Serena Williams. This chapter considers the history of female runners, the founding and corporate culture of Nike, the arguments of the mother-athletes, and then applies public relations and broader communication concepts to the case.

Background

More than 2,000 Years of History

This section encapsulates female athletes' exclusion from competitive running as a result of sexism and the founding of Nike, during the time of the United States' Women's Liberation Movement of the 1960s and 1970s.

While running as a sport originated during the ancient Olympic Games, women were intentionally excluded from competition for more than 2,000 years for reasons mostly centered around maintaining traditional femininity and the misguided belief that running would make women too muscular, promote the growth of facial hair, and/or make them infertile (Burfoot, 2016; Cahn, 2015). In 1928, after much advocacy, women were finally allowed to run up to 800 meters in the Olympic Games. Nine women from across the globe competed, but

DOI: 10.4324/9781003316763-20

because they looked "tired" after the race, women were banned from competing in anything longer than 200 meters for the next 20 years.

The 1960s and 1970s were marked by the Women's Liberation Movement, which took place largely in the United States, and the push for women's equality in all domains of society – including sports. In 1967, Kathrine Switzer (in an act of rebellion) registered for the Boston Marathon using only her first and middle initials and gained national notoriety when she was accosted by race organizers, while competing, when they recognized she was a woman (Switzer, 2009).

In 1972, Congress enacted the Title IX Education Amendment that legally prohibited sex discrimination in any federally funded educational program or activity in the United States. As a result, girls' national participation in high school sports increased from only 294,000 in 1971 to more than 3.5 million girls in 2018 (National Federation of State High School Associations, 2019). By 2019, about 44% of all college athletes identified as female[1] (National Collegiate Athletic Association, 2021). This legislation revolutionized the landscape of U.S. sports in general and women's running in particular. Today, the majority (61%) of all registrants in road races are girls or women (Running USA, 2020).

The Evolution of Nike

At this same time, during the U.S. Women's Liberation Movement, the sports brand Nike began modestly as Blue Ribbon Sports, a small distributor of Japanese-made running shoes operated by 25-year-old Phil "Buck" Knight and his former University of Oregon track coach Bill Bowerman. Knight's father, a newspaper publisher, financed his son's travel to Japan to make initial contact with officials at Onitsuka Tiger, a Japanese sports shoe company. As Blue Ribbon Sports grew and eventually changed its name to Nike in 1971, Knight surrounded himself with a group of male colleagues whom he affectionately referred to as his "Band of Brothers" (Knight, 2016, p. 239). Today, Nike employs more than 76,000 people worldwide, generating $39 billion in sales in 2019 (Nike, 2020a, 2021a).

Nike has struggled with its social justice image over the years, including a scandal related to pay and worker safety in overseas factories in the 1990s (see Greenhouse, 1997). Nike has improved on this front in recent years, publicly promoting a more inclusive image and taking positive positions related to social justice and activism. Most notably, in late 2018, the company featured former National Football League (NFL) quarterback Colin Kaepernick in its "Dream Crazy" campaign. The choice of Kaepernick surprised many people, considering his controversial decision to kneel instead of stand during the "Star Spangled Banner" at NFL games in protest of police killings of unarmed Black citizens (Handley, 2019). In the "Dream Crazy" ad, the activist encourages viewers to "Believe in something, even if that means sacrificing everything" (Rivas, 2018). Anti-Kaepernick consumers reacted negatively to the commercial by boycotting Nike products and unloading considerable Nike stock (Germano, 2021); however, the stock rebounded quickly, and the "Dream Crazy" campaign won an Emmy Award (Vera, 2019).

Perhaps coincidentally, the "Dream Crazy" campaign premiered 6 months after female employees at Nike complained of pay inequities and inappropriate workplace behavior by male executives. The organization was described, in an internal memo, as a boys' club and a toxic environment for female employees (see Campbell, 2018; Germano & Lublin, 2018). Many onlookers blamed Nike's male-dominated culture as the primary reason the organization failed to keep up with other retail competitors in women's shoe and apparel categories, the fastest-growing segment of the market (Creswell et al., 2018). In an attempt to take control of their brand, Nike declared 2019 its year for women (see Danziger, 2019) and conducted several advertising campaigns with female empowerment as its central theme (Danziger, 2019; Felix, 2019; Handley, 2019).

One such video entitled "Dream Crazier" premiered during the Academy Awards in early 2019. Narrated by tennis star Serena Williams, the video focuses on some of the greatest achievements of female athletes in U.S. history, including Williams' own two dozen grand slam victories (Brito, 2019). Though "Dream Crazier," coupled with Kaepernick's "Dream Crazy" ad, proved too much for some of Nike's former sponsored athletes. They called out Nike's hypocrisy as it pertained to women's empowerment, particularly its policies on motherhood.

The Case

Female Athletes Speak Out against Nike

On Mother's Day 2019, *The New York Times* published a 6-minute video narrated by Olympic gold medal sprinter and former Nike athlete Alysia Montaño in which she alleged discrimination by Nike as a result of her pregnancy 5 years earlier (Montaño, 2019). She satirically used the "Dream Crazier" language of Williams and the "sacrifice everything" rhetoric of Kaepernick to expose Nike officials for threatening to pause her contract and not pay her, instead of allowing her paid maternity leave, for example, when discussing her pregnancy plans. Montaño asserted that Nike viewed pregnancy as an injury and a major setback. She left Nike for another sponsor before having her first child in 2014.

Montaño's video was accompanied by an article with accounts of other female athletes who described similar experiences. Olympic runner Kara Goucher shared that Nike would not pay her until she started racing again after giving birth in 2010[2]. A couple of days after Montaño's video was released, Nike offered the following response:

> Nike is proud to sponsor thousands of female athletes. As is common practice in our industry, our agreements do include performance-based payment reductions. Historically, a few female athletes had performance-based reductions applied. We recognized that there was inconsistency in our approach across different sports and in 2018 we standardized our approach across all sports so that no female athlete is penalized financially for pregnancy.
>
> *(Cited in O'Kane, 2019, para. 7)*

About a week after Nike's response, another track and field star and former Nike-sponsored athlete, Allyson Felix, released another tell-all video and article for *The New York Times* in which she explained: "It was really difficult for me to see the 'Dream Crazier' campaign . . . Alysia and Kara bravely spoke out" (Felix, 2019, 3:13). Felix shared her maternity-related discussions with Nike, which mirrored those of Montaño and Goucher. Felix, who became a mother in 2018, stated she was currently negotiating a new contract with Nike. Felix added that even though company officials quickly responded to Montaño's video promising to address the issue, Nike would not guarantee that Felix's compensation would not be reduced, or entirely eliminated, if she became pregnant again. "This is a great opportunity for Nike to really spell out what the new agreement is. What protection do women have? What does that look like?" (Felix, 2019, 3:34).

A few months later, in August 2019, Nike offered more specifics about the new agreement, clarifying that pregnant athletes would be guaranteed regular pay and bonuses spanning 8 months before the athlete's due date and 10 months after (Kilgore, 2019). In addition to Nike, competitors including Altra, Nuun, Brooks, and Burton promised to add similar contractual guarantees for their sponsored athletes (see Clemmons, 2019; Moore, 2020; West, 2019). By 2021, Nike spotlighted pregnant athletes in its "Toughest Athlete" campaign, and the company launched its first-ever maternity collection (Hambleton, 2021; Nike, 2020b, 2021b; Young, 2021). Montaño, who never returned to Nike, responded to the "Toughest Athlete" campaign on social media and in *Runner's World*, pointing out that Nike never offered an apology for the damage they caused her, Goucher, Felix, or any other mother-athletes (Montaño, 2021). Goucher and Felix expressed similar sentiments on their social media platforms (Hambleton, 2021). In June 2021, Felix launched her own apparel company, Saysh, with a shoe designed by two former Nike employees (Boateng, 2021). Wes Felix, Allyson's brother and agent, explained in a 2021 podcast interview: "We really hope that Saysh as a brand will – I wish I could say *restore* balance – but will *create* a balance from a gender equity standpoint within this footwear space" (emphasis added, cited in Chavez, 2021).

In another case involving Nike, in late 2021, distance runner Mary Cain filed a $20 million lawsuit against her running coach Alberto Salazar for abuse, which involved weight shaming, and Salazar's employer, Nike, for its lack of intervention (Manning, 2021). Salazar was also Goucher's coach many years earlier. Goucher went to the FBI a decade earlier, alleging Salazar gave her unprescribed drugs to lose weight following the birth of her first child (Strout, 2019). When Cain brought her abuse to the world's attention in a 2019 video in *The New York Times*, she encouraged Nike to hire more women: "Part of me wonders if I would have worked with more female psychologists, nutritionists, and even coaches, where I'd be today. I got caught in a system designed by and for men, which destroys the bodies of young girls" (Cain cited in *The New York Times*, 2019, 5:56).

You Make the Call

Image Restoration Theory and the Culture of Nike

In this section, the historical context of women's liberation, the evolution of Nike as a corporation, and the concerns voiced by the aforementioned female athletes are synthesized and analyzed to better understand communication lessons learned and practical applications for large corporations claiming to care about social justice in today's political climate.

Communication tactics employed by Nike executives in response to negative allegations over the years, including those brought forward by mother-athletes in 2019, can be explained by applying image restoration theory (IRT) (see Benoit, 1997). IRT offers five strategies for addressing crisis situations and is considered by many public relations practitioners as the ideal method to "reduce, redress, or avoid damage" to an organization's public reputation (Burns & Bruner, 2000, p. 27). IRT argues that public perceptions are more important than reality or intentions of a corporation or organization. Namely, it is more important to determine if the public believes that the organization is responsible for the act, rather than analyze if the act is truly offensive. Furthermore, the most important question when developing a crisis response is whether the targeted *audience* believes the act is/was offensive (Benoit, 1997).

In general, organizations like Nike answer to many audiences, or stakeholders (i.e., consumers, stockholders, employees, sponsored athletes), each connected to specific goals and interests (financial and otherwise) of the organization. As respondents to crises, IRT argues that company executives must identify and prioritize its most important stakeholders (Benoit, 1997). When analyzing the 2019 mother-athlete case, it appears Nike identified the key audience as their female consumer base and, in response, declared 2019 the year for women. Through subsequent advertising campaigns – like "Dream Crazier" and "Toughest Athlete" –and the introduction of the new maternity collection, Nike ensured that the ongoing crisis response targeted and fulfilled the needs of the female shoe – and apparel – buying audience.

Benoit (1997) offered five key strategies that can be utilized when responding to crises: (1) Denial, (2) evasion of responsibility, (3) reducing offensiveness, (4) corrective action, and/or (5) mortification (confession/forgiveness). The strategies can stand alone, or two or more can be engaged simultaneously. In recent years, it appears that Nike effectively engaged two of these options – reducing offensiveness and corrective action (Benoit, 1997). However, it is their lack of mortification that has put them at odds with their loudest critics. Simply put, Nike's lack of authenticity does not align well with the social justice values they espouse.

> *Denial:* Organizations may choose to deny any wrongdoing and/or shift the blame to another organization or person. Companies use this strategy to "deny that the act occurred, that the [organization] performed the act, or

that the act was harmful" (Benoit, 1997, p. 179). In the 1990s, when a coalition of women's groups accused Nike of violating worker safety regulations and giving inadequate compensation to overseas workers, a Nike spokesperson rebuffed the coalition saying that the women's group "misunderstood Nike's role" (Greenhouse, 1997, para. 6). The spokesperson neither used language that took ownership of any wrongdoing nor did they explicitly deny the coalition's allegations; rather, they deflected, stating Nike paid their workforce considerably more than other factories located within the same regions.

Evasion of Responsibility: Organizations may attempt to evade responsibility by stating that a negative act resulted, despite good intentions, by accident, because of a lack of information or as a response to another's action. This response strategy differs from denial in that an organization acknowledges an act occurred, rather than refute its existence. In response to the doping scandal surrounding disgraced former coach Alberto Salazar, Nike utilized evasion of responsibility when addressing Cain's 2019 allegations. While Nike publicly stated they found the allegations "deeply troubling," they evaded responsibility by blaming Cain and her parents for not bringing their concerns to Nike's attention earlier (cited in Chappell, 2019).

Reducing Offensiveness: This strategy aims to place the crisis in a positive light by emphasizing other, more appealing aspects of the organization (i.e., highlighting community contributions, promising to learn from mistakes). Many executives prefer this strategy as it effectively shifts focus away from crises (Benoit, 1997). In response to Montaño and the other athlete-mothers' accusations of discrimination, Nike began each written response to stakeholders with the phrase they are "proud to sponsor thousands of female athletes" (cited in O'Kane, 2019, para. 7). This was an attempt to shift the focus away from "a few outspoken athletes" and focusing on to its larger commitment of sponsoring thousands of female athletes.

Corrective Action: When an organization makes a promise to remedy a problem, they are engaging in corrective action. The focus is on returning to a pre-crisis state and/or preventing future occurrences of similar offensive acts (Benoit, 1997). In further reviewing Nike's written response to the athlete-mothers, Nike utilized aspects of corrective action by acknowledging the company's "inconsistency" and by implementing a new policy to standardize their "approach . . . so that no female athlete is penalized financially for pregnancy" (cited in O'Kane, 2019, para. 7). Additionally, Nike launched a new maternity collection, thereby striving to resolve any sentiments of anti-pregnancy or the mentality that pregnancy is an "injury" (see Montaño, 2019) and worked to restore and reinforce Nike's reputation of inclusivity for everyone, including pregnant athletes.

Mortification: Organizations may find it necessary to confess to the accused act and/or ask for forgiveness. After corrective action was taken on the part of Nike for their alleged involvement in discriminating against pregnant athletes, Montaño (2019) quickly pointed out Nike never formally apologized to any of the athlete-mothers. In addition, the organization has never apologized or otherwise asked for forgiveness from overseas workers or from Mary Cain.

Each of the five crisis response strategies offered by IRT can help organizations, like Nike, develop effective and comprehensive messages that aim to restore and maintain positive corporate images. While Nike employed many of the strategies mentioned in IRT through multiple crises, their actions failed to resolve an overarching, and seemingly recurring, flaw woven into its organizational culture – there is a misalignment of corporate deeds with the social justice values they espouse within public forums, including their advertising. In its responses to the countless crises mentioned in this chapter, Nike's most recent go-to strategies appear to be reducing offensiveness and corrective action. By implementing these strategies, Nike hopes to repair its reputation and corporate image by drawing on the overall company mission and values it wants to embody – those of fairness, equity, and inclusion. It is clear though that Nike's leadership has no interest in admitting wrongdoing or apologizing to affected stakeholders.

Leadership and Social Justice

Recently, Nike executives have used media campaigns (e.g., "Dream Crazy", "Dream Crazier", "Toughest Athlete") to convince their stakeholders they are committed to social justice, against the advice of company employees with marginalized identities. In February 2020, Nike's newly appointed CEO John Donahue, a White male born in 1960, put together a Diversity Working Group made up of high-level Black employees. The group selected advised Donahue to hold off on any more social justice campaigns until Nike publicly addressed internal deficiencies, in effect exercising the IRT's mortification strategy. Donahue ignored the suggestion and proceeded with the campaigns (Germano, 2021). And, therein lies the problem. Until the Nike executive team comprises people truly committed to equity and inclusion – even when finding and hiring such a team are difficult – the marketing campaigns aimed at reducing offensiveness or taking corrective action will likely continue to fall flat, and key stakeholders – including athletes like Montaño, Felix, Goucher, and Cain – will be misunderstood and mistreated by the organization. The company could also be labeled as disingenuous or appear guilty of "virtue signaling," defined as "making a statement because you reckon it will garner approval, rather than because you actually believe it" (Shariatmadari, 2016, para. 5).

The callous boys' club culture under which Phil Knight founded and operated Nike in the 1970s worked poorly then as now. Knight (2016) affectionately referred to the early Nike leadership team as his "Band of Brothers" (p. 239), but he more commonly referred to them as "buttfaces" (p. 251). He described the culture of the company in 1976 this way: "Our meetings were defined by contempt, disdain, and heaps of abuse . . . We called each other terrible names . . . The last thing we took into account was someone's feelings" (Knight, 2016, p. 253).

Sanford (2020) wrote that leadership centered on social justice requires five commitments – good communication skills, the desire to call out injustices, willingness to be vulnerable, an ability to see people as individuals and share power with them, and involvement in the community outside of the organization. The leaders at Nike were certainly deficient in the first four commitments: Internal communication was admittedly hostile and abusive, the leadership was too homogenous and privileged to recognize injustices, the environment was hypermasculine and did not allow for humility and vulnerability, and the company structure discouraged power-sharing with entry-level employees or sponsored athletes. The environment described by Knight (2016) does not portray an inclusive, creative, safe space to work for most people, especially people with non-privileged identities (i.e., feminine, LGBTQIA+, BIPOC).

Not surprisingly, there were very few women at the company in the early days. By 2018, women represented only 38% of directors and 29% of vice presidents within the company (Creswell et al., 2018). At the end of 2019, nearly 80% of the vice presidents were White (Germano, 2021). In Felix's video in *The New York Times*, the former sponsored athlete noted a barrier in contract negotiations with Nike, stating, "the individuals who are negotiating these contracts are all men, and it might be more difficult for them to understand what we are going through, and what we have been through, and what we need" (Felix, 2019, 3:56).

In 1978, Nike ran a series of ads featuring women's running shoes on the back cover of *Runner's World*, declaring that "the idea of a woman athlete has come" and "women runners are every bit men's equal" (see Nike, 2015). In the same year, at a meeting of the top leadership, Knight (2016) called the meeting to order with a speech that included these phrases: "Our industry is made up of Snow White and the Seven Dwarfs! And next year . . . finally . . . one of the dwarfs is going to get into Snow White's pants!" (p. 276–277). Knight went on to explain that a rival shoe company was Snow White, and Nike represented the person getting into her pants. The early days of the company set the tone, as many of Knights' "buttfaces" continued to work for Nike for decades (Creswell et al., 2018; Germano, 2021) and had responsibilities for hiring and supervising employees.

Knight retired in 2016 and published his memoir, *Shoe Dog*, the same year. The book included troubling references to objectifying women (Knight's student later became his wife); the excessive drinking of Nike executives; body shaming overweight colleagues; making fun of the English used by second-language speakers; and Knight's tendency to ignore his employees, most notably Nike's "first employee" Jeff Johnson.

Although Knight's 400-page memoir thoroughly covers the time period between 1962 and the time until Nike was first publicly traded in 1980, there is no mention of the. U.S. Women's Liberation Movement; Title IX; the *Runner's World* women's campaign of 1978; or Nike's first female sponsored athlete Mary Decker (a runner signed in 1978). However, there are many pages dedicated to the first sponsored athlete Ilie Nastase (a male tennis player signed in 1972) and Steve Prefontaine (a male runner signed in 1973). When Nike went public in 1980, each "buttface" became an instant millionaire – not one female employee received any stock (Strasser & Becklund, 1991).

Discussion Questions

1. In what ways might the founding of Nike in the 1970s and its evolution in the 1980s and 1990s impact the organizational culture today?
2. Review some of the Nike advertising campaigns of the late 2010s discussed in this chapter. What are your initial reactions? How do the ads make you feel about the company? (See Nike, 2015 for pictures of some of the ads.)
3. Discuss any new developments of the treatment of female-identifying athletes by corporations such as Nike. Have there been any recent instances of discrimination against female-identifying athletes by their sponsors?
4. Consider a company or organization in the news that is currently responding to a crisis. Which of the five strategies of IRT (Denial, Evasion of Responsibility, Reducing Offensive, Corrective Action, Mortification) have they utilized or are they utilizing? Now, gauge their effectiveness.
5. Describe what the IRT's mortification step might look like for Nike in this case, as suggested by its own internal committee. What are the advantages and disadvantages of this approach for the company? For its stakeholders?

Notes

1 Women continue to experience inequality in running today. For example, in college cross country, women typically run 6k while men compete in 8k or 10k.
2 This ultimatum resulted in several health issues for Goucher after she felt pressured to run the Boston Marathon just 7-months postpartum.

References

Benoit, W.L. (1997). Image repair discourse and crisis communication. *Public Relations Review*, *23*(2), 177–186. https://doi.org/10.1016/s0363-8111(97)90023-0

Boateng, G. (2021, July 14). Allyson Felix launches a new athletic brand, Saysh, after cutting ties with Nike. *Forward Times*. https://forwardtimes.com/allyson-felix-launches-a-new-athletic-brand-saysh-after-cutting-ties-with-nike/

Brito, C. (2019, February 25). Nike's new Serena Williams ad encourages girls to 'dream crazier.' *CBS News*. www.cbsnews.com/news/serena-williams-oscars-2019-nike-ad-colin-kaepernick-dream-crazier/

Burfoot, A. (2016). *First ladies of running*. London: Rodale.

Burns, J.P., & Bruner, M.S. (2000). Revisiting the theory of image restoration strategies, *Communication Quarterly*, *48*(1), 27–39. https://doi.org/10.1080/01463370009385577

Cahn, S. (2015). *Coming on strong: Gender and sexuality in women's sport* (2nd ed.). Chicago, IL: University of Illinois Press.

Campbell, A.F. (2018, April 30). Report: Human resource managers at Nike ignored complaints from women employees for years. *Vox.* www.vox.com/policy-and-politics/2018/4/30/17302130/nike-women-harassment-discrimination-survey

Chappell, B. (2019, November 8). Nike to investigate runner Mary Cain's claims of abuse at its Oregon Project. *NPR.* www.npr.org/2019/11/08/777542988/nike-to-investigate-mary-cains-claims-of-abuse-at-its-nike-oregon-project#:~:text=In%20response%20to%20Cain%27s%20allegations%2C%20Nike%20says%2C%20%22We,nor%20her%20parents%20had%20previously%20raised%20the%20allegations

Chavez, C. (Host). (2021, July 12). Why Wes Felix and Allyson Felix started Saysh as a lifestyle, footwear company built for women. [Audio podcast episode]. *CITIUS MAG Podcast with Chris Chavez.* CITIUSMAG.com. https://podcasts.apple.com/us/podcast/citius-mag-podcast-with-chris-chavez/id1204506559?i=1000528665671

Clemmons, A.K. (2019, June 17). Are women athletes forced to choose between sponsorship and motherhood? *ESPN.* www.espn.com/espnw/life-style/story/_/id/26964549/are-women-athletes-forced-choose-sponsorship-motherhood

Creswell, J., Draper, K., & Abrams, R. (2018, April 28). At Nike, revolt led by women leads to exodus of male executives. *The New York Times.* www.nytimes.com/2018/04/28/business/nike-women.html

Danziger, P.N. (2019, March 1). Nike declares 2019 its year for women. *Forbes.* www.forbes.com/sites/pamdanziger/2019/03/01/nike-the-worlds-most-valuable-fashion-brand-declares-2019-its-year-for-women/?sh=7e3cdd8c419d

Felix, A. (2019, May 22). My own Nike pregnancy story. *The New York Times.* www.nytimes.com/2019/05/22/opinion/allyson-felix-pregnancy-nike.html

Germano, S. (2021, January 6). Can Nike keep its cool? *Financial Times.* www.ft.com/content/d4cbf3a8-77ec-4f0a-95ae-35f4e974d518

Germano, S., & Lublin, J.S. (2018, April 2). Inside Nike, a Boys-Club culture and flawed HR. *Wall Street Journal.* www.wsj.com/articles/inside-nike-a-boys-club-culture-and-flawed-hr-1522509975

Greenhouse, S. (1997, October 26). Nike supports women in its ads but not in its factories, groups say. *The New York Times.* www.nytimes.com/1997/10/26/us/nike-supports-women-in-its-ads-but-not-its-factories-groups-say.html

Hambleton, B. (2021, March 16). Athletes react to Nike pregnancy ad. *Canadian Running.* https://runningmagazine.ca/the-scene/athletes-react-to-nike-pregnancy-ad/

Handley, L. (2019, May 16). Nike's 'inclusive' image at risk if it fails women athletes, brand experts say. *CNBC.* www.cnbc.com/2019/05/16/nikes-inclusive-image-at-risk-if-it-fails-women-athletes-say-experts.html

Kilgore, A. (2019, August 16). Under fire, Nike expands protections for pregnant athletes. *The Washington Post.* www.washingtonpost.com/sports/2019/08/16/under-fire-nike-expands-protections-pregnant-athletes/

Knight, P. (2016). *Shoe dog: A memoir by the creator of Nike.* New York: Scribner.

Manning, J. (2021, October 12). Distance runner Mary Cain sues former coach Alberto Salazar, Nike over alleged abuse. *The Oregonian.* www.oregonlive.com/business/2021/10/distance-runner-mary-cain-sues-former-coach-alberto-salazar-nike-over-alleged-abuse.html

Montaño, A. (2019, May 12). Nike told me to dream crazy, until I wanted a baby. *The New York Times.* www.nytimes.com/2019/05/12/opinion/nike-maternity-leave.html

Montaño, A. (2021, March 19). Here's what Nike got wrong with its new maternity ad. *Runner's World.* www.runnersworld.com/runners-stories/a35877784/alysia-montano-nike-maternity-ad/

Moore, P. (2020, February 10). Why Altra signing two pregnant runners is a big deal. *Outside.* www.outsideonline.com/health/running/altra-pregnant-runners-alysia-montano-tina-muir/

National Collegiate Athletic Association. (2021). NCAA demographics database. www.ncaa.org/sports/2018/12/13/ncaa-demographics-database.aspx

National Federation of State High School Associations. (2019). 2018–19 high school athletics participation survey. www.nfhs.org/media/1020412/2018-19_participation_survey.pdf

Nike. (2015). Nike puts women front and center for 40 years and counting. https://news.nike.com/news/nike-women-advertising-a-40-year-journey

Nike. (2020a). 2020 annual report and notice of annual meeting. https://s1.q4cdn.com/806093406/files/doc_financials/2020/ar/363224(1)_16_Nike-Inc_Combo_WR_R2.pdf

Nike. (2020b). Creating a bond between motherhood and sport. https://news.nike.com/news/nike-m-maternity-collection

Nike. (2021a). Fortune. https://fortune.com/company/nike/

Nike. (2021b). Nike's film on motherhood celebrates female strength. https://news.nike.com/featured_video/nike-m-maternity-film-the-toughest-athletes

O'Kane, C. (2019, May 14). Nike responds to backlash over maternity leave policy. *CBS News.* www.cbsnews.com/news/nike-response-to-backlash-over-maternity-leave-policy/

Rivas, A. (2018). Here's the full-length Nike ad featuring Colin Kaepernick. *ABC News.* https://abcnews.go.com/US/full-length-nike-ad-featuring-colin-kaepernick/story?id=57623877

Running USA. (2020). U.S. running trends. www.wpr.org/sites/default/files/running_usa_trends_report_2019-r4.pdf

Sanford, A.A. (2020). *From thought to action: Developing a social justice orientation.* San Diego, CA: Cognella Academic Publishing.

Shariatmadari, D. (2016, January 20). 'Virtue-signaling' – The putdown that has passed its sell-by date. *The Guardian.* www.theguardian.com/commentisfree/2016/jan/20/virtue-signalling-putdown-passed-sell-by-date

Strasser, J.B., & Becklund, L. (1991). *Swoosh: The unauthorized story of Nike and the men who played there.* London: Harcourt Brace Jovanovich Publishers.

Strout, E. (2019, October 16). Kara Goucher on Alberto Salazar's doping violations ban: "I feel at peace." *Women's Running.* www.womensrunning.com/culture/people/goucher-on-alberto-salazar-doping-violations/

Switzer, K. (2009). *Marathon woman: Running the race to revolutionize women's sports.* Boston, MA: Da Capo Press.

The New York Times. (2019, November 7). I was the fastest girl in America, until I joined Nike [Video]. *Youtube.* www.youtube.com/watch?v=qBwtCf2X5jw

Vera, A. (2019, September 15). Colin Kaepernick's Nike ad wins Emmy for outstanding commercial. *CNN Entertainment.* www.cnn.com/2019/09/15/entertainment/nike-ad-emmy-win-trnd/index.html

West, J. (2019, May 24). Athletes speak out against Nike's lack of maternity leave protection, other companies make change. *Sports Illustrated.* www.si.com/olympics/2019/05/24/nike-maternity-protection-sponsorships-contract-allyson-felix-alysia-montano#:~:text=Athletes%20Speak%20Out%20Against%20Nike's,big%E2%80%94until%20they%20get%20pregnant.&text=Nike%20wants%20women%20to%20dream%20big%E2%80%94until%20they%20get%20pregnant.,-Nike%20prides%20itself

Young, S.M. (2021, March 16). Nike's new ad celebrating pregnant athletes falls flat, given its own history of mistreating them. *Yahoo Sports.* https://yhoo.it/3ihIWof

18

LET THEM WEAR SHORTS! ANALYZING THE NORWEGIAN WOMEN'S BEACH HANDBALL TEAM'S UNIFORM CODE PROTEST

Megan R. Hill, Karen T. Erlandson and Katey A. Price

Introduction

On July 20, 2021, the European Handball Federation fined each member of the Norwegian women's beach handball team by €150 Euros (about $170 USD) – a team total of €1500 – for violating the International Handball Federation's (IHF) uniform policy during their bronze medal match against Spain at the European Beach Handball Championships in Varna, Bulgaria (Gross, 2021a). The policy, which required female athletes to wear bikini bottoms "with a close fit and cut on an upward angle toward the top of the leg" (Gross, 2021a, para. 2), covering no more than 10 cm of the buttocks (International Handball Federation, 2014), had been an ongoing point of contention for the Norwegian team since as early as 2006, with players citing concerns about being sexualized and feeling personal discomfort and embarrassment, as well as issues related to cultural insensitivity and gender double standards (Gross, 2021a).

The Norwegian team's protest, in the form of wearing shorts during competition, was simple and timely, as women broadly, and female athletes in particular, continue the call for equity and inclusion reinvigorated by the #MeToo and other social justice movements. Against this backdrop, news of the rule and resulting fine spread quickly, generating a global public relations crisis for the IHF best epitomized by an IHF spokeswoman's revelation that she was unaware of the rule's origin and unable to explain its purpose (Gross, 2021a).

This case study examines how the IHF responded to this crisis through the lens of organizational legitimacy theory. As a sport governing body (SGB), the IHF possesses the ability to establish and regulate uniform policy (Vamplew, 2007). However, as an organization, the IHF does not and cannot operate with impunity. Rather, to maintain their legitimacy as an organization in society, their activities

DOI: 10.4324/9781003316763-21

and policies must align with societal expectations (Sethi, 1975; Suchman, 1995). In this case, the fine and, ultimately, the rule that generated the fine violated society's expectations regarding female athletes' rights, exposing the IHF's uniform code as socially undesirable and morally illegitimate, and damaging the organization's long-term legitimacy.

This chapter goes on to contextualize the Norwegian women's team's protest within female athletes' historic struggle for equity in sport, particularly as it relates to dress codes, highlighting how arguments regarding male viewership and the male gaze, although unfounded in today's media landscape, continue to be used to support a gender double standard in uniform policies. Public opinion on this issue has shifted, however, positioning the Norwegian athletes as empowered women taking control of their image on an international stage.

Background

The IHF, founded in 1946, is the administrative and governing body for the sport of handball, including beach handball (Krieger & Duckworth, 2021). As such, the IHF is tasked with a variety of duties, from organizing and overseeing international events, such as the Men's and Women's Handball Championships, to creating and/or amending the rules of the game (International Handball Federation, 2021). It is in this latter capacity that the IHF came under fire in July 2021.

Among the four categories of rules a SGB oversees are regulatory rules, which "place restraints on behaviour independent of the sport itself" (Vamplew, 2007, p. 845). Regulatory rules thus have no direct impact on a particular game or competition; rather, they are solely designed to reinforce particular types of athlete behavior. A sport's dress code, including whether there is a uniform and what it should look like, epitomizes this type of rule (Vamplew, 2007).

The IHF's uniform code, which required female athletes to wear bikini bottoms during play, had been a point of contention for the Norwegian Women's Beach Handball team for at least 15 years (Gross, 2021a). In 2006, the Norwegian Handball Federation (NHF) wrote a letter to the IHF arguing the IHF's "requirement for women to wear bikini bottoms was insensitive to some countries' cultural norms and could be embarrassing for those who did not want so much of their bodies exposed" (as cited in Gross, 2021a, para. 16). Moreover, the letter made the case that the sport itself, a fusion of soccer and basketball, necessitated changes to goalkeepers' uniforms in order to maintain player safety, as goalies block shots with all parts of their bodies (Gross, 2021a). Despite the Norwegian delegation's arguments, the IHF made no changes to the uniform code.

Then, in April 2021, during a meeting of the European Handball Federation, the NHF formally proposed changing the uniform code for the sport's female athletes. The motion was expected to be discussed at the IHF's international conference in November (Gross, 2021a), after both the European Beach Handball

Championships and Tokyo Summer Olympics took place. The timing meant the sport's female athletes would be required to wear bikini bottoms at both international events.

Organizational Legitimacy and Reputation

The IHF was within its rights as a SGB to delay making a final decision on women's uniforms until its November 2021 meeting. However, as the organizational legitimacy theory asserts, the IHF does not and cannot operate with impunity. Rather, to maintain their legitimacy as an organization in society, their activities and policies must align with societal expectations (Sethi, 1975; Suchman, 1995). If a discrepancy emerges between an organization's actions and society's expectations of their actions, a legitimacy gap may appear, fundamentally threatening the organization's legitimacy and reputation (Sethi, 1975).

As Suchman's seminal model of legitimacy (1995) asserts, "Legitimacy is a generalized perception or assumption that the actions of an entity are desirable, proper, or appropriate within some socially constructed system of norms, values, beliefs, and definitions" (p. 574). Legitimacy then, as a *generalized* perception, is an amalgamation of three primary types that are pragmatic (self-interest), moral (normative approval), and cognitive (comprehensibility), with "each type . . . rest[ing] on a somewhat different behavioral dynamic" (Suchman, 1995, p. 577).

Principally, pragmatic legitimacy's focus on the audience's self-interest means it can, literally and figuratively, be bought by providing rewards to specific stakeholders. Neither moral nor cognitive legitimacy may be attained in this way. Rather, because moral and cognitive legitimacies involve "larger cultural rules," engaging in such practices would serve to further delegitimize an organization along these dimensions (Suchman, 1995, p. 585). Similarly, perceptions of pragmatic and moral legitimacy are directly tied to an organization's participation in public discourse whereas cognitive legitimacy is not, meaning publicly defending one's actions and choices may serve to build an organization's pragmatic and moral legitimacy while simultaneously diminishing its cognitive legitimacy (Suchman, 1995).

Importantly, Palazzo and Scherer (2006) argue that among the three primary types of legitimacy, "moral legitimacy has become the core source of societal acceptance" as cognitive legitimacy is "eroding (e.g., shareholder value ideology, free and open market narratives, normative homogeneity)," and pragmatic legitimacy "provokes growing resistance (e.g., anti-globalization movement, no logo movement)" (p. 78).

Within this theoretical framework, SGBs, like the IHF, "should be in an enviable position, enjoying strong legitimacy, insulated from criticism on specific actions" (Anastasiadis & Spence, 2020, p. 31). This is due, in large part, to the way(s) in which the public continues to perceive sport(s) as "enhance[ing] social and cultural life by bringing together individuals and communities" (Council of Europe, 2022, para. 30). Such positive, collective sentiment toward sports is, in effect, a subtype of pragmatic legitimacy known as dispositional legitimacy, whereby organizations are regarded as individuals, "possessed of goals, tastes, styles, and personalities" (Suchman, 1995, p. 578). Organizations perceived as possessing positive attributes should thus possess additional moral legitimacy and be shielded from "the deligitimating effects of isolated failures, miscues, and reversals" (Suchman, 1995, p. 579)

Yet, organizations such as the International Olympic Committee (IOC), International Football Federation (FIFA) (e.g., Anastasiadis & Spence, 2020), and the National Football League (NFL) (e.g., Woods & Stokes, 2018) have all faced significant challenges to their legitimacy in the past few years. The crises these sports organizations have faced all stem from legitimacy gaps, which have subsequently affected each organization's reputation.

Organizational reputation is itself a combination of three factors that are personality (what the organization really is), identity (what the organization says it is), and image (what people view the organization as) (Abratt, 1989; Davies, 1998). The alignment of each of these factors is equally vital for building and sustaining an organization's reputation; similar to organizational legitimacy theory, where gaps occur among these three factors, reputational problems follow (Bernstein, 1984).

In this case, the IHF's inability to provide an explanation for its uniform code, along with its decision to enforce the code during the European Championships and Tokyo Summer Olympics, violated society's moral expectations regarding female athletes' rights, creating a legitimacy gap for the IHF. This gap was directly attributable to both the IHF uniform code's failure to meet societal standards and the organization's failure to adequately respond to the public's outrage. The IHF's slow and unsympathetic reaction to this crisis illustrated they were not only oblivious to the public's changing expectations of female athletes and their empowerment but indifferent to them as well, threatening the IHF's legitimacy as an organization and creating a reputational gap between the organization's identity and image. Simply put, the public's outrage was their way of telling the IHF: Let them wear shorts!

Sportswomen's Uniforms

The "let them wear shorts" sentiment represents a significant departure from how women's participation in sport has historically been regarded. In fact, women's participation in sport has largely been predicated on controlling how their bodies look, particularly through the use of austere uniform codes (Friedman, 2021). Such codes, created and enforced by SGBs composed solely of men, were justified with claims to respectability (Rosoff, 2021) and the need to differentiate female bodies from male bodies so audiences would not be confused about the athletes' gender. Exercising such control, however, has always been a hypocritical act, as SGBs have sought to both cover up female bodies so they are not indecent or too distracting to male audiences while also exposing more of the female body to attract a larger male audience (Friedman, 2021).

Women's sport history is replete with examples of female athletes being policed for their *decency* in uniforms even when subjected to uniform codes that stress the importance of looking good, and feminine, while they play. For example, the tennis manual from 1903 advises women to "look their best on the court, for all eyes are on them. Many an onlooker understands nothing about the game, and then the next thing generally is to criticize the player and her looks" (as cited in Chrisman-Campbell, 2019, para. 6). In 1919, Suzanne Lenglen directly and defiantly challenged tennis's uniform code by wearing a calf-length skirt with no petticoat and corset to Wimbledon, along with flat rubber-soled shoes. The press called her outfit "indecent" (Chrisman-Campbell, 2019). She won Wimbledon that year anyway. Almost 40 years later, in 1955, a 12-year-old Billie Jean King generated even more controversy after wearing shorts rather than a traditional tennis skirt to an amateur tennis tournament. Her attire was once again considered "inappropriate," and she was subsequently excluded from a group photo with her fellow competitors (Friedman, 2021).

More recently, in 2014, Angie Tatiana Rojas Suarez, a member of the Colombian women's cycling team, designed the team's uniforms, which were highly criticized (Chappell, 2014). The uniforms included a middle portion that was beige and made the women appear nude from their middle torso to their upper thighs, leading the head of the Union Cycliste Internationale to tweet that the uniforms were "unacceptable by any standard of decency" (Chappell, 2014, para. 7). The Colombian cycling program responded with a tweet of its own, posting a picture of a professional men's team wearing a similar uniform with the caption, "It's cycling, not fashion" (Chappell, 2014, para. 9).

The policing of female athletes' bodies via claims to decency belies the simultaneous means by which uniform codes stress femininity and sexuality as a means of attracting the male audience member's gaze (Benchetrit, 2021). The assumption here is that people (i.e., men) will not be interested in watching female athletes compete if they do not also look like a woman; specifically, a feminine woman. For example, in 2011, the Badminton World Federation tried to make women wear skirts and dresses (Friedman, 2021). According to the head of the federation, "TV ratings are down . . . We want [the women athletes] to look nicer on the court and have more marketing value for themselves. I'm surprised we got a lot of criticism" (Benchetrit, 2021, para 21).

As these examples illustrate, female athletes have repeatedly protested the hegemonic femininity imposed upon them by uniform codes but doing so comes at a price. As Krane (2001) asserts:

> Consequences of nonconformity to hegemonic femininity in sport often include sexist and heterosexist discrimination. This leads many sportswomen to emphasize feminine characteristics to avoid prejudice and

discrimination. However, females perceived as too feminine are then sexualized and trivialized, leaving women to carefully balance athleticism with
hegemonic femininity.

(p. 1)

Nevertheless, as this case illustrates, the assumptions (i.e., the male gaze) driving the uniform codes female athletes must follow are flawed, particularly in the
21st century. Not only do men no longer dominate sport viewership, but fans
are as interested in women's sports as men's sports as well, with recent research
indicating Millennials and members of Generation Z are both more likely than
other generations to identify as fans of women's sports (Silverman, 2021). Wom-
en's sports are also growing at six times the rate of men's (Sports Innovation
Lab, 2021). These numbers clearly indicate that women's sports are the future of
sports, and that future is now (Sports Innovation Lab, 2021).

Subsequently, the sport consumer is changing, as are their attitudes toward
female athletes. It is against this backdrop that the Norwegian Women's Beach
Handball team wore shorts to protest the IHF's uniform code.

The Case

Following the IHF's decision to table the uniform code change until its November 2021 meeting, the Norwegian Women's Beach Handball team set in motion
a plan to demonstrate just how irrational and sexist the uniform code was for the
sport's female athletes; they would wear shorts, rather than the required bikini
bottoms, during their bronze medal match against Spain at the European Championships (Gross, 2021a).

In doing so, the Norwegian team willfully, visibly, and unequivocally violated
the IHF's uniform code, leading the European Handball Federation to enforce the
rule, fining each player €150 Euros (Gross, 2021a). Rather than quietly resolving
the situation, news of the fine, which was publicly delivered just as the Tokyo
Summer Olympics were starting, went viral, generating "widespread condemnation, a petition against the rule and an offer from the singer Pink to pay the fine"
(Gross, 2021a, para. 7). That offer, in the form of a tweet (P!nk, 2021), succinctly
captured the public's general sentiment:

> I'm VERY proud of the Norwegian female beach handball team FOR
> PROTESTING THE VERY SEXIST RULES ABOUT THEIR "uni-
> form." The European handball federation SHOULD BE FINED FOR
> SEXISM. Good on ya, ladies. I'll be happy to pay your fines for you. Keep
> it up.

The initial response by the IHF further underscored the fact that the uniform code
contained no rationale related to legitimate, competitive advantage. Not only did

the IHF spokeswoman, Jessica Rockstroh, not know the reason for the rule but apparently neither did anyone else at the organization, which was "'looking into it internally'" (Gross, 2021b, para. 3.). The federation's inability to explain its own rule throughout this global public relations crisis further exposed the uniform code as fickle, as lacking any sport-specific rationale and, therefore, as illegitimate. This fact, combined with the IHF's inept response, increased the organization's legitimacy gap, as its actions in response to the critique were slow and apathetic (Sethi, 1978), underscoring the degree to which the rule, and the IHF's response, failed to promote a sense of social well-being (i.e., moral legitimacy).

The IHF neither made additional statements, nor engaged in any additional actions to close the legitimacy gap created by its uniform code for an entire month. Then, in August 2021, Hassan Moustafa, president of the IHF, divulged that the uniform code was derived from beach volleyball and conceded that under such intense, international outrage, the federation was "'very likely'" to change its rules (Gross, 2021a, para. 6) but could not do so until its international conference in November (Gross, 2021a).

Importantly, Moustafa did not explain why, if the uniform rule was based on beach volleyball, the IHF did not also follow the lead of that sport's ruling federation and provide women more, not fewer, uniform choices (FIVB, 2019). Rather, by attempting to shift blame for the policy to beach volleyball, Moustafa implicitly asserted that wearing bikinis instead of shorts enhanced the women's beach handball players' performance. There is, however, no evidence to support this argument. As Dr. Janice Forsyth, associate professor of sociology at Western University in Canada and former director of the University's International Center for Olympic Studies made clear, "I don't see how that argument holds any weight. To say that wearing less clothing, as the women are required to do, allows them to be better athletes is just silly" (Gross, 2021a, para. 22).

Moreover, in the IHF's extremely limited and delayed communication in regard to the case, the organization suggested it was "unfortunate" the protest had overshadowed the athletes' achievements (Gross, 2021b). Statements like these reinforce the contention the IHF was tone deaf in regard to the athletes' motivation, the public's outrage, and the continuing threat to the organization's legitimacy and reputation.

You Make the Call

On October 3, 2021, the IHF published a new set of uniform rules for female athletes. The new rules, effective January 1, 2022, state that "Female athletes must wear short tight pants with a close fit" (Gross, 2021c, para. 2).

From the start of this case, on July 20, 2021, to passage of the new rule, on October 3, 2021, 74 days passed. During that time frame, the IHF neither addressed the Norwegian team's motivation for its protest, nor provided a rationale for the resulting rule change (Gross, 2021c). In fact, by passing the rule change prior to their November international conference, the IHF undermined what little justification it had for not changing or amending the rule earlier, say in April 2021 or in July 2021, when news of the rule and fine generated international outrage.

The IHF's failure to implement any legitimacy repair or reputation management strategies during this crisis only exacerbated the damage done to both. The organization repeatedly demonstrated no resolve to address the crisis, a fact underscored by remarks made by the IHF president in August 2021, when he implied the rule would have likely remained in place had public outrage not reached such extraordinary levels. Such inaction flies in the face of legitimacy repair strategies, which argue that the first action to be taken is to address the crisis (Suchman, 1995), as well as crisis management strategies, which argue that the organization's response within the first few hours of a crisis is critical because it "set[s] the stage for how the organization is remembered for handling the event" (Ward & Aggozino, 2021, section 2).

Moreover, by supporting the European Handball Federation's fine and attempting to deflect responsibility for its own rule (unfairly) to another sport (i.e., beach volleyball), the IHF's attempt at a normalizing account (Suchman, 1995) backfired. Rather than distancing itself from the crisis, including from any moral responsibility associated with the rule's creation and enforcement, the IHF further undermined their cognitive legitimacy by appearing unwilling to acknowledge their repeated internal failures to address this issue, and their moral legitimacy, by failing to understand that the rule and fine were simply wrong. After all, beach volleyball changed its uniform rules in 2019; the IHF could have easily followed suit then, as well as at any point before or during this crisis.

Their failure to do so, as well as their failure to recognize the growing chasm being created between their identity and image, led to even more self-inflicted wounds, allowing this public relations crisis to continue to spiral out of control. The organization's repeated missteps during this crisis therefore damaged both its long-term legitimacy and reputation, and no rule change, however important, is likely to repair that.

In the end, the Norwegian team's protest was a crucial catalyst to prompt this change, leading Kare Geir Lio, head of the Norwegian Handball Federation, to say that he was proud of the women for "choos[ing] the right moment to say 'Enough is enough'" (Gross, 2021c, para. 9). In this case, the simple, yet powerful act of wearing shorts illustrated the growing influence of women in sport and society's recognition and validation of women's rights as athletes.

You Make the Call Questions

1. Who should decide what athletes wear during competition? Who actually decides?
2. Organizational legitimacy theory emphasizes that organizations attempt to enhance their legitimacy by aligning their values, and by extension their

rules and policies, with those of other organizations and the larger social system. What does this case say about the value system of the IHF? Of the NHF?

3. How, if at all, has the increased understanding of the science of performance affected the conversation about athletes' uniforms?

4. Many have argued that sex sells. Does it? What does this case tell us about the sexualization of female athletes in the 21st century and audience reactions and perceptions of that practice? How might being sexualized impact athletes' performances or perceptions of themselves?

5. In 2020, the International Ski Federation (FIS) updated its uniform rules to no longer require additional hip panels be sewn into female ski jumpers' suits. What happened to female competitors participating in the mixed team ski jump final during the 2022 Beijing Winter Olympics, and how, if at all, does this case's discussion inform your perception of the athletes' and the FIS' legitimacy and reputation, respectfully?

References

Abratt, R. (1989). A new approach to the corporate image management process. *Journal of Marketing Management, 5*(1), 63–76.

Anastasiadis, S., & Spence, L.J. (2020). An Olympic-sized challenge: Effect of organizational pathology on maintaining and repairing organizational legitimacy in sports governing bodies. *British Journal of Management, 31*, 24–41. https://doi.org/10.1111/1467-8551.12345

Benchetrit, J. (2021, July 30). Women athletes are pushing back against the uniform status quo. *CBC.* www.cbc.ca/news/entertainment/women-athletes-uniform-changes-1.6122725

Bernstein, D. (1984). *Company image and reality: A critique of corporate communications.* London: Holt, Rinehart & Winston, Ltd.

Chappell, B. (2014, September 15). 'Nude' or not, women's cycling team uniform makes waves. *NPR.* www.npr.org/sections/thetwo-way/2014/09/15/348714775/nude-or-not-womens-cycling-team-uniform-makes-waves

Chrisman-Campbell, K. (2019, July 9). Wimbledon's first fashion scandal. *The Atlantic.* www.theatlantic.com/entertainment/archive/2019/07/suzanne-leglen-wimbledon-fashion-scandal-tennis/593443/

Council of Europe. (2022). *Manual for human right education with young people: Culture and sport.* www.coe.int/en/web/compass/culture-and-sport

Davies, G. (1998). Reputation management: Theory versus practice. *Corporate Reputation Review, 2*(1), 16–27.

FIVB. (2019). *Beach volleyball teams' uniform guidelines for Games of the XXXII Olympiad Tokyo 2020.* www.fivb.org/en/beachvolleyball/Document/2020/Rule50/FIVB_BVB_OG_Teams Uniform_Guidelines_FINAL.pdf

Friedman, V. (2021, July 29). Who decides what a champion should wear? *The New York Times.* www.nytimes.com/2021/07/29/fashion/olympics-dress-codes-sports.html

Gross, J. (2021a, July 20). Women's handball players are fined for rejecting bikini uniforms. *The New York Times.* www.nytimes.com/2021/07/20/sports/norway-beach-handball-team.html

Gross, J. (2021b, August 12). Facing outrage over bikini rule, handball federation signals 'likely' change. *The New York Times.* www.nytimes.com/2021/08/12/sports/norway-beach-handball-team.html

Gross, J. (2021c, November 1). Handball federation ends bikini bottom requirement for women. *The New York Times.* www.nytimes.com/2021/11/01/sports/women-beach-handballbikini.html?campaign_id=2&emc=edit_th_20211102&instance_id=44361&nl=todaysheadlines&regi_id=51056587&segment_id=73273&user_id=df8ea14aa2ecd1b2654f5e0fcbbe8540

International Handball Federation. (2014). Rules of the game. www.ihf.info/sites/default/files/2019-05/0_09%20-%20Rules%20of%20the%20Game%20%28Beach%20Handball%29_GB.pdf

International Handball Federation. (2021). Rules of the game. www.ihf.info/sites/default/files/2021-10/09B%20-%20Rules%20of%20the%20Game_Beach%20Handball_E_0.pdf

Krane, V. (2001). We can be athletic and feminine, but do we want to? Challenging hegemonic femininity in sport. *Quest, 53*, 115–133. https://doi.org/10.1080/00336297.2001.10491733

Krieger, J., & Duckworth, A. (2021). Annexation or fertile inclusion? The origins of handball's international organisational structures. *Sport in History.* https://doi.org/10.1080/17460263.2021.1927810

Palazzo, G., & Scherer, A.G. (2006). Corporate legitimacy as deliberation: A communicative framework. *Journal of Business Ethics, 66*, 71–88. https://doi.org/10.1007/s10551-006-9044-2

P!nk [@P!nk]. (2021, July 24). *I'm VERY proud of the Norwegian female beach handball team FOR PROTESTING THE VERY SEXIST RULES ABOUT THEIR "uniform".* The [Tweet]. Twitter. https://twitter.com/pink/status/1419127641068630016?lang=en

Rosoff, N.G. (2021). "Exercise requires the greatest freedom"; Athletic clothing for American women, 1880–1920. In L.K. Fuller (Ed.), *Sportswomen's apparel in the United States* (pp. 19–33). Hoboken, NJ: Palgrave Macmillan.

Sethi, S.P. (1975). Dimensions of corporate social performance: An analytic framework. *California Management Review, 17*, 58–64.

Sethi, S.P. (1978). Advocacy advertising: The American experience. *California Management Review, 11*, 55–67.

Silverman, A. (2021, June 14). Olympics buck trend of interest gap for men's and women's sports. *Morning Consult.* https://morningconsult.com/2021/06/14/womens-sports-olympics/

Sports Innovation Lab. (2021). The Fan Project. www.sportsilab.com/blog/thefanprojectishere

Suchman, M.C. (1995). Managing legitimacy: Strategic and institutional approaches. *Academy of Management Review, 20*, 571–610.

Vamplew, W. (2007). Playing with the rules: Influences on the development of regulation in sport. *The International Journal of the History of Sport, 24*(7), 843–871.

Ward, J., & Aggozino, A. (2021). PR principles: Current proven practical. [eBook]. *Stukent.* www.stukent.com/higher-ed/pr-principles/

Woods, C.L., & Stokes, A.Q. (2018). Patching a crisis with CSR: How the NFL fumbled its handling of domestic violence. In T.L. Rentner & D.P. Burns (Eds.), *Case studies in sport communication: You make the call* (pp. 21–31). New York: Routledge.

19

SPORTS NEWS MEDIA, MAJOR LEAGUES, AND INTIMATE PARTNER VIOLENCE

*Steve Ingham, Jade Metzger-Riftkin
and Tara McManus*

Introduction

In 2019, the National Football League (NFL) exceeded $15.25 billion in revenue (Gough, 2021). That same year, Major League Baseball (MLB) continued its 17th year of consecutive fiscal growth, collecting nearly $10.7 billion (Brown, 2019). Beyond the impressive monies garnered by the leagues for their owners and the residual profits accrued by municipal, state, and regional businesses, the NFL and MLB are long-established cultural institutions in the United States. Players are elevated to celebrity status and presented as role models and relatable hometown heroes to a national audience (Fields, 2016; Lynch, Adair, & Jonson, 2014). However, that comes at a cost.

Card and Dahl (2011) found an increase in domestic assault reports connected with team loss. Adubato (2015) reported a strong correlation between NFL game days and an increase in the reporting of domestic violence. Gantz, Wang, and Bradley (2009) supported a similar link between football games and domestic violence reports. Given these connections, it is vital to understand how sports organizations attempt to frame athletes who have engaged in intimate partner violence (IPV).

In this chapter, we examined how sports organizations, including the National Football League, Major League Baseball, and sports news media, framed, negotiated, and contextualized how athletes accused of IPV should be understood within their respective situations. Using image repair theory (IRT) (Benoit, 2014, 2018) as a theoretical frame, we analyzed the IPV scandals of four athletes and the fallout from each, focusing particularly on how sports organizations utilized athletes' cultural capital to justify their interpretations of the athletes, the events, and the punishments (or lack thereof) that occurred as a result of the IPV.

DOI: 10.4324/9781003316763-22

Background

IPV became a cultural focal point in U.S. sports after the release of video footage showing Baltimore Ravens running back Ray Rice assaulting his then-fiancée Janay Palmer in an elevator in 2014 (Doerer, 2018; McCollough, 2019). The NFL and MLB responded to subsequent public outcry about player IPV by developing and implementing stricter league-wide domestic abuse policies. The NFL's 2014 updated Personal Conduct Policy and MLB's 2015 Joint Domestic Violence, Sexual Assault and Child Abuse Policy allowed league commissioners to punish players accused of domestic abuse, regardless of the results of a criminal investigation (McCollough, 2019; Pilon, 2017). Since 2014, more than two dozen players have been accused of IPV, with several arrested (Skrbina, 2018). However, responses by leagues, teams, fans, and sports journalists have varied widely based on the perceived value of the player in their respective sport (Doerer, 2018; Gonzalez, 2021; Pilon, 2017).

Because of the public nature of athletes in the NFL and MLB, players must navigate legal proceedings, journalistic investigations, and public perception as they leverage their cultural capital to maintain success and employment within their respective leagues. However, as MacGregor (2018) identifies, sexual assault is not an outlier among professional athletes as a population; instead, it is a function of sports culture. Her research found that athletes were involved in more sexual assaults than the general population and examined potential explanations for this, including toxic masculinity, the belief they are sexually entitled to women, and a belief that they can act with impunity (MacGregor, 2018). MacGregor believed that the language, which supports the athlete at the expense of the accuser, especially when used by the media, significantly impacts the narrative surrounding the event and contributes to a sports culture that glorifies violence (MacGregor, 2018). One of the factors that influences a player's ability to withstand accusations of IPV is cultural capital.

Cultural capital, a non-physical form of capital, is achieved through performance and social recognition (Bourdieu & Passeron, 1977). Sports organizations and news media, especially sports journalists, control information about athletes (McCombs & Shaw, 1972; 1993), becoming a source of information about organizations for audiences (Carroll, 2013). The way sports journalists report IPV scandals impacts the public image of athletes, teams, and sports organizations (Brown-Devlin, 2018). Therefore, cultural capital (and fiscal capital) can be gained or lost through how sports journalists frame the actors involved in an IPV scandal and the responses of organizational leadership to the IPV scandal.

Benoit (2014, 2018) developed a typology, known as IRT, to explain the various strategies and tactics people and organizations use to reduce or repair damaged reputations with audiences. There are five general strategies of denial, mortification, corrective action, reduce offensiveness, and evade responsibility. Additionally, there are six tactics to reduce offensiveness that are bolstering, minimization, differentiating, transcendence, attack accuser, and compensation (see Table 19.1).

Normally, when an organization's image is damaged, its public relations practitioners engage in image repair strategies to restore the company's reputation

TABLE 19.1 Sports Image Repair Strategies

Image Repair Strategy	Definition	Example from Sports	Relevant Example from Case Studies
Denial			
Simple denial	Did not perform act	Lance Armstrong denied doping	Addison Russell denied attacking his wife
Shift the blame	Another performed act	Athlete says trainer gave drugs	
Evasion of Responsibility			
Provocation	Responded to act of another	You fouled me, so I fouled you back	
Defeasibility	Lack of information or ability	We didn't know the stadium roof leaked	Montee Ball argued that his demons, including alcoholism, removed his agency to affect positive change
Accident	Mishap	Fall while skating was an accident	
Good intentions	Meant well	We wanted to help fans with new menu	
Reducing Offensiveness of Event			
Bolstering	Stress good traits	Armstrong helped through charitable donations	Hal Steinbrenner highlighted positive qualities of Aroldis Chapman
Minimization	Act not serious	Calling a person names is not as bad as causing physical injury	Kareem Hunt claimed the attack was not as bad as people believe
Differentiation	Making the act seem less offensive than the public perceives	Point shaving is not as bad as throwing a game	
Transcendence	More important values	It is OK to cheat if we help build a child's confidence	

Image Repair Strategy	Definition	Example from Sports	Relevant Example from Case Studies
Attack accuser	Reduce accuser's credibility	You can't believe my accuser; he/she just wants to keep me from participating	
Compensation	Reimburse victim	If you don't report athlete's misdeeds, we will give you season tickets	
Corrective Action	Plan to solve/prevent recurrence of problem	Athlete promises never to take performance-enhancing drugs again	Chiefs released Kareem Hunt after learning he lied to them
Mortification	Apologize; express remorse	Armstrong is sorry he lied about doping	Montee Ball stated that he is working to correct his imperfections

From Benoit, W. L. (2018). Image repair theory and sport. In A. C. Billings, W. T. Coombs, & K. A. Brown (Eds.). *Reputational challenges in sport: Theory and application* (pp. 25–38). Routledge. DOI: 10.4324/9781315165608

(Benoit, 2014, 2018). For the purpose of our case study, it is important to understand that news media, particularly sports media, act as a mechanism through which an organization, team, and athlete's reputation can be both injured and repaired.

Each strategy and tactic can occur in tandem with one or more of the others and can be simultaneously deployed differently by an athlete, team, and organization. For example, an athlete might deny involvement in an IPV scandal while emphasizing all the positive things they do for their community, engaging in both denial and bolstering strategies. As described in the next two sections, organizations, including sports news media and the NFL/MLB, utilized image repair strategies as they interpreted a player's IPV scandal. We included examples of four professional athletes: Addison Russell, Montee Ball, Kareem Hunt, and Aroldis Chapman. More information on each athlete is found in Table 19.2).

The Case

Sports News Media

Both Addison Russell and Montee Ball were embroiled in IPV scandals, and both men could be considered exceptional athletes in their respective fields. Russell was drafted by the Oakland Athletics directly from high school, with a sign-on bonus of

TABLE 19.2 Players, IPV, Position, and Team at Time of Incident

	IPV Scandal	*Position*	*Team*
NFL Players			
Montee Ball	June 28, 2014	Running Back	New England Patriots
Kareem Hunt	February 10, 2018	Running Back	Kansas City Chiefs
MLB Players			
Jose Reyes	October 31, 2015	Shortstop/Utility Player	Colorado Rockies
Addison Russell	June 7, 2017	Shortstop	Chicago Cubs
Aroldis Chapman	October 30, 2015	Closing Pitcher	Cincinnati Reds

$2.6 million (Ostler, 2014). He was traded to the Chicago Cubs in 2014. Two years later, he was the starting shortstop for the MLB All-Star Game and hit a Grand Slam home run in the sixth game of the World Series. In 2016, he played 151 games, hit 21 home runs, and had 95 runs batted in (RBIs) (MLB). In 2017, however, Russell's on-field performance began to slip. By mid-June "Russell was batting 209 with 3 home runs and 19 RBIs." (Rogers, Steele, & the AP, 2017, para. 16)

IPV allegations and a subsequent MLB investigation also began in June of 2017, prompted by a comment on an Instagram post made by Russell's then-wife, Melisa Reidy, initially alleging infidelity by Russell. The comment, written by a friend of Reidy, accused Russell of being "mentally and physically [abusive]" toward Reidy (AP, 2017a, para. 1). Reidy later went public with the abuse on her personal blog, detailing both the abuse during her marriage and the subsequent stalking she experienced once she decided to separate from Russell.

The news reporting around the IPV accusation emphasized Russell's denial of the allegation and the sympathetic actions of MLB leadership. Russell responded to allegations stating: "Any allegation I have abused my wife is false and hurtful. For the well-being of my family, I'll have no further comment" (AP, 2017a, para. 2). Then-Cubs Manager Joe Maddon said that "I have not lost confidence in him as a player," and Theo Epstein, then-Cubs president, stated that "Russell's comments to him after Wednesday's game were 'very consistent' with the statement" (Rogers, Steele, & the AP, 2017, para. 11). Kris Bryant, the 2017 National League Most Valuable Player, expressed shock when stating:

> I want to be a good teammate. Always want to be there to help. Addy is going to find a way to handle it. Like I said, we are all going to learn from it, hopefully be better for it. We don't know what happened. I don't know what's happened. It's early. . . . It is just unfortunate.
>
> *(Rogers, Steele, & the AP, 2017, para. 13)*

Despite the seriousness of these allegations, the headlines of these articles were "Cubs SS Addison Russell Returns to Lineup against Rockies" and "Russell's

'Serious Allegation,' Pedroia Returns," respectively. Neither headline lent credence to these allegations, and the single quotation marks around "Serious Allegation" in the latter title further reinforced the notion that the reporting of the IPV event seemed more obligatory than mandatory for the journalists.

Russell received a significant boost to his reputation when journalists heavily covered his mishap with a fan during a September 25, 2017 game against the St. Louis Cardinals:

> Russell helped the Cubs get to starter Luke Weaver (7–2) early, then made some friends out of rival fans. After diving into the stands chasing a foul ball down the third-base line and spilling a man's tray of chips, Russell emerged from the dugout a few innings later with a plate of nachos and delivered it to the fan. Russell stopped to take a selfie before heading back to play shortstop.
>
> *(Mayes, 2017, para. 2)*

This incident was referenced positively and repeatedly by journalists (AP, 2017b; Flaten, 2017; Mayes, 2017; Lyons, 2017; Kelly, 2017). Journalists highlighted his "apologetic" actions, detailing how Russell posed for a selfie and treated the group to beer and Italian ice (AP, 2017b, para. 3). Direct quotations from Russell's subsequent interviews and Twitter account showed him joking good-naturedly about the incident (Uria, 2017). The detailed and lighthearted reporting portrayed Russell as a positive influence on fans and overlooked the ongoing MLB investigation. Besides citing the Instagram post, Reidy and her council were rarely mentioned, no experts in IPV were sought out for a statement, and MLB's new domestic violence policy was rarely mentioned in news reporting on this incident between June and September 2017.

Montee Ball's circumstances were similar to Russell's. In high school, he was recognized by *Sports Illustrated* magazine (Fenwick, 2012) and was acknowledged as the Offensive Player of the Year by the *St. Louis American* (Austin, 2008). He played for the University of Wisconsin Badgers, setting the National Collegiate Athletic Association (NCAA) record for most points scored by a non-kicker, and tying the record for the most touchdowns in a season (Owczarski, 2012). He was a second-round draft pick by the Denver Broncos in 2013. However, his collegiate successes did not translate to the professional league. He finished his rookie year in the NFL with only 559 rushing yards and four touchdowns. He was released by the Broncos in September 2015 and signed by the New England Patriots in December. Despite this disappointing start, journalists consistently played up his previous college success and high draft selection into the pros (Wisconsin State Journal, 2015; Schultz, 2016).

In February of 2016, Ball was arrested on felony battery charges for assaulting his girlfriend. According to the police report, Ball threw his girlfriend across the room into a table where she sustained cuts to her leg. When questioned about a bruise on her lip, she stated Ball had backhanded her days prior. Ball was sentenced to 60 days of house arrest, 18 months of probation, and counseling (Schultz, 2016). In January 2017, TMZ released graphic photos of her injuries (TMZ Sports, 2017).

Journalists, especially those located in Madison, WI, where Ball attended the University of Wisconsin (UW), were keen to include his record-breaking college performances in their reporting of his criminal and NFL IPV investigations:

> At the UW, Ball was given the Doak Walker Award as the nation's most outstanding college running back in 2012 after he finished his career at the school as the NCAA's all-time leader in touchdowns with 82 and rushing touchdowns with 76.
>
> *(Schultz, 2016, para. 25)*

Reporters in follow-up articles about Ball discussed his family's history of alcoholism and his subsequent treatment for alcohol abuse.

At trial, Ball's attorney, Erika Bierma, told presiding Judge William E. Hanrahan that Ball was receiving alcohol counseling and his lack of criminal history made him a strong candidate for probation. Ball told Hanrahan he had a son living in Denver and counseling helped him "correct my imperfections. I understand I made a few mistakes in my life and I'm willing to do whatever I need to help myself" (Schultz, 2016, para. 10).

Ball's utilization of mortification and defeasibility strategies via the journalists allowed him to enter into an important redemption narrative. Unlike Russell, who deployed simple denial in a circumstance devoid of concrete evidence, Ball's actions were legally documented and thus subject to public record. Although both leagues would ultimately release these players (due to lack of performance, the IPV scandal, or both), journalists continued to reference the titles they had won, records they had broken, and their peak performances on their respective sports fields.

Sports Organizations

Kareem Hunt, running back for the Kansas City Chiefs, was accused of assaulting a woman in the hallway of a Cleveland hotel in 2018 (Conway, 2018).[1] Key members of the Chiefs, and the NFL overall, had different reactions to Hunt's IPV event. When news first broke about his assault, the NFL activated their domestic abuse policy to investigate Hunt (Conway, 2018). While no immediate punishment was handed down, they did engage in corrective action (Benoit, 2014, 2018) to remediate the situation. The Chiefs instigated their own investigation (de la Cretaz, 2018), asking Hunt about his actions on that day. Hunt told leadership that the allegations were not true (denial). While the Chiefs did not publicize this interview with Hunt by taking him at his word, they, too, engaged in denial (Benoit, 2014, 2018). Similarly, months after the event took place, the Chiefs attempted to minimize and redirect the act in an August statement:

> They're [players] not always going to make the best decisions, but we have a strong support system, both with the coaching staff and also with our player development department that works with young guys and talks to them about the situations they want to be in.
>
> *(de la Cretaz, 2018, para. 6)*

This quote barely acknowledges that a woman was assaulted by Hunt and focuses more on the youthfulness and inevitability of mistakes from NFL players. As de la Cretaz (2018) identifies, "this statement is testament to the redemption narrative that athletes are so often given," (para. 6) which ignores the health of women.

Only after TMZ published the video of Hunt attacking the woman (TMZ Sports, 2018) did the Chiefs release him. However, the statement issued by the Chiefs organization stated that Hunt was released because he lied to them about the incident, rather than for the incident itself (Chiefs Public Relations, 2018). While the Chiefs eventually engaged in corrective action (Benoit, 2014, 2018), the reasoning for Hunt's release still focused more on truthfulness between players and the organization rather than the assault itself.

After the Chiefs released Hunt on November 30, 2018, he did not wait long for a second chance. The Cleveland Browns signed Hunt on February 11, 2019, while he was still under investigation by the NFL (Patra, 2019). The general manager of the Browns, John Dorsey, knew that Hunt would face suspension, yet believed Hunt deserved a "second chance [to move] forward to be a better person" (Patra, 2019, para. 13). In an article about Hunt's signing with the Browns by Kevin Patra, the phrase "second chance" was used four times, twice by Dorsey and twice by Patra, reinforcing the idea that Hunt is a good man who acted badly, and is therefore deserving of redemption, even though the NFL investigation was still ongoing.

By framing Hunt as a good man who acted badly, Dorsey and the Browns engaged in a subcategory of IRT – bolstering. While Dorsey recognized that Hunt acted poorly, and that the Browns recognized and accepted the punishment for Hunt's actions, Dorsey consistently highlighted how Hunt had learned his lesson and would move forward as a better man. No mention of the woman's health or well-being was made, and there was no recognition of Hunt's violent actions. Instead, Dorsey focused on the upside of signing Hunt and adding his athletic value to the Browns, rather than the downside. The clear take-away message: If an athlete is good enough, he can be definitively caught assaulting someone and suffer no real negative consequences to his career or his life.

A second example of IRT and IPV applied at the sports organization level comes from MLB regarding Aroldis Chapman. Chapman was accused of assaulting his girlfriend and discharging firearms in an empty garage to intimidate her

(Brown & Passan, 2015, as cited in Gartland, 2015). This event was first reported by Dan Gartland in the midst of a potential Chapman trade between the Cincinnati Reds and the Los Angeles Dodgers, with the Dodgers subsequently backing out of the trade (Gartland, 2015). Similarly, Gartland reported that the Boston Red Sox were also interested in Chapman until they learned of the allegations (2016). While the organizations did not provide statements for avoiding this trade, their choices to not pursue the trades exemplified corrective action, an aspect of IRT (Benoit, 2014, 2018), by showing a refusal to accept Chapman, and his allegations, regardless of his talent.

The New York Yankees, on the other hand, did trade for Chapman, despite likely knowing about the allegations against him. As he began his career as a Yankee, Chapman faced an investigation by MLB. Hal Steinbrenner, owner of the Yankees, defended this decision by citing the "innocent until proven guilty" precedent of the U.S. legal system (McCarron, 2016, para. 2). He further justified his position by identifying positive aspects of adding Chapman, mainly that he has the talent to offset the potential negatives:

> Obviously, as a player, he's tremendous. We looked at him in July at the trade deadline . . . . A lot of thought was put into it. But the benefits for the organization as a player, if you look at the baseball side of it, is tremendous upside, needless to say.
>
> *(McCarron, 2016, para. 10)*

Implicit in this argument is that "benefits for the organization" rest solely on athletic performance rather than character, regardless of the results of the investigation. One of the first articles to report on Chapman's domestic violence investigation by Jorge L. Ortiz referred to it as the "latest, most disturbing stumble" (Ortiz, 2015, para. 4) for Chapman, referencing past infractions, such as speeding. The allegation referenced, however, was serious bodily violence (choking) and intimidation with a weapon (firing a gun eight times). By using this language, Yankee's owner Steinbrenner, as well as sports journalist Ortiz (among other journalists), engaged in the bolstering strategy of IRT as they identified Chapman's positive qualities while downplaying his negative actions (Benoit, 2014). After several months of investigation, MLB handed down a suspension of 30 games to Chapman, the first punishment under the new policy (Kroh, 2016).

As being players within a major professional sports league in the United States, athletes have tremendous power over their own narratives, particularly regarding their behaviors. However, organizations have even more power to frame, reinterpret, evaluate, punish, and reward players on a variety of factors. As outlined in these two examples, the NFL and MLB utilized their new domestic abuse policies to punish players for violations regardless of the outcome of a police investigation (neither Hunt nor Chapman faced criminal charges). At the team level, the Chiefs, Browns, Dodgers, Red Sox, and Yankees controlled how the actions of the player and the organization were interpreted. Similarly, when releasing, signing, or trading for an athlete who is being investigated, organizations must engage in strategies identified in IRT to justify their actions (Benoit, 2014, 2018).

Just like sports news media, sports organizations can control the narrative of their actions, repair their image, and move on as if the underlying problem no longer exists, even though IPV is still a highly prevalent and relevant issue in sports. There is no shortage of recent examples, including Frank Clark, Tyreek Hill, and Chad Wheeler (NFL) (Gonzalez, 2021); Sam Dyson and Roberto Osuna (MLB) (Lacques, 2021); and Alex Galchenyuk and Patrick Kane (NHL) (Skrbina, 2018). Players continue to commit IPV, and organizations continue to engage in IRT to alter how the public understands and perceives these events (Benoit, 2014, 2018).

You Make the Call

As discussed earlier, the NFL, MLB, and their respective teams must repair their image after one of their players is investigated for IPV. Organizations employ several strategies to do this, including denial (Russell), mortification (Ball), bolstering (Chapman), and corrective action (Hunt). These organizations have incredible power to control their own narratives, particularly the interpretation that athletic capability is more important than off-field misconduct. Additionally, sports news media, seen here through the lens of an organization as well, have incredible power to interpret and frame athletes in a similar manner. Through language like "second chance" (Patra, 2019, paras. 1, 14), "stumble" (Ortiz, 2015, para. 4), and a similar focus on athletic ability (Schultz, 2016), sports news media frame athletes as "good men who acted badly" rather than perpetrators of violent acts against women and children.

While these organizations did not specifically state whether their strategies were successful or not, we can infer much about their communication choices. Hunt has amassed 2,169 total yards and 19 touchdowns with the Browns since arriving in 2019 (Kareem Hunt – Stats, n.d.), signing a 2-year contract extension in 2020 (Ulrich, 2020). Based on his continued production, presence on the team, and the lack of conversation regarding his IPV accusations, it is possible to surmise that the Browns successfully repaired their image regarding this situation.

Although Chapman was traded to the Cubs in 2016, eventually winning the World Series, he re-signed with the Yankees in 2017, signing a new 5-year, $86 million contract. He amended his contract with the Yankees in 2019 for an extra 3 years, worth another $48 million (AP, 2019). Since returning to the Yankees, Chapman has pitched in 258 games (going 133/150 in save opportunities) with an earned run average of 3.03 (MLB Baseball – Aroldis Chapman, n.d.). We can infer that the Yankees (and Cubs), like the Browns, were successful in repairing their image after Chapman's accusation, investigation, and suspension. As mentioned previously, Ball and Russell are no longer in their respective leagues.

It was more difficult to measure sports news media's success at repairing the image of athletes since journalists and their organizations do not earn compensation or prestige based on how successfully they repair images. Instead, we can make the same inference regarding the athletes from other organizations, in that sports news journalists can frame, negotiate, and contribute to the image repair of athletes successfully based on the continued success of the athletes they support and failure of the athletes they demonize.

Athletes in the United States are positioned as heroes and icons, providing them opportunities not given to most people in the country (Fields, 2016; Lynch, Adair, & Jonson, 2014). Not only are they given more fame, fortune, and notoriety, they are also seemingly given more latitude for wrongdoing, particularly regarding IPV. However, athletes are not the only actors responsible for the interpretation of their actions. While most people accused of a crime or of wrongdoing argue they are innocent, they do not have organizational support. However, athletes, particularly in the NFL and MLB, are supported by those organizations, the teams for which they play, and by sports news media, if their athletic potential is deemed high enough. While the NFL and MLB have instituted and punished players under their respective domestic abuse policies, in reality, those policies have done very little to change the perception that athletes seemingly can get away with anything.

Discussion Questions

1. What is the responsibility of sports news organizations to include the voices of survivors of IPV while balancing privacy, legal proceedings, and readership?
2. What role do performance anxiety and stress play with regards to athletic performance and IPV, particularly when engaging in mortification and defeasibility strategies? Are factors like these ever justifiable excuses for an athlete's violent actions or reasons for leniency?
3. What responsibility do sports organizations, specifically the NFL and MLB, have in ensuring that their players are being cared for physically, emotionally, and mentally? Is it up to the NFL and MLB to institute mandatory programs, or are they allowed to follow other businesses that only step in (either to punish someone or force them into rehabilitation programs) when their issues/addictions affect their work?
4. How do other, more recent IPV scandals from professional athletes build on, develop further, or fall outside of this image repair typology?
5. How else could the decisions and actions made by sports organizations, including sports news journalists, be explained other than through the lens of IRT?

Note

1   While this technically falls outside the definition of intimate partner violence, we include it here because Hunt was punished under the same domestic abuse policy as Ball and organizations responded by engaging in image repair strategies, mirroring other examples as well.

References

Adubato, B. (2015). The Promise of violence: Televised, professional football games and domestic violence. *Journal of Sport and Social Issues, 40*(1), 22–37. https://doi.org/10.1177/0193723515594209

Associated Press (AP). (2017a, June 9). Leading off: Russell's 'serious allegation,' Pedroia returns. *Fox Sports.* www.foxsports.com/stories/mlb/leading-off-russells-serious-allegation-pedroia-returns

Associated Press (AP). (2017b, September 27). 'Nacho man' relates Cub's collision with snacks in St. Louis. *USA Today.* www.usatoday.com/story/sports/mlb/2017/09/27/nacho-man-recounts-cardinals-cubs-game/106046552/

Associated Press (AP). (2019, November 3). Aroldis Chapman and the Yankees agree to a contract extension. *The New York Times.* www.nytimes.com/2019/11/03/sports/baseball/aroldis-chapman-yankees-contract.html

Austin, E. (2008, January 3). Montee Ball, Brandon Harold earn top 'All American' large team honors. *St. Louis American.* www.stlamerican.com/sports/local_sports/montee-ball-brandon-harold-earn-top-all-american-large-team-honors/article_8d016c67–0e6d-5b04–84f5–728264ecdd2f.html

Benoit, W.L. (2014). *Accounts, excuses, and apologies: Image repair theory and research* (2nd ed.). London: SUNY Press.

Benoit, W.L. (2018). Image repair theory and sport. In A.C. Billings, W.T. Coombs, & K.A. Brown (Eds.), *Reputational challenges in sport: Theory and application* (pp. 25–38). New York: Routledge. https://doi.org/10.4324/9781315165608

Bourdieu, P., & Passeron, J. (1977). *Reproduction in education, society and culture.* New York: Sage Publications.

Brown, M. (2019, December 21). MLB sees record $10.7 billion in revenues for 2019. *Forbes.* www.forbes.com/sites/maurybrown/2019/12/21/mlb-sees-record-107-billion-in-revenues-for-2019/?sh=24c30e465d78

Brown, T., & Passan, J. (2015, December 7). Aroldis Chapman's girlfriend alleged he choked her, according to police report. *Yahoo! Sports.* http://sports.yahoo.com/news/aroldis-chapman-s-girlfriend-alleged-he – choked – her – according-to-police-report-023629095.html?nf=1

Brown-Devlin, N. (2018). Experimentally examining, crisis management in sporting organizations. In A.C. Billings, W.T. Coombs, & K.A. Brown (Eds.), *Reputational challenges in sport: Theory and application* (pp. 41–55). New York: Routledge. https://doi.org/10.4324/9781315165608

Card, D., & Dahl, G. (2011). Family violence and football: The effects of unexpected emotional cues on violent behavior. *The Quarterly Journal of Economics, 126*(1), 103–143. https://doi.org/10.1093/qje/qjr001

Carroll, C. (2013). Corporate reputation and the disciplines of journalism and mass communication. In C.E. Carroll (Ed.), *The handbook of communication and corporate reputation* (pp. 1–10). Hoboken, NJ: John Wiley & Sons. https://doi.org/10.1002/9781118335529

Chiefs Public Relations. (2018, November 30). Statement from the Kansas City Chiefs on RB Kareem Hunt. *Chiefs*. www.chiefs.com/news/statement-from-the-kansas-city-chiefs-on-rb-kareem-hunt?sf203419367 = 1

Conway, T. (2018, December 2). NFL says Kareem Hunt investigation 'ongoing' after RB wasn't interviewed. *Bleacher Report*. https://bleacherreport.com/articles/2808860-nfl-says-kareem-hunt-investigation-ongoing-after-rb-wasnt-interviewed

de la Cretaz, B. (2018, December 3). Sports culture still does not see the female victims of star male athletes as valuable – and it shows. *Vice*. www.vice.com/en/article/nepdgm/kareem-hunt-and-a-sports-world-that-ignores-domestic-violence-victims-kansas-city-chiefs

Doerer, K. (2018, December 7). The NFL's problem with violence against women: A story of profit and apathy. *The Guardian*. www.theguardian.com/sport/2018/dec/07/the-nfls-problem-with-violence-against-women-a-story-of-profit-and-apathy

Fenwick, A. (2012, December 3). Faces in the crowd. *Sports Illustrated*. https://vault.si.com/vault/2012/12/03/faces-in-the-crowd

Fields, S. (2016). *Game faces: Sport celebrity and the laws of reputation*. Chicago, IL: University of Illinois Press. https://doi.org/10.5406/illinois/9780252040283.001.0001

Flaten, M. (2017, October 6). Decatur-area Cubs fans optimistic entering postseason. *Herald & Review*. https://herald-review.com/news/local/decatur-area-cubs-fans-optimistic-entering-postseason/article_a0d9642b-7466-5e1f-90f9-562ff902ffee.html

Gantz, W., Wang, Z., & Bradley, S. (2009). Televised NFL games, the family, and domestic violence. In A.A. Raney & J. Bryant (Eds.), *Handbook of sports and media* (pp. 396–415). New York: Routledge. https://doi.org/10.4324/9780203873670

Gartland, D. (2015, December 7). Report: Aroldis Chapman trade held up over domestic violence allegations. *Sports Illustrated*. www.si.com/mlb/2015/12/08/aroldis-chapman-domestic-violence-allegations-dodgers-trade

Gonzalez, T.D. (2021, April 16). Seahawks' stance against domestic abuse continues to fall on deaf ears. *Sports Illustrated*. www.si.com/nfl/seahawks/news/seahawks-stance-against-domestic-abuse-continues-to-fall-on-deaf-ears

Gough, C. (2021, September 8). Total revenue of the National Football League 2001–2020. *Statistica*. www.statista.com/statistics/193457/total-league-revenue-of-the-nfl-since-2005/

Kareem Hunt – Stats. (n.d.). NFL. www.nfl.com/players/kareem-hunt/stats/career

Kelly, M. L. (2017, September 26). Dive for pop fly sends baseball fan's nachos flying [Radio broadcast transcript]. *NPR*. www.npr.org/2017/09/26/553661935/dive-for-pop-fly-sends-baseball-fans-nachos-flying

Kroh, K. (2016, March 4). The problem with focusing on Major League Baseball's first domestic violence punishment. *Think Progress*. https://archive.thinkprogress.org/the-problem-with-focusing-on-major-league-baseballs-first-domestic-violence-punishment-91d040512c20/

Lacques, G. (2021, March 5). MLB pitcher Sam Dyson suspended entire 2021 season for domestic violence. *USA TODAY*. www.usatoday.com/story/sports/mlb/2021/03/05/sam-dyson-suspended-2021-mlb-domestic-violence/4599542001/

Lynch, S., Adair, D., & Jonson, P. (2014). Professional athletes and their duty to be role models. In M. Schwartz, H. Harris, & A. Tapper (Eds.), *Research in ethical issues in organizations: Achieving ethical excellence* (Vol. 12, pp. 75–90). Emerald Group Publishing Limited. https://doi.org/10.1108/S1529-209620140000012012

Lyons, J. (2017, September 27). Cubs clinch division title with 5–1 win over Cards. *St. Louis Post-Dispatch*. www.stltoday.com/sports/baseball/professional/cardinal-beat/dejong-rbi-wacha-k-s-have-cards-up-/article_1726840d-8a96-5111-aa08-bb24964cf682.html?mode=comments

MacGregor, W. (2018). It's just a game until someone is sexually assaulted: Sport culture and the perpetuation of sexual violence by athletes. *Education & Law Journal, 28*(1), 43–73.

Mayes, W. (2017, September 26). Russell makes food run, Cubs beat Cards to near clinch. *AP*. https://apnews.com/article/49fae3a3c8e5429fb915f44ed3b0ca15

McCarron, A. (2016, January 20). Yankees owner Hal Steinbrenner says alleged domestic abuser Aroldis Chapman 'innocent until proven otherwise.' *New York Daily News*. www.nydailynews.com/sports/baseball/yankees/yankees-owner-chapman-innocent-proven-article-1.2503820

McCollough, J.B. (2019, May 17). Sports leagues hope to win where criminal justice system hasn't on domestic violence. *Los Angeles Times*. www.latimes.com/sports/dodgers/la-sp-sports-domestic-violence-policy-julio-urias-dodgers-20190518-story.html

McCombs, M., & Shaw, D. (1972). The agenda-setting function of mass media. *The Public Opinion Quarterly, 36*(2), 176–187. www.jstor.org/stable/2747787

McCombs, M., & Shaw, D. (1993). The evolution of agenda-setting research: Twenty-five years in the marketplace of ideas. *Journalism of Communication, 43*(2), 58–67. https://doi.org/10.1111/j.1460-2466.1993.tb01262.x

MLB Baseball – Aroldis Chapman. (n.d.). MLB Baseball – Aroldis Chapman. *The Washington Post*. http://stats.washingtonpost.com/mlb/playerstats.asp?id=8616

Ortiz, J.L. (2015, December 8). Chapman's latest stumble may prove his costliest. *USA Today*. www.usatoday.com/story/sports/mlb/2015/12/08/aroldis-chapman-domestic-violence/76968672/

Ostler, S. (2014, February 24). Shortstop Russell is taking fast track to big leagues. *SFGate*. www.sfgate.com/athletics/ostler/article/Shortstop-Russell-is-taking-fast-track-to-big-5264171.php

Owczarski, J. (2012, November 20). Is Montee Ball one of the greatest of all time? *OnMilwaukee*. https://onmilwaukee.com/articles/monteeballgreatest

Patra, K. (2019, February 11). Cleveland Browns sign running back Kareem Hunt. *NFL*. www.nfl.com/news/cleveland-browns-sign-running-back-kareem-hunt-0ap3000001017583

Pilon, M. (2017, January 31). Inside the NFL's domestic violence punishment problem. *B/R Mag*. https://mag.bleacherreport.com/nfl-domestic-violence-policy-suspensions/

Rogers, J., Steele, M., & the Associated Press. (2017, June 8). Cubs' Addison Russell denies domestic violence accusation. *ESPN*. www.espn.com/mlb/story/_/id/19578868/mlb-investigating-domestic-violence-accusation-chicago-cubs-addison-russell

Schultz, R. (2016, August 5). Former UW running back Montee Ball gets 60 days in jail for domestic violence incidents. *The Wisconsin State Journal*. https://madison.com/news/local/crime-and-courts/former-uw-running-back-montee-ball-gets-60-days-in-jail-for-domestic-violence-incidents/article_b5228676-fe41-5647-b813-a2c95fd3e1b6.html

Skrbina, P. (2018, September 18). When pro athletes are accused of abuse, how often does punishment follow? *Nashville Tennessean*. www.tennessean.com/story/sports/nhl/predators/2018/09/19/nfl-domestic-violence-sexual-assault-child-abuse-nba-mlb-nhl/1335799002/

TMZ Sports. (2017, January 7). Ex-NFL RB Montee Ball bloody photos from female battery case released. *TMZ*. www.tmz.com/2017/01/07/montee-ball-victim-injuries-photos/

TMZ Sports. (2018, November 30). Kareem Hunt cut by the Chiefs for brutalizing woman on video . . . team says he lied. *TMZ*. www.tmz.com/2018/11/30/kc-chiefs-kareem-hunt-attacked-kicked-woman-surveillance-video/

Ulrich, N. (2020, September 8). Kareem Hunt agrees to two-year, $13.25 million extension with Cleveland Browns. *USA TODAY*. www.usatoday.com/story/sports/nfl/browns/2020/09/08/kareem-hunt-contract-extension-cleveland-browns-running-back/5748936002/

Uria, D. (2017, September 26). Baseball fan loses nachos to acrobatic fielder. *UPI*. www.upi.com/Odd_News/2017/09/26/Baseball-fan-loses-nachos-to-acrobatic-fielder/1141506451279/

Wisconsin State Journal. (2015, December 15). NFL: Patriots sign former Badgers running back Montee Ball to practice squad. *The Wisconsin State Journal*. https://madison.com/wsj/sports/football/professional/nfl-patriots-sign-former-badgers-running-back-montee-ball-to/article_afc26bd0–4ef7–54c6-a358–482e877340ed.html

20

"PLAY LIKE THE LADY YOU ARE"

Marketing Women's Gaelic Football

Niamh Kitching

Introduction

Discourses of sports media and communication can both reflect and construct attitudes and prejudices to wider society, and these narratives are evident in research on the representation and portrayal of sportswomen. Sport is overwhelmingly constructed as a male domain in the media; when women do appear, they are framed differently to men and in ways that retain the hegemonic position of men in sport (Bruce, 2016). Similarly, strategies used in the marketing and advertising of women's sport have reduced it to a sexualized, infantilized, hyper feminized, "pinkified" pursuit, at all times inferior to and less serious than men's sport (Esmonde et al., 2015; Toffoletti, 2017). Subsequently, these representations can restrict the public's imagination about women's sport and what women can achieve. Following on from other media representation work by Kitching and others (Kitching et al., 2021; Bowes and Kitching, 2021; Kitching et al., 2020; Kitching and Bowes, 2020), this case study chapter considers how one women's sports organization and its partner sponsor chose to depict women's presence in sport through a faux media and advertising campaign.

Gaelic games are gaining prominence globally, with the sports of hurling and Gaelic football in particular growing in all parts of the world. With over 2,200 clubs, the volunteer-led sports organization, the Gaelic Athletic Association (GAA), is the most prominent cultural and sporting institution on the island of Ireland. Almost 100 years after its initiation, the GAA's sister organization the Ladies Gaelic Football Association (LGFA) was founded in 1974 and is the largest sports organization for women and girls in Ireland, with its rate of membership growth described at a governmental hearing as "exponential" (Government of Ireland, 2021). The increasing prominence of intercounty

DOI: 10.4324/9781003316763-23

women's Gaelic football has attracted corporate and commercial attention from global brands such as AIG insurance. In 2022, global supermarket giant Lidl announced an extension of their partnership with the LGFA until 2025, bringing their investment to €10 million over 10 years. The original extension of the deal was already one of the largest sponsorship investments in women sports in Europe (Ladies Gaelic Football Association, 2018). In the period since Lidl partnered with the LGFA, the participation of girls has increased by 73%, perhaps demonstrating the continued growth of the sport in this period (Ladies Gaelic Football Association, 2022a).

The LGFA–Lidl partnership was uniquely initiated in 2016 via a faux media campaign, the center of which was a fabricated pink ball product called "Ladyball." The "outrage marketing" stunt was accompanied by 360-degree advertisements, and the product was described as "fashion-driven for a woman's style" and "specially designed for a lady's game." While the Lidl/LGFA partnership has been somewhat unprecedented in its support for the broad participant base in women's and girls' Gaelic football, and while the ensuing Lidl/LGFA #SeriousSupport campaigns were more in line with Bruce's (2016) new rules for female athlete representation, elite LGFA players still lag behind their male equivalents in the GAA in terms of government grants, media attention, and match attendance. This case study draws attention to the gendered communication and advertising strategy used to launch the LGFA–Lidl partnership, with particular focus given to how sports organizations choose to frame and represent both their athletes and women's sport.

Background

The professionalization and commercialization of women's sport in recent years have attracted much attention from corporate sponsors (Nielsen Sports, 2018), and a small number of studies have outlined the motivation, potential, and strategies used in these partnerships. Morgan's (2019) study on women Australian rules football found that sponsors were motivated by a desire to promote gender equality and that this aim converged with their corporate social responsibility goals. Lough and Greenhalgh (2019) suggest that women's sport could offer sponsors flexibility and the ability to achieve their marketing objectives more efficiently and effectively than their competitors. From a marketing strategy point of view, Doyle et al. (2021) suggest that women's sport can differ from men's sport by promoting players as role models and their teams as champions of diversity and inclusion. There is no doubting the potential for sponsors of women's sport, but of concern in this case are the strategies employed to maximize revenue for the associated brands.

As previously mentioned, there are many studies confirming the lack of coverage dedicated to women's sport, along with the gendered representation and framing techniques employed particularly by sports media (e.g., Domeneghetti,

2018). Fink (2015) suggests that women's sport receives starkly disparate treatment by the sport media commercial complex, compared to male athletes and sport. Bruce (2008) posits that when women receive media coverage, specific approaches, more in line with cultural ideas about femininity, are used (e.g., gender marking, compulsory heterosexuality, appropriate femininity, infantilization, and the downplaying of women's sport). Studies on the portrayal of both women's sport and individual female athletes in public relations and advertising campaigns are fewer in number, though they carry much of the same outcomes.

In a study of how Nike advertising reified gender stereotypes in sport over the past decade, Rasmussen et al. (2021) found that Nike commercials continued to treat sport as a predominantly masculine domain. In a study examining how instant noodle giant Nissin Foods represented its sponsored athlete Naomi Osaka, Ho and Tanaka (2021) found the advertisements' representations of Osaka reflected the same gendered ideologies apparent in homogenous Japanese society. Franklin and Carpenter (2018) argue that while surfing companies prosper on sexualized images used in the marketing and sponsorship of female professional surfers, they do little to promote women's surfing prowess and ability. In relation to fitness advertising, Drake and Radford (2021) found that advertisements glorify the pursuit of the ideal female body, thereby discounting women's potential in, and contributions to, sport. In summary, the available evidence from marketing and public relations indicates the same triviality with which brands are representing both female athletes and women's sport more broadly.

Gaelic games have grown in significance on local, national, and global levels in recent years. Gaelic football is one of the two primary Gaelic field sports, the other being the stick sport of hurling (men)/camogie (women). The governing body for men's Gaelic football and hurling —although an amateur sports organization – the GAA attracts sponsorship, endorsements, and media coverage at unprecedented levels for a national sport. While there are over 2,000 GAA grounds in Ireland, the participation of LGFA and camogie teams at these venues is at the behest of arrangements made with the local club. While the chief executives of the LGFA and Camogie Association have been non-voting members in recent years, it was only in 2021 that the first woman full member was appointed to the GAA's central management committee.

It is clear that the GAA remains a normatively male organization, while the LGFA and Camogie Association often come off second best in terms of visibility and access to pitches, facilities, stadiums, and large and long-term sponsorship. In this way, GAA discourses set the parameters for what is possible for women's Gaelic games. For example, commentary around Gaelic games often assumes ladies football and camogie as part of, rather than separate to, the GAA. One such instance occurred when the Limerick men's hurling team won the all-Ireland final in 2018. After the win, Limerick's benevolent sponsor and philanthropist, JP MacManus, donated €100,000 to each of the 32 GAA county boards, which was then to be distributed to every club, a magnanimous display of generosity toward Gaelic games. Or was it? LGFA and Camogie Association clubs do not occupy seats on GAA county boards and, thus, may have received nothing from the MacManus donation.

The LGFA was formed in 1974 at a symbolic time when the position of women in Irish society was improving, but the LGFA was only officially recognized by the GAA in 1982 (Kilgallon, 2021). In the initial decades, women's Gaelic football grew slowly, but key to its development was the interception of the Irish language television station TG4. The channel has broadcast games live, free to air since 1995 and became one of the sport's first big sponsors also supporting the all-Ireland intercounty championship since 2001. The 2021 All-Ireland final between Meath and Dublin was the second most watched program on TG4 in 2021. Women's Gaelic football continued to grow incrementally but steadily. In 2007, the LGFA had 132,182 members; that figure increased to over 188,000 by 2018. Today, LGFA membership is expected to be over 200,000.

Similarly, match attendances have grown immensely; while finals in the 1970s attracted as few as 3,000 people (Kilgallon, 2021), by 2015, the attendance at the All-Ireland final had grown to 31,083 – the highest attendance for any women's sporting event in Europe that year. Prior to the COVID-19 pandemic, the record attendance was over 56,000 for the 2019 finals, while the 2021 final was capped at 40,000 spectators due to COVID-19 restrictions. In summary, while it has always operated in the shadow of the GAA, women's Gaelic football is growing participation and gaining visibility and profile.

While the commercialization of women's sport has grown significantly in recent years, this growth was still in its infancy at the time of the Ladyball campaign in early 2016. To help put into context, the campaign took place prior to equal pay and treatment protests in women's elite sport, such as the Irish women's soccer team strike over team equipment and remuneration (2017) and, more broadly, the initiation of legal action by members of the U.S. women's national soccer team (2016). Around the time of the Ladyball campaign, the prolific Cork men's hurling team had just won their tenth All-Ireland championship in 11 attempts, and they went on to win the 2016 final as well. As such, LGFA and women's Gaelic football may not have been as appealing a proposition for sponsors then, compared with the time of this writing.

The Case

The subject of this chapter is the initial launch of Lidl's longer running partnership with the LGFA. In January 2016, advertisements of a fabricated pink ball product called "Ladyball" began to appear on national television, radio, newspapers, online, and throughout social media, with consumers directed to the-ladyball.com and various social media channels. The Ladyball ball product was placed in pink, shiny packaging, accompanied by slogans such as "Don't break a nail, break boundaries." The product was described as "eazi-play for a woman's ability" and "fashion-driven for a woman's style." A PR event was held and a press release issued, with the photocall depicting scantily clad women models dressed in pink. The models were accompanied by a well-known male GAA footballer who endorsed the product commenting, "I have no doubt the softer texture will be welcomed by all the ladies out there." *As is the aim with "outrage" marketing, the appearance of Ladyball stimulated conversation over social media. Within three days, the Ladyball video garnered over 300,000 views; it topped Twitter trends in Ireland and reached over 8.5 million users on social media (The Institute of Creative Advertising and Design, 2016).* The campaign was even discussed in *Fortune* magazine (Zarya, 2016) and *The Washington Post* (Bonesteel, 2016). Three days later, both Lidl and the LGFA owned up to the faux campaign, which led to the second stage of the promotion, a wide-reaching campaign called #SeriousSupport which was accompanied by a television advertisement featuring LGFA players competing in various Gaelic football scenarios.

The company employed by Lidl to carry out the marketing promotion outlined their "agitate" approach to this phase of the outrage campaign, whereby Ladyball aimed to create a pool of negative support they hoped they could then re-distribute to the "support" phase (i.e., #SeriousSupport) (The Institute of Creative Advertising and Design, 2016). From the LGFA point of view, the stated aim of the campaign was to put "the spotlight on women in sport in Ireland and raise awareness of the difficulties female sports persons have in getting the same recognition as their male counterparts" (Ladies Gaelic Football Association, 2016, para 2). The President of the LGFA, Marie Hickey, commented:

> This is a very significant announcement for our sport and one that will see a huge investment in the game from a major brand . . . we hope to see everyone who spoke so passionately when defending women in this debate . . . channel that same energy into pitch side support during the coming season.
> *(Ladies Gaelic Football Association. (2016, para 4)*

The CEO of the LGFA said that "My one wish out of the campaign would be that people would put their energies into supporting not only our sport but women in sport in general" (Lidl Ireland, 2016). In summary, the LGFA appeared pleased with the campaign, and particularly so with the long-term partnership they made with their new sponsor.

You Make the Call

What requires further explication in the Ladyball case are the choices made in the first phase of the marketing campaign. Depictions of sexualized and hyper-feminized women models have long since been part of the narrative in promoting and advertising men's sport, particularly in the likes of motorsport and combat sports. Ladyball is not the first case of old tropes of sexualization being used in advertising related to Gaelic games. In 2011, a potato crisp company called Hunky Dory ran an advertisement in Ireland with images of scantily clad models portrayed as Gaelic footballers and with images focused on the women's cleavage and midriffs with the captions, "proud supporters of Gaelic football", "still staring", "bursting with flavour", and "taaaasty" (Stack, 2011). The advertisement received over 80 complaints before it was taken down. In terms of player representations, in 2013, injured Wexford camogie player Katrina Parrock gained the unwanted attention of television media when she appeared in denim shorts and a vest/t-shirt top while providing water for her teammates at a match. Putting the focus on women's bodies deflects attention away from women's athletic performance and positions them as objects for the attention of men. In this way, sport is positioned as "by" and "for" heterosexual men (Channon et al., 2018), while women's sport is deemed unimportant or not worthwhile. In terms of consumer views on the representation of women's sport, there is evidence to show that sports fans rate athletic prowess and sports performance-related images more positively than sexualized images of athletes or "sexy babes" (Daniels et al., 2021; Kane & Maxwell, 2011). The choice of a male GAA player alongside hyperfeminized and sexualized women models accompanying him in the press photos further emphasized how male opinions and views are valorized in the Gaelic games environment, and how women are othered or positioned as objects in the context of the male domain of sport.

Gendered marketing practices such as the "pinkification" of women's sport have become commonplace in the marketing and merchandising of sport to women. Esmonde et al. (2015) suggest that though these practices are sometimes considered inclusive efforts, they serve only to infantilize and hyperfeminize women sports fans, strategies that often 'other' female followers of sport. Sveinson et al. (2019) suggest that sports organizations should recognize the more diverse nature of women's gender identities and provide a wider range of products that demonstrate their status as authentic fans of sport. In analyzing the responses to the U.S. Soccer Federation's promotion of feminized fan clothing, Sveinson and Allison (2021) found an overwhelming dislike for hyperfeminized items that were marketed to women and girls and suggested that this indicated organizational cultural issues within the U.S. Soccer Federation. Using girls to market women's soccer in the United States (Allison, 2021), while marketing women's football to a heteronormative family target audience in England both illustrate the hackneyed, tunnel-visioned marketing practices that are currently employed through women's sports (Fielding-Lloyd et al., 2020). There is a need for sports organizations to recognize their fan base, particularly when much research is now available indicating the wide typology of female fans (e.g., Richards et al., 2020). The choice of a pink product only served to encourage the "pinkification" of sport for women, and it is possible that these marketing decisions are perpetuating traditional stereotypes and cultural values around sport for both women and girls.

Further, the Ladyball case illustrates the risks and choices for sports organizations and athletes in engaging in marketing and advertising campaigns. While the LGFA, at least publicly, indicated no reputational damage arising from Ladyball, the perils of sponsorship were also laid bare through Ladyball. In a separate 2015 advertisement controversy, this time linked to an LGFA sponsor, television station TG4 tweeted an image of a player holding a football at her abdomen, in a pose reminiscent of a pregnant woman, with the caption "the most important nine months of a woman's life . . . January to September." The LGFA reported the ad was created years before by an agency and was never meant to be aired (Irish Examiner, 2015). The research around representation strategies found that, for elite women athletes, they preferred being portrayed as competent in sponsorship campaigns (Fink et al., 2014). The premise behind the Ladyball campaign was that marketing women's sport required a shock or agitate campaign however, evidence from consumers of sport shows indicate that these approaches are no longer necessary. Interestingly, what may be disappointing from a woman athletes' viewpoint is that old stereotypes remain embedded in their own worldviews. In examining how elite female athletes responded to their portrayals in sports media, the same authors (Kane et al., 2013) found that competence was the best representative strategy; however, many respondents chose "soft porn" to best increase interest, thereby confirming athletes' beliefs that "sex sells" women's sports, particularly to male audiences. More recently, in interviews with professional soccer players, Allison (2021) found that many of the women athletes believed in gender essentialism, the scientifically discredited lay theory that males and females are fundamentally, biologically different. In summary, this research indicates the importance attached to sports organizations in engaging with both their athletes and their fan bases and choosing marketing and communication strategies that are best suited to supporting women and women's sport.

Following the Ladyball first phase, the #SeriousSupport campaign received much attention, and there followed a prolonged sponsorship deal between Lidl and the LGFA. In 2022, Lidl extended their partnership with the LGFA to the end of the 2025 season with a total investment of €10 million over 10 years. The deal includes sponsorship of a wide range of initiatives from schools' football programs, the Lidl National football leagues, the One Good Club program, and the Gaelic for Mothers and Others initiative.

Later marketing campaigns did not employ "outrage" but were just as eye-catching, particularly the "Level the Playing Field" television advertisement from 2021, depicting a women's team working together on a playing pitch with a steep slope that the team must work to overcome. The 20×20 campaign in Ireland proved a rising tide with a shift occurring in women's sports. From expanded media coverage, an influx in sponsorships, to an increased visibility for women athletes and commentators, there has been a change in Irish culture. The Women's Gaelic players association (WGPA) was initiated in 2015, which amplified the voices of Gaelic football and camogie players. Even more recently, several top women footballers have signed contracts with women's Australian rules football leagues, allowing them to compete in professional sport during the LGFA off season.

In 2021, the WGPA merged with the Gaelic Players' Association (GPA), following which Ireland's leading sponsorship agencies pledged pay equity to female and male intercounty players for their promotional work. Also in 2021, the Government of Ireland announced that individual intercounty women Gaelic games players will receive the same monetary grant as male GAA players; until then, women received just a third of what men Gaelic players received annually.

In summary, the signs are positive for the LGFA and women's Gaelic football. One of the major challenges ahead for the organization is managing its relationship with the GAA. Ahead of the annual congress of each organization in Spring 2022, the GPA brought forward a motion that all three organizations should discuss immediate consolidation. Given the increased coordination and collaboration between the organizations in recent years around child welfare and protection, membership registration, volunteer leadership education, and coach education and training, it came as no surprise that the motion carried with overwhelming success. However, the LGFA chief executive commented that while the organization is open-minded about amalgamation and ensuring it is done in proper fashion, "integration may not be the silver bullet that some would imagine" (Ladies Gaelic Football 2022b, p. 42). Just like the LGFA's marketing and communication decisions, any merger discussions carry risk and rewards, particularly so when the organization operates both in the shadow and at the bosom of the GAA.

Discussion Questions

1. In the period since this publication, have any similar marketing campaigns taken place around women's sport, and what has been the reaction?
2. What values, stereotypes, or norms did the Ladyball campaign communicate in relation to women's sport?
3. How are sports organizations choosing to frame or represent women athletes and participants in their marketing and communications?
4. What methods of representation could sponsors, and sports organizations, use to enhance the visibility of women athletes?
5. How could campaigners and sponsors/marketeers work together to end pay inequality for women athletes?

References

Allison, R. (2021). Privileging difference: Negotiating gender essentialism in U.S. women's professional soccer. *Sociology of Sport Journal, 38*(2), 158–166. https://doi.org/10.1123/ssj.2020-0016

Bonesteel, M. (2016, January 19). What does the fake 'Ladyball' campaign say about women's sports? *Washington Post.* www.washingtonpost.com/news/early-lead/wp/2016/01/19/what-does-the-fake-ladyball-campaign-say-about-womens-sports/

Bowes, A., & Kitching, N. (2021). 'The Solheim Cup: media representations of golf, gender and national identity'. In K. Dashper (Ed.), *Sport, gender and mega-events* (pp. 201–219). London: Emerald Publishing Limited. https://doi.org/10.1108/978-1-83982-936-920211017

Bruce, T. (2008). Women, sport and the media: A complex terrain. In C. Obel, T. Bruce, & S. Thompson (Eds.), *Outstanding research about women and sport in New Zealand* (pp. 51–71). Hamilton: Wilf Malcolm Institute of Educational Research.

Bruce, T. (2016). New rules for new times: Sportswomen and media representation in the third wave. *Sex Roles, 74,* 361–376.

Channon, A., Quinney, A., Khomutova, A., & Matthews, C. (2018). Sexualisation of the fighter's body: Some reflections on women's mixed martial arts. *Corps, 16,* 383–391. https://doi.org/10.3917/corp1.016.0383

Daniels, E.A., Hood, A., LaVoi, N.M., & Cooky, C. (2021). Sexualized and athletic: Viewers' attitudes toward sexualized performance images of female athletes. *Sex Roles, 84*(1), 112–124. https://doi.org/10.1007/s11199-020-01152-y

Domeneghetti, R. (2018). 'The other side of the net': (re)presentations of (emphasised). femininity during Wimbledon 2016. *Journal of Policy Research in Tourism, Leisure and Events, 10*(2), 151–163. https://doi.org/10.1080/19407963.2018.1403164

Doyle, J.P., Kunkel, T., Kelly, S.J., Filo, K., & Cuskelly, G. (2021). Seeing the same things differently: Exploring the unique brand associations linked to women's professional sport teams. *Journal of Strategic Marketing,* 1–15. https://doi.org/10.1080/0965254X.2021.1922489

Drake, C., & Radford, S.K. (2021). Here is a place for you/know your place: Critiquing "biopedagogy" embedded in images of the female body in fitness advertising. *Journal of Consumer Culture, 21*(4), 800–826. https://doi.org/10.1177/1469540519876009

Esmonde, K., Cooky, C., & Andrews, D.L. (2015). "It's supposed to be about the love of the game, not the love of Aaron Rodger's eyes": Challenging the exclusions of women sports fans. *Sociology of Sport Journal, 32*(1), 22. https://doi.org/10.1123/ssj.2014-0072

Fielding-Lloyd, B., Woodhouse, D., & Sequerra, R. (2020). 'More than just a game': Family and spectacle in marketing the England Women's Super League. *Soccer & Society, 21*(2), 166–179. https://doi.org/10.1080/14660970.2018.1541799

Fink, J. (2015). Female athletes, women's sport and the sport media commercial complex: Have we really "come a long way, baby"? *Sport Management Review, 18*(3), 331–342.

Fink, J., Kane, M.J., & La Voi, N., M. (2014). The freedom to choose: Elite female athletes' preferred representations within endorsement opportunities. *Journal of Sport Management, 28,* 207–219.

Franklin, R., & Carpenter, L. (2018). Surfing, sponsorship and sexploitation: The reality of being a female professional surfer. In Lisahunter (Ed.), *Surfing, sex, genders and sexualities.* New York: Routledge.

Government of Ireland. (2021, April 27). *Issues facing women in sport: Discussion* (Joint Committee on Media, Tourism, Arts, Culture, Sport and the Gaeltacht). www.oireachtas.ie/en/debates/debate/joint_committee_on_media_tourism_arts_culture_sport_and_the_gaeltacht/2021-04-27/3/

Ho, M.H.S., & Tanaka, H. (2021). How Nissin represented Naomi Osaka: Race, gender, and sport in Japanese advertising. *Communication & Sport.* https://doi.org/10.1177/21674795211040213

Irish Examiner. (2015, July 22). Controversial ladies football ad was released accidentally. www.irishexaminer.com/sport/gaa/arid-30687710.html

Kane, M.J., La Voi, N. M., & Fink, J. (2013). Exploring elite female athletes' interpretations of sport media images: A window into the construction of social identity and "selling sex" in women's sport. *Communication & Sport, 1*(3), 269–298.

Kane, M.J., & Maxwell, H.D. (2011). Expanding the boundaries of sport media research: using critical theory to explore consumer responses to representations of women's sports. *Journal of Sport Management, 25*(3), 202–216. https://doi.org/10.1123/jsm.25.3.202

Kilgallon, H. (2021). From novelty act to national association: The emergence of Ladies' Gaelic Football in the 1970s. *Studies in Arts and Humanities, 7*(1). https://doi.org/10.18193/sah.v7i1.204

Kitching, N., & Bowes, A. (2020) 'Top of the Tree': Examining the print news portrayal of the world's best female amateur golfer during her transition to professional golf. In M. Free & N. O'Boyle (Eds.), *Sport, media and cultural industries in Ireland*. Cork: Cork University Press.

Kitching, N., Bowes, A., & MacLaren, M. (2021) 'Online activism and athlete advocacy in professional women's golf: risk or reward?' In R. Magrath (Ed.), *Athlete activism: Contemporary perspectives* (pp. 181–192). London: Routledge Research in Sport, Culture and Society, Routledge.

Kitching, N., Bowes, A., & Maclaren, M. (2020) 'Write when it hurts. Then write till it doesn't': athlete voice and the lived realities of one female professional athlete. *Qualitative Research in Sport, Exercise and Health*. https://doi.org/10.1080/2159676X.2020.1836507

Ladies Gaelic Football Association. (2016, January 15). Lidl behind 'Ladyball' concept to promote partnership with LGFA. https://ladiesgaelic.ie/lidl-and-lgfa-behind-ladyball-concept/

Ladies Gaelic Football Association. (2018, May 6). Lidl Ireland commits to an additional €3 million investment in ladies Gaelic football. https://ladiesgaelic.ie/lidl-ireland-commits-to-an-additional-e3-million-investment-in-ladies-gaelic-football/

Ladies Gaelic Football Association. (2022a, February 8). A decade of #serioussupport as Lidl pledges commitment of €10 million investment in Ladies Gaelic Football in 10 years of sponsorship. https://ladiesgaelic.ie/a-decade-of-serioussupport-as-lidl-pledges-commitment-of-e10-million-investment-in-ladies-gaelic-football-in-10-years-of-sponsorship/

Ladies Gaelic Football Association (2022b, March 4). Congress 2022: National reports. https://ladiesgaelic.ie/wp-content/uploads/2022/03/Congress-2022-National-Book.pdf

Lidl Ireland (2016, January 15). Lidl and LGFA behind "Ladyball" concept [Video]. www.youtube.com/watch?v=ufU_KSDyVqA

Lough, N., & Greenhalgh, G. (2019). Sponsorship of women's sport. In N. Lough & A. Geurin (Eds.), *Routledge handbook of the business of women's sport*. New York: Routledge. https://doi.org/10.4324/9780203702635

Morgan, A. (2019). An examination of women's sport sponsorship: A case study of female Australian Rules football. *Journal of Marketing Management, 35*(17–18), 1644–1666. https://doi.org/10.1080/0267257X.2019.1668463

Nielsen Sports. (2018, 1 October). The rise of women's sports: Identifying and maximising the opportunity. https://www.nielsen.com/insights/2018/the-rise-of-womens-sports/

Rasmussen, K., Dufur, M.J., Cope, M.R., & Pierce, H. (2021). Gender marginalization in sports participation through advertising: The case of Nike. *International Journal of Environmental Research and Public Health, 18*(15), 7759. www.mdpi.com/1660-4601/18/15/7759

Richards, J., Parry, K., & Gill, F. (2020). "The guys love it when chicks ask for help": An exploration of female rugby league fans. *Sport in Society*. https://doi.org/10.1080/174 30437.2020.1809380

Stack, S. (2011, November 23). Hunky Dory red carded for foul play in adverts. *Irish Examiner*. www.irishexaminer.com/news/arid-20174782.html

Sveinson, K., & Allison, R. (2021). "Something seriously wrong with U.S. soccer": A critical discourse analysis of consumers' twitter responses to U.S. Soccer's Girls' apparel promotion. *Journal of Sport Management*, 1–13. https://doi.org/10.1123/jsm.2021-0127

Sveinson, K., Hoeber, L., & Toffoletti, K. (2019). "If people are wearing pink stuff they're probably not real fans": Exploring women's perceptions of sport fan clothing. *Sport Management Review*, *22*(5), 736–747. https://doi.org/https://doi.org/10.1016/j.smr.2018.12.003

The Institute of Creative Advertising and Design. (2016). *Lidl – LGFA #Serious Support*. https://icad.ie/award/lidl-lgfa-serious-support-3/

Toffoletti, K. (2017). Advertising the 2015 cricket world cup: Representing multicultural female sports fans. *Communication & Sport*, *5*(2), 226–244. https://doi.org/10.1177/2167479515601868

Zarya, V. (2016, January 15). This genius marketing campaign says everything about women's sports. *Fortune*. https://fortune.com/2016/01/15/lidl-ladyball-womens-sports/

21

TRANS INCLUSION IN SPORTS

Assumed Advantages, (Un)Fairness, and Athlete Well-Being

Aaron W. Gurlly

Introduction

Athletics remains one of the few cultural institutions in the United States, which maintains a strict sex/gender binary and makes different opportunities available to people based on sex. Though schools and workplaces have largely ended the practice of sex-based segregation, sports continue to use physical sex as a way to categorize participants into different sports teams. This ongoing practice of segregation is widely seen to be necessary to ensure fairness in competition. Implicit in this belief is the idea that people designated male at birth possess inherent physical advantages that make them better suited to athletic activity.

In the past, it was believed that gender equality in sport would be achieved by providing separate but equal opportunities for people of different genders. While Title IX requires educational institutions in the United States to ensure that students are given equal athletic opportunities regardless of gender, sports outside of the school environment have voluntarily maintained separate athletic opportunities for males and females. In some cases, sports are separated into two separate leagues, such as the NBA and WNBA for basketball. In other cases, athletes are directed toward entirely different sports, with, for example, male athletes playing football and female athletes playing field hockey. Other sports divide male and female athletes into different groups and establish different rules for the "men's" and "women's" versions of the sport. Artistic gymnastics, for example, is divided into separate disciplines for men and women. There is a significant overlap between men's and women's gymnastics, but there are also profound differences between the two disciplines.

Where do trans athletes fit into the picture? Strict interpretations of the traditional sex/gender binary appear to leave no room for trans participation in sports.

DOI: 10.4324/9781003316763-24

As society gains increasing awareness of trans persons and demonstrates greater inclusivity for people who do not neatly fit into the traditional binary, sports face a challenge: To include trans and nonbinary athletes and to offer them fair opportunities to participate in their chosen sports.

In light of newly emerging ideas about sex and gender, *who* gets to compete in which sports becomes an issue. This question is complicated by the somewhat controversial assumption that maleness confers athletic advantages over femaleness. This chapter will explore the assumptions made about gender identity, physical sex, testosterone, and athletic ability in order to highlight the complexity of the issue of fairness and equity in sports. In particular, the chapter will focus on the competition rules of artistic gymnastics, a sport where athletic performances require agility, control, and a high degree of precision, in addition to strength and power. Those rules, which include restrictions that limit who is allowed to compete, reflect the macro-level assumptions held by the governing bodies of sports and potentially negatively impact trans athletes (Cunningham, 2012). Finally, the chapter will ask readers to consider whether the existing regulations on transgender gymnasts provide access to all athletes, without providing unfair advantages to participants on the basis of sex or gender.

Background

Traditionally, physical sex has divided people into two categories, male and female. Membership in either group is determined by physical attributes. Genitalia, hormone levels, and chromosomes have all been treated as biological facts that indicate one's maleness or femaleness. In this view, the meaning of our body parts is predetermined. Gender, on the other hand, is understood as a social construct. "Men" and "women" (or "boys" and "girls") are assumed to be social roles; as such, they are defined less by physical attributes than by behaviors. At various times in history, men have been expected to act as protectors and providers, while women have been expected to act as nurturers and caregivers. Because social roles are arbitrary, societies have long recognized that these roles could be performed in nontraditional ways.

In the United States, we have historically theorized physical sex as the primary criteria for determining gender identity. People whose bodies are labeled male were called boys and men; those labeled as female were called girls and women. Transgender and non-binary people highlight the limits of this thinking. They show that people whose physical attributes are deemed male can identify as women or girls (and vice versa), or that a person might identify as neither a man nor a woman (non-binary), or as both at the same time. This newer way of thinking is still based on the traditional idea that physical sex is a biological fact. Body parts, in this theory, are still considered to have predetermined biological meaning.

Judith Butler (1990) challenged the traditional theory of physical sex when she argued that sex, like gender, is socially constructed. To Butler, physical sex is arbitrary in the same way as gender roles. According to Butler's reasoning, our body parts do not come with predetermined meaning; we assign meaning to them. In Butler's theory of sex, a physical attribute such as high testosterone level does not have to signify maleness. If we, in American society, think of high testosterone as a male characteristic, it is because we have decided to think of it that way.

Butler's theories express two seemingly contradictory ideas. One, if physical sex is arbitrary, it can be changed. Bodies can be altered to display traits associated with either sex. Gender confirmation procedures modify a physical body to make it fit with our expectations of maleness and femaleness. A person could, for example, have surgery and/or begin hormone therapy in order to gain a body that looks and performs more like a body that is traditionally associated with maleness or with femaleness. However, since Butler's theory considers these physical traits to be arbitrary, these medical procedures are not strictly necessary, because no physical trait inherently signifies maleness. Thus, according to Butler's theory, a person who identifies as male is not required to possess any particular physical trait in order to be male.

Butler's work in sex and gender studies influenced a generation of theorists who expanded upon her ideas. Westbrook and Schilt (2014) argued that we use different theories for understanding sex and gender; sex-segregated activities, such as sports, tend to treat physical sex as a biological fact, while integrated activities are more likely to demonstrate the notion that sex is socially constructed. Enke (2012) similarly argues that most gender analysis perpetuates the idea that physical sex is a biological fact, even when attempting to break down traditional ideas regarding gender.

Sports reflect the larger cultures in which they operate, and the sex/gender politics described earlier influence the ways in which sports organizations deal with sex and gender within sports. As Cunningham (2012) claims in his discussion of the Multilevel Model for understanding LGBT athlete experiences, "Cultural norms and standards within a given context can shape the prevalence of heterosexism and the specific sexual prejudice athletes encounter" (p. 8). That is to say, when biases against LGBT athletes exist within sports organizations (meso-level factors, in Cunningham's model), those biases are a manifestation of bias against LGBT persons in society at large (macro-level factors).

The sports world has generally separated participants based on a traditional sex/gender binary. Because of this tradition of sex-based segregation, sports have been ill-prepared to address questions about sex and gender as Butler and other scholars define them. In their recent guidance for trans inclusion, the International Olympic Committee (IOC) and USA Gymnastics, after intense media coverage and pressure from key stakeholders, sought to create space for trans athletes to participate in high-level competition. However, their efforts reinforced traditional beliefs about what makes a person male or female.

The rules that sought to establish provisions for trans athletes required trans women competing in Olympic sports to (1) declare their intention to compete as women and to maintain this declaration for at least 4 years, (2) demonstrate serum testosterone levels below 10 nmol/L for at least 12 months prior to her first competition, and (3) undergo repeated testing to ensure that testosterone levels remain below the aforementioned-listed threshold. (International Olympic Committee, 2015, pp. 2–3).

These IOC regulations assume that male persons and others with higher testosterone levels possess inherent physical advantages over female persons and that such people must, for the sake of fairness, be excluded from women's competition.

Fairness for whom, one might ask? An unlikely alliance of progressive feminists, conservative critics (Stebbings et al., 2021), and scientists (Anderson et al., 2019) has argued that the inclusion of trans athletes (trans women, in particular) unfairly disadvantages women athletes designated female at birth. On one hand, some critics argue that the efforts of women in sport should not be diminished or obscured by others – while excluding trans women from their definition of "woman." Other critics argue that women who are designated female at birth are inherently worse at sports and are simply unable to compete directly against persons whose legally recognized sex is male (Roberts et al., 2020). Others question whether these rules do enough to place males and females designated at birth on a level playing field (Hilton & Lundberg, 2021; Ivy & Conrad, 2018). Yet, others question whether a sex-based advantage exists at all (Jones et al., 2017; Torres et al., 2020).

Regardless of the basis of these arguments, the outright exclusion of trans and non-binary persons from sports is patently unfair to them. The challenge lies in making room for all athletes to compete in high-level competition without doing a disservice to anyone. New policies from the IOC and USA gymnastics seek to address this issue. This type of intervention is called for, given that 79% of trans athletes report having experienced structural discrimination against them as a significant problem they have faced while training and competing in sports (Braumuller, Menzel, and Hartmann-Tews, 2020).

The Case

In November 2021, the IOC issued its "Framework on Fairness, Inclusion and Non-Discrimination on the Basis of Gender Identity and Sex Variations." This policy supersedes an older IOC policy that required trans women athletes to undergo hormone therapy or otherwise reduce testosterone to levels at or below 10 nmol/L and to maintain this lower level for at least one year (International Olympic Committee, 2015). The IOC's new rules eliminate the hormone therapy requirement and replace it with a loose set of guidelines that encourage each sport to establish its own eligibility rules for women's competition. The new statement, which went into effect in March 2022, reads:

In issuing this Framework, the IOC recognizes that it must be in the remit of each sport and its governing body to determine how an athlete may be at a disproportionate advantage against their peers, taking into consideration the nature of each sport. The IOC is therefore not in a position to issue regulations that define eligibility criteria for every sport, discipline or event across the very different national jurisdictions and sport systems.

(International Olympic Committee, 2021, p. 1)

The new policy also includes a statement on fairness, which reads:

4.1 Where sports organizations elect to issue eligibility criteria for men's and women's categories for a given competition, they should do so with a view to:

(a). Providing confidence that no athlete within a category has an unfair and disproportionate competitive advantage (namely an advantage gained by altering one's body or one that disproportionately exceeds other advantages that exist at elite-level competition);

(b). Preventing a risk to the physical safety of other athletes; and

(c). Preventing athletes from claiming a gender identity different from the one consistently and persistently used, with a view to entering a competition in a given category (International Olympic Committee, 2021, pp. 3–4).

The IOC statement further notes that no athlete should be presumed to have such an advantage unless evidence of such advantage is provided (p. 4).

It is worth noting that these rules place no particular obligations on trans men who, according to conventional wisdom, may be at a competitive disadvantage by vying against men who were designated male at birth. Because these regulations assume that trans women have a competitive advantage, by virtue of having been designated male at birth, the old rules place onerous burdens on them, including invasive tests that might result in the publicizing of private information about their gender identity.

Gender testing has a long, sordid history in sports. Women athletes have been ridiculed for the ways in which they failed to exhibit normative sex traits. Track and field star Caster Semenya faced an unacceptable level of derision when she underwent gender testing that ultimately resulted in the publication of private information about her sex and gender identity. Scores of other women have received such treatment in the past, particularly those representing Germany and Russia, whose high levels of athleticism were considered unnatural for women (Heggie, 2017). When rules like this exist, they potentially harm all women athletes. Oddly, the assumptions on which these rules are based may produce negative consequences for women athletes who are deemed too good at their respective sports. To avoid negative scrutiny, and to maintain privacy, high-level athletes may be pressured to perform below their capacity (Fischer & McClearen, 2019), which diminishes the spirit of competition and perpetuates the mistaken notion that "real women" lack athleticism.

USA Gymnastics policy, most recently updated in April 2022, defers to the IOC and to the Federation Internationale de Gymnastique (FIG), the international governing body for competitive gymnastics, for rules regarding gender/sex and eligibility for competition. Until this update, USA Gymnastics' transgender policy cited the old IOC policy, which stated:

> International track athletes: Transgender boys or men are eligible to compete in the male category without restriction. Transgender girls or women who, in the next 12 months, intend to qualify for Junior or Senior National Team, those who may represent USA Gymnastics internationally, or those who qualify to any event where a National Team is selected, must meet the requirements for transgender and non-binary athletes put forth by the International Olympic Committee. Testosterone level documentation is indicated for a transgender girl or woman who has been evaluated by a physician and determined to be post-pubescent.
>
> *(USA Gymnastics. Policy for Transgender and Non-Binary*
> *Athlete Inclusion, 2020, p. 3)*

And

The athlete has declared that her gender identity is female. The declaration cannot be changed, for sporting purposes, for a minimum of four years.

> The athlete must demonstrate that her total testosterone level in serum has been below 10 nmol/L for at least 12 months prior to her first competition (with the requirement for any longer period to be based on a confidential case-by-case evaluation, considering whether or not 12 months is a sufficient length of time to minimize any advantage in women's competition).
>
> The athlete's total testosterone level in serum must remain below 10 nmol/L throughout the period of desired eligibility to compete in the female category.
>
> Compliance with these conditions may be monitored by testing. In the event of non-compliance, the athlete's eligibility for female competition will be suspended for 12 months.
>
> Additional Note: To require surgical anatomical changes as a precondition to participation is inconsistent with developing legislation and notions of human rights.
>
> *(USA Gymnastics. Policy for Transgender and Non-Binary*
> *Athlete Inclusion, 2020, p. 5)*

You Make the Call

Since USA Gymnastics' regulations are based on a defunct IOC policy, it remains to be seen what changes USA Gymnastics may make now that it is no longer bound by the old Olympic regulations listed before. The new USA Gymnastics guidelines, updated in April 2022, now defer to the FIG, which, for the time being, has no stated policies regarding trans inclusion. So the new IOC framework provides guidance but no clear ruling on the eligibility for trans gymnasts competing at the elite level.

For advocates of trans inclusion in sports, the new IOC framework demonstrates the limited strides that have been made. On one hand, the new policy empowers each sport to determine its own rules, taking into account the specific nature of each sport. This approach allows a sport such as artistic gymnastics to establish rules that consider the sport's unique physical demands. On the other hand, granting such freedom to each sport's governing bodies risks producing uneven results if some sports adopt simple, inclusive policies while other sports impose harsh restrictions on trans athletes.

The sport of artistic gymnastics presents a particularly complicated set of considerations for those seeking trans inclusion in athletics. For one, gymnasts – particularly those competing in women's gymnastics – tend to be quite young. Those who are below the age of majority may not have the authority to make relevant medical decisions; their parents or guardians maintain that authority. Likewise, gymnasts from different parts of the world – or parts of the United States – might face legal barriers that prevent them from choosing medical procedures that confirm their gender identity.

Another complicating factor emerges from the fact that men's and women's gymnastics differ significantly from one another. Men's gymnastics includes six events – floor exercise, vault, pommel horse, still rings, parallel bars, and high bar. Women's gymnastics includes four events – floor exercise, vault, balance beam, and uneven bars.

Training for elite level gymnastics, which typically begins many years before athletes actually compete at that level, is event-specific. Years of preparation for competing on still rings or pommel horse (men's events) do little to prepare a gymnast to compete on balance beam or uneven bars (women's events). Because men's and women's gymnastics include different events, a young gymnast needs to start training on events early in life, perhaps before understanding their gender identity and their options for medical intervention. The existing requirement that trans women should maintain the reduced testosterone levels for at least 1 year before becoming eligible to compete means that participants must plan their gender transitions at very young ages, perhaps before they are able to make the best decisions for their physical and mental health.

Likewise, these rules may pressure young athletes to delay or avoid a gender transition that they might otherwise undergo. A teenager who has already invested years of training in men's gymnastics might feel obligated to continue competing in that discipline, regardless of their actual gender identity (Drescher & Byne, 2014).

Even the two events that are shared by men's and women's gymnastics differ from one another in significant ways. As an example, compare the descriptions of men's and women's floor exercise from each sex's codes of points, from the international rule book for gymnastics competition.

From the men's Code of Points:

> A Floor Exercise is composed predominantly of acrobatic elements combined with other gymnastic elements such as strength and balance parts, elements of flexibility, handstands, and choreographic combinations all forming a harmonious rhythmic exercise which is performed utilizing the entire floor exercise area (12 m × 12 m).
>
> *(Federation Internationale de Gymnastique, Men's Code of Points 2022–2024a, p. 37)*

From the women's Code of Points:

> An artist performance is one in which the gymnast demonstrates her ability to transform her floor exercise from a well-structured composition into an artistic performance. In so doing, the gymnast must demonstrate a strong choreographic flow, artistry, expressiveness, musicality and perfect technique. The main objective is to create and present a unique and well-balanced artistic gymnastic composition by combining the body movements of the gymnast harmoniously with theme and character of the music.
>
> *(Federation Internationale de Gymnastique, Women's Code of Points 2022–2024b, section 13, page 1)*

Note the increased emphasis on choreography and the rules for music and artistic expression that exceed the expectation set forth for men. Floor exercise in women's gymnastics requires the athlete to perform choreography to music and limits the amount of difficult acrobatic skills for which a gymnast may receive credit. Even if we accept the still-questionable belief that trans women athletes possess a strength and power advantage over cisgender women, increased strength and power do not offer any artistic advantages and, therefore, do not grant any unfair advantages based on the judging criteria listed earlier.

It is important to credit the efforts of the IOC and USA Gymnastics to reduce or eliminate the significance of sex and gender and their impact on the sport. New rules that allow athletes more freedom to wear clothing they deem appropriate, requirements for protecting the privacy of athletes, and the invalidation of any rules that require surgical intervention do matter, even if these rules fall short of addressing all of the underlying problems associated with sport's gender binary.

Though gymnastics is a particularly complex example, trans athletes in many other sex-segregated sports face a similar conundrum. Even if one accepts the assumption that people designated male at birth do possess greater strength and speed, we are still left with the question of how to include trans people fairly, in ways that place no onerous burdens on trans athletes.

Discussion Questions

1.   Discuss whether people designated male at birth really have advantages in sports. Besides advantages from higher levels of testosterone, what other factors might explain an athlete's dominance in a sport (i.e., strength-building regimens)?
2.   Discuss the merits and demerits to the requirement for trans women to undergo hormone treatment in order to compete in sports.
3.   If people designated male at birth do have advantages over other people in terms of strength and speed, discuss whether those advantages matter in *all* sports. Give examples of sports where increased strength and speed would not *necessarily* confer any significant, consistent advantages. Discuss the IOC's action to rescind its specific rules about trans women and, instead, encouraging each sport to determine for itself which rules would make the most sense.
4.   Discuss other ways to balance out physical advantages other than by strict sex segregation. Wrestling and boxing provide examples of how sports might separate athletes into different classes based on body size. Several martial arts separate participants into different ranks based on experience. How might these approaches be used in other sports to mitigate any supposed physical advantages conferred by higher testosterone levels?
5.   What new developments have arisen in sports that affect how you think about this issue? How have other sports sought to deal with the issue of trans inclusion?

References

Anderson, L., Knox, T., & Heather, A. (2019). Trans-athletes in elite sports: Inclusion and fairness. *Emerging Topics in Life Sciences, 3*(6), 759–762. https://doi.org/10.1042/ETLS20180071

Braumuller, B., Menzel, T., & Hartmann-Tews, I. (2020). Gender identities in organized sports – athletes' experiences and organizational strategies of inclusion. *Frontiers in Sociology, 5.* https://doi.org/10.3389/fsoc.2020.578213

Butler, J. (1990). *Gender trouble: Feminism and the subversion of identity.* New York: Routledge.

Cunningham, G. (2012). A multilevel model for understanding the experiences of LBGT sports participants. *Journal for the Study of Sports and Athletes in Education, 6*(1), 5–20. www.tandfonline.com/doi/abs/10.1179/ssa.2012.6.1.5

Drescher, J., & Byne, W. (2014). *Treating transgender children and adolescents: An interdisciplinary discussion.* New York: Routledge.

Enke, F. (2012). *Transfeminist perspectives in and beyond transgender and gender studies.* Philadelphia, PA: Temple University Press.

Federation Internationale de Gymnastique. (2022–2024a). Code of points, men's artistic. *Gymnastics.* www.gymnastics.sport/publicdir/rules/files/de_MAG%20CoP%202022-2024.pdf

Federation Internationale de Gymnastique. (2022–2024b). Code of points, women's artistic. *Gymnastics.* www.gymnastics.sport/publicdir/rules/files/en_WAG%20CoP%202022-2024.pdf

Fischer, M., & McClearen, J. (2019). Transgender athletes and the queer art of failure. *Communication & Sport, 8*(2), 147–167. *https://doi.org/10.1177%2F2167479518823207*

Heggie, V. (2017). *Subjective sex: Science, medicine and sex tests in sports.* In E. Anderson & A. Travers (Eds.), *Transgender athletes in competitive sport.* New York: Routledge.

Hilton, E.N., & Lundberg, T.R. (2021). Transgender women in the female category of sport: Perspectives on testosterone suppression and performance advantage. *Sports Medicine, 51,* 199–214. https://doi.org/10.1007/s40279-020-01389-3

International Olympic Committee. (2015, November). IOC consensus meeting on sex reassignment and hyperandrogenism. https://stillmed.olympic.org/Documents/Commissions_PDFfiles/Medical_commission/2015-11_ioc_consensus_meeting_on_sex_reassignment_and_hyperandrogenism-en.pdf

International Olympic Committee. (2021). IOC framework on fairness, inclusion, and non-discrimination on the basis of gender identity and sex variations. https://stillmed.olympics.com/media/Documents/News/2021/11/IOC-Framework-Fairness-Inclusion-Non-discrimination-2021.pdf?_ga=2.24159481.2125256659.1645483831–267546066.1645483831

Ivy, V., & Conrad, A. (2018). Including trans women athletes in competitive sport: Analyzing the science, law, and principles and policies of fairness in competition. *Philosophical Topics, 46*(2), 103–140.

Jones, B.A., Arcelus, J., Bouman, W.P., & Haycraft, E. (2017). Sport and transgender people: A systematic review of the literature relating to sport participation and competitive sport policies. *Sports Medicine, 47,* 701–716.

Roberts, T.A., Smalley, J., & Ahrendt, D. (2020). Effect of gender affirming hormones on athletic performance in transwomen and transmen: Implications for sporting organisations and legislators. *British Journal of Sports Medicine, 55*(11), 577–583.

Stebbings, G., Herbert, A., Heffernan, S., Pielke, R., Tucker, R., & Williams, A. (2021). The BASES expert statement on eligibility for sex categories in sport: Trans athletes. *The Sport and Exercise Scientist, 68,* 14–15.

Torres, C.R., Javier, F., Frias, L., & Martínez Patiño, M.J. (2020). Beyond physiology: Embodied experience, embodied advantage, and the inclusion of transgender athletes. *Competitive Sport, Sport, Ethics and Philosophy, 16*(1), 33–49. https://doi.org/10.1080/17511321.2020.1856915

USA Gymnastics. (2020). Policy for transgender & non-binary athlete inclusion. https://web.archive.org/web/20220210174650/https://usagym.org/PDFs/About%20USA%20Gymnastics/transgender_policy.pdf

USA Gymnastics. (2022). Policy for transgender & non-binary athlete inclusion. https://usagym.org/PDFs/About%20USA%20Gymnastics/transgender_policy.pdf

Westbrook, L., & Schilt, K. (2014). Doing gender, determining gender: Transgender people, gender panics, and the maintenance of the sex/gender/sexuality system. *Gender & Society, 28*(1), 32–57.

PART IV

Mental Health
and COVID-19 Pandemic

22

ATHLETE INFLUENCE IN REGARD TO MASK WEARING

An Application of Social Cognitive Theory

Lindsey J. DiTirro and Jennifer R. Allen Catellier

Introduction

Wearing a mask has become a controversial issue in the United States during the COVID-19 pandemic. The Centers for Disease Control and Prevention (2021) encourages individuals to wear a mask that covers the mouth and nose in order to prevent the spread of COVID-19. In addition, U.S. President Joe Biden has been a strong proponent of mask wearing. He even issued an executive order requiring mask wearing for the federal workforce (The White House, 2021). Even with support from top government authorities, many people still resist wearing masks. One study reported by *Newsweek* (Fearnow, 2021) found that only 51% reported wearing a mask in public at the height of the pandemic. This number is significantly lower, only 21%, when people are gathering with friends and family outside their households (Fearnow, 2021).

To help keep sports in action during the pandemic, many professional leagues required athletes to wear masks on the sidelines, or face penalties (Boren, 2020; Cwik, 2020; NHL Public Relations, 2020; Smith, 2021). In 2020, the NBA employed a bubble where the league sequestered players to a location, the NFL had a season with no fans in the stands, and the NHL ended its season early at two sites in Canada. While not all athletes regularly wore or encouraged the use of face masks, several prominent athletes could be seen wearing masks on the sidelines or on the field. Major League Baseball players Clint Frazier, currently of the Chicago Cubs and previously with the New York Yankees, and Mike Trout of the Los Angeles Angels were notable for wearing their masks and publicly acknowledging the importance of mask wearing in the early days of the COVID-19 pandemic.

This study asks whether mask-wearing professional athletes influenced fans to do the same. An exploratory survey was used to gather data about social and

DOI: 10.4324/9781003316763-26

environmental factors that influenced mask wearing. The survey used social cognitive theory (SCT) to help understand what factors influenced respondents' intentions to wear masks.

Background

Athlete Influence on Behaviors

Athletes and sports have become a major part of today's culture and receive significant media coverage. Beyond their sport, athletes are seen in a range of advertisements, such as Tiger Woods and Nike, LeBron James and McDonald's, and Peyton Manning and Wheaties (Lee, 2013). Advertisers use athletes as spokespeople because they are seen as role models (Bush et al., 2004). Bush et al. (2004) found that athletes are influential to adolescents when making brand choices. Through their research, Bush et al. (2004) found that adolescents see athletes as role models who can be influential in selling products.

Another area where athletes have influence is donating their time and money to charitable organizations. Kim and Walker (2013) found that athlete identification, positive perceptions toward the athlete, trust in the athlete, and an individual's pre-existing involvement with the athlete's cause made it more likely that a person would donate to that athlete's organization. This research shows how individuals model athlete's behaviors when it comes to charitable giving.

Athletes have also served as models for healthy behaviors. For example, Brown, Basil, and Bocarnea (2003) found that young adults who idolized baseball player Mark McGuire were also more knowledgeable about health issues and causes that were relevant to McGuire. These young adults, who looked up to McGuire, paid special attention to topics he discussed. While McGuire's reputation was later damaged after it was found that he used performance-enhancing drugs, at the time of Brown et al. (2003) study, McGuire was revered by many. Additionally, while the research on McGuire specifically involved young adults, other researchers, like Kim and Walker (2013), have shown that adults are also influenced by athletes.

Social Cognitive Theory

Social cognitive theory posits that media influence can lead to behavior change in individuals. SCT describes "the process of learning through observation and imitation" (Connolly, 2017, p. 24) and how individuals learn behaviors through the media and other individuals. This is the dual path of influence in which change can occur. In the direct pathway, the media promote "changes by informing, enabling, motivating, and guiding audience individuals" (Bandura, 2004a, p. 76). Through this pathway, the media directly influence behavior change. The other pathway is through social mediation. In this pathway, the media influence connections between individuals and social networks. People consume the media and then share what they learn with others to influence them to change.

In this instance, people are resistant to change until they see the benefits of others exhibiting the behavior. When others show the positive aspects of a behavior, this can change the observer's beliefs about that behavior (Bandura, 2001). Also, "In some instances the media both teach new forms of behavior and create motivators for action by altering people's value preferences, efficacy beliefs, outcome expectations, and perception of opportunity structures" (Bandura, 2001, p. 286).

People learn through social modeling which is the process of learning by observing from the successes and failures of others (Bandura, 2004b). This can be done through the observation of characters in the media. Social modeling consists of four functions – instructive, motivational, social prompting, and social construction (Bandura, 2004b). Through social modeling, people change their behaviors based on what they see other individuals doing (Bandura, 2004b). By watching athletes wear masks during professional sporting events, people may learn to copy that same behavior and wear masks themselves.

Bandura (2004b) applied SCT to entertainment-education serial dramas. Through these dramas, he noted three types of modeling – positive, negative, and transitional. Positive modeling shows attractive and aspirational characters modeling beneficial lifestyles. Negative modeling shows characters portraying negative lifestyle behaviors. And last, transitional modeling shows characters overcoming unfavorable life choices (Bandura, 2004b). Athletes could be seen as positive models for mask wearing. Athletes are aspirational to many people. They also exhibit beneficial lifestyle choices by wearing masks when they are not playing their respective sports.

Vicarious motivators in television programming illustrate the benefits of participating in positive lifestyle changes and the consequences of negative lifestyle choices (Bandura, 2004b). This can be seen in the sports world, specifically the National Football League (NFL) where many teams were fined for not following COVID-19 protocols. For example, the Baltimore Ravens were fined $250,000 for COVID-19-related infractions (Rapoport, 2020).

The research shows that SCT can successfully predict a number of health behaviors. Therefore, it is a strong framework for understanding intentions to wear masks as a COVID-19 mitigation strategy.

Stages of Change

Another theory that can also explain behavior change is the stages of change model, which suggests that individuals begin contemplating an action, like mask wearing, and then move through a series of phases including determination, action, maintenance, and potential relapse (Prochaska & DiClemente, 1983). This model may help to explain how individuals move from intention to wear masks to actual mask wearing. While it was originally designed to study smoking cessation (Prochaska & DiClemente, 1983), it has also been used to study behaviors such as diabetes management and physical activity (Dutton et al., 2008), bullying prevention (Evers et al., 2007), and HIV risk reduction (Gazabon et al., 2007) among others. It may also help to explain why individuals begin wearing masks and either maintain mask-wearing behaviors or stop wearing masks throughout the pandemic.

Stages of change differs from other models in that it looks at behavior change not as something that happens at one specific point in time, but as something that occurs over time and not always in a linear fashion (Prochaska et al., 2015). This begins with the precontemplation stage in which people do not see the behavior as something that needs to be addressed (Raihan & Cogburn, 2021). It is either not something they are interested in or not something they see as a problem. Once they begin to see the issue as something that needs to be addressed, they enter the contemplation stage, where they begin to consider behavior change. They begin to consider pros and cons or costs and benefits of the behavior (Prochaska et al., 2015). When one is ready to make a behavior change, they enter the preparation phase where they plan and gather information (Raihan & Cogburn, 2021). This is followed by the action phase, where behavior change takes place, and the maintenance phase, where the behavior change is sustained. At this point, some people will continue with the change while others will relapse or terminate the behavior.

Recent research has applied stages of change to study behaviors related to climate change (Inman et al., 2021) and fruit and vegetable consumption (Vilamala-Orra et al., 2021). These articles showed that the stages of change model accurately reflects how individuals move through the behavior change process. The research also points to the importance of communicating appropriately to increase motivation throughout the behavior change process (Vilamala-Orra et al., 2021). Tailoring education strategies to each stage may increase the success of the intervention. When applying this to mask wearing, it is important to consider things like consciousness raising, environmental reevaluation, social support, and stimulus control when communicating to the public (Prochaska et al., 2015).

The Case

Masks and Safety in Major League Baseball

In March 2020, Major League Baseball players were well into spring training when the United States reported its first cases of COVID-19. On March 12th, the remainder of spring training was canceled, and the season was delayed by at least 2 weeks. Just a few days later, on March 16th, MLB announced the season's indefinite postponement, after the CDC recommended that events of more than 50 people be restricted to prevent the spread of the virus. This marked the first time that an MLB game had been postponed since the terrorist attacks on 9/11. Eventually, MLB announced baseball's return on July 23 for a shortened, 60-game season, with a variety of precautions in place.

In addition to regular testing and social distancing, at the start of the abbreviated season, players were required to wear face masks at the ballpark, with the exception of time on the field, in the dugout, or while engaging in strenuous activity (Baccellieri, 2020). Individual players could choose to wear their masks during games. However, after 21 games were postponed or canceled in the first 2 weeks of the season due to positive COVID-19 cases, the league stepped up its mask requirements, making masks mandatory for players at all times, except when on the field (Boren, 2020).

Many players stepped up to the challenge, wearing their masks on and off the field. Notable MLB players like Mike Trout, all-star outfielder for the Los Angeles Angels, made headlines for wearing a mask on the field. His mother posted an image of Trout running bases while wearing a mask. Along with the picture, she wrote, "If Mike Trout can wear a mask while running the bases, you can wear a mask going out in public," with the hashtag #WearAMask (Stump, 2020). During the 2020 season, Trout's wife was pregnant with their first child. Trout stated that he wanted to protect his wife and unborn child from COVID-19 and that is why he decided to wear a mask on the field (Townsend, 2020). Trout stated, "Honestly, I still don't feel comfortable with the baby coming. There's a lot of things on my mind. I'm trying to be the safest and most cautious to get through the season. It's going to be tough" (Nightengale, 2020, para.2).

Players like Clint Frazier, at the time a New York Yankees outfielder, wore his mask on and off the field during games in the 2020 season, the only player on the Yankees to consistently do so. He was quoted as saying, "I'm just trying to overall make sure that I can do the best part that I can and make sure that our team does stay healthy" (Red, 2020, para. 3). At that time, MLB required masks for personnel in the dugout and bullpen, but Frazier stated that he wanted to set a good example for the public and therefore wore his mask both on and off the field (Hoch, 2020).

However, Frazier's efforts were not without criticism. In an interview with ESPN (2020) Frazier said, "I got a lot of positive feedback. I got a lot of negative feedback, as well, just from wearing the mask. A lot of people have their own opinions. I got called a sheep by some people, but it's all good." He added:

> With the situation that we're in, with how fragile this virus is for some people, I'm not really too worried about the negative feedback because moving forward, I think it's the right thing to protect myself, others around me and everyone else that everyone goes home to. It has affected us, and we want to win the World Series. The way to do that is to be healthy.
>
> *(ESPN, 2020, para. 4)*

Study: Social Cognitive Theory and Athlete Influence on Mask Wearing

The question of interest here is whether athletes like Trout and Frazier influenced public opinions and behaviors related to mask-wearing. As noted earlier, SCT suggests that cognitive, social, and environmental factors can influence our behaviors (Bandura, 2004a). To test this, an online survey was distributed in March 2021 via Amazon MTurk to collect data related to COVID-19 attitudes and behaviors. Participants were paid a small sum to complete the survey, and all procedures were approved by the university Institutional Review Board. The final dataset included 257 individuals. The sample was predominantly male (62.6%), White (45.9%), and highly educated (77.7% earned a bachelor's degree or higher). The average age of participants was 33.22.

To assess the influence of athletes on mask-wearing behaviors, two scales were created. The first scale included three items that asked generally about whether athletes influenced behaviors. We asked if individuals paid attention to athletes and if they supported products and causes promoted by athletes. All items used Likert scales where 1 indicated strongly disagree and 5 indicated strongly agree. These items were checked for reliability and averaged into a scale titled "General Athlete Influence" ($\alpha = .89$). The second scale included three items specific to COVID-19. These items used the same five-point Likert scale. Specifically, we asked if seeing professional athletes wear masks, engage in general preventive health behaviors related to COVID-19, or receive a COVID-19 vaccine encouraged them to do the same. Three items were checked for reliability and averaged into a scale titled "COVID-19 Athlete Influence" ($\alpha = .91$).

SCT measures were based on research by Dewar and colleagues (2012) and adapted to assess COVID-19 behaviors and mask-wearing intentions. All items were measured using a five-point Likert scale. Measures included self-efficacy ($\alpha = .57$), situation ($\alpha = .73$), outcome expectations ($\alpha = .84$), behavioral strategies ($\alpha = .70$), and social norms ($\alpha = .62$). While reliability estimates for self-efficacy and social norms were lower than expected, we proceeded with analysis because the scales had been previously validated (see Dewar et al., 2012).

Descriptive statistics for the athlete influence and social cognitive variables are presented in Table 22.1. In general, participants rated their attitudes and behaviors very positively, with most items having a mean score of 4 or greater. The influence of athletes on COVID-19 behaviors was slightly higher than general athlete influence ($m = 3.25$ and $m = 3.03$, respectively).

The first model examined demographic characteristics, the second model added athlete influence variables, and the final model added SCT variables. When looking at the second model, the athlete influence variables explained 20% of the variance in mask-wearing behaviors, suggesting that athletes have the ability to influence our behaviors related to masks. As expected, "General Athlete Influence" was positively related to intention to wear masks ($\beta = .24$, $p < .05$).

TABLE 22.1 Athlete Influence Descriptive Statistics

	m(sd)
Athlete Influence – General	3.03(1.26)
Athlete Influence – COVID	3.35(1.23)
Self-Efficacy	4.23(0.57)
Situation	4.14(0.85)
Outcome Expectations	4.11(0.76)
Behavioral Strategies	4.19(0.87)
Social Norms	3.96(0.94)
Mask Intention	3.97(0.86)

To test the relationship of SCT and athlete influence, a series of regression analyses were run. Results are provided in Table 22.2.

TABLE 22.2 Mask-Wearing Intentions

	Mask-Wearing Intentions		
Controls	β	β	β
Age	−.16*	−.10	−.14**
Gender	.11	.18**	.08
Race	.19*	.10	.01
Education	−.05	−.08	−.04
Income	.05	.00	.03
Marital Status	−.23**	−.20**	−.16**
Children in Household	.02	−.06	.01
Political Views	.07	.13*	.05
Predictors			
Athlete Influence General		.24*	.38***
Athlete Influence COVID		.17	−.18*
Self-Efficacy			.02
Situation			.09
Outcome Expectations			.32***
Behavioral Strategies			.28***
Social Norms			.11
Adjusted R²	.10	.20	.63

*$p < .05$, **$p < .01$, ***$p < .001$

However, "COVID-19 Athlete Influence," while in the expected direction, was not a significant predictor of intention to wear masks ($\beta = .17$, $p = .15$). It is possible that at the time this survey was conducted, people were tired of hearing celebrities, including athletes, talk about mask wearing and COVID-19 preventive behaviors. Celebrities did not seem to be impacted as much as the general public since they often live in larger homes and have access to more resources.

Therefore, hearing them talk about wearing masks or staying home may have felt like a hollow request to some.

In regard to SCT, in the final model, self-efficacy, situation, and social norms were not predictive of intention to wear masks. Outcome expectations (β=.32, p <.001) and behavioral strategies (β = .28, p < .001) were both significant predictors of intention to wear masks. Results showed that the "General Athlete Influence" variable was positively related to intention to wear a mask (β = .38, p < .001) suggesting that athletes could be influential in encouraging mask-wearing behaviors.

However, when we examined the "COVID-19 Athlete Influence" variable in the final model, it was negatively related to intention to wear masks (β = −.18, p < .05). Recall that the "COVID-19 Athlete Influence" variable asked participants not only about mask wearing, but also about athletes being vaccinated, or engaging in general preventive behaviors. In the second model, without the SCT measures, this relationship was positive, although not significant (β = .17, p = .15). However, when the SCT measures were added in the final model, the relationship reversed. This is likely caused by a confounding relationship between the COVID-19 Athlete Influence variable and the SCT variables. The most likely explanation for this is high collinearity between these variables. A correlation analysis shows strong, significant correlations between COVID-19 Athlete Influence and the SCT variables. Statistically, this can affect the direction of a predictor variable. See Table 22.3.

In this case, because the SCT variables and the COVID-19 Athlete Influence variable were highly correlated, it changed the direction of the athlete influence variable from positive to negative between model two and model three. This relationship is worth exploring further in future research.

This exploratory study provides some evidence that the behaviors of athletes may positively influence the behaviors of sports fans. When athletes step up and

TABLE 22.3 Pearson Correlations for Continuous Variables

Measure	1	2	3	4	5	6	7
Self-Efficacy	—						
Situation	.38***	—					
Outcome Expectation	.39***	.75***	—				
Behavioral Strategies	.32***	.72***	.72***	—			
Social Norms	.21***	.55***	.54***	.61***	—		
Athlete Influence General	−.12	.06	.15*	.04	.16*	—	
Athlete Influence COVID	−.07	.18**	.30***	.17**	.30***	.81***	—

*p < .05, **p < .01, ***p < .001

speak out, they have an opportunity to be role models for public health efforts. Seeing a favorite athlete like Trout or Frazier wear a mask may make it more comfortable for people to wear their own masks.

You Make the Call

In summer 2020, COVID-19 was still a relatively new phenomenon. There were no vaccines, and little was known about the efficacy of mask wearing. However, some athletes, like Trout and Frazier, stood out as positive role models, using traditional and social media to provide their reasons for wearing masks. Their reasons were the same as many other Americans – to keep themselves, their families, and their communities healthy. While Trout spoke out about wearing his mask to keep his pregnant wife healthy, Frazier specifically pointed to his intention to keep his teammates healthy.

The results from this study found that athletes can have a positive influence on intentions to wear masks. Those who indicated that athletes were generally influential were also more likely to intend to wear masks. Those who did not find athletes influential were less likely to intend to wear masks. While intention does not always lead to behavior change, there is a strong correlation (Webb & Sheeran, 2006; Armitage & Conner, 2001; Floyd et al., 2000). Knowing that people may be influenced by athletes who wear masks provides an opportunity for athletes to encourage behavior change.

We know from previous literature that many people look up to athletes as role models. Therefore, it is important to consider the ways that athletes can be used as role models for public health behaviors. Using these athletes in public health campaigns or public service announcements might help to normalize behaviors like mask wearing or getting vaccinated for COVID-19. In the future, we may look up to athletes to promote other public health behaviors, becoming a face for issues that will benefit the health and safety of the general public.

In public health, theory-based campaigns are standard. Using theory helps to understand the factors that need to be addressed to ensure behavior change. Both SCT and stages of change are proven models for health behavior change. Either can be used to successfully design interventions that encourage individuals to change behaviors like mask wearing. For example, in SCT, social and environmental factors, like athlete influence and mass media, are driving forces behind behavior change. In the stages of change model, seeing athletes wearing masks may encourage others in the pre-contemplation phase to move to the completion stage and consider mask wearing. Seeing these athletes wearing their masks can be a call to action for sports fans to put on their masks as well.

These athletes received a great deal of media attention for their decision to wear a mask on and off the field. However, neither Trout nor Frazier directly encouraged others to wear face masks, only doing what they felt was the right thing to do. This approach has pros and cons. Fans saw these and other players wearing masks, which helped normalize mask-wearing behaviors. Although this is a good thing, speaking out directly about mask wearing may have made a stronger statement, letting fans know that the athletes they admire believe mask-wearing is important. In this instance, MLB missed an opportunity to use well-known athletes to be the face of an important topic.

There are also ethical implications to consider. Do athletes have a responsibility to be role models for public health behaviors? There is not a clear answer here. While some believe that athletes and celebrities, who are admired by children and adults, have a responsibility to be role models, others believe that they should be able to live their lives and make decisions like everyone else. Is there an ethical responsibility to be a good role model, particularly in the midst of a public health crisis? This may be an avenue for future studies.

To fully understand how athletes influence public health behavior, it would be useful to examine specific athletes and their effects on fans. For example, were fans of Mike Trout more likely to wear their masks after seeing him do the same? And, would they have been even more likely to wear their masks if he spoke out directly about the importance of mask wearing? Future research should test theory-based messaging to determine the most effective communication strategies for athletes to use in a public health crisis. Using SCT or stages of change is a good starting point for this research.

Discussion Questions

1. Update the chapter based on the current state of the COVID-19 pandemic. What role do athletes currently play in encouraging other preventive behaviors like vaccinations? Are there examples of athletes who have been vocal about these behaviors and have they influenced behavior change?
2. What role can professional sports teams play in encouraging mask wearing? Is this different from the role that individual athletes might play in encouraging mask wearing?
3. Consider the role that mask wearing may have on the reputation or image of an athlete. Discuss the possibility that athletes consider their reputation when making decisions about preventive health behaviors and the potential influence they have on their fans.
4. How would you design a campaign using professional athletes to promote mask wearing? Consider the elements of SCT or the stages of change model in your campaign. What are the benefits and disadvantages to creating a public health campaign using professional athletes? Would you recommend this approach or a more passive approach like that used by Trout and Frazier?
5. Discuss the ethical responsibility of high-visibility athletes who become role models during a public health crisis. If you were in charge of a sports league, how would you handle an athlete who is not being a good role model?

References

Armitage, C.J., & Conner, M. (2001). Efficacy of the theory of planned behaviour: A meta-analytic review. *British Journal of Social Psychology, 40*(4), 471–499.

Baccellieri, E. (2020, June 25). New MLB operations manual offers glimpse into negotiations for 2020 season. *Sports Illustrated.* www.si.com/mlb/2020/06/26/mlb-season-2020-operations-manual-changes

Bandura, A. (2001). Social cognitive theory of mass communication. *Media Psychology, 3*(3), 265–299.

Bandura, A. (2004a). Health promotion by social cognitive means. *Health Education & Behavior, 31*(2), 143–164.

Bandura, A. (2004b). Social cognitive theory for personal and social change by enabling media. *Entertainment-Education and Social Change: History, Research, and Practice, 54,* 75–96.

Boren, C. (2020, August 6). MLB tightens coronavirus rules, requiring masks in dugouts and compliance officers. *The Washington Post.* www.washingtonpost.com/sports/2020/08/06/mlb-tightens-coronavirus-rules-requiring-masks-dugouts-compliance-officers/

Brown, W.J., Basil, M.D., & Bocarnea, M.C. (2003). The influence of famous athletes on health beliefs and practices: Mark McGwire, child abuse prevention, and androstenedione. *Journal of Health Communication, 8*(1), 41–57.

Bush, A.J., Martin, C.A., & Bush, V.D. (2004). Sports celebrity influence on the behavioral intentions of generation Y. *Journal of Advertising Research, 44*(1), 108–118.

Centers for Disease Control and Prevention. (2021). *COVID-19:* Considerations for wearing masks. *Centers for Disease Control and Prevention.* www.cdc.gov/coronavirus/2019-ncov/prevent-getting-sick/about-face-coverings.html#:~:text=People%20may%20choose%20to%20mask,with%20COVID%2D19%20Data%20Tracker

Connolly, G.J. (2017). Applying social cognitive theory in coaching athletes: The power of positive role models. *Strategies, 30*(3), 23–29.

Cwik, C. (2020, August 2). Report: NBA warns teams it will punish players for not wearing masks. *Yahoo! Sports.* www.yahoo.com/video/report-nba-warns-teams-it-will-punish-players-for-not-wearing-masks-005343372.html

Dewar, D.L., Lubans, D.R., Plotnikoff, R.C., & Morgan, P.J. (2012). Development and evaluation of social cognitive measures related to adolescent dietary behaviors. *International Journal of Behavioral Nutrition and Physical Activity, 9*(1), 1–10.

Dutton, G.R., Provost, B.C., Tan, F., & Smith, D. (2008). A tailored print-based physical activity intervention for patients with type 2 diabetes. *Preventive Medicine, 47*(4), 409–411.

ESPN News Services (2020, July 18). Yankees' Clint Frazier brushes off criticism for wearing a mask during coronavirus pandemic. *ESPN.* www.espn.com/mlb/story/_/id/29486073/yankees-clint-frazier-brushes-criticism-wearing-mask-coronavirus-pandemic

Evers, K.E., Prochaska, J.O., Van Marter, D.F., Johnson, J.L., & Prochaska, J.M. (2007). Transtheoretical-based bullying prevention effectiveness trials in middle schools and high schools. *Educational Research, 49*(4), 397–414.

Fearnow, B. (2021, January 23). 83 percent of Americans support wearing masks, but only HALF wear THEM: POLL. *Newsweek.* www.newsweek.com/83-percent-americans-support-wearing-masks-only-half-wear-them-poll-1563944

Floyd, D.L., Prentice-Dunn, S., & Rogers, R.W. (2000). A meta-analysis of research on protection motivation theory. *Journal of Applied Social Psychology, 30*(2), 407–429.

Gazabon, S.A., Morokoff, P.J., Harlow, L.L., Ward, R.M., & Quina, K. (2007). Applying the transtheoretical model to ethnically diverse women at risk for HIV. *Health Education & Behavior, 34*(2), 297–314.

Hoch, B. (2020, July 12). Frazier plans to wear mask during games. *MLB.* www.mlb.com/news/clint-frazier-plans-to-wear-mask-during-games

Inman, R.A., Moreira, P.A., Faria, S., Araújo, M., Cunha, D., Pedras, S., & Correia Lopes, J. (2021). An application of the transtheoretical model to climate change prevention: Validation of the climate change stages of change questionnaire in middle school students and their schoolteachers. *Environmental Education Research*, 1–20.

Kim, M., & Walker, M. (2013). The influence of professional athlete philanthropy on donation intentions. *European Sport Management Quarterly, 13*(5), 579–601.

Lee, A. (2013, February 11). 25 athletes who have been in a million commercials. *Bleacher Report.* https://bleacherreport.com/articles/1524474-25-athletes-who-have-been-in-a-million-commercials

NHL Public Relations. (2020). Capitals fined $100,000 by NHL for COVID-19 violations. *NHL.com.* www.nhl.com/news/washington-capitals-fined-by-nhl-for-covid-19-violations/c-320514680

Nightengale, B. (2020, July 3). With pregnant wife, Angels star Mike Trout unsure if he'll play in 2020: 'Playing it by ear.' *USA Today.* https://amp.usatoday.com/amp/5371712002?__twitter_impression=true"

Prochaska, J.O., & DiClemente, C.C. (1983). Stages and processes of self-change of smoking: Toward an integrative model of change. *Journal of Consulting and Clinical Psychology, 51*(3), 390–395. https://doi.org/10.1037/0022-006X.51.3.390

Prochaska, J.O., Redding, C.A., & Evers, K.E. (2015). The transtheoretical model and stages of change. In K. Glanz, B.K. Rimer & K. Viswanath (Eds.), *Health behavior: Theory, research, and practice* (4th ed., pp. 97–121). Jossey-Bass.

Raihan, N., & Cogburn, M. (2021). *Stages of change theory.* New York: StatPearls Publishing.

Rapoport, I. (2020, December 27). NFL fines Baltimore Ravens $250,000 for COVID-19 violations. *NFL.com.* www.nfl.com/news/nfl-fines-baltimore-ravens-250-000-for-covid-19-violations

Red, C. (2020, July 22). Masks halt COVID, but pro-sports athletes are divided on wearing them. *NBC News.* www.nbcnews.com/news/us-news/masks-halt-covid-pro-sports-athletes-are-divided-wearing-them-n1234575

Smith, M.D. (2021, August 26). NFL has issued $14,650 fines to 25 players for failing to wear masks or tracking devices. *NBC Sports.* https://profootballtalk.nbcsports.com/2021/08/26/nfl-has-issued-14650-fines-to-25-players-for-failing-to-wear-masks-or-tracking-devices/

Stump, S. (2020, July 6). Mike Trout's mother shares photo of him playing baseball in mask with important message. *Today.* www.today.com/health/mike-trout-s-mother-shares-photo-him-playing-baseball-mask-t185889

Townsend, M. (2020, July 8). As Mike Trout decision looms, Angels commit to wearing masks and avoiding crowds. *Yahoo.* www.yahoo.com/now/angels-answer-mike-trouts-concerns-by-committing-to-wear-masks-and-avoid-crowds-022828327.html

Vilamala-Orra, M., Vaqué-Crusellas, C., Foguet-Boreu, Q., Guimerà Gallent, M., & del Río Sáez, R. (2021). Applying the stages of change model in a nutrition education programme for the promotion of fruit and vegetable consumption among people with severe mental disorders (DIETMENT). *Nutrients, 13*(6), 1–15.

Webb, T.L., & Sheeran, P. (2006). Does changing behavioral intentions engender behavior change? A meta-analysis of the experimental evidence. *Psychological Bulletin*, *132*(2), 249.

The White House (2021, January 20). Executive order on protecting the Federal workforce and requiring mask-wearing. *The White House.* www.whitehouse.gov/briefing-room/presidential-actions/2021/01/20/executive-order-protecting-the-federal-workforce-and-requiring-mask-wearing/.

23

CONTROLLING THE NARRATIVE

NBC, USA Gymnastics, and Simone Biles at the 2020 Summer Olympic Games

Aaron W. Gurlly

Introduction

On July 27, 2021, American gymnast Simone Biles stunned the world when she withdrew from the women's team competition at the 2020 Summer Olympic Games (held in 2021 due to COVID-19). To date, Biles had been considered an unstoppable force in women's artistic gymnastics. From her first world championship titles in 2013 through her victories at the 2019 world championships, Biles was undefeated in major all-around competitions, ultimately winning a record-setting five world all-around titles. She also served as a mentor to her teammates in many competitions, leading the U.S. women's team to four world championship gold medals and one Olympic team gold medal. Her successes in individual events also set her apart from the other legends of the sport; her medal winning performances on the balance beam, uneven bars, floor exercise, and vault have made her the most decorated gymnast in history.

Off the competition floor, Biles is also a celebrity. Hers is a household name – a relatively rare accomplishment for a gymnast in the United States. She has a well-established media presence, both traditional media and social media. She has used her fame to promote her sport and to advocate for important causes, including the widely publicized sexual abuse scandal in which hundreds of girls and young women were assaulted by team doctor Larry Nassar. As perhaps his most high-profile victim, Biles spoke alongside other courageous women to bring Nassar' crimes to light and to hold USA Gymnastics, the sport's official governing body in the United States, accountable for its failure to protect its athletes.

This chapter focuses on the media discourses surrounding Biles' withdrawal from the competition by examining American broadcast network NBC's coverage of the Olympics, public statements from Simone Biles, responses from press

DOI: 10.4324/9781003316763-27

outlets, and public responses from other elite-level gymnasts and coaches. It considers different communication strategies used by Biles and by USA Gymnastics to mediate the issue of Biles' withdrawal and the consequences of Biles's public revelation of the health concerns that led her to walk away from the competition floor. The chapter applies impression management theory and third-level agenda setting theory to argue that Biles' and USA Gymnastics' conflicting goals in managing the press coverage of the competition exacerbated the ongoing conflict between the organization and Biles, whose success and notoriety have immensely profited USA Gymnastics, but whose public criticism threatens the public image of that organization. NBC, official broadcaster of the Games, also has a vested interest: To ensure high levels of viewership. Sections of the chapter explore how these competing interests created a complex media spectacle that highlighted the concerns that have been expressed about competition, celebrity, and the push for success at all costs.

Background

When Biles suddenly stepped away from Olympic competition after an uncharacteristic error in the first rotation of the women's team final, the world was shocked. After all, the unstoppable force of gymnastics, the Greatest of All Time (as she had been dubbed), revealed another aspect of her identity to the public – her humanity. Public discourse that treated Biles as if she were a superhero led the world to believe her impervious to stresses that would affect any person, let alone a person competing in a dangerous sport in front of more than a billion spectators around the globe.

Performance anxiety, which can affect any athlete at any level of competition, was not the only challenge Biles faced at her second Olympic Games. Even while the Olympics were going on, Biles was involved in ongoing proceedings regarding the Nassar case and seemingly in incessant conflict with USA Gymnastics over its perceived reluctance to implement further safeguards for the well-being of American gymnasts. Additionally, Biles faced a mountain of expectations. Being labelled unbeatable places an immense burden on athletes who supposedly "cannot lose." In retrospect, it seems almost inevitable that something would happen to upset the pre-established narrative of Biles's assumed victory in Tokyo. Biles' subsequent withdrawal from the all-around competition and from three of the four event final competitions for which she had qualified further complicated the situation.

Theoretical Framework

Impression management theory, initially conceived by sociologist Erving Goffman (1956), assumes that people attempt to influence the way they are seen by others. Jones (1982) defined five strategies of impression management:

- Self-Promotion – publicizing one's supposed positive qualities (p. 241)
- Ingratiation – leading others to attribute positive qualities to oneself (p. 235)
- Exemplification – highlighting one's integrity and moral worth (p. 245)
- Intimidation – seeking to appear dangerous or frightening (p. 238)
- Supplication – seeking mercy from others (p. 247)

The theory has since been expanded by other scholars who have shown that organizations, like individuals, also use strategies to exert control over their public image (Gardner & Martinko, 1988; Bolino & Turnley, 1999; Watkins Allen & Caillouet, 1994). Later parts of this chapter explore how Biles and USA Gymnastics differ in their use of these strategies in their public statements made during the 2020 Games.

Third-level agenda setting (McCombs, Shaw & Weaver, 2014) posits that media influence the cognitive associations made by audiences between different media stories. That is, the media can affect the ways in which viewers mentally connect information presented in different media stories. This is not to suggest that media determines *exactly* what people will think; third-level agenda setting merely suggests that media can influence audiences to perceive links between different news events. By covering different issues at the same time, media encourage audiences to see connections between those issues. Third-level agenda setting suggests that news stories and television coverage discussing Biles' departure from competition circulating alongside media coverage of the ongoing controversies in gymnastics may lead audiences to see Biles' departure as related to those ongoing controversies.

As already mentioned, Biles faced an array of pressures at the beginning of the 2020 Games. USA Gymnastics also faced many challenges at the onset of competition. The aforementioned sexual abuse scandal not only resulted in Nassar's conviction; it also led to the arrest of Steve Penny, former CEO of USA Gymnastics, and the indictment of John Geddert, head coach of the American women's gymnastics team at the 2012 Olympics. As of January 2022, Penny awaits trial for his alleged attempts to cover up the rampant abuse committed by Nassar, and Geddert committed suicide soon after abuse allegations were made against him. While only those two USA Gymnastics officials were charged with crimes related to the scandal, numerous other officials left the organization or were asked to resign, including the national team coordinator, training camp officials, and the entire Board of Directors of USA Gymnastics. It would, perhaps, be an understatement to claim that USA Gymnastics faced a public relations nightmare.

The Nassar sexual abuse scandal is just the latest in a series of negative press events that has threatened the USA Gymnastics image for decades. Despite the ongoing success of the United States in competition, the sport's governing body has long been criticized for endangering – or failing to adequately protect – the well-being of its gymnasts. Former team coordinator Marta Karolyi and her husband, long-time coach Bela Karolyi, have been criticized since the 1980s for pushing young athletes to win medals at the expense of their physical and mental health. Similar allegations have been made against several other prominent coaches. Gymnastics is also known for having a longstanding problem with disordered eating. Though the press no longer reports the height and weight of gymnasts during broadcasts – a common practice that persisted through the 1990s – Tan, Bloodworth, McNamee, and Hewitt (2012) note that eating disorders remained common among gymnasts, long after Joan Ryan's *Little Girls in Pretty Boxes* (1995) publicized the risks facing participants of the sport.

The Case

As the 2020 Games approached, USA Gymnastics needed positive media stories to draw attention away from the negative press that threatened the reputation of the organization. Likewise, Biles, as an outspoken critic of USA Gymnastics, was motivated to use the press to tell her own stories. Those stories became intertwined when, because of Biles' sudden departure from competition, questions about gymnasts' mental health began to dominate the media coverage.

Pre-Olympic press coverage of the U.S. women's gymnastics team was overwhelmingly optimistic and positive. NBC's coverage of the U.S. National Championships and the subsequent team selection process highlighted the team's prowess. The team, led by Biles, was predicted to be the most successful team in the history of women's gymnastics. The U.S. magazine *International Gymnast*, a leading publication in the sport, reported, "Undoubtedly the U.S. women will capture their third consecutive Olympic team gold medal" (IG Staff, 2021, para. 2). The NBC broadcast of the pre-Olympic selection process also depicted the team as a group of happy, successful, and thriving young women who would go on to win America's third consecutive team gold medal. The coverage even highlighted the racial diversity of the team, demonstrating the inclusivity of the sport since the time when nearly all high-level gymnasts were White. Little mention was made of the organization's troubles. With new staffing in place, and new policies designed to address athlete safety, USA Gymnastics was receiving the positive coverage it needed, including some positive acknowledgment from Biles herself (Clarke, 2020).

Biles was the recipient of overwhelmingly positive coverage going into the Games. Though her competitive record alone would elicit praise from across the media landscape, Biles herself played an active role in shaping media narratives. She is active on social media and is featured in numerous television commercials, including spots for Uber Eats and Powerade, the latter of which focuses on mental health issues affecting athletes. She earns millions from endorsement deals with major companies such as Visa and United Airlines and with sports and fitness companies such as Core Power Fitness and GK Elite, a gymnastics apparel company. She has testified before Congress, been interviewed countless times, appeared on major talk shows, and has published a book. Her ability to influence the media rivals that of USA Gymnastics itself. She, more than other athletes represented by USA Gymnastics, is able to bypass the organization and speak through the media to a large swath of the public, in addition to her nearly 7 million Instagram followers.

However, once the competition began, the rosy press coverage wilted. NBC's coverage of the first phase of competition in Tokyo revealed a U.S. women's gymnastics team facing uncharacteristic problems. Biles stumbled repeatedly in the initial qualification round, but still finished in first place as an individual. Her teammates uncharacteristically committed more errors than usual in competition as well, and the team finished the qualifying round in second place, behind the gymnasts from Russia. NBC's coverage seemed ill-prepared to cover an insurgent team from Russia; neither the official livestream nor the primetime broadcast showed all of the routines performed by the ultimately victorious Russian gymnasts. Instead, the production team for the broadcast seemed better prepared to broadcast images of the American gymnasts on the sidelines, chatting with one another between performances.

This focus on American athletes and the exclusion of athletes from other countries seemed particularly odd, given the Russian gymnasts' successes at recent meets. It also proved problematic when NBC's planned coverage was thrown into disarray by Biles' departure. Since NBC's central game plan was to spotlight Biles, her sudden absence forced the production team to quickly re-strategize in order to (1) provide updated reports on Biles' condition and her plans for the rest of the competition and to (2) determine which gymnasts to spotlight in place of Biles in its coverage. Because Olympic gymnastics is popular among American television viewers, NBC allots significant airtime for the sport. Biles' popularity only increased the amount of airtime NBC scheduled for the sport, with the 2020 Games including more livestream coverage and network coverage for gymnastics than it did for the previous Games in 2016. With Biles in the lineup, NBC assumed that viewership would be high; in her absence, that assumption was less certain. If viewership was low, NBC might fail to gain a return on its $7.75 billion long-term investment in the Games.

USA Gymnastics, like NBC, also depends on high levels of viewership during the Olympics. Generally, enrollment in gymnastics programs increases in the months after an Olympics, particularly in years when the American team wins gold medals (Gilroy Dispatch Staff, 2012; Meyers, 2016; Swink, 2021). Outside of the Olympics, gymnastics lacks the popularity of other sports such as basketball and baseball. The Olympics function as a recruiting tool for USA gymnastics because, for a large part of the public, the Olympics are the only time when they watch the sport. Declining viewership might, for USA Gymnastics, lead to reduced gymnastics participation in future years.

Biles also benefits from the outsize role she plays in Olympic gymnastics. Her fame is based primarily on her successes in competition. By leaving the competition, Biles risked tarnishing her public image and reducing her perceived value to her sponsors. But, unlike USA Gymnastics and NBC, Biles also risked personal losses when she stepped away. Biles has spoken repeatedly about the pressure she faces to maintain her success. Walking out during a competition does not only threaten her status as a champion, it also threatens her sense of self. Given these stakes, Biles, like USA Gymnastics, is motivated to protect her public image.

When the unexpected happens, underlying assumptions are revealed. As Biles, on a rolling basis, withdrew from multiple phases of competition, NBC was left to confront its mistake in basing its women's gymnastics coverage on one athlete – Biles – and their belief in her inevitable victory. Though Biles' unparalleled record might explain why her victory was assumed to be guaranteed, it is a major risk for a broadcaster to plan several days of athletic coverage around the appearance of a single athlete culminating in a happy ending.

After all, Olympic gymnastics has a long history of upsets. In 1992, for example, none of the gymnasts favored by the American press (Svetlana Boginskaya, Kim Zmeskal, Cristina Bontas) medaled in the all-around competition. Injuries have disrupted competitions and resulted in sudden changes to the athlete roster. In addition, the COVID-19 pandemic threatened to create last-minute chaos that should have been anticipated by the network. For all these reasons, it is fair to question NBC's scheduling strategy – and the inherent need to balance the uncertainty of a gymnastics competition – with the anticipated boost in viewership Biles brings to events in which she participates.

NBC garnered criticism for its response to Biles' absence. Though it seems reasonable that the network would cover every update from Biles during her absence, it is less clear what the network was hoping to achieve by aborting planned livestreams of some gymnastics events. Did NBC truly believe Biles was the only reason viewers would tune in to those early morning video feeds? Likewise, NBC was chastised for altering its delayed primetime broadcast to broadcast old news. NBC's evening coverage dedicated significant airtime to Biles' ongoing story, despite the fact that, by the time the broadcast aired, Biles' updates would already have been made available to the public.

You Make the Call

NBC, USA Gymnastics, and Simone Biles each found themselves in an unanticipated media frenzy when Biles suddenly withdrew from portions of her second Olympic Games. The unexpected departure created a complex set of public relations issues for each of those stakeholders. NBC, as official broadcaster for Olympic coverage, generally dedicates some portion of its gymnastics coverage to explaining the sport's complex rules to a viewing public that is largely unfamiliar with some of the sport's more esoteric regulations. Biles' decision presented the network with an opportunity to explain what happens when a gymnast drops out of an ongoing competition. Unfortunately, this opportunity was largely missed by the on-air commentators. First, athletes who withdraw during the team competition cannot be replaced. This rule makes it even more difficult for an athlete in Biles' position to decide to withdraw; her absence from the team will almost certainly have a negative impact on the team. Next, athletes who, like Biles, withdraw from the all-around competition or from an event final are replaced by the gymnast with the next highest qualifying score, which means that an athlete who withdraws is unlikely to be replaced by a gymnast from their team. Finally, decisions for withdrawal are scheduled around the timing of each event; gymnasts do not immediately withdraw from every part of the competition. This causes a delay in reported withdrawals for an athlete who sits out of multiple phases of competition. Thus, an athlete may withdraw from competition once but must *officially* withdraw from competition multiple times and over multiple days. These rules create a situation in which an athlete can be blamed for being selfish and harming their team. They also create the appearance that the athlete is forcing the public to wait for them to make an official decision regarding their participation.

Because these rules are generally unknown to the public, clarification from NBC might have helped the public better understand the process and might have provided the needed context for Biles' decision. NBC commentators might also have explained, as Biles herself did during her televised interviews, that her decision was based on her belief that her performances – had she continued in the competition – would have jeopardized the team's chances at medaling, which it ultimately did. In making this statement, Biles shatters the assumption that she is destined to perform well and, instead, indicates her awareness of her human limitations.

NBCs commentators also described the competition as "wide open" after Biles' departure, again reinforcing the notion that Biles would have been assured victory – and that every other competitor was destined to lose to her. This framing, combined with NBC's decision not to air performances by other talented gymnasts, made the Russian gymnasts' victory seem to come from nowhere, despite that team's recent competitive results and despite their first-place ranking after the qualifying round. Unfortunately, this fed into a narrative of blame for members of Team USA. Biles was, of course, criticized by segments of the public for being "a quitter" (Constantine, 2021). Jordan Chiles, another member of the team who, like Biles, is a woman of color, was also singled out for chastisement due to a few errors in the early round of competition. Whether intentional or not, these two women received disproportionate public vitriol for events that are relatively common in gymnastics. Gymnasts do sometimes withdraw from competition for health reasons, as Biles did here. Top-tier gymnasts, like Chiles, also sometimes stumble.

In response to this criticism, Biles was steadfast. She turned to social media and to traditional media (television, in particular) in an attempt to manage the emerging discourse. Her strategies included public disclosure of the health issue that caused her to leave the competition. "The twisties," as the condition is called, causes a gymnast to spontaneously lose their sense of place while tumbling. Though the cause is unknown, mental stress is thought to exacerbate the problem. When performing skills as difficult as those performed by Biles (or any high-level gymnast), this condition can be incredibly dangerous. Gymnasts have been gravely injured in training and in competition when they have lost the ability to orient themselves in the middle of a high-flying skill. USA Gymnastics is still haunted by the death of Julissa Gomez from injuries sustained during the 1987 World Championships. Because the danger of "the twisties" is so well-known in the gymnastics community, several former elite gymnasts spoke out in support of Biles after her disclosure. This prompted a large-scale public discussion about mental health in gymnastics specifically, and in sports more broadly.

Biles's candid disclosures, along with her skillful responses to unwarranted criticism from outsiders, helped shape the larger narrative emerging from the Olympics (Scott, 2021). In the time since the games, other high-profile athletes, including multiple Olympic Champion Michael Phelps, have also made public health disclosures, and some have, like Biles, walked away from important competitions in order to care for themselves. Subsequent to Biles' experience, alternative framings have emerged that emphasize the importance of ensuring athlete safety and health over victory.

Throughout the Games, USA Gymnastics remained relatively quiet. Their strategy was based in ingratiation, or allowing others to say and do things that reflect well on the organization. If Team USA performed well, and if NBC provided images of a happy, healthy group of gymnasts, USA Gymnastics could indirectly benefit from the positive coverage. It might appear that the organization had finally gotten past its controversies. Biles' withdrawal for mental health reasons complicated this plan.

First, Biles' absence threatened the anticipated victory that would help improve USA Gymnastics' image. Second, because she reported having mental health issues, her withdrawal raised more questions about the organization's commitment to athlete health and safety. Third, Biles' public criticism left USA Gymnastics in a bind. If the organization encouraged Biles to remain in the competition, it would confirm that USA Gymnastics values gold medals over an athlete's well-being. If the organization encouraged Biles to sit out of the competition, it might appear as retaliation against her. If the organization prioritized mental health, it could raise questions about why Biles and her teammates were not already receiving this kind of support from USA Gymnastics. This left the organization with little to say, except for a message included in its official press release issued after the women's team final competition. The release reads:

> Biles made the difficult decision to withdraw out of an abundance of caution for her mental and physical well-being. Her World Champions Centre teammate Chiles stepped in on uneven bars and balance beam, while Lee competed on floor exercise in Biles' stead. "We could not be prouder of how this team handled things tonight," said USA Gymnastics CEO Li Li Leung. "From Simone's bravery and selflessness to the team's ability to adapt quickly and perform so well, these young women inspired us all."
>
> *(USA Gymnastics, July 27, 2021d, paras. 3–4)*

Other press releases issued during the Olympics mention Biles' withdrawal but offer no commentary (USA Gymnastics, July 29, 2021e; USA Gymnastics, August 1, 2021a; USA Gymnastics, August 2, 2021b; USA Gymnastics, August 3, 2021c). The press release that discusses Biles' bronze-medal winning performance in the balance beam finals does not mention her withdrawal from earlier phases of competition.

Given the constraints on USA Gymnastics and its public statements, the organization was limited in its ability to deploy any of the five strategies of impression management described before. NBC, as broadcaster, was likewise limited in its strategies. Because the network was responsible for generating so much hype surrounding Biles, NBC might, like USA Gymnastics, seek to avoid drawing attention to itself and its role in exacerbating the stress she felt during the competition.

Biles, as a savvy media figure, used multiple strategies for impression management in this situation. As seen in NPR's (Chappell 2021) transcript of Biles' withdraw statement, Biles presented an image of herself as a supportive teammate and advocate for persons struggling with mental health concerns (exemplification) and highlighted her own ongoing struggles as a result of a wide range of stress associated with her affiliation with USA Gymnastics (supplication).

In her social media feed, Biles speaks directly about herself and her value (self-promotion). Her accolades and her advocacy have elicited support and praise from large swaths of the public (ingratiation). Biles has also demonstrated to USA Gymnastics that, even while competing under their auspices, she was willing and able to stand up to the organization and, if necessary, walk away from it, taking her legions of fans with her (intimidation).

This last point was exemplified in Biles' decision to start the Gold over America tour, a post-Olympic tour for gymnasts. Biles' tour, which includes four of her 2020 Olympic teammates alongside a cast of other renowned gymnasts, replaces the post-Olympic tour usually held by USA Gymnastics. The tour usually generates revenue in the millions of dollars for USA Gymnastics; those funds now going to Biles' tour, which, at Biles' insistence, has no connection with USA Gymnastics. This sends a clear message to USA Gymnastics that Biles is not only able to influence fans, she is also able to influence other gymnasts to stand in opposition to the organization. In so doing, Biles exerts control over significant amounts of revenue USA Gymnastics needs for its development and continued existence.

Discussion Questions

1. How have other sports responded to athlete concerns about mental health? How have athletes in other sports brought attention to mental health concerns in their sport?
2. What do you think of the impression management strategies used by Biles, NBC, and USA Gymnastics? How might each party have addressed this situation differently?

3. Discuss possible resolutions that could allow all parties involved to improve their public image. In what ways could third-level agenda setting play a part in these situations?

4. In what ways was the narrative of the Olympics shaped by several different news events (the abuse scandal, the lawsuits against USA Gymnastics, NBC's pre-Olympic hype)? How might public opinion be influenced by a combination of these stories? Discuss the possibility that each story could stand on its own in the public imagination.

References

Bolino, M.C., & Turnley, W.H. (1999). Measuring impression management in organizations: A scale development based on the Jones and Pittman Taxonomy. *Organizational Research Methods, 2*(2), 187–206. *https://doi.org/10.1177/109442819922005*

Chappell, Bill (2021, July 28). Read what Simone Biles said sfter her withdrawal from the Olympic Final. *NPR.* www.npr.org/sections/tokyo-olympics-live-updates/2021/07/28/1021683296/in-her-words-what-simone-biles-said-after-her-withdrawal

Clarke, Liz. (2020, January 20). Simone Biles calls USA Gymnastics interim training base 'a good start' on road to Tokyo Olympics. *The Washington Post.* www.washingtonpost.com/sports/2020/01/20/simone-biles-calls-usa-gymnastics-interim-training-base-good-start-road-tokyo-olympics/

Constantine, T. (2021, July 31). Simone Biles is no hero. She is a quitter. *The Washington Times.* www.washingtontimes.com/news/2021/jul/31/simone-biles-no-hero-she-quitter/

Gardner, W.L., & Martinko, M.M. (1988). Impression management in organizations. *Journal of Management, 14*(2), 321–338.

Gilroy Dispatch Staff. (2012, July 20). Gymnastics: Olympics leave impact on local gyms. *Gilroy Dispatch.* https://gilroydispatch.com/gymnastics-olympics-leave-impact-on-local-gyms/

Goffman, E. (1956). *The presentation of self in everyday life.* London: Anchor.

IG Staff (2021, July 20). Tokyo Olympics: IG's medal predictions, part ii – Women's competition. *International Gymnast Media.* www.intlgymnast.com/tokyo-2020/tokyo-olympics-igs-medal-predictions-part-ii-womens-competition/

Jones, E.E. (1982). Toward a general theory of strategic self-presentation. In J. Suis (Ed.), *Psychological perspectives on the self: Volume 1* (pp. 231–262). Hoboken, NJ: Lawrence Erlbaum Associates.

McCombs, M.E., Shaw, D.L., & Weaver, D.H. (2014). New directions in agenda-setting theory and research. *Mass Communication and Society, 17*(6), 781–802. https://doi.org/10.1080/15205436.2014.964871

Meyers, S. (2016, August 16). Gymnastics see increase during Olympics. *The Dispatch.* www.the-dispatch.com/story/business/2016/08/16/gymnastics-see-increase-during-olympics/25630853007/

Ryan, J. (1995). *Little girls in pretty boxes.* London: Doubleday Religious Publishing Group.

Scott, K.D. (2021). Repurposing black women's strength and normalizing "strong sista self-care" on social media. *Women's Studies in Communication, 44*(4), 484–490. https://doi.org/10.1080/07491409.2021.1987823

Swink, S. (2021, July 15). Wings Gymnastics opening west side location thanks to Olympics, growth. *Argus Leader*. www.argusleader.com/story/news/business-journal/2021/07/15/olympics-and-growth-has-wings-gymnastics-opening-second-location-soon/7963612002/

Tan, J., Bloodworth, A., McNamee, M., & Hewitt, J (2012). Investigating eating disorders in elite gymnasts: Conceptual, ethical and methodological issues, *European Journal of Sport Science, 14*(1), 60–68. https://doi.org/10.1080/17461391.2012.728632

USA Gymnastics. (2021a, August 1). Skinner, Lee medal on first night of artistic gymnastics event finals at 2020 Tokyo Olympic Games. *USA Gymnastics*. https://usagym.org/pages/post.html?PostID=26478

USA Gymnastics. (2021b, August 2). Carey golden on floor exercise at 2020 Tokyo Olympic Games. *USA Gymnastics*. https://usagym.org/pages/post.html?PostID=26484

USA Gymnastics. (2021c August 3). Biles takes bronze on balance beam on final night of Olympic artistic gymnastics. *USA Gymnastics*. https://usagym.org/pages/post.html?PostID=26487

USA Gymnastics. (2021d, July 27). U.S. women capture hard-fought silver medal at 2020 Tokyo Olympic Games. *USA Gymnastics*. https://usagym.org/pages/post.html?PostID=26460

USA Gymnastics. (2021e, July 29). Lee captures Team USA's fifth-straight Olympic women's all-around title. *USA Gymnastics*. https://usagym.org/pages/post.html?PostID=26467

Watkins Allen, M., & Caillouet, R.H. (1994). Legitimation endeavors: Impression management strategies used by an organization in crisis. *Communication Monographs, 1*, 44–62.

24

"WE HOPE TO SEE YOU SOON"

The Green Bay Packers' Crisis Management through a Letter to the Fans during COVID-19 Mega-Crisis

Julia C. Richmond

Introduction

In the wake of the COVID-19 global pandemic, professional sports teams, like the world at large, were forced to adopt new rules and regulations to adhere to emerging policies in public health (Hartman, 2020). Following the trend in the NFL, the Green Bay Packers announced that they would not allow fan attendance during the 2020 season. As a result of this announcement, Packers fans were dejected, disillusioned, and dissatisfied, endangering the relations between the Green Bay Packers organization and its fans. From a public relations and reputation management perspective, the Packers needed to act quickly to restore the relations with key constituents.

On September 12, 2020, the Packers responded to fan disappointment by publishing a letter to the fans on the team's official website. As an act of crisis response, letters to fans are important strategic communication tools which provide perspective from the organization and act as a mechanism to restore trust (Compton & Compton, 2014). The Packers used the letter to improve relations with key constituents during a season marred by the physical absence of the fans through web-based strategic communication. The organization constructed the message to acknowledge fan disappointment with the realities of the new season, express adoration for the loyal fans – also known as "Cheeseheads," and offer virtual alternatives for continued fan engagement.

Although the Packers organization did not hold responsibility for the COVID-19 pandemic, they did need to repair and reinforce the fractured relationships between the organization and its fans due to the changes in physical fan presence during the 2020 season. The need for communication between the organization and the fans demonstrates the unique characteristics of fans

DOI: 10.4324/9781003316763-28

as a highly engaged and invested public (Phua, 2010). Ultimately, the letter strengthened ties by underpinning the situated identities of fans, recalling shared sports experiences through social language, and appealing to the heritage of the organization.

Background

The Packers, unlike other teams in the NFL, are a publicly owned franchise. Fans can own stock in the team becoming shareholders. Packers shareholders are offered the unique opportunity to vote to elect a board of directors but do not have a voice in team decisions (Bolluyt, 2018). The main advantage of the Packers ownership structure is the community and public identity of the fan-centered organization. The strong commitment to fans built into the structure of the organization underpins the necessity for an appropriate response to crises such as the COVID-19 pandemic. The response is important since the fans are structurally integrated into the organization.

During the 2020 season, COVID-19 created a mega-crisis which shut down many regular operations in the professional sports industry and beyond. A mega-crisis is characterized by far- reaching effects, incomprehensible impacts, and capacity overload (Young & Rentner, 2018). As a mega-crisis (Parrott, 2020), COVID-19 would greatly alter the game day experience for fans. Thus, the Packers needed to implement a crisis response strategy to maintain positive relations with stakeholders during this crisis (Coombs, 1995). Crisis response must meet the situation and circumstances of the crisis, specifically crisis type, severity of damage, crisis history, and relationship history (Coombs, 2007b).

Public relations professionals must ensure trusting relations between the organization and their constituents (Doorley & Garcia, 2015; Jackson, 2004). These trusting relationships endure over time through successful interactions with an organization, which results in increased reputational capital (Doorley & Garcia, 2015). Within public relations in sport, fans are characterized as a unique type of highly engaged public. Fans often bolster their self-esteem by relating to a team and fan community (End, 2001; Phua, 2010). As such, teams have a responsibility to uphold and maintain authentic relationships during times of crisis. Fans are also unique communities with distinct social practices. During the shutdown of sporting events in the United States, teams were faced with the challenge of maintaining authentic fan relationships in the absence of events that usually stimulate the bulk of organization-to-fan relations. Sports organizations, like the Packers, relied on mediated communication to connect with isolated fans. The COVID-19 pandemic, as a mega-crisis, greatly altered the regular Packers operations, which resulted in disruptions in the game day experiences. Thus, a robust public relations response was necessary.

Theoretical Considerations

Public relations practitioners attempt to measure, influence, and predict public opinion to positively influence widespread perceptions of the brand, institution, or organization. Public opinion is formed through the measurement of human attitudes toward social and political topics. One of the definitions of public opinion is the aggregation of individual opinions (Glynn et al., 2015). Under this definition, public opinion can be measured through polling and survey research. As such, public relations practitioners must understand the individual in order to understand the collective.

On the individual level, people tend to form inferences, assumptions, and guesses about the motivations, actions, or behaviors of others, referred to as attributions (Weiner, 1985). Attribution theory explains how an individual's inferences about the motivation behind other's actions or opinions affect their own agreement with these actions or opinions (Coombs, 2007). Attribution theory refers to the tendency to assign characteristics to observable behavior. Consider if you observed a co-worker who always comes to work on time, communicates with you about expectations, and regularly completes job tasks. You may "attribute" underlying characteristics such as hardworking, reliability, or diligence to that individual. In this example, observable behavior is attributed to unseen characteristics. This same dynamic can be applied to organizations or companies.

In public relations, attribution theory is often used in crisis communication. Crisis communication is information sharing during a crisis (Doorley & Garcia, 2015). A crisis occurs when there is a public challenge to an organization's reputation due to an unexpected negative occurrence. During a crisis, individuals will attribute blame to make sense of the crisis and hold responsible parties accountable to wrongdoing (Coombs, 2007). The perception or attributes assigned to a crisis affect the situational particularities of a crisis.

Situational crisis communication theory (SCCT) applies attribution theory by exploring the specific aspects of a crisis, crisis response, and crisis outcome. SCCT posits that each crisis holds a measurable and predictable amount of attributed responsibility for the organization (Coombs, 2007). If publics attribute responsibility to the organization for the crisis, there is a serious reputational threat facing the organization. For example, if a company is experiencing a crisis due to pollution, there is a high-level organizational responsibility since they acted to pollute. The public will assign blame to the organization, and the crisis will have damaging reputational effects.

Following SCCT, the Packers needed to acknowledge the magnitude of the crisis and connect with stakeholders to avoid reputational damage (Coombs, 2007b). Within SCCT, a crisis response must be proportional to the threat of the crisis (Coombs & Holladay, 2002). SCCT emphasizes the influence of attribution theory in crisis management, that is, the tendency for stakeholders to attribute responsibility to an organization considering situational factors (Coombs, 1995; Coombs, 2007). While the Green Bay Packers did not hold any responsibility for the COVID-19 global pandemic, the management of the pandemic did present reputational risks for the organization as fans could attribute disappointment with the 2020 season to the organization. The risks associated with the pandemic warranted clear and carefully crafted communication.

Letters to fans are a form of strategic communication that connects the organization to the fans in an informal and congenial manner. A letter to fans is well positioned to express emotions by collapsing private and public communication, creating a strong connection between the organization and fans (Compton & Compton, 2014). This unique form gives internal and external stakeholders a glimpse into contextual information about decision-making and attitudes. As a form of image repair (Benoit, 1997), letters to fans have become increasingly digitized over time (Wallace et al., 2011).

The Case

The Green Bay Packers published a letter to the fans about the 2020 season. The letter appeared on the team's official Facebook and Twitter accounts, was emailed to current ticket holders, and was sent to local papers including the *Appleton Post-Crescent, Green Bay Press-Gazette,* and *Wausau Daily Herald* (K. Hermsen, personal communication, April 12, 2022). See Appendix C.

The message afforded fans the opportunity to reconnect with their team and share disappointment. The first part of the short letter acknowledged the far-reaching effects of COVID-19 beyond the scope of the team and organization. Through the recognition of the disruption of COVID-19, the organization positions itself as relatable and connected to their fans beyond football. The message goes on to state how the organization has missed the fans during key events that lead into the season. The organization carefully crafted the letter to encourage virtual fan interaction and to build ties to the organization since physical attendance was not permitted. Finally, the letter captures the emotion of being at the game while acknowledging the pain fans feel for not being present for a game this season. The letter ends by calling to mind the successful legacy of the organization.

When responding to the COVID-19 pandemic crisis, the Green Bay Packers needed to consider internal and external stakeholders. Through the adoption of an honest tone and authentic expression, this letter captures the state of the organization and the grief felt by fans, players, and employees alike. Through this analysis, the effectiveness of the letter is evaluated, along with dynamics of situated identities of fans (Gee, 2004), the use of football jargon called "coachtalk" (Enterline, 2010; Llewellyn, 2003), and appeals to heritage through paradigmatic/ syntagmatic choices (Chandler, 1994). Fans reacted by expressing strong virtual support for the team, frustration for missing out on physical presence, and adoration from abroad. Social media responses also deflected toward other issues facing the team like activism and social justice issues.

Situated Identities: The Fans

One effective strategy implemented in the Packers' letter to the fans is the appeal to the situated identity of the reader as a fan. A situated identity is a social position or role enacted in a particular setting or through linguistic choices (Gee, 2004). An individual's identity, for discursive psychologists, is enacted by social dialogue internalized through social interactions (Mead, 1934; Bakhtin, 2010; Jorgensen & Phillips, 2002). Therefore, the language used to identify fans is meaningful in the construction of fan identity. Moreover, organizations that wish to connect with their fans must find ways to reinforce and enact the reader's position as a fan. Fans carry with them an association with the team, a level of commitment, and social practices associated with the organization (Gray et al., 2017). The letter states, "Although we may not have you cheering us on in person, we can still feel your support from afar, and we will carry your energy with us" (para. 1). In this quote, the organization identifies and strengthens the importance of the fan community and claims the *presence* of the fans through their continued engagement even if it is through an unfamiliar virtual context. The situated identity is confirmed in this message as the reader is identified as a fan. Importantly, fan community building is effective for both internal and external stakeholders, especially in the case of the Packers, a fan-owned team.

Social Language and Coachtalk

Another effective aspect of the Packers' letter to the fans is the strategic use of language to craft a letter capturing the spirit of the organization and the sport of football at large. Social language, as a tool used in communication to recognize the position of the audience (Gee, 2004), was effectively used throughout the letter to strike the appropriate tone. An example of social language is the organization's repeated use of the pronoun "we." The emphasis on 'we' and the contraction "we've" positions the letter as collective, conversational, and casual highlighting the proximity between the Packers and the fans. Further, the Packers organization echoed and emphasized the term "kick off (para. 1)." The phrase "kick off" is used to refer to an active, exuberant movement which discursively links the reader to the physicality of sport. Moreover, in football, the kick off indicates the literal start of the game which further reinforces the social language in the letter through the lens of football. The use of this phrase, and other football jargon, would be characterized as coachtalk (Enterline, 2010; Llewellyn, 2003), which is a linguistic approach used to construct sports norms and instill enthusiasm. By labeling the start of the season the "kick off," the organization further positions the fan as part of the game.

Appeals to Heritage

A further effective aspect of this letter is through appeals to the heritage of the team. Heritage, along with history, traditions, and legacy, is an important branding anchor to build relations between organizations and their publics (Rose et al., 2021).

Teams can appeal to fans through nostalgia by evoking through strategic messaging the events, emotions, and engagements of the team's past (Ramshaw, 2011). The Packers are able to appeal to claims of heritage by offering in the letter that this year's season will be "one unlike any of the previous 101 [years]" (para. 3). By stating the long history of the organization, the letter brings to mind the enduring nature of the players, fans, and community. Through the use of language, coupled with the experiences of the fans, the community is characterized as being persistent, storied, and tested but nevertheless enduring. The appeal in this phrase is also one of commitment to a shared reputation and common legacy. The sense of shared experiences and legacy is reinforced by the image of Lambeau Field that accompanies the letter to the fans. From the perspective of public relations and reputation management, the letter helps to repair an otherwise unstable, fractured fan–organization relationship. By calling to mind the lineage of the Packers, the letter underpins and celebrates the past, provides a sense of calm and order during the turbulent present, and instills confidence in the future.

Discourses in Reaction to Letter

The Green Bay Packers' letter appealed to fans on social media platforms such as Twitter and Facebook. Previous research has found that social media platforms provide virtual spaces for organizations to build their reputation (L'etang, 2013). Additionally, social media platforms afford users the ability to engage in social discourse (Novak & El-Burki, 2016). Fans and other key constituents responded to the letter via social media. In public relations, organizations, like the Green Bay Packers, can track and recognize fan message patterns in real time through the analysis of responses, reposts, and reactions to the message. These patterns can help the organization to understand how fans are responding and what topics are prevalent in social media discourse. Social media platforms aid public relations professionals in understanding the direction and intensity of reaction from the fan base and other constituents instantly. Like most social media posts, the main response was "likes" to the original posts. The likes indicate a minimum amount of positive engagement which boosts the overall content. Besides the likes, there were also written responses from fans in the form of retweets, comments, and shares which provide a richer understanding of fan reaction. Given in the next section are some of the key discourses that emerged in reaction to the original letter. Facebook posts in response to the letter are included to demonstrate the discourses.

Discourse of Fan Understanding

Throughout the social media reactions, there was a sense that the new season was not an ideal situation for fans looking to enjoy game day events. Users mirrored the tone of the original letter offering that this season would be unique, but the fan community was strong. Many fans expressed support and gratitude for the precautions. Within this discourse, fans posted content that demonstrated a connection to the team even though the season would not feel the same during the games. Mostly, users would post hearts in the team colors or simply write "Go Pack Go," a popular cheer for the team. One user conveyed their support for the team by posting "Love my Packers! Let's go boys! Thank you for being responsible and doing what is necessary! Go Pack Go!!" (Talkington, 2020). The user here is establishing a strong relationship with the team and commitment to the fan community. Some supportive fans offered examples of how they planned to watch the game alternatively. Another user posted "So excited! Will be enjoying a wonderful brunch with the family decked out in Packer gear! Go Pack Go!" (Nabholz, 2020). Within these posts, there is an expressed relationship with the team. Some committed fans even stated an intention to perform fan behavior while social distancing in isolation. One fan offered "Go Pack Go! We'll be cheering enthusiastically from our home . . . complete with Lambeau leaps!" (Abler, 2020). The Lambeau Leap is a specific touchdown celebration performed at Lambeau Field. Such posts demonstrated the strong commitment to fan practices, communities, and the team.

Discourse of Fan Frustration

For other users, the announcement to change the fan experience during the new season was frustrating, and they expressed anger toward the Packers' policy. One critique was that the team overreacted to the pandemic. A user posted, "Imagine shutting down the entire planet for the common cold" (Rieth, 2020). This post minimized the threat of COVID-19. The frustration from fans centered on the team being too precautious in the wake of the COVID-19 public safety threat. Another common criticism was in comparison to other teams. A user posted, "I don't understand why they can't have fans in the stands [like] they did [in] Kansas City, they had 6 months to figure this out" (Fischer, 2020). This post expressed frustration with the team's inability to find a better solution to the pandemic in the months leading up to the season. The fan was comparing the Green Bay Packers to Kansas City Chiefs, a team that was allowing fan attendance. Others offered anger about the lack of nuance in the approach "Why are they closing VIP box seats[?] It's clearly only one family . . . in there. Plus there [sic] already boxed off" (Jackman, 2020). Such posts expressed frustration with the team's handling of the situation but still demonstrated a commitment to the team.

Discourse of Global Cheering

Another discourse that emerged in response illustrated the range of committed fans. As previously mentioned, the Green Bay Packers have a highly invested global fandom. Thus, on the social media posts, there was a communal practice of supporting the team and identifying where that user was watching the game. One user posted, "Go Pack Go! for 21 years from Pasadena, CA" (Benn, 2020). Such posts included the location of the fan. In these posts, the user is expressing a strong connection with the team, demonstrating a long-term commitment to fandom, and identifying where they are watching the team. This practice of checking-in was very common, and individuals would be posting that they would be watching the game from all over the world. Another user offered, "Have a great season. Supporting fans from the UK" (Hughes, 2020). This practice of cheering virtually from afar is important because it demonstrates the value of social media in modern fandom. Fans have the ability to watch games, engage on social media platforms, and wear team gear from distant places. Public relations professionals should be aware of such global communities to understand the types of fans they serve.

Discourse of Fan Activism

Another reaction to the letter to the fans was deflecting the conversation toward other issues facing the organization. During the 2020 season start, there was an increased commitment to Black Lives Matter activism from the organization, the coaches, and players following the deaths of Jacob Blake, Breonna Taylor, and George Floyd due to police brutality (Kilgore & Adelson, 2020). Throughout the social media threads, there was a deflection from the issue of the pandemic to racism in policing. Some users were in support of the activism, posting in part "Proud of the team for standing up to injustice! 100% Support!" (VanWormer, 2020). Others did not share the support for activism by posting, "If BLM shows up we're done I'm so tired of the news and how bad everything & everybody is. I would like to just enjoy the moment for a change" (Chez, 2020). The deflection toward other important issues impacting the organization illustrates how users can change topics in virtual spaces. It is critical for public relations professionals to understand the dynamics of an online discussion since such posts provide insights into conversations happening in fan communities. Further, fans can use virtual spaces for social and political activism.

These discourses provide a case study in social media responses. Social media platforms are spaces for fans to express grievances with the organization. While announcing public safety policies that will drastically change the experience of the fan, public relations professionals can expect push back and frustration from even their most loyal and engaged fans. Additionally, the virtual spaces constructed on social media platforms enable global discussion and fan expression. In the case of the Green Bay Packers, fans post globally. Finally, the Green Bay Packers case study demonstrates the power of users to shape conversations. While the Packers wanted to share COVID-19-related information, users directed the conversation to Black Lives Matter activism.

Legacy Media Reporting

In addition to the social media responses from fans, there were also responses from news outlets in reaction to the policies. In the days following the announcement, legacy media outlets, such as local newspapers including the *Appleton Post-Crescent, Green Bay Press-Gazette,* and *Wausau Daily Herald,* covered the story. The newspapers focused the reporting on the financial losses to the tourism industry due to the lack of game day experiences (Green Bay Packers offering, 2020). Some reporting highlighted the difference between the expected mass crowds normally in attendance with the quiet during the season with COVID-19 protocols in place (Rubesky, 2020). The newspapers also covered the ongoing discussion about player protests and activism (Ryman, 2020).

You Make the Call

The mega-crisis that faced public relations professionals at the start of the COVID-19 global pandemic was swift, far-reaching, and uncompromising. The pandemic enacted an uncertain future for teams, players, and fans while simultaneously displacing key fan communities, uprooting fan practices, and disrupting scheduled sporting events. While the Packers organization was not uniquely affected by the consequences of the pandemic, the team found a way to reinforce relationships with their uniquely positioned fans. The Packers leveraged situated identities of fans, utilized coachtalk, and appealed to heritage to maintain positive ties with fans during an uncertain global mega-crisis. While the letter is just one aspect of the strategic messaging during the pandemic, it offers insight into how direct correspondence to a key stakeholder – like a letter – can effectively engage fans. As advances in digital platforms continue to alter and shift the landscape of public relations, the future of the letter to the fans is unclear. As teams rely on microblogging platforms such as Twitter or video-sharing platforms such as TikTok, there are fewer opportunities for long-form written communication to the fans.

Discussion Questions

1. What are other examples of letters to fans in sport communication? Discuss these examples and how they were employed.
2. In an age of social media, video sharing, and microblogging, discuss a letter's efficacy or suggest other methods for communicating with a fan base.
3. Suggest other actions the Green Bay Packer could have performed to maintain their relationships with fans and other stakeholders. Why would these other actions be suitable?
4. In your opinion, what other crises, events, and occurrences might warrant the use of mass communication with fans?

References

Abler, J. (2020, September 12). Go Pack Go! We'll be cheering enthusiastically from our home . . . complete with Lambeau leaps! *Facebook*. www.facebook.com/Packers/posts/10158281506435073?comment_id=10158282 57915073

Bakhtin, M.M. (2010). *The dialogic imagination: Four essays* (Vol. 1). Austin, TX: University of Texas Press.

Benn, A. (2020, September 12). Go Pack Go! For 21 years from Pasadena, CA. *Facebook*. www.facebook.com/Packers/posts/10158281506435073?comment_id=101582857 915073

Benoit, W.L. (1997). Image repair discourse and crisis communication. *Public Relations Review, 23*(2), 177–186. https://doi.org/10.1016/S0363-8111(97)90023-0

Bolluyt, J. (2018, September 9). Who owns the Green Bay Packers? Why the team is unique in the NFL. *Sportingcasting*. www.sportscasting.com/who-owns-the-green baypackers/

Chandler, D. (1994). Semiotics for beginners [DX Reader version]. www.aber.ac.uk/media/Documents/S4B/semiotic.html

Chez, J. (2020. September 12). If BLM shows up we're done I'm so tired of the news and how bad everything & everybody is. *Facebook*. www.facebook.com/Packers/posts/10158281506435073?comment_id=10158282 57915073

Compton, J., & Compton, J.L. (2014). College sports, losing seasons, and image repair through open letters to fans. *Communication & Sport, 2*(4), 345–362. https://doi.org/10.1177/2167479513503542

Coombs, W.T. (1995). Choosing the right words: The development of guidelines for the selection of the "appropriate" crisis-response strategies. *Management Communication Quarterly, 8*(4), 447–476. https://doi.org/10.1177/0893318995008004003

Coombs, W.T. (2007). Attribution theory as a guide for post-crisis communication research. *Public Relations Review, 33*(2), 135–139. https://doi.org/10.1016/j.pubrev.2006.11.016

Coombs, W.T. (2007). Protecting organization reputations during a crisis: The development and application of situational crisis communication theory. *Corporate Reputation Review, 10*(3), 163–176. https://doi.org/10.1057/palgrave.crr.1550049

Coombs, W.T., & Holladay, S.J. (2002). Helping crisis managers protect reputational assets: Initial tests of the situational crisis communication theory. *Management communication quarterly, 16*(2), 165–186. https://doi.org/10.1177/089331802237233

Doorley, J., & Garcia, H.F. (2015). *Reputation management: The key to successful public relations and corporate communication*. New York: Routledge.

End, C.M. (2001). An examination of NFL fans' computer mediated BIRGing. *Journal of Sport Behavior, 24*(2).

Enterline, L. (2010). *Apologia in Coaches' Post-game Rhetoric* [Doctoral dissertation] Wake Forest University, Winston-Salem, NC.

Fischer, D. (2020, September 12). I don't understand why they can't have fans in the stands they did a Kansas City, they had 6 months to figure this out. *Facebook*. www.facebook.com/Packers/posts/10158281506435073?comment_id=10158282 57915073

Gee, J.P. (2004). *Discourse analysis: What makes it critical? An introduction to critical discourse analysis in education* (pp. 49–80). New York: Routledge.

Glynn, C.J., Herbst, S., Lindeman, M., O'Keefe, G.J., & Shapiro, R.Y. (2015). *Public opinion*. Boulder, CO: Westview Press.

Gray, J., Sandvoss, G., & Lee Harrington, C. (2017). *Fandom: Identities and communities in a mediated world*. New York: New York University Press.

Green Bay Packers. (2020, September 12). A letter to fans of the Green Bay Packers. Packers.com. www.packers.com/news/a-letter-to-fans-of-the green-bay-packers

Green Bay Packers Offering Game Day Meals "To Go." (2020, September 14). *WSAW-TV*. www.wsaw.com/2020/09/14/green-bay-packers-offering-game-day-meals- to-go/

Hartman, K.L. (2020). The elephant in the room: How COVID-19's financial impact further threatens title IX compliance. *International Journal of Sport Communication, 13*(3), 399–407. https://doi.org/10.1123/ijsc.2020-0242

Hughes, M. (2020, September 12). Have a great season. Supporting fans from the UK. *Facebook.* www.facebook.com/Packers/posts/10158281506435073?comment_id= 10158282 57915073

Jackman, M. (2020, September 12). Why are they closing VIP box seats. Its clearly only one family is in there. Plus there already boxed off. *Facebook.* www.facebook.com/ Packers/posts/10158281506435073?comment_id=101582824 57915073

Jackson, K.T. (2004). *Building reputational capital: Strategies for integrity and fair play that improve the bottom line.* Oxford: Oxford University Press.

Jorgensen, M.W., & Phillips, L.J. (2002). *Discourse analysis as theory and method.* London: Sage.

Kilgore, A., & Adelson, E. (2020, September 13). On the first NFL Sunday of the pandemic, a mix of silence, protests and unfamiliar scenes. *The Washington Post.* www. washingtonpost.com/sports/2020/09/13/first-nfl-sunday-pandemic-scene/

L'etang, J. (2013). *Sports public relations.* London: Sage.

Llewellyn, J.T. (2003). Coachtalk: Good reasons for winning and losing. *Case Studies in Sport Communication,* 141–157.

Mead, G.H. (1934). *Mind, self and society* (Vol. 111). Chicago, IL: University of Chicago Press.

Nabholz, D.L (2020, September 12). So excited! Will be enjoying a wonderful brunch with the family decked out in Packer gear! Go Pack Go! *Facebook.* www.facebook. com/Packers/posts/10158281506435073?comment_id=10158282 57915073

Novak A., & El-Burki, I.J. (2016). *Defining identity and the changing scope of culture in the digital age.* Hershey, PA: IGI Global.

Parrott, B. (2020). The American Mega-Crisis: COVID-19 and Beyond. *Challenge, 63*(5), 245 -263.

Phua, J.J. (2010). Sports fans and media use: Influence on sports fan identification and collective self-esteem. *International Journal of Sport Communication,* 3(2), 190–206. https:// doi.org/10.1123/ijsc.3.2.190

Ramshaw, G. (2011). The construction of sport heritage attractions. *Journal of Tourism Consumption and Practice, 3*(1), 1–25.

Rieth, M. (2020, September 12). Imagine shutting down the entire planet for the common cold. *Facebook.* www.facebook.com/Packers/posts/10158281506435073?comment_ id= 0158282457915073

Rose, M., Rose, G.M., Merchant, A., & Orth, U.R. (2021). Sports teams heritage: Measurement and application in sponsorship. *Journal of Business Research, 124,* 759–769. https://doi.org/10.1016/j.jbusres.2020.03.040

Rubesky, C. (2020, September 15). Packers to close parking lots to tailgaters for Sunday's game. *Fox 11 News.* https://fox11online.com/news/local/packers-to-close-parking-lots-to-tailgaters-for-sundays-game.

Ryman, R. (2020, September 12). Green Bay Packers fans have strong, but divided, feelings on player protests, Black anthem. *Green Bay Press-Gazette.* www.greenbaypress-gazette.com/story/news/2020/09/12/player-protests-divide- green-bay-packers-fans/ 5705572002/.

Talkington, D. (2020, September 12). Love my Packers! Let's go boys! Thank you for being responsible and doing what is necessary! Go Pack Go!!. *Facebook.* www.facebook.com/ Packers/posts/10158281506435073?comment_id=10158282 57915073.

Van Wormer, Y. (2020, September 12). #GoPackGo from Michigan!! Proud of the team for standing up to injustice! 100% Support! *Facebook*. www.facebook.com/Packers/posts/10158281506435073?comment_id=10158282 57915073

Wallace, L., Wilson, J., & Miloch, K. (2011). Sporting Facebook: A content analysis of NCAA organizational sport pages and Big 12 conference athletic department pages. *International Journal of Sport Communication, 4*(4), 422–444. https%3A//doi.org/10.1123/ijsc.4.4.422

Weiner, B. (1985). An attributional theory of achievement motivation and emotion. *Psychological Review, 92*(4), 548.

Young, C.L., & Rentner, T.L. (2018). The NFL as a mega-crisis: Applications of fractal theory. In *Proceedings of the international crisis and risk communication conference* (pp. 42–45). Orlando, FL: Nicholson School of Communication.

25

BLAMING BILES

Intersectionality and Organizational Obligations to Mental Health

Jeff Nagel and Scott J. Varda

Introduction

During the 2020 Summer Olympics in Tokyo (held in the summer of 2021 due to COVID-19), Simone Biles, the greatest gymnast of all time by consensus, unexpectedly withdrew from the team finals (Marks, 2021). Days later, citing stress and mental exhaustion, she also withdrew from the women's individual all-around (Kindelan, 2021). Numerous critics loudly panned Biles' decision, labeling her a "quitter" and demanding she "apologize to her teammates" (Leitner, 2021, para. 1). Biles's withdrawal came on the heels of professional tennis player Naomi Osaka's well-publicized mental health struggles during both the 2021 French Open and the Summer Olympics. Then ranked as the world's number two women's tennis player, Osaka had both drawn attention to the issue of mental health struggles in sport and received much public criticism for her decision to withdraw in France (Caroyal, 2021). Moreover, while both Biles and Osaka eventually received verbal support from a number of professional commentators and athletes, some questioned whether American Olympic officials or French Open organizers offered enough support to Biles or Osaka, respectively (Campbell, 2021; Jenkins, 2021).

In addition, as the Biles' saga was unfolding, Novak Djokovic, arguably the greatest men's tennis player ever, was also competing at the Olympics (Wertheim, 2021). When asked about pressure and mental health, Djokovic responded that "pressure is a privilege" (Ganguly, 2021, para. 1). Expanding on this, Djokovic explained, "If you are aiming to be at the top of the game you better start learning how to deal with pressure and how to cope with those moments – on the court but also off the court, all the expectations" (Ganguly, 2021, para. 7). However, when Djokovic himself failed to medal individually, he reacted in a

DOI: 10.4324/9781003316763-29

racket-destroying rage before withdrawing prior to his mixed doubles medal match, citing his own mental exhaustion. Despite his public actions, Djokovic received little criticism in comparison to Biles' and Osaka's severe public scrutiny.

Given these highly publicized events, and the growing discourse around competitive athletics and mental health, this chapter considers the racial and gender implications of this differential treatment in the media. Following Kimberlé Crenshaw's (1991) notion of intersectionality, and guided by more recent analyses in the fields of rhetorical and organizational communication, this chapter considers the convergence of sport, race, gender, and mental health to investigate the limited communicative support Biles received from American Olympic officials, as well as the raced and gendered treatment her mental health concerns received.

Background

It nearly goes without saying that sports are a fundamental part of modern society. Moreover, despite claims from some media members about how (mostly Black or female) athletes should just "shut up and dribble," sports remain a vibrant site for thinking about and contesting politics and public culture (Sullivan, 2018). Much of this is because "sports are imbued with political meanings. From the financing of stadiums through public tax dollars . . . to the display and veneration of the flag, sports are inherently political" (Kaufman & Wolff, 2010, p. 165). On the one hand, we imagine sports to be an ideal vacuum through which we can affirm and debate the basic aspects of American culture like fairness, teamwork, and perseverance (Butterworth, 2010). On the other hand, sports are also a unique social dynamic in that "identities that might be marginal in previous sporting times or in contemporary non-sporting places might find a place of sanctuary with sport" (Aitchinson, 2007, p. 1). To say this in a different way, we imagine sports to be reflective of larger social issues and concerns even when such a comparison underrepresents those most marginalized identities who often end up participating.

Why do we imagine sports as this fertile testing ground, however, and from where does such an idea originate? Communication scholar Debra Hawhee (2005) explains how, for ancient Greeks and Romans, the idea of the agora – the public marketplace where speeches and deliberation often occurred – shares a similar root and meaning with agonism – constructive debate and the clash of ideas. These ideas about the intersection of communication as a physical and embodied act are further institutionalized through the creation of the Olympic Games in which rhetorical practice, physical betterment, and competition are combined (Poulakos, 1995). Although the substance and format of the Olympics has evolved significantly over several millennia, there nevertheless remain key elements in this formation and maintenance of identity, especially within media coverage.

American athletes are framed by media reports as exceptional, heroic, and the embodiment of American ideals (Billings & Zengaro, 2021). In contrast, Western media projects ideas about other countries onto their athletes, often reflecting international political tensions as represented through the triumphs and tribulations of international competition (Hubbard & Wilkinson, 2015). Most importantly for the purposes of this chapter, regardless of international location of origin, the coverage of athletes is often racialized and gendered and frequently extrapolates questions of success and failure through discourses of effort, genetics, and intelligence (Angelini et al., 2012; Oates, 2012).

In the case of sports, governing organizations have unique rhetorical abilities to shape the culture of the sport, as well as the public's understanding of the sport and athletes (Kassing & Matthews, 2017). In regard to the Olympics, identifying the governing institution is difficult enough to answer. The International Olympic Committee (IOC) regulates much of the drug testing, site selection, coordination of media, and other administrative tasks one often thinks to be synonymous with the running of "the Olympics" (Chappelet & Kübler-Mabbott, 2008). Beside the IOC, however, global sport is regulated by 35 international federations, National Olympic Committees (NOCs), and national governing bodies regulating domestic sport within a particular nation. The United States Olympic and Paralympic Committee (USOPC), which covers the American athletes competing in Olympic qualifying sports, is one such NOC (Lenskyj, 2000). Although these various organizations often possess similar goals, conflicts over revenue-sharing, bids for hosting Games, and accusations of unfairness or corruption reveal a number of conflicting agendas and differences in organizational leadership and direction (IOC, USOC, 2012; Lenskyj, 2000).

These differences are clearest at the moments of institutional conflict or crisis. Consider briefly the struggle to properly handle the case of Larry Nassar's sexual abuse of athletes. In 2016, after a lengthy investigation, Larry Nassar, a doctor working as the national medical coordinator for USA Gymnastics (USAG), was arrested and charged with sexually assaulting female athletes for decades despite several women reporting abuse and informing his superiors (Levenson, 2018). He eventually pled guilty to 10 counts of sexual assault as well as possession of child pornography and evidence tampering and has been sentenced to several consecutive life sentences. Nassar was able to continue his abuse for decades in part because of a cascading series of institutional failures that saw dozens of sexual abuse complaints ignored. As such, by the time of his arrest, Nassar's victims included an estimated number in the hundreds including virtually every single American Olympic gymnast between 1980 and 2016 (Lavigne & Noren, 2018).

In the United States, the USOPC has delegated authority over Olympic gymnastics to USAG – an independent body regulating American gymnastics. FBI reporting found that this structure allowed plausible deniability and intentional ignorance across organizations as various actors failed to heed reports about Nassar (Lavigne & Noren, 2018). In the wake of the Nassar investigation, the entire

18-member board of USAG resigned, and several former officials, including former coaches, were arrested on charges stemming from the investigation (Levenson, 2018). Although the extent of these institutional failures is beyond the scope of this chapter, it is important to note that the athletes themselves believe these institutions failed them. As Biles herself testified, "I blame Larry Nassar, and I also blame the entire system that enabled and perpetrated his abuse" (*Simone Biles: "I Blame System that Enabled Larry Nassar Abuse"*, 2021, para. 4).

Although mental health has always been an important part of competitive athletic success, open conversations about the balance between personal well-being and on-field performance are more recent. Despite this trend, "mental toughness and mental health are seen as contradictory" such that the benefits of asking for help are seen by many to be "outweighed by the negative consequences of appearing mentally weak" (Bauman, 2015, p. 135). The highly public nature of modern professional athletes forces the construction of a "persona" or brand that must be maintained constantly through public performance (Delayo, 2021). More than ever, athletes are scrutinized off the field – for their pregame attire, political opinions, social media presence, and so on – as on it. In part due to this feeling of online connectedness and unmediated interaction with fans, there exists a growing demand for an athlete's "authentic voice," including insights into their lives and everyday struggles (Mendis et al. 2021).

Most of those garnering sustained media attention for their mental health struggles, however, are men. In 2018, NBA star Kevin Love, for example, talked publicly about his pre-game panic and his ongoing struggles with depression and anxiety (Lavelle, 2020). Dallas Cowboys quarterback Dak Prescott opened up about dealing with anxiety and depression, as well, following the suicide of his brother and the struggles of COVID-19 quarantine (Conway, 2020). Although criticized by some media figures like Fox Sports' Skip Bayless, Prescott's disclosure led in part to the NFL's 2020 "It Takes All of Us" campaign, which includes an ongoing testimonial video series by current players, coaches, and staff ("Player Health").

Stephanie Salazar, a medical professional who manages outreach programs for athletes, notes that these examples are especially important because "as more athletes speak out, it gives others permission to ask for help and normalizes mental health as part of the conversation" (Gavin, 2021, para. 12). Although many of these individuals still received some media criticism, initiatives by the NBA, NFL, and NCAA (the collegiate sport regulatory body) all highlight acceptance and the various resources available to these (mostly male) athletes.

These growing trends represent a positive step for open and frank discussions about mental health and the struggles athletes face on and off the field. Despite this improved trend, however, significant racial and gendered barriers remain. One notable example, mentioned in the introduction, is tennis player Naomi Osaka. Osaka made headlines for openly discussing her own struggles with anxiety and depression, including a request to skip post-match press conferences during the 2021 French Open (Futterman, 2021). French Open officials and news media were both outraged at the suggestion that Osaka would refrain from interacting with them. After she – as promised – skipped her first post-match conference, the tournament fined her $15,000 and threatened further penalties including expulsion from the competition. In response, Osaka withdrew from the tournament on her own and announced via Instagram that she would step away from tennis for some time to recover mentally.

Compared to other athletes who have shared their struggles or asked for accommodation, the response to Osaka by tournament officials, media members, and her fellow competitors was overwhelmingly negative. French Open officials, joined by representatives of the three other major tournaments, wrote an open letter condemning Osaka for failing to meet with them and framed her refusal to attend media events as a competitive advantage (Futterman, 2021). Media members also criticized Osaka's refusal to subject herself to press conferences. Even commentator John McEnroe, who initially was supportive of Osaka's openness, criticized her after her loss at the 2022 Australian Open and noted that she had invited an increased scrutiny of herself going forward (Watson, 2022). As Julie DiCaro, a senior editor at *Deadspin*, noted in an interview that "The rules have always been very different for . . . women of color who are playing tennis" and while most members of the press corps are professional, there are still significant issues with racism and sexism in international tennis coverage (Martin, 2021, para. 10). Women – especially women of color who are labeled controversial, or who set boundaries uncomfortable to dominant ideologies – are almost always labelled "ungrateful" or sacrilegious to sports' ideals (Webster, 2009).

Intersectional Communication Theory

Intersectionality, as a political and communication theory, might help explain why the organizational and communicative structures work for some athletic organizations, but not others. Historically, emerging partially from the Combahee River Collective Statement, intersectionality was coined by Kimberlé Crenshaw as a way to better apprehend the interlocking axes of oppression structurally leveled at particular social categories (race, class, gender, etc.) (Bauer et al., 2021). As early organizational communication was overly managerial – and hence viewed racial and gender differences as problems to be solved – only in the last few decades have intersectional analyses in organizational communication interrogated power and privilege (McDonald, 2019). The last decade, however, has seen a concerted effort to incorporate intersectionality into considerations of conflict, public relations, management, and more (McDonald, 2019). As an analytic tool, intersectionality allows researchers to better identify and understand the structural power relations contouring public interactions. Communicative practices – be they social media posts, press releases from organizational rhetors, or podcasts from sport commentators – help shape the structures of power that affect how we craft our own identities and understand the identities of others (Palczewski et al., 2016). Moreover, those ideologies help shape our understanding of reality (Hall, 1989). For example, the circulation of raced and gendered communication can reinforce the racism and sexism of institutions, organizations, or culture more generally.

The Case

Among the major stories covered by Western media in the lead up to the 2020 Olympics was American gymnast Simone Biles' continued dominance, with pundits and athletes alike acknowledging her greatness (Gibbs, 2021). Biles' reputation was not unearned. Over the 8-year period since her 2013 debut, she won four Olympic golds, 19 world championship medals, and had never lost a single major competition. She pioneered four gymnastic maneuvers, all named after her, leading many, including USAG officials, to believe Biles was *under*scored because she was the only gymnast on the planet capable of performing some aspects of her routines (Abad-Santos, 2021). She was routinely described as "superhuman," and the only question leading up to the Tokyo games was simply by how much would Biles win (Ruiz, 2021).

For many American audience members, team qualifying was the first time they had seen Biles compete in 4 years. When Biles struggled on three of her four apparatuses in qualifying, and Team USA finished in second place, professional analysts and armchair social media commenters alike expressed significant surprise (Mizoguchi, 2021). During the day off before the team finals competition, Biles posted on social media, "I truly do feel like I have the weight of the world on my shoulders at times. I know I brush it off and make it seem like pressure doesn't affect me but . . . sometimes it's hard" (Mizoguchi, 2021, para. 16). The next day, during the first apparatus of the team finals, Biles made another mistake on a landing and soon exited, before eventually returning to cheer on her teammates. In subsequent days, Biles would withdraw from all four individual event finals for which she had qualified.

In the wake of Biles' initial withdrawal from the team final, confusion and vitriol reigned in equal measure. Much of the confusion could be blamed on the USAG, which communicated tersely. In a single tweet, the official USAG Twitter account noted, "After further medical evaluation, Simone Biles has withdrawn . . . to focus on her mental health" (USA Gymnastics, 2021, para. 1). Biles herself also commented briefly following the team medal ceremony, noting that as she began competing she realized her "mental is not there, so I just need to let [my teammates] do it and focus on myself" (Maine, 2021, para. 10). Given the overwhelming coverage of the Olympics in the United States and of women's gymnastics in particular, the lack of additional information for several days created a vacuum for speculation and confusion that ultimately turned into anger toward Biles herself.

Without knowing the full extent of Biles' condition, many professional journalists and well-circulated social media commenters hyperbolically framed her withdrawal as being "devastating" to American fans (Nolan, 2021), while some went so far as to describe her as a villain (Niesen, 2021). Some columnists undercut the seriousness of her injury by explicitly framing her withdrawal as a "mental issue" and "not believed to be injury-related" (Nolan, 2021). Ignoring the ableist construction of mental health as neatly separated from physical health, in gymnastics (and likely all sports), the two are closely related. When the 4-foot-8-inch Biles is at the height of her routine, she launches herself as much as 10 feet in the air, upside-down, twisting multiple times, at a rotational speed of more than 150 revolutions per second – a third that of a helicopter's blades (Radnofsky et al., 2021). As Biles would later reveal, her condition, known as "the twisties," "can cause a person to lose their sense of space and dimension as they're in the air, causing them to lose control of their body and do extra twists or flips that they hadn't intended" (Nagesh, 2021, para. 6). At best, the twisties make safe execution and landing of gymnastic maneuvers impossible, and continuing to compete could risk concussions, spinal injuries, or even paralysis.

Despite the seriousness of Biles' condition, ableist mocking remained something of an unofficial event for some commenters into the second week of Olympic coverage. Several factors likely contributed to this outrage, including the nationalistic context of the Olympics itself and the idea that Biles represented the commentator or viewer as much as herself. Furthermore, the collective national disappointment of the US women's team winning silver instead of the projected gold, and perhaps missing out on other medals, meant that Biles had hurt not just her team, but also in a cultural sense where the Olympic medal count displayed the symbolic greatness of a nation – the country as a whole (Gastellum, 2021). While sports media have long engaged in intentionally inflaming and eliciting outrageous emotional "takes" on topics (Nemeth, 2021), those "takes" must be at least tangentially grounded in a set of actual cultural ideologies to be believed by audiences.

Media obsession with medal counts has long dominated Olympics media coverage, and Biles' "transgression" of failing to win gold likely reinforced harmful racist and sexist rhetorical tropes (Billings, 2008). Racist and gendered tropes resurfaced in online sports commentary, as memes and conservative websites more broadly portrayed Biles as a "villain" who allowed the Russian team to win while betraying her teammates, her fans, and her country due to her own weakness (Niesen, 2021). For those insistent on framing her negatively, Biles now existed at an intersection of contradiction in the culture war, both as a Black woman and an Olympic athlete. Through their depictions of Biles, these individuals constructed her persona as simultaneously representing America and betraying it through her choice to prioritize her own mental health over the health of the nation.

Given the crescendo of commentary and criticism that continued even as American gymnast Sunisa Lee won all-around individual gold, Biles was forced to turn to social media to defend and explain herself (Mizoguchi, 2021). In a series of posts, she explained the severe stress she was under, and how it began manifesting itself through the twisties. Biles even included videos and images from practice, attempting to illustrate how her mental struggles could still manifest as physical risk.

Seemingly compelled to justify her mental health struggles, Biles detailed the many aspects of mutually reinforcing pressures she faced not only as a role model and as the "universally acknowledged greatest gymnast of all time," but also as the last of Nassar's victims still competing (Ruiz, 2021). In that capacity, she was a public face not simply for sexual assault survivors, but for U.S. gymnasts who had been doubly betrayed by both a team doctor and the parent organization ostensibly charged with protecting them. "I'm still here, so it's not going to disappear," she announced, clarifying that she needed to compete in Tokyo to remind USA Gymnastics and the world that more is still needed to be done for sexual assault victims. "If I let them rule me, then they're winning," she said (VanHoose, 2021, para. 4).

Although all elite athletes must confront significant pressures to compete, women and athletes of color like Biles and Osaka face unique challenges brought about by intersecting axes of oppression. Recent social science and medical data evidence how media and fans approach the subject of mental health differently depending on an athlete's race and gender (Rosenfield, 2012). Black women especially appear to face increased scrutiny from medical and public figures alike, making it more difficult to get the help they need. For Simone Biles, and for Naomi Osaka a month prior, the controversies around their mental health and what, if anything, they owe to fans, competitors, and organizers sustain conversation and debate alike. Rarely do these deliberations, especially by their critics, mention their race or gender explicitly. And yet, it seems impossible to ignore the differences in how media covered Biles and Osaka as compared to Novak Djokovic's tantrum-like, racket-destroying loss and subsequent withdrawal and exit from the Olympics.

You Make the Call

This chapter discusses the relationship between athletes' mental health and several factors that may influence how media and organizations respond to mental health issues in sport. Of course, the situations surrounding Simone Biles, Naomi Osaka, or any other athlete are all different and present unique considerations for the organizations at play. In Biles' case, USAG may have privately supported her but publicly did very little in the aftermath to clarify its messaging or support her and the growing vitriol against her. The IOC and Japan, as hosts, publicly did nothing and chose instead to defer responsibility and support to the relevant national team. Because the IOC is structured such that it defers most responsibilities to the team level, it sidesteps the responsibilities or concerns of its athletes beyond satisfying the most basic conditions allowing the Olympic event to occur.

Culture is created, however, in the discourses that constitute it. That USAG's short statement was insufficient support for Biles is nearly beyond question. At a minimum, the absence of a strong defense from the athlete's governing body, at the height of highly publicized and frenzied media coverage, created a narrative vacuum, which was filled, at least partially, by nationalistic fervor that demanded ownership of Biles' achievements and denounced her as a cowardly villain when she rejected the demand. But the structural failure to prevent abuse, as well as the communicative failure to support their athletes, is also reminiscent of the mutually reinforcing nature of organizational communicative practices and structures of inequality that organizational inquiry has observed (McDonald, 2019). If organizations are truly committed to protecting their athletes, they must treat differences of race, class, gender, or the like in a meaningful way by actually hearing the voices articulating how those differences are being treated and acting to protect those athletes.

Discussion Questions

1. Media and public responses create ethical demands on corporate communicators, but how and to what extent can sport organizations better support athletes and communicate about mental health?
2. Race and gender differences often correlate with poor treatment and support for mental health. What, if any, additional obligations should organizations have to act with a differential response? In other words, should organizations populated with more women, or athletes of color, be expected to be more attuned to mental health concerns?
3. How should organizations be better prepared to publicly defend their governed athletes when raced or gendered attacks on those athletes occur? Moreover, for an event like the Olympics, which organization should take responsibility? For example, how might the United States Olympic and Paralympic Committee be better prepared to publicly defend their governed athletes when raced or gendered attacks on those athletes occur?
4. Which, if any, athletes have recently disclosed mental health challenges? How have their leagues or organizations responded? Discuss whether their experiences with organizations and the media support or refute the examples from this chapter. Discuss how these interactions may have changed since Simone Biles' public disclosure.

Acknowledgments

The authors acknowledge and thank Baylor University's Department of Communication, Pennsylvania State University's Department of Communication Arts and Sciences, and Pennsylvania State University's Center for Humanities and Information for their support.

References

Abad-Santos, A. (2021, July 24). The Simone Biles scoring controversy, explained. *Vox.* www.vox.com/22575301/simone-biles-olympics-scoring-explained-gymnastics-yurchenko-double-pike

Aitchinson, C.C. (2007). Gender, sport and identity: Introducing discourses of masculinities, femininities and sexualities. In C.C. Aitchinson (Ed.), *Sport and gender identities: Masculinities, femininities and sexualities* (pp. 1-4). London: Routledge.

Angelini, J.R., Billings, A.C., & MacArthur, P.J. (2012). The nationalistic revolution will be televised: The 2010 Vancouver Olympic games on NBC. *International Journal of Sport Communication, 5*, 193–209.

Bauer, G.R., Churchill, S.M., Mahendran, M., Walwyn, C., Lizotte, D., & Villa-Rueda, A.A. (2021). Intersectionality in quantitative research: A systematic review of its emergence and applications of theory and methods. SSM – *Population Health, 14*, 100798.

Bauman, N.J. (2015). The stigma of mental health in athletes: Are mental toughness and mental health seen as contradictory in elite sport? *British Journal of Sports Medicine, 50*, 135–136.

Billings, A.C. (2008). *Olympic media: Inside the biggest show on television.* London: Routledge.

Billings, A.C., & Zengaro, E. (2021). The biggest double-edged sword in sport media: Olympic media and the rendering of identity. In M. Butterworth (Ed.), *Communication and sport,* (pp. 405–420). London: De Gruyter Mouton.

Butterworth, M.L. (2010). *Baseball and rhetorics of purity: The national pastime and American identity during the War on Terror.* Alabama: University of Alabama Press.

Campbell, J. (2021, June 1). Event organisers failed Naomi Osaka, who has now withdrawn from French Open. *Women's Health.* www.womenshealth.com.au/naomi-osaka-has-withdrawn-from-french-open-amid-battle-over-press-conferences/.

Caroyal, T. (2021, May 31). Naomi Osaka withdraws from French Open amid row over press conferences. *The Guardian.* www.theguardian.com/sport/2021/may/31/naomi-osaka-withdraws-french-open-press-conference-fines-tennis

Chappelet, J., & Kübler-Mabbott, B. (2008). *International Olympic Committee and the Olympic system: The governance of world sport.* London: Routledge.

Conway, T. (2020, September 10). Cowboys' Dak Prescott discusses mental health after Skip Bayless' comments. *Bleacher Report.* https://bleacherreport.com/articles/2908555-cowboys-dak-prescott-discusses-mental-health-after-skip-bayless-comments

Crenshaw, K. (1991). Mapping the margins: Intersectionality, identity politics, and violence against women of color. *Stanford Law Review, 43*(6), 1241–1299.

Delayo, M. (2021). *"I definitely want to thank my psychiatrist": Digital mental health disclosures in professional sports.* [Master's thesis, The Pennsylvania State University]. Electronic Theses and Dissertations for Graduate School. https://etda.libraries.psu.edu/catalog/18958mud528

Futterman, M. (2021, July 27). Naomi Osaka quits the French Open after news conference dispute. *New York Times.* www.nytimes.com/2021/05/31/sports/tennis/naomi-osaka-quits-french-open-depression.html

Ganguly, S. (2021, July 28). Tennis-'pressure is privilege' for history-chasing Djokovic. *Reuters.* www.reuters.com/lifestyle/sports/tennis-pressure-is-privilege-history-chasing-djokovic-2021-07-28/

Gastellum, A. (2021, August 8). Team USA passes China on final day for most gold medals at Tokyo Olympics. *Sports Illustrated.* www.si.com/olympics/2021/08/08/team-usa-wins-gold-medal-count-tokyo-olympics-china

Gavin, K. (2021, July 29). A game-changer for mental health: Sports icons open up. *Michigan Medicine*. https://healthblog.uofmhealth.org/brain-health/a-game-changer-for-mental-health-sports-icons-open-up

Gibbs, D. (2021, July 27). Tokyo Olympics: Why is Simone Biles called the GOAT? USA Gymnastics star has special leotard and own Twitter emoji. *Eurosport*. www.eurosport.com/artistic-gymnastics/tokyo-2020/2021/tokyo-olympics-why-is-simone-biles-called-the-goat-usa-gymnastics-star-has-special-leotard-and-own-t_sto8445691/story.shtml

Hall, S. (1989). Ideology and communication theory. In B. Dervin (Ed.), *Rethinking communication theory* (pp. 40–52). London: SAGE publications.

Hawhee, D. (2005). *Bodily arts: Rhetoric and athletics in ancient Greece*. Austin, TX: University of Texas Press.

Hubbard, P., & Wilkinson, E. (2015). Welcoming the world?: Hospitality, homonationalism, and the 2012 London Olympics. *Antipode*, 47, 598–615.

IOC, USOC Finalize Revenue Deal. (2012, May 4). *ESPN.com*. www.espn.com/olympics/story/_/id/7967000/ioc-usoc-resolve-differences-revenues

Jenkins, S. (2021, July 29). Simone Biles was abandoned by American Olympic officials, and the torment hasn't stopped. *Washington Post*. www.washingtonpost.com/sports/olympics/2021/07/29/simone-biles-larry-nassar-fbi/

Kassing, J., & Matthews, R. (2017). Sport and organizational communication. In A.C. Billings (Ed.), *Defining sport communication* (pp. 137–149). London: Routledge.

Kaufman, P., & Wolff, E.A. (2010). Playing and protesting: Sport as a vehicle for social change. *Journal of Sport and Social Issues*, *34*, 154–175.

Kindelan, K. (2021, July 28). Simone Biles puts spotlight on mental health after 2nd withdrawal at Tokyo Olympics. *ABC News*. https://abcnews.go.com/GMA/Wellness/simone-biles-surprise-withdrawal-tokyo-olympics-puts-spotlight/story?id=79088278

Lavelle, K.L. (2020). The face of mental health: Kevin Love and hegemonic masculinity in the NBA. *Communication and Sport*, 9(6), 954–971.

Lavigne, P., & Noren, N. (2018, January 25). OTL: Michigan State secrets extend far beyond Larry Nassar case. *ESPN.com*. www.espn.com/espn/story/_/id/22214566/pattern-denial-inaction-information-suppression-michigan-state-goes-larry-nassar-case-espn

Leitner, W. (2021, July 28). Clay Travis: Simone Biles should apologize for quitting on her team. *Fox Sports Radio*. https://foxsportsradio.iheart.com/content/2021-07-28-clay-travis-simone-biles-should-apologize-for-quitting-on-her-team/

Lenskyj, H.J. (2000). *Inside the Olympic industry: Power, politics and activism*. London: SUNY Press.

Levenson, E. (2018, February 5). Larry Nassar apologizes, gets 40 to 125 years for decades of sexual abuse. *CNN*. www.cnn.com/2018/02/05/us/larry-nassar-sentence-eaton/index.html

Maine, D. (2021, July 28). Simone Biles withdraws from individual all-around gymnastics competition at Tokyo Olympics to focus on mental well-being. *ESPN.com*. www.espn.com/olympics/gymnastics/story/_/id/31902290/simone-biles-withdraws-individual-all-competition-tokyo-olympics-focus-mental-health

Marks, M. (2021, August 4). What makes Simone Biles the greatest gymnast of all time? *Texas Standard*. www.texasstandard.org/stories/what-makes-simone-biles-the-greatest-gymnast-of-all-time/

Martin, M. (Host). (2021, May 29). "Sidelined" author's take on Naomi Osaka's media Boycott [Audio podcast episode]. In all things considered. *NPR*. www.npr.org/transcripts/1001603733

McDonald, J. (2019). Difference and intersectionality. In A.M. Nicotera (Ed.), *Origins and traditions of organizational communication* (pp. 270–287). New York: Routledge.

Mendis, D., Steward, C., & Cox, K. (2021, August 16). Social media has helped Gen Z athletes find their "authentic voice." *The Conversation.* https://theconversation.com/social-media-has-helped-gen-z-athletes-find-their-authentic-voice-165926

Mizoguchi, K. (2021, August 2). Timeline of Simone Biles' Tokyo Olympics: From skipping Opening ceremony to exiting her event finals. *People.* https://people.com/sports/tokyo-olympics-simone-biles-timeline-withdrawals-event-finals/?slide=5764d95a-f846–441d-b93b-8149558f7c8b#5764d95a-f846–441d-b93b-8149558f7c8b

Nagesh, A. (28 July, 2021). Simone Biles: What are the twisties in gymnastics? *BBC News.* www.bbc.com/news/world-us-canada-57986166

Nemeth, M. (2021, September 16). The calculated outrage of the news media. *Medium.* https://medium.com/the-graph/the-calculated-outrage-of-the-news-media-9b17d1455092

Niesen, J. (2021, July 28). In a divided US, it's no surprise some see Simone Biles as a villain. *The Guardian.* www.theguardian.com/sport/2021/jul/28/simone-biles-withdrawal-olympics-gymnastics-tokyo-media-reaction

Nolan, E. (2021, July 27). Simone Biles' Olympics exit devastates Team USA fans. *Newsweek.* www.newsweek.com/simone-biles-olympics-exit-devastates-team-usa-fans-reaction-1613457

Oates, T.P. (2012). Representing the audience: The gendered politics of sport media. *Feminist Media Studies, 12,* 603–607.

Palczewski, C.H., Ice, R., & Fritch, J. (2016). Rhetoric in civic life. Strata Pub. *Player health and wellness: Mental health.* nfl.com. www.nfl.com/playerhealthandsafety/health- and-wellness/mental-health/?campaign=sp-tu-lp-bm-gg-2000058

Poulakos, J. (1995). *Sophistical rhetoric in classical Greece.* Columbia, SC: University of South Carolina Press.

Radnofsky, L., Gomez, J., Cole, D., & Beaton, A. (2021, July 26). How Simone Biles performs her most difficult gymnastics moves at the olympics. *Wall Street Journal.* www.wsj.com/articles/how-simone-biles-does-her-most-difficult-gymnastics-moves-11627320600#:~:text=Biles%20reaches%20her%20maximum%20height,the%20rate%20of%20helicopter%20blades

Rosenfield, S. (2012). Triple jeopardy? Mental health at the intersection of gender, race, and class. *Social Science & Medicine, 74*(11), 1791–1801.

Ruiz, M. (2021, July 27). Simone Biles doesn't have to be superhuman. *Vogue.* www.vogue.com/article/simone-biles-doesnt-have-to-be-superhuman

Simone Biles: "I Blame System that Enabled Larry Nassar Abuse" (2021, September 15). Simone Biles: "I blame system that enabled Larry Nassar abuse." *BBC.com.* www.bbc.com/news/world-us-canada-58573887

Sullivan, E. (2018, February 19). Laura Ingraham told LeBron James to shut up and dribble; He went to the hoop. *NPR.* www.npr.org/sections/thetwo-way/2018/02/19/587097707/laura-ingraham-told-lebron-james-to-shutup-and-dribble-he-went-to-the-hoop

USA Gymnastics [@USAGym]. (2021, June 28). *After further medical evaluation, Simone Biles has withdrawn from the final individual all-around competition. We wholeheartedly support Simone's decision and applaud her bravery in prioritizing her well-being. Her courage shows, yet again, why she is a role model for so many* [Tweet]. *Twitter.* https://twitter.com/USAGym/status/1420266286441922562?s=20

VanHoose, B. (2021, June 15). Simone Biles reveals the 'hardest part' of returning to gymnastics as sexual assault survivor. *People.* https://people.com/sports/simone-biles-on-returning-gymnastics-after-coming-forward-sexual-abuse-story/

Watson, F. (2022, January 22). Naomi Osaka's decision to speak up about her mental health questioned by John McEnroe. *Express*. www.express.co.uk/sport/tennis/1554096/Naomi-Osaka-John-McEnroe-tennis-news

Webster, S.P. (2009). It is a girl thing: Uncovering the stylistic performance of female athleticism. In B. Brummett (Ed.), *Sporting rhetoric: Performance, games, and politics* (pp. 48–63). London: Peter Lang.

Wertheim, J. (2021, August 3). Mailbag: The Olympic twist to Novak Djokovic's complicated reputation. *Sports Illustrated*. www.si.com/tennis/2021/08/03/mailbag-novak-djokovic-olympics-complicated-reputation.

26

HOW CAN ORGANIZATIONS BETTER SUPPORT ATHLETES? A CASE STUDY OF THE IMPACT OF COVID-19 ON MINORITIZED COMMUNITIES IN INTERCOLLEGIATE SPORT

Yannick Kluch, Shaun M. Anderson, and Tomika L. Ferguson

Introduction

From cancellations of major sporting events and devastating staff layoffs by sports organizations to alterations of athletes' everyday lives and changing consumption habits of sport fans, the COVID-19 pandemic has altered many aspects of the sport industry since its documented emergence at the end of 2019. As critical sport scholars with experience working in sport contexts and with sport organizations in a variety of capacities to promote equity, diversity, and inclusion in sport and beyond, our attention was soon drawn to crucial questions that emerged from a (sport) world that had changed significantly over the course of a few weeks.

Our immediate concerns were perhaps best captured by the succinct observation shared in Greco's (2020) opinion piece in which they noted so aptly that in the context of COVID-19 "the Diversity and Inclusion (D&I) needle that was so hard to move before has now turned into a 12,000-pound elephant" (para. 3). How does the global pandemic affect those communities within sport that have already been marginalized, stigmatized, or minoritized prior to this global health crisis? What implications and consequences does this crisis have when it comes to inclusive excellence in sport? Perhaps most importantly, what can sport professionals do to (re-) envision sport in ways that take into account issues related to promoting diversity, pursuing equity, and fostering inclusion at a time where a visible commitment to each of these axioms may seem less relevant for powerful actors within the institution of sport?

Background

As a microcosm of society, it has been well established that the institution of sport has the ability to serve as a lens through which social worlds can be documented, explored, critiqued, and sometimes changed for the better. Because sport often

DOI: 10.4324/9781003316763-30

reflects larger inequities in society, scholars across various academic disciplines turn their attention to matters of diversity and representation in sport. As a group-level concept, diversity can be defined as the various ways in which difference is constructed in society, often based on social identity categories such as race, ethnicity, gender, sexuality, socio-economic class, nationality, or religion. In addition to social identity categories, a comprehensive approach to diversity also takes into account differences on the basis of individuals' values and belief systems, upbringings, perspectives, and ideological leanings (Harrison & Klein, 2007).

In sport, discourses surrounding effective diversity work have become part of the industry's cultural fabric since the late 1990s (Doherty & Chelladurai, 1999), and sport organizations specifically have used it as a metric to determine their overall success and efficiency (Herring, 2009). However, it is important to note that diversity in itself is no more than a descriptor capturing matters of representation; it "is a fact; either it exists or it does not" (UC Berkeley Strategic Plan for Equity, Inclusion, and Diversity, 2009, p. 5). The process of *doing diversity* (i.e., increasing diversity in representation) at an institutional level often leads individuals to identify the institutions they operate in as the root of the problem (Ahmed, 2012), and to change institutions often means changing the discriminatory and systemic inequities that continue to persist in these contexts. As Ahmed (2012) convincingly argues, as drivers for diversity "we might need to be the cause of the obstruction. . . . We might need to become the blockage points by pointing out the blockage points" (p. 187).

During a time that is marked by global institutional interruptions due to COVID-19, it is particularly crucial to follow Ahmed's call for dismantling discriminatory practices and institutional barriers to diversity; yet, diversity in itself can rarely change systemic imbalances of power. Rather, it is principles of *equity* and *inclusion* that allow us to serve as *blockage points* to such imbalances and become driving forces for change on our campuses, in sport, and society at large during times of crises. In its strategic plan for equity, inclusion, and diversity, the University of California – Berkeley defines equity as the "guarantee of fair treatment, access, opportunity, and advancement for all . . ., while at the same time striving to identify barriers that have prevented the full participation of marginalized groups" (UC Berkeley Strategic Plan for Equity, Inclusion, and Diversity, 2009, p. 5). Inclusion, in extension, is "the act of creating environments in which any individual or group can feel welcomed, respected, supported, and valued" (UC Berkeley Strategic Plan for Equity, Inclusion, and Diversity, 2009, p. 5).

Because the COVID-19 pandemic changed the landscape of higher education and intercollegiate sport significantly, the goal of this case study is to offer considerations of equity, diversity, and inclusion for (re-)envisioning the community of intercollegiate sport in the context of a global health crisis. Considering our experience working in and researching U.S. intercollegiate sport, along with recent findings that show athletic departments in the United States can serve as powerful agents of social change (Cunningham, 2015; Wright-Mair et al., 2021), throughout this chapter we use collegiate athletes in the United States as an example population to (1) highlight the impact of COVID-19 on marginalized populations in sport and (2) identify strategies to counteract oppressive and harmful practices affecting vulnerable populations in sport during times of crises.

We draw primarily from Jolly et al.'s (2021) transformational allyship framework to examine how institutions – and the individuals within them – can advocate for minoritized groups and drive positive social change, especially during times of crisis. Rooting the development of their framework in the inequities revealed by the intersecting crises of COVID-19 and ongoing systemic racial injustice, Jolly et al. (2021) developed the concept of *transformational allyship* to

> [P]osit that allyship needs to rely on centralising practices of transformation . . . intentional, culturally conscious, and critically reflexive allyship as activism on an individual and institutional level will further enhance social justice movements by reducing the decentering of oppressed voices.
>
> *(p. 231)*

As a framework committed to centering the experiences of minoritized groups, Jolly and colleagues (2021) distinguish between individual allyship and institutional allyship as forms of activism leading to transformational change. They explain:

> [A]t the individual level, one has to develop a conscious, intentional plan to utilise their privileged identity (or identities) to challenge hegemonic structures and empower oppressed groups. Similarly, at the institutional level, individuals in an organisation have to create a methodical and strategic action plan to use their institutional power to challenge the status quo and deconstruct systemic barriers that undermine equality and equity. We posit that while there is power in individual allyship as activism that can drive institutional change, a combination of individual and institutional activism is needed for allyship to be transformational.
>
> *(p. 236)*

Following their call, this chapter focuses on the latter form of activism – institutional activism – to illustrate how organizational efforts can center the experiences of minoritize groups and create more equitable organizational praxis that removes systemic barriers to belonging, equity, inclusion, and ultimately positive social change.

The Case

Impact of COVID-19 on Marginalized Populations in Intercollegiate Athletics

Like most entities in the world of organized sport, the National Collegiate Athletic Association (NCAA) in the United States was affected by the COVID-19 pandemic, leaving the over 500,000 collegiate athletes competing across three divisions at over 1,100 NCAA member institutions unsure of what their future may hold. For instance, multiple universities have used the pandemic as an excuse to cut programs: The University of Cincinnati announced the elimination of its men's soccer program (Anderson, 2020); Florida International University cut its men's indoor track and field program (Nivison, 2020); and the University of Akron discontinued its men's cross country, men's golf, and women's tennis programs (Cobb, 2020). In addition, dozens of schools announced furloughs and layoffs of athletics staff (Pilon, 2020), and some schools, such as MacMurray College, a small liberal arts school in Illinois, closed indefinitely due to the financial loss resulting from the pandemic (Hobson & Hagan, 2020).

At the organizational level, the coronavirus has further implications for arguably the most vulnerable population within the NCAA – collegiate athletes. For instance, a survey conducted by Temple University's Hope Center for College, Community, and Justice found that of the 3,506 collegiate athletes in the study, 24% of athletes competing at the Division I level, 26% of athletes in Division II, and 21% of Division III athletes suffered from food insecurity in the fall of 2019 (Goldrick-Rab et al., 2020). Similarly, between 13 and 19% of athletes (depending on division) experienced homelessness during the fall of 2019 (Goldrick-Rab et al., 2020). The study does not provide insight into respondents' demographics, but research indicates that racially and sexually minoritized students are more likely to experience food insecurity compared to their peers (Willis, 2019). In fact, a recent *Sports Illustrated* article reported that food insecurity and homelessness among collegiate athletes could increase if the pandemic is not controlled (Desai, 2020). Findings like these are particularly alarming as the world continues to deal with the pandemic, which is why this case study highlights the *additional* impact COVID-19 may have on marginalized populations within intercollegiate sport.

Racially Minoritized Athletes

The Centers for Disease Control and Prevention (CDC) acknowledges racial disparities among COVID-19 infections. Early on in the pandemic, Black Americans represented over 27% of those infected, based on knowledge of race and ethnicity for about half of those tested (CDC, 2020), while being only 13% of the larger U.S. population (U.S. Census Bureau, 2021). The racial disparity is of grave concern within intercollegiate athletics, particularly in revenue-generating sports with large numbers of Black collegiate athletes.

While making up only 16% of all NCAA collegiate athletes, Black collegiate athletes comprise 56% and 49% of Division I men's basketball and football players, respectively (NCAA, 2020). Teams with Black collegiate athletes likely worry about the racial disparities among COVID-19 infections. Teams travel to, or host competitors from, other states with varied, individual levels of response to COVID-19, with some in phases of re-opening and others without state-wide restrictions. Further, there are differences among accessible testing, hospitalization rates, and treatment for People of Color (Garg et al., 2020). National racial disparities may be reflected among student populations at all colleges and universities, thereby increasing the importance of institutions to think about the needs of minoritized collegiate athletes. Black collegiate athletes in revenue-generating sports need institutions to weigh both the need and desire for profits from sporting events and the social implications of racial health disparities due to COVID-19. Without balanced consideration, Black collegiate athletes may remain an at-risk population due to COVID-19.

Racially and ethnically minoritized populations across the United States face unseen COVID-19 challenges as well. The Native American community experienced the highest number of COVID-19 cases by population compared to any other racial/ethnic community. While only 1% of the U.S. population (U.S. Census Bureau, 2021), Native American/Alaska Native populations represent around 5% of those infected (CDC, 2020).

The spread of the virus cancelled the 2020 Native American Basketball Invitational, an event co-founded by former Phoenix Suns' player Mark West (Weiner, 2020). This event is pivotal for many Native American collegiate athletes dependent on college scholarships to access higher education. The tournament included college fairs to increase interest in going to college. However, the cancellation of the June tournament represented a significant loss to collegiate athletes hoping to make a transition to intercollegiate athletics. Native American collegiate athletes are often invisible in intercollegiate sports, and fewer than 1% compete in NCAA sports (NCAA, 2020). Their lack of visibility and dependence on a single, significant event highlights the existing disparity of this population despite the impact of COVID-19. Yet, with competing challenges faced by Native American, Black, and other collegiate athletes of color, there must be a consideration about the importance of invisibility of marginalized student populations.

Women Collegiate Athletes

In a scholarly commentary in *Managing Sport and Leisure*, Clarkson and colleagues have already outlined some of the repercussions of the COVID-19 crisis on women's sport (Clarkson et al., 2020). Specifically, they highlighted organizational and economic consequences for women's sport in England; the impact of the global crisis on player contracts, migration, investment; and the threat to these athletes' well-being and welfare due to uncertainty associated with COVID-19 (Clarkson et al., 2020).

For collegiate athletes, specifically, the financial implications of COVID-19 at the U.S. college level cannot be ignored. Institutions have cut sports and salaries to respond to the financial loss. For women collegiate athletes, Title IX provides protections related to equitable sport participation and scholarship funding. Institutions must adhere to these federal protections despite the difficulty when facing grim projections for tuition dollars and delayed starts for fall sports.

Women collegiate athletes have decreased professional sport opportunities post-college, and many find opportunities overseas. The international response to COVID-19 has financial implications for collegiate women athletes' sporting opportunities across the globe, impacting those collegiate athletes who rely on senior seasons to boost their ability to compete for contracts with professional teams and those looking to join an Olympic team. The long-term impact of COVID-19 on women's intercollegiate sports has yet to be revealed, yet institutions, such as the University of Akron, have already begun to cut women's sport teams among others.

Historically, women's intercollegiate sport teams have struggled to maintain high levels of attendance across all sports. COVID-19 presents an opportunity for enhanced creativity for institutions to re-imagine how to market the benefits of intercollegiate sports to their stakeholders, including sharing the value of women's sports.

LGBTQ+ Collegiate Athletes

As captured accurately in a statement released by member states of the intergovernmental Equal Rights Coalition (2020), LGBTQ+ persons are "amongst the most marginalized and excluded because of historic and ongoing stigma, discrimination, criminalization and violence against them, and they are and will continue to be among those most at risk during this crisis" (para. 2). College is often an important time for individuals identifying as members of the LGBTQ+ community. Compared to their straight peers, students identifying as LGBTQ+ tend to perceive their environment in college to be safer and more inclusive compared to the settings they grew up in (Renn, 2017). While still being far from perfect, in athletics specifically – a domain that has historically been dominated by White, straight men in positions of power (Fink et al., 2001) – the inclusion of LGBTQ+ athletes has improved over the past decade (Cunningham, 2019). When interviewing LGBTQ+ athletes who identify as activists, for instance, participants frequently praise their athletic departments for being supportive and for empowering them to live authentically (Kluch, 2020). Given that COVID-19 led to campus closures across the country, the need to move back home for many

LGBTQ+ athletes at times exposed them to less welcoming, and potentially unsafe, environments. By its very nature, the pandemic can have a drastic impact on the well-being of LGBTQ+ collegiate athletes.

Moving beyond physical safety and well-being, LGBTQ+ individuals are also more likely to experience mental health issues as compared to their straight peers (Lipson et al., 2019). As such, spending an indefinite amount of time in physical quarantine can lead to feelings of social isolation and thus can be particularly harmful for LGBTQ+ collegiate athletes struggling with their mental health. While these athletes may have developed coping mechanisms on campus, ranging from finding support systems, utilizing mental health services on campus, or using LGBTQ-specific resource centers, COVID-19 has made it harder for these individuals to access such resources as they might seem less readily available. Due to the stigma attached to LGBTQ+ identities in society generally, and in sport specifically, it can be harder for LGBTQ+ collegiate athletes to access health care and other services needed to cope with issues related to mental health even if they should decide to seek help.

Collegiate Athletes with Disabilities

Early on in the pandemic, universities across the globe converted to online learning. Consequently, students who depended upon campus resources (i.e., living, eating, computer labs) were told to gather their belongings and find shelter elsewhere as a way to avoid further spread of the virus. In an already restricted lifestyle due to various NCAA regulations, collegiate athletes may find that the COVID-19 pandemic intensifies underlying issues. While adjusting to online or remote learning, collegiate athletes with disabilities face even more issues of accessibility. For example, collegiate athletes with learning disabilities may require extra support regarding daily class activities and facilitation. They may need notetakers, teaching assistants, and access to campus resources, not readily available to them off campus. Additionally, these students may be accustomed to having their academic counselors more accessible. The lack of security within this situation may negatively affect the mental health of these athletes.

Those collegiate athletes with physical disabilities faced even starker consequences of the COVID-19 crisis, as they no longer had campus resources (i.e., team nurses, athletic trainers) available that could help them with their everyday needs. In addition, COVID-19 protocols such as washing hands and social distancing may prove difficult for collegiate athletes with physical disabilities. For example, these athletes may have in-home health care needs that may not be as accessible off campus. Additionally, adequate testing and protective masks during this crisis may also not be as available to these athletes, making them more susceptible to the disease. Overall, sustainable efforts to assure collegiate athletes with disabilities have a more equitable and inclusive experience remain lacking. While efforts are being made to ameliorate this issue (Comerford, 2018), the pandemic further showcases the need for rules, regulations, and other forms of tangible support to be established for collegiate athletes with various disability and accessibility issues.

You Make the Call

Organizational Efforts for Driving Inclusive DEI in the Context of COVID-19

For collegiate athletes, the COVID-19 crisis showcases the ineptitudes of university support – or *institutional support*, as Jolly et al. (2021) call this type of support – in the United States. Following Jolly et al.'s (2021) framework of identifying strategies of support at the institutional level, this section maps out some ways in which the institutions within collegiate athletics (e.g., universities or the NCAA) can utilize institutional power to support and advocate for those on the margins. As mentioned, food shortages and homelessness are continual issues for some collegiate athletes. In fact, the pandemic illuminates the increased need for developing more efficient campus-level policies to handle such shortages, especially for those collegiate athletes who receive partial or no scholarship offerings. Without institutional support, these athletes may also have to deal with socialization issues that could affect their mental health. Consequently, this pandemic could force these athletes to break NCAA violations as a means of survival. More so, for marginalized and minoritized collegiate athletes, lack of university support could prove detrimental to their overall well-being.

For example, with collegiate athlete disability issues being mostly handled through the university's office of disability/accessibility, universities should create new institutional policies and contingencies to mediate the crisis. For collegiate athletes as a whole, to lose out on essential needs due to forces beyond their control can be harmful to them if left unchecked. To be proactive in times of global crises, universities first and foremost should increase their lobbying initiatives on the local, state, and federal levels to increase funding and improve policy initiatives for collegiate athletes in general and minoritized collegiate athletes in particular. For example, collegiate athletes are not allowed to receive benefits under the Supplemental Nutrition Assistance Program (SNAP) as it is considered a violation of NCAA regulations.

The Group of 5 Commissioners (G5), a group of Division I athletic commissioners representing mid-major universities (i.e., University of Houston, University of Memphis, Arkansas State University), suggested that the NCAA should decrease the number of sport programs a university sponsors in order to keep Division I status (DeBoer et al., 2020). Further, their suggestion focuses on allocating remaining funds to sport programs that are high-revenue generating (e.g., football, men's basketball). If enacted, universities would be forced to cut less-visible programs such as volleyball, baseball, and tennis. While it is unlikely that universities will comply with this suggestion, the notion of eliminating some sport programs over others marginalizes collegiate athletes who seek to have the same college experience as others. Finally, universities must focus on collegiate athlete sustainability, especially for those who have a history of being marginalized.

Prior to COVID-19, collegiate athletes were already considered vulnerable to psychological issues. Collegiate athletes have decreased help-seeking behaviors due to discomfort with receiving mental health services (Moore, 2017). COVID-19 caused trauma for these athletes, coaches, and administrators. This may lead to a labyrinth of unaddressed and unfamiliar feelings among all sport teams. Intercollegiate administrators and coaches are often not trained to identify mental health behaviors (de Souza et al., 2021), preventing them from giving a sound guidance on how to respond to trauma-induced or unhealthy behaviors. Sport program cuts, the devastation of months of social distancing, loss of seasons, and fear of the unknown may drive athletes to think their sport is not valued by their institution. Efforts to support athlete well-being and mental health, financially and administratively, should be protected at all costs. Policies created in the midst of COVID-19 should position athletes as crucial stakeholders; decisions should not decrease their value and sense of belonging within their sport. Indeed, equity-minded practice is reflected in leadership that identifies systemic inequities within an organization, takes responsibility for it, and seeks to eliminate it within policies and practices (Malcom-Piqueux & Bensimon, 2017).

More specifically, implications of COVID-19 include the need for a race-conscious approach to drive inclusive excellence in decision-making. Earlier points highlighted current and future challenges facing Black student-athletes and racial health disparity with COVID-19 infection rates and accessible testing. At the governance level, consideration must be given to an athlete's home location, how their state and local communities dealt with COVID-19, and the impact of this virus on their families. For instance, if Black student-athletes from a community still facing tremendous consequences to COVID-19 feel forced to leave their families, they may feel guilt or anxiety about their families and their own well-being. These feelings can impact their performance (Reardon & Factor, 2010). Marginalized athletes from various backgrounds deserve safe athletic environments, informed by equitable and inclusive policies and practices. Decisions about when seasons and practices start may be ethical decisions, influenced by financial responsibilities and social expectations. Industry leaders must be equity-focused, considering both the short- and long-term impact of COVID-19 decisions on individual students, and sport-wide policies must consider the mental well-being of student-athletes. Further, because marginalized populations continue to face stark barriers when it comes to accessing higher education, governing bodies need to continue to deconstruct and eliminate such barriers and advocate for those who struggle to have their voices heard in times of this crisis. Therefore, they must (re-)envision a post-COVID-19 community of sport that embraces diversity, ensures equity, and encourages inclusion at all levels.

Discussion Questions

1. Given the COVID-19 pandemic's trajectory, how have recent developments affected organizational efforts to protect minoritized populations in intercollegiate athletics? What are some of the recent developments on this issue?
2. In this case study, the focus is on three minoritized populations (i.e., racially minoritized athletes, LGBTQ+ athletes, and athletes with disabilities). How might other marginalized or minoritized populations be affected by the COVID-19 pandemic (e.g., women, international athletes)? How may the pandemic further marginalize them and hinder their development of a sense of belonging in athletics?
3. The case study maps out recommendations for organizations to support minoritized populations. On an individual level, what can athletic administrators, coaches, faculty, or other stakeholders in the collegiate athlete experience do to protect minoritized athletes and eliminate structural barriers to their belonging, inclusion, and/or overall success on campus?
4. At the institutional level, what have organizations in the intercollegiate sport system (e.g., NCAA institutions, conference offices, the association as a whole) recently done to protect minoritized athletes from the repercussions of the pandemic? What more can these organizations do?
5. How does the impact of the COVID-19 pandemic differ for non-minoritized athletes? What are similarities in the experiences of privileged/non-minoritized athletes and of those identifying as members of minoritized groups?

References

Ahmed, S. (2012). *On being included: Racism and diversity in institutional life.* Durham, NC: Duke University Press.

Anderson, G. (2020, April 24). Pandemic hits college sports. *InsideHigherEd.com.* www.insidehighered.com/news/2020/04/24/financial-crisis-related-coronavirus-hits-athletic-departments

Center for Disease Control (CDC). (2020, May 15). Case in the U.S. www.cdc.gov/coronavirus/2019-ncov/cases-updates/cases-in-us.html

Clarkson, B.G., Culvin, A., Pope, S., & Parry, K.D. (2020). Covid-19: Reflections on threat and uncertainty for the future of elite women's football in England. *Managing Sport & Leisure, 27*(1–2), 50–61. https://doi.org/10.1080/23750472.2020.1766377

Cobb, D. (2020, May 14). Akron eliminates three sports programs for financial reasons amid COVID-19 crisis. *CBSsports.com.* www.cbssports.com/college-basketball/news/akron-eliminates-three-sports-programs-for-financial-reasons-amid-covid-19-crisis/

Comerford, D.M. (2018). A call for NCAA adapted sports championships: Following the Eastern College Athletic Conference's lead to national collegiate athletic opportunities for student-athletes with disabilities. *Marquette Sports Law Review, 28*(2), 525–552.

Cunningham, G.B. (2019). Understanding the experiences of LGBT athletes in sport: A multilevel model. In M. Anshel (Ed.), *APA handbook of sport and exercise psychology: Sport psychology* (Vol. 1, pp. 367–383). Washington, DC: American Psychological Association.

Cunningham, G.B. (2015). LGBT inclusive athletic departments as agents of social change. *Journal of Intercollegiate Sport, 8*(1), 43–56. https://doi.org/10.1123/jis.2014-0131

DeBoer, K., Earhart, G., Kehoe, R., & Moyer, M. (2020, April 27). COVID-19 and the future of college sports. *University Business.* https://universitybusiness.com/covid-19-and-the-future-of-college-sports/

Desai, P. (2020, April 21). Coronavirus pandemic magnifies an all-too-real issue for some NCAA athletes. *Sports Illustrated.* https://www.si.com/college/2020/04/21/ncaa-athletes-food-nutrition-study-coronavirus

de Souza, N.L., Esopenko, C., Conway, F.N., Todaro, S.M., & Buckman, J.F. (2021). Patterns of health behaviors affecting mental health in collegiate athletes. *Journal of American College Health, 69*(5), 495–502. https://doi.org/10.1080/07448481.2019.1682591

Doherty A., & Chelladurai, P. (1999). Managing cultural diversity in sport organizations: A theoretical perspective. *Journal of Sport Management, 13*(4), 280–297. https://doi.org/10.1123/jsm.13.4.280

Equal Rights Coalition. (2020, May 15). ERC statement on COVID-19 and the human rights of LGBTI persons. *Government of Canada.* www.international.gc.ca/world-monde/issues_development-enjeux_developpement/human_rights-droits_homme/2020-05-15-erc_statement-declaration_ced.aspx?lang=eng

Fink, J.S., Pastore, D.L., & Riemer, H.A. (2001). Do differences make a difference? Managing diversity in division IA intercollegiate athletics. *Journal of Sport Management, 15*(1), 10–50. https://doi.org/10.1123/jsm.15.1.10

Garg, S., Kim, L., Witaker, M., O'Halloran, A., Cummings, C., Holstein, R., Prill, M., Chai, S. J., Kirley, P.D., Alden, N.B., Kawaski, B., Yousey-Hindes, K., Niccolai, L., Anderson, E.J., Openo, K.P., Weigel, A., Monroe, M.L., Ryan, P., Henderson, J., . . . Fry, A. (2020). Hospitalization rates and characteristics of patients hospitalized with laboratory-confirmed coronavirus disease 2019 – COVID-NET, 14 states, March 1–30, 2020. *US Department of Health and Human Services/Centers for Disease Control and Prevention Morbidity and Mortality Weekly Report, 69*(15), 458–464.

Goldrick-Rab, S., Richardson, B., & Baker-Smith, C. (2020). Hungry to win: A first look at food and housing insecurity among student-athletes. *The Hope Center for College, Community, and Justice.* https://hope4college.com/wp-content/uploads/2020/04/2019_StudentAthletes_Report.pdf

Greco, A. (2020, May 4). Keeping diversity & inclusion alive in times of crisis: adapt, survive, thrive. *Tlnt.com.* www.tlnt.com/keeping-diversity-inclusion-alive-in-times-of-crisis-adapt-survive-and-thrive/

Harrison, D.A., & Klein, J.K. (2007). What's the difference? Diversity constructs as separation, variety, or disparity in organizations. *Academy of Management Review, 32*(4), 1199–1228. https://doi.org/10.5465/amr.2007.26586096

Herring, C. (2009). Does diversity pay? Race, gender, and the business case for diversity. *American Sociological Review, 74*(2), 208–224. www.jstor.org/stable/27736058

Hobson, J., & Hagan, A. (2020, May 13). Coronavirus may mark the end for many small liberal arts colleges. *Wbur.org.* www.wbur.org/hereandnow/2020/05/13/coronavirus-small-college-closures

Jolly, S., Cooper, J.N., & Kluch, Y. (2021). Allyship as activism: advancing social change in global sport through transformational allyship. *European Journal for Sport and Society, 18*(3), 229–245. https://doi.org/10.1080/16138171.2021.1941615

Kluch, Y. (2020). "My story is my activism!": (Re-)definitions of social justice activism among collegiate athlete activists. *Communication & Sport, 8*(4–5), 1–25. https://doi.org/10.1177/2167479519897288

Lipson, S.K., Raifman, J., Abelson, S., & Reisner, S.L. (2019). Gender minority mental health in the U.S.: Results of a national survey on college campuses. *American Journal of Preventive Medicine, 57*(3), 293–301. https://doi.org/10.1016/j.amepre.2019.04.025

Malcom-Piqueux, L., & Bensimon, E.M. (2017). Taking equity-minded action to close equity gaps. *Peer Review, 19*(2), 5–8.

Moore, M. (2017). Stepping outside of their comfort zone: Perceptions of seeking behavioral health services amongst college athletes. *Journal of Issues in Intercollegiate Athletics,* 130–144.

National Collegiate Athletic Association (NCAA). (2020, March). Demographics by race/ethnicity. www.ncaa.org/about/resources/research/ncaa-demographics-database

Nivison, A. (2020, May 6). Report: FIU cuts men's indoor track and field. *247sports.com.* https://247sports.com/Article/FIU-cut-mens-track-and-field-program-coronavirus-146885146/

Pilon, M. (2020, May 13). Can millionaire college coaches defend their salaries during Covid-19? *TheGuardian.com.* www.theguardian.com/sport/2020/may/13/can-millionaire-college-coaches-defend-their-salaries-during-covid-19

Reardon, C., & Factor, R. (2010). Sport psychiatry: A systematic review of diagnosis and medical treatment of mental illness in athletes. *Sports Medicine, 40*(11), 961–980. https://doi.org/10.2165/11536580-000000000-00000

Renn, K. (2017, April 10). LGBTQ students on campus: issues and opportunities for higher education leaders. *HigherEdToday.org.* www.higheredtoday.org/2017/04/10/lgbtq-students-higher-education/

UC Berkeley Strategic Plan for Equity, Inclusion, and Diversity. (2009). Executive summary. https://diversity.berkeley.edu/sites/default/files/executivesummary_webversion.pdf

U.S. Census Bureau. (2021). 2020 census results: Quick facts. *Census.gov.* https://www.census.gov/quickfacts/fact/table/US/PST045221

Weiner, A. (2020, April 20). NABI cancellation means much more to Native American community than just loss of basketball. *Cronkite News.* https://cronkitenews.azpbs.org/2020/04/20/native-american-basketball-tournament-cancelled/

Willis, D.E. (2019). Feeding the student body: Unequal food insecurity among college students. *American Journal of Health Education, 50*(3), 167–175. https://doi.org/10.1080/19325037.2019.1590261

Wright-Mair, R., Kluch, Y., Swim, N., & Turick, R. (2021). Driving systemic change: Examining perceptions of high-impact practices for advancing diversity, equity, and inclusion in intercollegiate athletics. *Journal of Issues in Intercollegiate Athletics, 14,* 599–625.

APPENDIX A

Drew Brees' Written Apology

I would like to apologize to my friends, teammates, the City of New Orleans, the black community, NFL community and anyone I hurt with my comments yesterday. In speaking with some of you, it breaks my heart to know the pain I have caused. In an attempt to talk about respect, unity, and solidarity centered around the American flag and the national anthem, I made comments that were insensitive and completely missed the mark on the issues we are facing right now as a country. They lacked awareness and any type of compassion or empathy. Instead, those words have become divisive and hurtful and have misled people into believing that somehow, I am an enemy. This could not be further from the truth, and is not an accurate reflection of my heart or my character. This is where I stand:

I stand with the black community in the fight against systemic racial injustice and police brutality and support the creation of real policy change that will make a difference. I condemn the years of oppression that have taken place throughout our black communities and still exists today. I acknowledge that we as Americans, including myself, have not done enough to fight for that equality or to truly understand the struggles and plight of the black community. I recognize that I am part of the solution and can be a leader for the black community in this movement. I will never know what it's like to be a black man or raise black children in America but I will work every day to put myself in those shoes and fight for what is right. I have ALWAYS been an ally, never an enemy. I am sick about the way my comments were perceived yesterday, but I take full responsibility and accountability. I recognize that I should do less talking and more listening . . . and when the black community is talking about their pain, we all need to listen. For that, I am very sorry and I ask your forgiveness (Brees, 2020).

Reference

Brees, D. (2020, June 4). I would like to apologize to my friends, teammates, the City of New Orleans, the black community, NFL community [Facebook page]. *Facebook*. www.facebook.com/permalink.php?story_fbid=10163708482215461&id=207038895460

APPENDIX B

Transcript from Drew Brees' Video Apology

I know there's not much that I can say that would make things any better right now. But I just want you to see in my eyes how sorry I am for comments that I made yesterday. I know that it hurt many people, especially friends, teammates, former teammates, loved ones, people that I care and respect deeply. That was never my intention. I wish I would have laid out what was on my heart in regards to the George Floyd murder, Ahmaud Arbery, the years and years of social injustice, police brutality and the need for so much reform and change in regards to legislation, so many other things to bring equality to our black communities. I am sorry. And, I will do better. And, I will be part of the solution. And, I am your ally. And I know no words will do that justice (Brees, 2020).

Reference

Brees, D. (2020, June 5). Drew Brees apology video [Video]. *YouTube*. www.youtube.com/watch?v=Ig83FIxGv00

APPENDIX C

Green Bay Packers' Letter to the Fans

Dear Green Bay Packers Fans,

As we begin the 2020 NFL season, nothing in our everyday routines – let alone our favorite sports – has been untouched by the COVID-19 pandemic. Since March, we all have faced challenges, some more daunting than others. We've had to adjust in our homes, workplaces and schools as we learn to co-exist with the virus. For the Packers, the last six months have been dramatically different. We've missed seeing many of you at Lambeau Field and sharing your enthusiasm during the NFL Draft, minicamp, Shareholders meeting, training camp and preseason games. But your virtual engagement from all around Wisconsin, the country and the world has helped us prepare for the season in a new way, and we are extremely grateful for your support. You are the best fans in the NFL. As we prepare to kick off this weekend, we know that nothing can replace the true roar of the crowd and the feeling of having our fans in Lambeau Field or stadiums throughout the NFL. Although we may not have you cheering us on in person, we can still feel your support from afar, and we will carry your energy with us as we take the field on Sunday and in the weeks to come.

Thank you for your passionate support as we kick off another season of Packers football. One unlike any of the previous 101. We hope to see you soon. Sincerely, The Green Bay Packers

(Green Bay Packers, 2020)

Reference

Green Bay Packers. (2020, September 12). A letter to fans of the Green Bay Packers. *Packers.com*. www.packers.com/news/a-letter-to-fans-of-the green-bay-packers

INDEX

Note: Page numbers in **bold** indicate a table on the corresponding page.

Abbot, Mark 55, 58
Abdul-Jabbar, Kareem 10
Abdul-Rauf, Mahmoud 6
Academy Awards 193
accept (as taking responsibility) 70, 101, 164, 173
accident 172, 196, **214**
account (as 'taking into') 41, 44, 75–76, 164, 198, 244, 300–301
accumulate 55, 164
adapt 164, 271
addiction 5, 222
Adubato, Beth 212
AdvoCare 65
advocates 4, 46, 160, 162–163, 185, 244
African American 4, 30–31, 143–144, 147
agenda-setting 88, 265–266, 273
agora, idea of 288
alcohol abuse 5, 218
Ali, Mohammed 4, 77, 93
align 164, 195, 203–204
Allison, Rachel 232–233
ally 68, 70, 164, 312, 314
allyship 137, 302
Altra 194
Alves da Silva, Dani 132–138
Amazon MTurk 256
Ambrosie, Randy 114

American: athletes 264, 268, 289, 292–293, 299; customs/culture 17, 41, 64, 67, 88, 288; flag 66, 69, 71, 312; military 88, 90; professional sports 109, 111–112
American Academy of Neurology 43
analyze 26, 41, 54, 146, 160, 164, 195
Andrews, Ben 110–112
anti-American 86, 88, 90, 111
anti-gay sentiment 31
anti-racist 57–58, 132, 135m 137–138, 148
anxiety 5, 222, 265, 290, 308
appoint 164
Arbery, Ahmaud 70, 314
arbitration 46–47, 170, **171**
arenas. see stadiums
Armstrong, Lance 68, **214–215**
Ashe, Arthur 4
Asian Americans 11
Aspen Institute 120
Associated Press Sports Editors' (APSE) 98
athlete reputational crisis (ARC) 88, 90
athletes: activism 10, 86, 89–90; as activists 4, 305; collegiate 302, 305, 306–308; with disabilities (collegiate) 306; endorsements 8, 65, 123, 156, 184, 229, 267; female 8, 77, 156, 162, 170, 193, 202–207, 229, 238, 288; influence of

252, 256, **257**, 258–259; marginalized 302–303; patriotism 70, 90; pay equity/gap 8–9, 155–159, 182, 185, 234–159; professional 11, 22, 71, 213, 251, 260, 290; as role models 9–10, 184, 212, 228, 252, 259; as targets 5, 66, 75, 126, 134–135; transgender 6, 185
athleticism 77, 182, 184, 186, 207, 242
Atlanta Braves 110
Atlantic times 24
attack accuser 213, **215**
attribution theory 172, 277
Autism Speaks 125
Axios/Ipsos poll 11

Back, Les (et al 2001) 123
Bacon, Perry Jr. 22, 24
Badminton World Federation 206
Ball, Montee **214–215**, 215, **216**, 217–218, 222
Balotelli, Mario 134
Baltimore Ravens 213, 253
Band of Brothers 191–192; as buttfaces 197–198
baseball 4, 53, 181, 220, 268, 307
  see also MLB
Basil, Michael D. 252
Bayless, Skip 290
Baylor University 295
Beard, Amanda 5
behavior: change 252, 254, 259; fan 29, 34, 133, 281
Benoit, William L. 54, 59, 67, 69, 128, 195, **215**
Benzema, Karim 133
Berri, David 161
bicycling/cycling 180, 206
Biden, Joseph 251
Bieniemy, Eric 23–24
bigotry 75, 78, 80–81
Biles, Simone: mental health 267, 271–272, 288, 290, 292–294; withdrawal from competition 264, 269, 287, 292
Bird, Sue 91
Black: athletes 4, 11, 21, 31, 141, 146; coaches/head coaches 18, 23–24; coordinators 22–23; false assumptions 31; players 20, 22, 30, 40, 44–45, 123, 134, 144; quarterbacks 20
Black Americans 4, 141–142, 144, 303
Black and Brown 91, 133, 136

Black Lives Matter (BLM) 4, 8, 10, 31, 66, 79, 87, 91, 137, 142, 178, 282
Black Players for Change (BPC) 124–125
Black, Indigenous, and people of color (BIPOC) 98, 104, 178, 184
Blaikie, William 180
Blake, Jacob 92, 141, 143–144, 147–149, 282
Bloodworth, Andrew 267
Blue Ribbon Sports 192
Bocarnea, Mihai C. 252
bolstering 68, 102, 213, **214**, 215, 219–221
Boston Marathon 192
Boulaire, André 179
Bowerman, Bill 192
Bowman, Brian 114
Boyd, Josh 77
Boyer, Nate 88
Bradley, Samuel 212
Brady, Tom 65
brain injury 22, 43, 45, 48
brains diseases 41, 43
Brandt, Andrew 46
Brees Dream Foundation 66, 72
Brees Family Field 65
Brees, Drew 64–65, 67, 70
Brody, Anita 41, 45–47
Brown, Antonio 7
Brown, Sterling 144
Brown, William J. 252
Bruce, Toni 163, 228–229
Bryant, Kobe 68, 89
Bryant, Kris 216
Bucher, Timothy J. 47
Burchard, Peter 171–172
Butler, Judith 240
Butterworth, Michael L. 77

Cain, Mary 194, 196–197
Camogie Association 229–230
Campaya Lleo, David 133, 137
Canadian Football League (CFL): branding, as offensive 110, 113; Diversity is Strength campaign 114; Grey Cup 109, 112–113; origination of 109–110; social responsibility 108, 110, 116; Us *vs.* Them mindset 112; you make the call 116
Canadian Heritage 111
Canadianness 111–112, 117
candidate pool 24

Carastathis, Anna 42
Card, David 212
Carlos, John 4, 6
Carolina Panthers 23
Carpenter, Lorelei 229
Castile, Philando 66, 87
Catalan culture 76–77
cause marketing 123
cause washing 123, 125, 128–129
celebrity sports figures 10
Centers for Disease Control and
    Prevention (CDC) 251, 254, 303
centrality 20–21, 112
Centre for Sport and Human Rights 11
Chapman, Aroldis **214**, 215, **216**,
    219–221
Chara, Diego 127
Charland, Maurice 145, 147
Chicago: Bears 10; Blackhawks 10, 110;
    Bulls 10; Cubs 10, **216**, 216–217, 221,
    251; Fire 10; Red Stars 10; Sky 10;
    White Sox 10
Chicago Department of Public Health 10
Chicago Tribune 19
Chiles, Jordan 270–271
Chinese Communist Party 6
Christians 70
Chronic Traumatic Encephalopathy (CTE)
    41–44
Church of Jesus Christ of Latter-day Saints
    (LDS) 31
Ciletti, Dorene 187
Cincinnati Reds **216**, 220
Civil Rights Act 1991/1999 22, 44, 159
Civil Rights Era 64
Clark, Frank 221
Clarkson, Beth G. (et al 2020) 304
Cleveland: Browns 219; Cavaliers 120;
    Indians 110
climate: action 12; change 254
CNN (Cable News Network) 80
Coca-Cola Company 9, 115
code of conduct 33 *see also* Fan Code of
    Conduct
Collective Bargaining Agreement (CBA)
    45–46, 156, 159, 162
Colorado Rapids 126
Columbus Crew 57, 127
columnists 29, 66, 98, 293
Combahee River Collective
    Statement 291
combat sports 56, 87, 231
Commanders/Redskins controversy 7, 117

commentators 29, 233, 269–270, 287, 291
communication. *see* crisis communication;
    sport communication
communication capital 178, 181, 184
compensation (image repair) 67, 213, **215**
compensation (wages/pay) 22, 40, 156,
    159, 194
competition: eligibility 170, 241–244;
    phases of 77, 82, 265, 268–270, 272;
    withdraw from 6, 270
concussion: crisis 41–43, 45, 48; protocol
    40; reporting 44
Confederate flag 11
conflict: issue-specific 43–44, 54; potential
    for 77, 104
coordinator offensive/defensive 23–24
corporate: advocacy 135, 137–138;
    communication 109, 129; culture
    186, 191; internal practices 191;
    responsibility 37, 78, 228; sponsors 9,
    78, 115–116, 163, 228, 230
corporate responsibility to race (CRR) 30,
    33–37
corrective action 59–60, 67–70, 100, 121,
    195, 213, **215**, 221
COVID-19 7; athlete influence 251;
    crisis management 275, 306–307;
    fan disappointment 275; institutional
    support (lack of) 307; mask wearing
    protocol 251, 256, **257**, 258–260;
    protocols, you make the call 253, 259,
    283, 306; vaccine/vaccination 7, 10,
    256, 259
Creative Arts Emmy Award 9
Crenshaw, Kimberle 288, 291
crisis communication: image restoration/
    repair 55, 67; power to act, lack of 168;
    strategies 41–42; tools 275, *see also*
    situational crisis communication theory
critical discourse analysis (CDA) 145–146
Crowder, Jae 36
cultural: capital 212–213; domination 111;
    norms 36, 203, 240; stereotypes 233
Cunningham, George 240
Cuomo, Andrew 159
Curry, Steph 142

da Silva Santos Jr, Neymar 133–134
Dahl, Gordon 212
Dallas Cowboys 87, 290
Daniels, Deborah 159, 179
Davenport, Najeh 40, 42
Davis, Alvin 10

Davis, Demario 70
de la Cretaz, Britni 219
Deacon White, William 109
Decker, Mary 198
defeasibility 59, 67, 69–70, **214**, 218
deflect/deflection 46–47, 68, 209, 282
DeKnop, Paul 179
Delta Air Lines 9
dementia 22, 40, 44
Democrats 11
denial, strategy of 59, 69, 100, 173, 175,
    195, 213, **214**, 221
Denver Broncos 183, 217–218
depression 5, 290
DeRozan, DeMar 5
Detroit: Pistons 31; Tigers 10
Detroit Red Wings 10
Detroit Tigers 10
DiCaro, Julie 291
differentiation 67, 78, **214**
disabilities 306
disciplinary: action 45, 66, 126;
    procedures/policy 45–47, 124
discrimination: gender 155, 206; racial
    19, 67
disparity, silence of 155, 157, 161, 165
diversity initiatives 18, 20–21, 25, 78, 124,
    128, 301
Diversity Working Group 197
diversity, equity, and inclusion (DEI) 8,
    124–125, 307
Djokovic, Novak 7, 9, 287–288
Doak Walker Award 218
domestic abuse/violence 7, 42, 121,
    212–213, 218, 220, 222
Donahue, John 197
Donovan, Landon 78–80, 82–83
Dorsey, John 219
Dougall, Elizabeth 164
Douglas, Gabby 4
Doyle, Jason P. 228
draft selection 24, 217
Drake, Carly 229
Dream Crazy 9, 192, 197
Driving Under the Influence (DUI) 5
Dube, Kheli 127
Duerson, Dave 43
Dugan, Márie 42
Duggan, Meghan 8
Dyson, Sam 221

eating disorders 267
Ederle, Gertrude 183–184

Edmonton Elks 108, 116–117
Edmonton Eskimos 109–110, 113–115
Edwards, harry 21
Edwards, Mike 7
Elite Formation Coaching License 124
English Channel 183
English Premier League 8
Enke, Anne 240
Epstein, Theo 216
Equal Pay Act 158–159
Equal Rights Coalition 305
equity 8, 15, 35, 91 153 *see also* diversity,
    and inclusion; pay equity, equity
Equity Action Committee (EAC) 124
ESPN 5, 55; gender/racial inequality
    98–99; Kendrick Perkins 101–102;
    leadership failure 102; Maria Taylor
    103; privacy violations 101, 104;
    Rachel Nichols 100–101; reputation
    management 97, 99, 103
ESPY Awards 91
European Handball Federation 202–203,
    207, 209
evading responsibility 59, 67–70, 100, 121
evasion of responsibility 59, 121, 126,
    195–196, **214**
excellence theory 56, 108–110
exclusion 12, 191, 241, 268
exemplification 266, 272

Facebook 113–114, 134, 278, 280
fan behavior 29, 34, 133, 281
Fan Code of Conduct 54–55, 57–58, 60
fan community 276, 279, 281
fandom 29, 72, 133, 281–282
FC Cincinnati 57
FC Dallas 125–126
Fearn-Banks, Kathleen 54–55
Fédération Internationale de Football
    Association (FIFA) 53, 123 *see also* FIFA
    World Cup
Federation Internationale de Gymnastique
    (FIG) 243–244
Felix, Allyson 9, 194, 197
Felix, Wes 194, 197
female athletes: as advocates 162–163;
    wage disparities 155–160
feminine apologetic 184
femininity 77, 183, 191, 206–207, 229
Fields, Sarah K. 123
Fienberg, Harvey 10
FIFA World Cup: Men's 136; prize money
    157–158; Women's 155, 158

Fink, Janet S. 229
First Nations 110–111
Fisherman's Friend 115
Flores, Brian 17, 25
Florida 101, 104, 142
Florida International University 303
Floyd, George 36, 66, 70, 92, 116, 125, 142, 282, 314
Football Club Barcelona (FCB) 76–77
footballers 132, 232, 234
Forbes magazine 9, 65, 156, 161
Forsyth, Janice 208
Fox News 5, 71
Fox Sports 290
franchise 24, 75, 80, 91, 109–110, 115–116
Franklin, John 7
Franklin, Roslyn 229
Frazier, Clint 251, 255–256, 259
French Open 5, 183, 287, 291
Friedman, Michael T. 157
Fritz Pollard Alliance 18, 20

Gaelic Players' Association (GPA) 233–234
Galchenyuk, Alex 221
Gantz, Walter 212
Garber, Don 53–56, 59–61
Garner, Eric 66, 89
Gartland, Dan 220
Geddert, John 266
Geir Lio, Kare 209
gender: confusion 240; equality 4, 77, 155, 228, 238; fairness 12; inequalities 98; non-binary 239, 241, 243; testing 242
Germany 242
Gibson, Althea 4
Gill, Sam 46
Gilman, Charlotte Perkins 180
Girls Academy 124
Girls Athletic Association (GAA) 227, 229–232, 234
Giudicelli, Bernard 183
Global Sport Institute 23
Global Sports Matters 4
Goffman, Erving 265
Gomez, Julissa 271
good intentions 54, 59, 67, 69, 196, **214**
Good Morning America 79–80
Goodell, Roger 25, 46
goodwill building 56
Gorsevski, Ellen W. 77
Goucher, Kara 9, 193–194, 197

Green Bay Packers 7; crisis management 275; fan activism 282; fan response 281; global fan base 281; letter to fans 277; team heritage 279–280
Greenhalgh, Greg 228
Greenham, Craig 110–112
Greenlaw, Paul S. 21
Griffin, Rachel A. 31
Griner, Brittney 6, 8
Group of 5 Commissioners (G5) 307
Gruden, Jon 7
Grunig, James E. 108

Hadzic, Alen 168, 170, **171**, 172–175
Hallahan, Kirk 163
Hambrick, Marion E. (et al 2013) 71
hashtag activism 132–133, 137
hastags: #AUnitedFront 55; #BlackLivesMatter 137, 142; #BlackOutTuesday 137; #deflategate 121; #Elks/#Charge 116; #Equalpay 163; #ImWithKap 137; #MeToo 137, 162, 202; #SayHerName 137; #SeriousSupport 228, 231, 233; #SomosTodosMacacos 132, 134; #TakeAKnee 88, 137; #WearAask 255; #WeAreAllMonkeys 132, 137–138
hate groups: 211 Bootboys 127; Battalion 49 57, 127; Empire State Ultras 57; Proud Boys 57, 127
hate speech 34
Hawhee, Debra 288
hegemonic: femininity 184, 206–207; systems/structures 145–146, 302
Hellas Verona Football Club 134
Henry, Kevin 40–42
Hewitt, Jeanette 267
Hickey, Marie 231
Hill, George 144
Hill, Jamele 24
Hill, Tyreek 221
hiring: decisions 18–19; head coaches 21; policies 26
Hispanic 11
Hispanic Heritage Month 125
Hispanic Star 125
HIV/AIDS 4, 254
Ho, Michelle H.S. 229
Hodges, Craig 6
Holm, Holly 5
homophobia 34, 79, 82
homophobic slurs 75, 80, 82
human rights in sports 12, 243

Hunt, Kareem **214–215**, 215, **216**, 218–219, 221
Hurricane Katrina 65

I Can't Breathe 10, 89
identity: gender 58, 239, 241–245; identification 145; national 111–112, 117
image 5, 31, 59, 255
image repair theory (IRT) 65, 67, 120, 212
image restoration 33, 55–56, 67, 100, 195
impression management theory 265–266
inclusion. *see* diversity, equity, and inclusion; trans inclusion
Indiana Pacers 31
Indigenous Peoples 108, 110, 114, 116–117
inequality/inequalities: health 12; pay 163, 234; racial (*see* racial inequality)
Ingraham, Laura 71
ingratiation 266, 271–272
Instagram 10, 69, 134–135, 216–217, 268, 291
Institute for Diversity and Ethics in Sports 30, 98
institutional racism 12, 19
intercollegiate sport 301, 303–305, 309
International Football Federation (FIFA) 205 *see also* FIFA World Cup
International Handball Federation's (IHF): founding of 203; legitimacy/reputation of 204–205; uniform policy/challenge 202, 205–206, 207–208
International Olympic Committee (IOC) 205, 240–244, 289, 294
International Ski Federation (FIS) 210
International Swimming Federation (FINA) 6
intersectionality 99, 288, 291
intimate partner violence (IPV): athlete engagement 212, 218–221; criminal investigations 213, 216218; image repair/player **214–216**, 221–222
intimidation 220, 266, 272
Inuit communities 110, 113, 115
Inuit Tapiriit Kanatami 113
Ireland 227, 229–234
Irving, Kyrie 7, 142–143
issues management 88, 155, 157, 159, 163
Ithaca College Center for Faculty Excellence 49
Iveson, Don 114

Jackson, Stephen 29, 37n1
Jacksonville Jaguars 7
James, LeBron 5, 10–11, 65, 71, 89, 142–143, 252
Jeffres, Leo Wayne (et al 2013) 181
Jenkins, Malcolm 65
Jensen, Sanne S. 21
Jiffy Lube 115
Johnson, Jeff 198
Johnson, Magic 30
Jolly, Shannon (et al 2021) 302, 307
Jones, E.E. 265
Jones, Jerry 87
Jones, Terry 110, 116
Jordan, Cam 71
Journal of the American Medical Association (JAMA) 44
JP MacManus 229

Kaepernick, Colin 4–5, 9, 64, 66, 86
    see also take a knee; Kaepernick Publishing 91; take a knee/reputation demise 92–93
Kane, Patrick 221
Kansan City Chiefs 24, **216**, 218, 281
Karlis, Jack V. 88
Karolyi, Bela and Marta 266
Keifer, Lee 171
Kenosha Police Department 148
Kerr, Steve 34
Kilvington, Daniel 133
Kim, Minhong 252
King, Billie Jean 4, 8, 156–157, 206
Kitching, Niamh 227
Knight, Phil "Buck" 192, 197–198
Know Your Rights 91
Koe, Jordan 110
Korver, Kyle 36
Krane, Vikki 206

LA Clippers 30
LA Galaxy II 75, 78
Ladies Gaelic Football Association (LGFA): corporate sponsors, questionable choices 228, 230; Ladyball campaign 227, 230–231; media campaign and sponsorship 227–228, 231–232
Las Vegas Raiders 7
Lavelle, Katherine L. 31
Lead Together 36
Lee, Sunisa 271, 293
legitimacy: gap theory 157, 164; lack of 46; organizational 202–203, 204

Lenglen, Suzanne 206
Leonard, David J. 31
Leung, Li Li 271
Levitt, Daniel 20, 25
LGBTQ (Lesbian, Gay, Bisexual,
    Transgender) 123, 178, 184–185,
    240, 305
Lidl 228, 230, 233
Lipka, Fred 124
Lloyd, Carli 156
Loducca 134–135, 137
Logan, Doug 54
Logan, Nneka 33
Los Angeles Dodger 220–221
Los Angeles Sparks 8
Los Angeles Angels 251, 255
Lough, Nancy 228
Love, Kevin 5, 290
Loy, J.W. 20–21

MacGregor, Wendy 213
Madden, Janice Fanning 23
Madden, Pete 40
Maddon, Joe 216
Major League Baseball (MLB) 8, 144, 212,
    216, 221, 254
Major League Soccer (MLS):
    #AUnitedFront 55; Fan Code of
    Conduct 54–55, 58, 60; Iron Front
    crisis 53; MLS NEXT 120–122,
    124–125, 127–128; organizational
    hierarchy 121; origination of 54;
    preparedness/prevention plan 58; public
    acts of racism 126
Make America Great Again 55, 87
Manchin, Joe 159
Manning, Alex (et al 2021) 31
Manning, Peyton 65, 252
Market Forces concept 160–161
marketing: campaigns 112–113, 197, 233;
    cause/cause washing 123; gendered 232
Maroney, McKayla 4
Marshall, Bobby 20
Martin, Collin 75, 79–81
Martin, Elijah 78
Martin, Trayvon 32, 142
masculine/masculinity 30–31, 45, 77, 82,
    179, 198, 213, 229
Maxwell, Vernon 29
McElvogue, Joseph F. 20–21
McEntee, Jimmy 47
McGregor, Connor 9
McGuire, Mark 252

McHenry, Britt 99
McNamee, Mike 267
media 30; influence 252, 266; stories
    266–267
mediation 40–41, 45, 47–48, 252
Memphis Grizzlies 29
mental health: organizational responsibility
    287; pandemic/lockdown and 249
Messi, Lionel 156
Métis Federation 114
Meyer, Urban 7
Miami Marlins 10, 183
Michigan State University 5
Mild Traumatic Brain Injury Committee
    (MTBI) 43, 47
Miller, Gail 32–33, 35–36
Milwaukee Bucks: bubble basketball 142;
    labor strike/CDA 141, 145–146; racial
    injustice statement 144, 147–148; safe
    voting 143
minimization 59–60, 213, **214**
Minnesota United 57
minority: head coaches 18, 21; players 22
Mohandesi, Salar 41–42
Montana, Joe 65
Montaño, Alysia 9, 193–194, 196–197
Moore, Jack 20, 25
Morant, Ja 29–30, 32, 37
Morant, Tee 29, 37
mortification, as image repair 59, 67–71,
    100, 121, 195–196, **215**, 221
Motley, Marion 20
Moustafa, Hassan 208
Mueller, Max Perry 31
Muhammad Ali Legacy Award 93
Musburger, Brent 6

NASCAR 6, 11
Nassar, Larry 5, 169, 264–266, 289–290
    see also USA Gymnastics
Nastase, Ilie 199
National Basketball Association (NBA):
    acts of racism 29–30, 32; finals 97,
    102–103, 158; NBA bubble 141–143;
    player influence 5–6, 10, 142
National Collegiate Athletic Association
    (NCAA) 6, 77, 217, 303, 306
National Football League (NFL): Black
    head coach 23; Commissioner, role/
    duties of 45–46; counternarrative/
    denial 43; Diversity Advisory
    Committee 4, 17, 25; first female
    coach 183; leadership 18, 89; mission/

values statement 47; national anthem
controversy 4–6, 8, 64, 69, 86 *see also*
Kaepernick; Brees; Nest Model 47;
Personal Conduct Policy 45, 213; socio-
historical background of 41; Thursday
Night Football 160–161; win-or-face-
firing 25
National Governing Bodies (NGBs) 168,
170, 173
National Hockey League (NHL) 22,
221, 251
National Labor Relations Act 46
National Olympic Committees
(NOCs) 289
National Organization for Women and
Girls in Sport 179
National Women's Soccer League 182
National Women's Hockey League 159
Native American 11, 110, 304
Native American Basketball
Invitational 304
Navratilova, Marina 4
NBA Players Association (NBPA) 141
NBC (National Broadcasting Company):
athlete withdrawal, criticism of
267–269 *see also* Biles; Winter Olympics
coverage 160, 265, 267
NBC Sports 72, 104
neo-Nazi groups 53–54, 57
nested conflict 42
New England Patriots 17, **216**, 217
New England Revolution 127
New Orleans Saints 65, 70–72
New York City Football Club's (NYCFC)
57, 127
New York Mets 10
New York Times 72, 98–102, 104, 163,
193–194, 198
New York Yankees 220, 251, 255
NFL Players Association (NFLPA)·
26, 46
Ng, Kim 183
Nham, Kai 139
Nichols, Rachel 97–104 *see also* ESPN
Nielson Fan Insights study 9
Nike: boycott 9, 124; corporate hypocrisy
191; evolution of 192–193; female
inequality 9, 163, 193–194; image
repair 195–197; jersey sales 155, 158;
leadership/social justice campaigns
197–199
Northern Engagement Community
Program 115

Norwegian Handball Federation (NHF)
203, 270
Norwegian women's beach handball:
founding of 203; organizational
reputation 204–205; uniform protest
202, 205, 207–209

O'Conner, Peter 4
Oakland Athletics 215
Obed, Nathan 112
Ochoa, David 127
Ogwumike, Nneka 8
Ohio State University 7
Oklahoma City Thunder 29
Olympic Games: female exclusion 191;
sexual misconduct allegation 168, 170,
171, 264 *see also* Biles; USA Gymnastics
Omalu, Bennet 43
Omine, Mitsuharu 123
One World Fútbol 77
organizational: communication 41, 288,
291; legitimacy theory 202, 204–205,
209; obligations to athletes 287, 300;
practices 19, 24; responses 29, 126;
responsibility 277
Orlando Magic 141
Ortiz, Jorge L. 220
Ortiz, Stephanie M. 123
Osaka, Naomi 4–5, 156, 229, 287,
290–291, 294
Osuna, Roberto 221
Ottawa Redblacks 113

Paine, Neil 22, 24
Palazzo, Guido 204
Pannullo, Robert 46–47
Parks Pieper, Lindsay 181
Parlow Cone, Cindy 160
Parrock, Katrina 232
pay equity 8, 155, 157–159, 182, 234
Peacock (streaming service) 160
Pedroia Returns 217
Pennsylvania Communication Annual 187
Pennsylvania State University 295
Penny, Steve 266
people of color 17–19, 22, 30 *see also*
BIPOC
performance-enhancing drugs (PEDs) 252
Perkins, Kendrick 101–104 *see also* ESPN
personality 145, 205
Phelps, Michael 5, 271
Philadelphia Eagles 24
Phoenix Rising FC 75, 79–80, 82

Phoenix Suns 304
Pittsburgh Riverhounds 81
Pittsburgh Steelers 17, 41
Platt, Larry 4
player deaths 42, 66
podcast 29, 194
police brutality: call to action 144, 185, 282; protests 64, 86–87, 137; raising awareness 10, 66, 70, 142
police corruption 67
political: correctness 71; speech 54, 57–60; statements 59, 137
Pollard, Frederick Douglass "Fritz" 20
poorly kept secret 29
Portland Timbers 55, 58–60, 81, 127
power to act 168–169
Prefontaine, Steve 199
prejudice 19, 136, 183, 206, 240
Prescott, Dak 290
press conferences 88, 90, 290–291
PricewaterhouseCoopers 179
Pride Month 125
pro-life 31
profanity 32, 82
provocation 59, 67, **314**
public health 123, 259–260, 271, 275
public relations 26, 37, 40, 89, 93, 108–109, 135, 157, 163 *see also* image repair; image restoration
Purce, Margaret 8
Putna, Andrew 127

Querengesser, Tim 109–110
Quinn, Sam 143

Raab, Earl 3
race: correction 44; relations 33, 35, 136
racial: abuse 29, 80, 132–134, 136; inequality 9, 11, 65, 68, 70, 116; norming 21, 40, 44–47; oppression 33; profiling 185
racialization 19, 136
racialized organizations theory (ROT) 18–19, 25
racist: act/action 33–34, 134–135; incidents 29, 125; language 7, 125–127
Radford, Scott K. 229
Raisman, Aly 4–5
Ralston, Steve 127
Ramos Aguilera, Diego 139
Rapinoe, Megan 8, 91, 163, 178, 182 *see also* women–identified athletes
Rasmussen, Kirsten (et al 2021) 229

Ray, Angela G. 181
Ray, Victor 19
Real Colorado 125–126
Real Salt Lake 32, 126
reducing offensiveness 67–68, 70, 100, 121, 125, 195–196, **214**
Reece, Joshua A. 45
reform 70, 92, 142, 144, 147
Reidy, Melisa 216–217
Republican 11, 31
reputation: brand 11 *see also* Nike; management 41, 97, 99; organizational 48, 56, 104, 168, 172, 175, 195, 205, 277; person/personal 70, 90, 217, 292; relational 172–174; team 29–30, 37
Rex Chapman Show 29
rhetoric 32, 54, 87, 110, 112–113, 141, 145, 193
Rice, Ray 43, 121, 213
Richelieu, Christèle 179
Rivera, Ron 23
Robinson, Jackie 4, 8
Rodgers, Aaron 7, 9
Roethlisberger, Ben 68
Rojas Suarez, Angie Tatiana 206
Rooney Rule 17–19, 21, 24–25
Rose, Derrick 89
Rosenberg, Michael 67
Ross, Kyla 4
Rousey, Ronda 5
Ruminski, Elesha L. 187
Runner's World (magazine) 194, 198
running shoes 192, 198
running, competitive 191 *see also* Nike
Russell, Addison **214**, 215, **216**, 216–218, 222
Russia 242, 268
Ryan, Joan 267

Saeed, Amir 133
SafeSport 171
Salazar, Alberto 194, 196
Salazar, Stephanie 290
San Diego Loyal (SDL): anti-bigotry actions 81–83; facing racism 78–80; mens soccer team 75; stakeholder theory 75–78
Schantz, Rick 79, 82
Scherer, Andreas G. 204
Schilt, Kristen 240
Schmitt, Allison 5
Schultz, Jaime 18
Seattle Mariners 10

Seattle Sounders 55, 57, 81
Seau, Junior 43
Seeger, Christopher 41, 47
segregation 19–20, 136, 181, 238, 240
self-efficacy 256, **257–258**, 258
self-promotion 266, 272
Selznick, Gertrude Jaeger 3
sexism 34, 191, 207, 291–292
sexist tropes 231, 293
sexual: discrimination 12, 155–156, 192, 206–207; harassment 29, 137, 185; misconduct 168, 170, **171**, 174
sexual assault 5, 137, 213, 289, 294 *see also* intimate partner violence
shared accountability 68–69
Sherman, Richard 65
Sheskey, Rusten 148
shift the blame 195, **214**
Shuai, Peng 6
shut up and dribble 5, 11, 71, 288
Silver, Adam 89
Sirianni, Nick 24
situational crisis communication theory (SCCT) 169, 172, 277
Smith, Cyril 41
Smith, Ryan 36
Smith, Tommie 4, 6
Snow White 198
social: consciousness 110; distancing 209, 255, 281, 306, 308; issues 4–5, 7–11, 25, 67, 78, 82, 123, 288; language 276, 279; modelling 253; problem 3, 181; roles 239
social cognitive theory (SCT) 252, 256, 258–260
social justice: issues 31, 67, 89, 178, 278; protests 9, 71, 132, 135, 137–138
social media: platforms 10, 162, 194, 280, 282; posts 6–7, 280–281, 291
sport communication 89, 138
sport governing body (SGB) 202–205
sportification of society 179
sports culture 128, 213
Sports Illustrated (SI) 65, 67, 93, 217, 303
sports media/sports news media 98–99, 212, 215, 227, 233, 293
sports organizations 127, 160, 205, 212, 218, 232–233, 240, 276
sports reporter 24
sportswomen 205–206, 227
stadiums: empty 77–78; financing 288; as pooling places 125; racist imagery/ political speech forbidden 54, 58–60;

soccer-specific 54, 136, 161; vaccination hubs 10
Stahley, Melissa Bigam 77
stakeholder theory 75, 157
Standeven, Joy 179
State University of New York 11
Staurowsky, Ellen J. 181
Steinbrenner, Hal **214**, 220
Sterling, Alton 87
Sterling, Donald 30
strategic resistance 178
Street Soccer 125
Strode, Woody 20
Suchman, Mark C. 204
suicide 5, 43, 266, 290
Summer Research Grant 2021, Ithaca College Center for Faculty Excellence 49
Summers, Chuck 123
Super Bowl 24, 65, 160
supplication 266, 272
Supplemental Nutrition Assistance Program (SNAP) 307
surfing/surfer 229
Sveinson, Katie (et al 2015) 232
Switzer, Kathrine 192
systemic racism 5, 11, 17–18, 42, 45, 67

Tagliabue, Paul 43, 47
Take a Knee: controversy 9; movement 86
Tan, Jacinta 267
Tanaka, Hiroma 229
Taylor, Breonna 142, 282
Taylor, Frederick 45
Taylor, Maria 97–100, 103 *see also* ESPN
Tebow, Tim 7
Temple University 303
tennis greats 4–5, 7, 156–157, 287, 290
tennis uniforms 206
The Institute for Diversity and Ethics in Sport (TIDES) 124–125
The Jump 101–102
Thomas, Etan 29
Thomas, Lia 6
Thomas, Michael 70
Tillman, Pat 5
Time magazine 88
Title IX 156, 179, 192, 198, 238, 305
TMZ Sports 218–219
Toledo Blue Stockings 4
Toronto Argonauts 109
Toughest Athlete campaign 194–195, 197

toxic: environment 7, 193; masculinity 213
track and field 9, 194, 242, 303
trans inclusion 238, 240, 244
transcendence 67–68, 70, 121, 125, 213, **214**
transgender athletes 6, 185
trash talk 82, 121, 123
Trout, Mike 251, 255–256, 259
Trudeau, Justin 114
Trudeau, Pierre 111
Trump, Donald J. 67, 71, 87–88, 90–91, 185
twisties 6, 270–271, 293–294
Twitter 55, 79–81, 91, 102, 116, 122, 126, 217, 231, 278, 280, 292

U. S. national anthem 86
U.N. General Assembly 179
U.S. Census Bureau 31, 303–304
U.S. Center for SafeSport (USCSS) 168, 170, **171**
U.S. Patent and Trademark Office 110
U.S. Soccer Development Academy (USSDA) 121
U.S. Soccer Federation (USSF) 158, 161–162
U.S. Supreme Court 110
U.S. Women's Hockey Team 8, 157
U.S. Women's National Soccer Team (USWNT) 8, 137, 155, 158, 230
U.S. Women's Team Players Association 163
UFC (Ultimate Fighting Championship) 5
uniform code protests 202–208
Union Cycliste Internationale 206
United Nations Educational, Scientific, and Cultural Organization (UNESCO) 179
United Soccer League (USL) 75, 80–81
United States Olympic & Paralympic Committee (USOPC) 168–170, 289
University of Akron 303, 305
University of California-Berkeley 301
University of Cincinnati 303
University of Iowa 7
University of Wisconsin (UW) 144, 217–218
USA Fencing: board of directors meeting 171–172; communication, lack of effective 168, 173–174; crisis communication strategy 172–173; final team selection 170; organizational

mission statement 169; sexual misconduct allegations 168, 170, **171**
USA Gymnastics: communication strategies 265–266, 271 *see also* Biles; press coverage 267–268; sexual abuse allegations against team doctor 5, 264, 266; trans inclusion 240–241, 243–244
USA Hockey 8
USA Swimming 169
Utah Jazz: corporate responsibility to race 30, 33–37; fan code of conduct 32; negative racial reputation 30–31; public perception 35–36; racism/racist remarks 29, 31

Valentine, John 112
Vassiliadis, Andrew 78
Verizon 65
Vertinsky, Patricia 180
victim 172–173, **215**, 264
Vietnam War 4
voting: legislation (Georgia) 9, 11; polls 125, 143; rights 183–185

Wade, Dwayne 36
Walker, Matthew 252
Walker, Moses Fleetwood 4
Walker, Rod 67
Wallace, Bubba 6
Walt Disney World 142
Wambach, Abby 5, 68
Wang, Zheng 212
warrior mentality 46
Washington Commanders 7, 23, 117
Washington, Kenny 20
Washington Post 10, 22, 57, 231
Washington Redskins 7, 110, 113, 115
Waters, Andre 43
Watt, Allen 110
Webster, Mike 41
Westbrook, Laurel 240
Westbrook, Russell 29
Western University, Canada 208
Wheeler, Chad 43, 221
White Privilege 67
White supremacist propaganda 53–54, 57, 87, 184
White women 21, 181
Whiteness 19, 23, 31
Wieber, Jordyn 4
Wilbon, Michael 70
Wilkinson, Katharine 46
Willard, Frances E. 180

willful nostalgia 112, 114
Williams, Serena 5, 8, 156, 183, 191, 193
Williams, Venus 8
Willis, Bill 20
Wilson, Russell 91
Wimbledon 8, 206
Wingard, Jason 178
Wisconsin (Kenosha) 141, 143, 147–148
woke-washing 123
Wolpert, Julia 46
women-identified athletes (WIAs) 178, 182, 185
Women's Christian Temperance Union 180
Women's Gaelic players association (WGPA) 233–234
Women's Liberation Movement 191–192, 198
Women's National Basketball Association (WNBA) 6, 8, 144, 156, 161, 238
women's sports: collegiate athletes 304; coverage 155, 207, 228; inequity 157, 160–161; professionalization/ commercialization 228; sexualization of 231–232; suffrage 178, 181–182; threats to 185; uniforms 205
Women's National Basketball Association Players Association (WNBAPA) 8
Women's Professional Golf Tour 4
Woods, Tiger 9, 68, 252
World Series 216, 221, 255
World War II 20, 65
World's Highest Paid Athletes 65
Wright, Daunte 66

Yahoo Finance 64, 71
Yips 6
Youth soccer 120, 122, 124
YouTube 58

Zaler, Emily 183
zero tolerance policy 126–128
Zignal Labs 89
Zimmerman, George 142

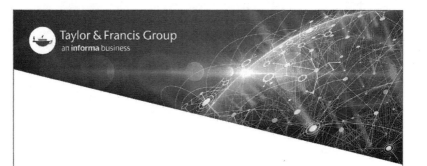

9781032288963